THE BOOK OF JOB AND THE IMMANENT GENESIS OF TRANSCENDENCE

Series Editors

Slavoj Žižek

Adrian Johnston

Todd McGowan

diaeresis

THE BOOK OF JOB AND THE IMMANENT GENESIS OF TRANSCENDENCE

Davis Hankins

Northwestern University Press
Evanston, Illinois

Northwestern University Press
www.nupress.northwestern.edu

Printed in the United States of America

10 9 8 7 6 5 4 3 2 1

Library of Congress Cataloging-in-Publication Data

Hankins, Davis, author.
    The Book of Job and the immanent genesis of transcendence / Davis
Hankins.
        pages cm. — (Diaeresis)
    Revised version of the author's dissertation—Emory University, 2011.
    ISBN 978-0-8101-3012-8 (cloth : alk. paper) — ISBN 978-0-8101-3018-0
(pbk. : alk. paper) — ISBN 978-0-8101-6806-0 (ebook)
    1. Bible. Job—Criticism, interpretation, etc. 2. Transcendence (Philos-
ophy) I. Title. II. Series: Diaeresis.
    BS1415.52.H36 2014
    223.106—dc23

                                                    2014026783

The paper used in this publication meets the minimum requirements of the
American National Standard for Information Sciences—Permanence of Paper
for Printed Library Materials, ANSI Z39.48-1992.

In memory of David C. Knauert

For Stephanie C. Hankins

Contents

Acknowledgments   ix

Introduction   The Book of Job: A Triumph for Today   3

Part 1. God, Wisdom, Sage: Immanent Emergences of Transcendence

1   Job's Critique of Transcendent Theology   11

2   Job 1–2: A Critique of Pure Fear   40

Part 2. Ideology, Resistance, Transformation

3   Ideology: The Wisdom of Job's Friends   77

    Excursus   Wisdom Ideology Beyond Job 4–5   99

4   Resistance: On Fear and Anxiety   105

5   Transformation: On Guilt and Shame   135

    Excursus   The Final Speeches   170

Part 3. Ontology, Aesthetics, Ethics

6   Ontology, Aesthetics, and the Divine Speeches   175

7   Ethics and the Ending   205

    Appendix   Job 4–5: Text and Translation   227

    Notes   233

    Works Cited   285

    Index of Names and Subjects   299

    Index of Ancient Sources   307

Acknowledgments

This project owes much to many for generous investments of time, resources, and energy. The idea for this book emerged in close collaboration with David Knauert during the cold summer of 2006, plus several subsequent seasons of cooperation. We each developed our shared idea in two dissertations, his on Proverbs at Duke and mine on Job at Emory University. I was not thinking about Job as David's sudden heart attack and death interrupted our lovely Saturday morning run in November 2009. But my subsequent thoughts about Job have all been articulated in the dark, tragic shadow of his traumatic death. I dedicate this book to David in the sorrow of profound loss and yet with gratitude for his abiding memory, through which he continues to enliven and inspire me.

I am enormously indebted to my advisor and advocate, Carol Newsom, who supported this project and helped carry it through its earlier iteration as a dissertation at Emory University. I have learned more about Job from Carol than anyone else, but so much more as well. She contributed to this book through countless conversations and invaluable criticism, which were always aimed at improving my argument, never at accommodating it to hers. I am also grateful to the other members of my dissertation committee, Brent Strawn, Deepika Bahri, and Adrian Johnston. Deepika, Carol, and I cherished our time together as fellows at the Fox Center for Humanistic Inquiry in Atlanta during the academic year 2010–2011. I completed the dissertation with the Center's generous support and profited richly from the conversations, space, and kindness that I savored there all year.

This book would not exist without the advocacy and intellectual labor of Adrian Johnston. The entirety of my theoretical orientation is profoundly indebted to him. Ever since I took his seminar on Jacques Lacan in 2006 Adrian has ceaselessly taught and surprised me with insight, grace, and generosity. To Adrian and the other editors of the Diaeresis series, Slavoj Žižek and Todd McGowan, I wish to acknowledge my heartfelt gratitude for their support. As the content of this book makes clear, Slavoj's centrality to this project extends far beyond his role as series editor, even to the very heart of my thought. The book is also much improved by the feedback of Tim Beal and other readers, both known and unknown to me, as well as by the helpful queries and clarifications of editors such as Martin Coleman, Anne Gendler, and others. To Henry Carrigan and all those at Northwestern University Press who participated in the production of this book, thank you for all you did to make this a truly superb and joyful publication experience.

I also would like to express my vast gratitude to those who have with love and support carried me and this project through many days and nights, gracing them all with joy and urgency. I would particularly like to mention Stephanie's and my parents, Ron and Vicki Hankins and Judy Lilly, as well as Harrison, Lily, David, and Leigh Knauert, plus Walter Brueggemann, Christine Yoder, and so many others at Columbia Theological Seminary and Emory University, and finally my colleagues in the Philosophy and Religion Department and in Women's Studies at Appalachian State University.

My ultimate acknowledgments I reserve for my family and Brennan Breed, who is about as close as it gets to family. Brennan has been a delightful and indispensable interlocutor since this project began, and I am thrilled to hunker down collaboratively with his ramifying and encouraging intellect as we begin our next book on Ecclesiastes. Finally, I am extremely grateful to Stephanie, whose companionship, care, and work profoundly bless and enrich the lives of so many, including myself and our sons, Miller and Nathaniel. I warmly dedicate this to you, Stephanie, with love and gratitude.

THE BOOK OF JOB AND THE IMMANENT
GENESIS OF TRANSCENDENCE

Introduction

The Book of Job: A Triumph for Today

§1 Rethinking Theology and Theory

The book of Job intervenes as an event into past and present theological, philosophical, ethical, and political discourse. JOB's[1] descriptions of God, human experience, and the material world speak volumes with uncanny relevance to contemporary philosophical debates about ontology and theories of subjectivity, as well as to traditional ethico-theological discourse. JOB's critique of traditional wisdom ideology attacks its transcendence in ways that challenge every appeal to transcendence; JOB's depictions of the world as dappled and of human experience as radically contingent leave behind rippling consequences for numerous contemporary political programs and theoretical debates.[2]

Many have described a "theological" or "post-secular turn" among American, British, and Continental critical theorists and philosophers at the end of the twentieth and beginning of the twenty-first centuries.[3] Different thinkers from different perspectives have overcome modern allergies to positive religion and to theological arguments in light of the deconstruction of the idea of the secular.[4] Theological discourse and religious texts have provided resources to think through political and ontological issues. Various scholars within religious studies have reciprocated by engaging theorists and philosophers in ways that move beyond the practice of application that seeks merely to demystify but does not disturb the founding categories of modern historical critical scholarship.[5] The dominant voices on this side are those of theologians and philosophers of religion, not biblical scholars.[6] These conversations regularly draw on biblical literature but rarely attend to critical biblical scholarship except in the most perfunctory way. In part this is because many biblical scholars remain preoccupied with achieving an appearance of objective scientism by insisting upon modernist boundaries between professional and confessional readings.[7] Many recent theoretical conversations about biblical literature and religion disregard these boundaries—finding, for example, a political universality in the religion of Paul, as does Alain Badiou—and thus are not easily integrated into contemporary biblical criticism.

These theoretical readings of the Bible have focused mostly on the New Testament, Paul in particular, largely because it was Badiou's controversial interpretation of Paul that drew other influential thinkers such as Giorgio Agamben into this reexamination of theology, religion, and sacred texts.[8] This book contributes to these ongoing conversations among philosophers, theorists, theologians, and biblical scholars by adding another voice from the underrepresented latter group. I read the Bible in the wake of theory as a site where modern ideological divisions—for example, between the professional subject and the confessional object—are disturbed and wherefrom a radical political (biblical) theology might take form. Indeed, in my opinion the writings collected in the Hebrew Bible offer better resources to these contemporary engagements with religious texts than the Greco-Roman writings collected in the New Testament, not only because they are shared across different faith traditions, but also because they are less marked by dualistic thought—especially of the emerging Neo-Platonic variety.

§2 Žižek and JOB: Ideology Critique

While the New Testament and Paul have received the lion's share of recent theoretical attention, JOB is far from the most neglected biblical text. In the last half century various thinkers beyond biblical studies have published engagements with JOB, including Slavoj Žižek, Gustavo Gutiérrez, Antonio Negri, Ernst Bloch, René Girard, Carl Jung, Philippe Nemo, and Emmanuel Levinas. While each of these is to some degree insightful, Žižek's work more than any other provides concepts and claims that have proven invaluable to this project.

Žižek has long been interested in exploring the significance of JOB for the traditional concerns of ideology-critique. Among other lessons he takes from JOB, Žižek regards JOB's relationship with the friends in the dialogue as:

> the first exemplary case of the *critique of ideology* in human history, laying bare the discursive strategies of legitimizing suffering: Job's properly ethical dignity lies in the way he persistently rejects the notion that his suffering can have any meaning, either punishment for his past sins or a trial of his faith, against the three theologians who bombard him with possible meanings—and, surprisingly, God takes his side at the end.[9]

Žižek's position, which I will nuance in part 2 of this book, is that Job refuses the discursive practices of the three friends that try to make his experience meaningful. Job's refusal exposes various ideological tactics. In the prose conclusion, Žižek thinks that God offers an important, anti-hermeneutical endorsement of meaninglessness against attempts to make meaning.

Žižek also reads the divine speeches as an exemplary critique of ideology. They strike him as a(n over)reaction typical of an emperor discovering his nakedness:

> Far from providing some kind of satisfactory account of Job's unde-
> served suffering, God's appearance at the end ultimately amounts to
> a pure argument of authority grounded in a breathtaking display of
> power: "You see all that I can do? Can you do this? Who are you, then,
> to complain?" So what we get is neither the good God letting Job know
> that his suffering is just an ordeal destined to test his faith, nor a dark
> God beyond the Law, the God of pure caprice, but, rather, a God who
> acts like someone caught in the moment of impotence—weakness, at
> least—and tries to escape his predicament by empty boasting. What we
> get at the end is a kind of cheap Hollywood horror show with lots of
> special effects.[10]

In the spectacle of the whirlwind God proves as weak and helpless as the friends' discursive strategies before the difficulties of human suffering. Žižek sees what is essentially Job's silence after God's speeches as an indication of Job's awareness of this dynamic. He asks why, if Job took God seriously, he would keep silent rather than answer, "'OK, if you can do all this, *why did you let me suffer in such a meaningless way?*' Do not God's thundering words make [Job's] silence, the absence of an answer, all the more palpable?"[11]

More recently Žižek takes a different direction, one that explicitly follows the lead of his favorite theologian, G. K. Chesterton.[12] Žižek sees God's speeches not as an attempt to answer or distract one from riddles but, as Chesterton says, "to propound them." Žižek now thinks that in the prose conclusion and the speeches God opposes the friends' attempts "to obfuscate the impact of the trauma with a symbolic semblance."[13] Chesterton writes, God "insists on the inexplicableness of everything . . . on the positive and palpable unreason of things." Chesterton goes on to claim, "God becomes for an instant a blasphemer; one might almost say that God becomes for an instant an atheist." Žižek explains why he thinks that the legacy of JOB in the image of a divine atheist is so important:

> The legacy of Job precludes such a figure of taking refuge in the standard transcendent figure of God as a secret Master who knows the meaning of what appears to us to be a meaningless catastrophe, the God who sees the entire picture in which what we perceive as a stain contributes to global harmony. When we are confronted with an event like the Holocaust, or the death of millions in Congo in recent years, is it not obscene to claim that these stains have a deeper meaning?[14]

This reading of the divine speeches allows Žižek to conclude that Job "remained silent neither because he was crushed by God's overwhelming presence, nor because he wanted thereby to indicate his continuous resistance—the fact that God avoided answering his question—but because, in a gesture of silent solidarity, he perceived the divine impotence."[15] In other words, Job realizes that God is not opposed to but beside him, equally impotent before and aware of the absence of any transcendent guarantee of meaning.

I argue below that God appears in JOB precisely when the impossibility, not just of a reference to transcendence, but also of a reference to any sort of closure or self-presence of the immanent, material conditions of life, appears. My reading is consitent with Žižek's at the most important level of his latest discussion: the legacy of JOB is fundamentally a rejection of transcendence that nonetheless does not abandon all reference to transcendence. Instead, JOB explores where, how, and why transcendence is related/immanent to an ontologically incomplete material world. JOB's theology is thus very different than what normally goes under that name. As will be evident, Žižek and Jacques Lacan are two of this project's closest intellectual allies because JOB's God operates within an ontology that is consistent with the later Lacan's assertions of a not-All, de-totalized Real for which no big Other exists.

My interpretation of JOB thus goes much further than Žižek's. Not only because I depart from his interpretation at various moments and remain much closer to the text than he, but also because I extend the implications of JOB beyond the issues of practical philosophy and into the domain of theoretical philosophy, in particular, of ontology. Even still, my analysis sanctions his interest in and enthusiasm for JOB. This book testifies in many ways to the productivity of those who have been the most important thinkers for Žižek's framework (such as Kant, Hegel, Freud, and Lacan), as well as of his framework itself, even as this project contributes to this framework through its deployment of these resources within the particular field of biblical criticism.

§3 Which Religion Will Triumph?

Lacan's 1974 remarks entitled "The Triumph of Religion" starkly oppose the theses Freud advances nearly fifty years prior in *The Future of an Illusion*.[16] Whereas Freud predicts that the desacralizing insights of reason through scientific advances will accompany the downfall of the illusion of religion, Lacan counters that religion will instead triumph alongside the instrumentalizing and disenchanting inroads made by science as people will increasingly turn to religion for a sense of ultimate meaning. However,

> Lacan also contends, using such examples as eighteenth-century French materialism and Darwinian evolutionary theory, that the sciences of modernity, although ostensibly atheistic, actually are suffused with theological images and sensibilities. These disciplines and their practitioners tend to imagine material Nature . . . [as a] totalizing big Other ruling the entirety of creation with its unbreakable laws . . . a thinly veiled replacement for the presumably dead-and-buried God of monotheisms.[17]

Johnston nicely suggests that we are thus left with two unsatisfactory options: either find a satisfying sense of ultimate meaning in techno-scientism's promises of exhaustive explanation (and/or in the gadgets that trickle down in capitalist economies from scientific advancements), or find satisfaction in the illusion of a God that could compensate for one's discontent with capitalist scientism.

Facing the failures of these two options, one feels an urgent need for two projects: (1) exorcise science of its ideological religiosity by constructing an ontology able to account for what tends to lure thought into supernaturalist and idealist metaphysics, and (2) exorcise religion of its reactionary deployment as palliative care for civilization's discontents. My wager in this book is that JOB, when read in light of various philosophical and psychoanalytic insights, supplies crucial resources for the latter. Through JOB's zealous attacks on various illusions—of transcendence, of a potentially fully-constituted subject, and of an organic totality in the form of an integrated cosmos—JOB exorcises theological discourse of two sets of ideological demons: reactionary conservatism and supernaturalist obscurantism. JOB speaks about God, subjectivity, ontology, and ethics in a way that one might even characterize as materialist insofar as JOB takes care to narrate the conditions out of which such more-than-material entities—subjectivity, God, wisdom, truth, etc.—immanently originate. In other words, JOB is critical of numerous varieties of idealisms as well as reductive materialisms, and JOB offers in their stead an account of the emergence of these more-than-material entities out of the material conditions that they become irreducible to and consequently influence. One might thus call JOB's account an "immanent theology" or a "transcendental materialism." The present project demonstrates the necessity, for a satisfactory understanding of the book of Job, of a dialectical and emergentist rather than a paradoxical conception of such notions. This dialectic is not the imposition of a modern conceptual framework on an ancient text—it grows out of JOB's own position, which refuses the framework it inherits from ancient Israel's wisdom tradition. In fact, the way that JOB forges a new, immanentist and emergentist framework for understanding God, subjectivity, the world, and so on, may also prove helpful to the first project mentioned above: the need to rethink ontology in light of the shortcomings of previous materialisms and idealisms in the face of recent scientific advancements.[18]

I do not think that one can disagree with Lacan's judgment that religion has and will continue to triumph along with the ever-accelerating economic energies and the forces of modernizing technologies launched in late capitalism. However, religion and theological discourse are far from monolithic, and so the future of religion will no less certainly remain a field of contestation. This book stems from my conviction that there is much at stake in the possibility that religious discourse could re-/dis-cover from ancient texts such as JOB a radical, immanent, political theology. In the final analysis, *The Book of Job and the Immanent Genesis of Transcendence* should be read as a plea that the religion and the theological discourse that will triumph in the future will be JOB's, not those that JOB opposes.

Part 1

God, Wisdom, Sage: Immanent Emergences of Transcendence

1

Job's Critique of Transcendent Theology

The eye with which I see God is the same with which God sees me.
  —Meister Eckhart

The human being is this night. . . . This night, this inner of
nature, that exists here—pure self—in phantasmagorical presentations, is night all around it, here shoots a bloody head—
there another white shape, suddenly here before it, and just
so disappears. One catches sight of this night when one looks
human beings in the eye—into a night, that becomes awful.
  —Georg Wilhelm Friedrich Hegel

§4 wisdom, Wisdom, and WISDOM

Ancient Israel's wisdom tradition endows "wisdom" with numerous meanings, many of which can be helpfully and usefully distinguished (for example, trade skills versus artistic learnings), and even categorized (for
example, practical knowledge versus ethical prudence).[1] Yet one distinction cuts across all others: there are the wisdoms that are available to
and through the imperfect, lacking, and temporal reality of human experience and understanding, and there is the Wisdom that is associated
with the divine and with transcendence, existing outside but not independently of human wisdoms.[2] Michael Fox discusses Lady/Woman Wisdom as the epitome of the transcendent, divine entity that he calls the
"wisdom-universal":

> Lady Wisdom symbolizes the perfect and transcendent universal of
> which the particulars of human wisdom are imperfect images or realiza-
> tions. Like a Platonic ἰδέα, the wisdom-universal exists objectively and
> not only as an abstraction or mental construct. It dwells in special prox-

imity to God—"before him," present to his mind—while maintaining a distinct existence. As a universal, it exists in both the supernal realm (universal, atemporal, extramundane) and the human (time-bound, wordly, belonging to particular peoples, realized in specific words). This transcendent wisdom now and ever presents itself to humanity, meaning that the wisdom that people can learn, such as the wise teachings of Proverbs, are manifestations or precipitates of a universal, unitary wisdom . . . It is the transcendent wisdom that is the universal of the infinity of wise things that humans can know and use.[3]

A tension divides the first two from the last three sentences in this quotation. Fox first speaks about the human's *mediated* access to transcendent Wisdom; then he says that transcendent Wisdom is *immediately* available within human wisdoms. The first two sentences distinguish a perfect, transcendent Wisdom-universal from its imperfect images in humanity's *particular*-wisdoms. The last three sentences claim that the transcendent Wisdom-universal "exists in" and "presents itself to" humanity's immanent particular-wisdoms. Fox's second claim reflects his rejection of any qualitative distinction between the Wisdom-universal and particular-wisdoms.[4] Ancient Israel's sages seem less interested—than, for example, some who are more influenced by Greek thought—in wholly separating the mundane realm of particular-wisdoms from the divine realm of transcendent truths.

Yet the entire sapiential enterprise that generates an "infinity of wise things" out of the Wisdom-universal depends upon taking such a qualitative distinction as axiomatic. To explain, let us ask a question that Fox himself poses: "how does the transcendent wisdom manifest itself in the mundane sphere?"[5] If Proverbs presents the extramundane, atemporal Wisdom-universal within the mundane and temporal reality of particular-wisdoms, then how and on what basis would Wisdom's difference from wisdom appear? Fox simply asserts that the Wisdom-universal is both present in particular-wisdoms and "transcends any human wisdom."[6] While Fox indicates his sense that something qualitative separates particular-wisdoms from the Wisdom-universal, he neither pursues why, when, or where the Wisdom-universal appears, nor how its appearances might be analyzed.[7]

Fox also fails to consider the statements from the sages about the limits of their wisdoms. While the sages do not always acknowledge the exclusion of the Wisdom-universal from their particular-wisdoms, they certainly reiterate the folly of ever considering particular-wisdoms as if they were "precipitates of the primeval, universal wisdom." Proverbs' principal admonition may be the teacher's to the son: "do not rely on your own understanding," to which one might add Proverbs' motto imperative: "Do not be wise in your own eyes; fear YHWH and turn from evil" (3:7; cf. 3:5; 12:15; 16:2; 21:2; 26:5, 12, 16; 28:11). Such admonitions and imperatives are the core of Proverbs' wisdom. They insist in no uncertain terms that human wisdom does not realize or present but is unequal and lacking with respect to divine Wisdom. The ethical axiom against being "wise in one's own eyes" ensures that the qualitative lack and imperfection that distance particular-wisdoms from the Wisdom-universal can never be considered overcome.

Fox's attention to the similarities and mutually enhancing relationship between particular-wisdoms and the Wisdom-universal leads him to reject any qualitative distinction between them. By treating particular-wisdoms as presentations of the Wisdom-universal, the limits of particular-wisdoms can only be seen negatively, either as indications of folly or of the absence of Wisdom. Yet the fear of YHWH and the recognition that one is not-wise preserve the limits of one's wisdom in ways that positively indicate the presence of wisdom. In fact, it is recognizing the limits to one's particular-wisdoms that provides the constitutive condition for what Fox rightly calls the "infinity of wise things that humans can know and use." Consider the common example of Prov 26:4a ("Do not answer a fool according to his folly . . .") and 26:5a ("Answer a fool according to his folly . . ."). Both are presented as if they were universal and unlimited, and yet their immediate juxtaposition indicates that they (and implies that all proverbs) are framed within a tradition that takes as axiomatic their distance from the Wisdom-universal.[8]

Furthermore, the presence of the transcendent Wisdom-universal is much more strongly indicated by these proverbs' juxtaposition than it would be by a straightforward claim that they somehow directly presented Wisdom. Indeed, the most effective way to manifest the Wisdom-universal is to present, as palpably as possible, the limit barring particular-wisdoms from identification with the Wisdom-universal. O'Connor puts it well in a section aptly entitled "Ambiguity as Revelatory": the wisdom literature "sees in ambiguity and confusion the opportunity for breakthrough into mystery . . . The point of highlighting ambiguity or paradox is not to bring the individual to an intellectual impasse but to lead her beyond the obvious into deeper, transcendent truth."[9] In the terms of Prov 21:31, the sage can be sure of God's presence in the event that all the preparations for battle have been made and yet the war is lost. The limits of particular-wisdoms open up spaces that allow one to imagine a beyond in which an unlimited, transcendent Wisdom is located.

My argument, then, is that the Wisdom-universal is not presented by any of the sages' particular-wisdoms—from the most sublime theological speculation to the most mundane technical calculation. The location of all such wisdoms within the sapiential framework compels the sage to treat them as penultimate, limited, competing, and conflicting claims that must be continually (re)negotiated and (re)discovered. Yet it remains useful to compare and distinguish the sages' limited, particular-wisdoms from their theological speculations about unlimited, universal Wisdom. In fact, one must identify the limits that beset both, limits that not only keep them from directly presenting Wisdom but also open up the spaces within which Wisdom's presence is indirectly indicated. We therefore need a third category of wisdom, which I indicate with small capitals: WISDOM. In short, (i) all sapiential articulations are particular-*wisdoms*, including those that speculate about the content of a (ii) *Wisdom* that may transcend and be indicated by the sages' particular-wisdoms. (iii) WISDOM thus refers to the internal limits of the sages' particular-wisdoms whose appearance may be taken as an indication of the (excluded) "presence" of a Wisdom that transcends wisdom. WISDOM thus answers Fox's question about how transcendent Wisdom can appear within the limited, particular-wisdoms of human thoughts, speech, and desire. WISDOM is what renders the discourse of wisdom ambiguous and paradoxical since it is the negative space that divides, limits, and opposes claims to particular-wisdoms. In its capacity as a gap, however, WISDOM also constitutes the sapiential discourse's seemingly infinite flexibility. Since wisdom's limits can be taken as WISDOM, and thus indicative of a transcendent Wisdom that it strives perpetually to approach, wisdom seems unlimited.

One can initially grasp the relationship among these three wisdoms as sequential: first the sage accumulates wisdom; at some moment he inevitably encounters WISDOM when he realizes his wisdom is limited; finally he imagines what unlimited Wisdom might exist beyond the limits of his cognizing abilities. This sequencing is partially misleading because, prior to the encounter with WISDOM that brings the sage some awareness of the limits of his wisdom, his "wisdom" is not coordinated enough to be called wisdom. The notion of WISDOM stands much critical and biblical doxa on its feet, according to which human, limited wisdom either arises from or generates divine, unlimited Wisdom. On this account, both wisdom and Wisdom emerge from WISDOM.

Some will detect the Hegelian contours of this conception of WISDOM. Just as the ancient sages reckoned the one who is wise in his own eyes a fool, so too did Kant deny that anyone has direct access to divine Wisdom. Kant referred to unlimited/divine Things-in-themselves as noumena. He insisted that limited/human knowledge and experience are cut off from noumenal Things-in-themselves, and are only capable of accessing phenomenal objects-as-appearances. Among the German idealists, Hegel's critique of Kant's noumena/phenomena distinction is best known. Hegel writes:

> No one knows, or even feels, that anything is a limit or defect, until he is at the same time above and beyond it . . . [T]o call a thing finite or limited proves by implication the very presence of the infinite and the unlimited . . . [O]ur knowledge of a limit can only be when the unlimited is *on this side* in consciousness.[10]

Kant adheres to a two-tiered model for speaking about the world that is similar to the critical conversation about wisdom up to now. Hegel makes the small but crucial step to say that, in order for the one (human/limited) to even speculate about the other (divine/unlimited), there must be something that indicates the latter *within* the former. In short, limitation precedes and is productive of transcendence, as the Slovenian philosopher Slavoj Žižek tirelessly reiterates in his narrations of the relationship between Kant and Hegel:

> For Hegel, the gap between phenomena and their transcendent Ground is a secondary effect of the *absolutely immanent* gap of/in the phenomena themselves. . . . immanence generates the specter of transcendence because it is already inconsistent in itself. . . . the tension between immanence and transcendence is . . . secondary with regard to the gap within immanence itself.[11]

The present project follows this fundamental Hegelian move to shift our critical focus from the tension between immanence (limited, human wisdom) and transcendence (unlimited, divine Wisdom), to the appearance of transcendence within immanence (WISDOM). This study asks, to use Hegel's words, where does "the very presence of the infinite and the unlimited" appear in JOB?

Why has one not heard much about this third category of WISDOM prior to this study?[12] In part because WISDOM often functions as a "vanishing mediator," a gap momentarily opened and then (usually) filled in, either by the interpreter's presumption of some figure of Wisdom as its referent, or by the text's offering of some figure of Wisdom as its referent.[13] JOB, however, is often directly concerned with this third category of WISDOM and with its active role in generating the appearance of a external split between (immanent) wisdom and (transcendent) Wisdom.[14] Thus, while it is true that WISDOM has not yet been adequately conceptualized, I attend throughout to its inchoate appearances in scholarly and biblical literature.

§5 "Short-Circuiting" Conventional Wisdom

Within these first pages I have already begun what will be an ongoing practice throughout this study: "short-circuiting" the usual categories of biblical interpretation with concepts drawn from other fields in order to organize and encapsulate the textual material and ancient ideas. While some of the concepts and categories I develop will be familiar (for example, Kant's notion of the sublime) or well-established in critical biblical interpretation (for example, tragedy, comedy), I try to explicate them as clearly as possible to the extent required by my use of them. Given my presumably mixed audience of biblical scholars and those more trained in critical theoretical discourses, I try neither to belabor nor truncate my discussions of issues arising from either field. In the end the theoretical elaborations produce concepts and categories that are unavailable in current biblical studies, and yet allow the text to be heard and seen to say and do things of which biblical studies has remained unaware. Conversely, as stated in the preface, the close analysis of texts from the Hebrew Bible contributes an important voice to recent conversations among critical theorists and theologians.

This project reassesses the conventional idea that the wisdom of the book of Job explicitly and implicitly challenges the tradition in which it stands. Wisdom can be initially approached as a discourse understood as a social link that structures and constitutes relations among subjects, of subjects to objects, and of subjects and objects to wisdom and the divine. JOB's wisdom is made possible by but is not present in the book of Proverbs—commonly considered the normative expression of Israel's traditional wisdom. JOB's new wisdom remains missing from or suffers unfortunate misreadings in contemporary interpretations.

Admittedly, to claim that JOB challenges traditional wisdom is close to hackneyed. But perhaps it is for this very reason that we stand to learn so much by reexamining it. One way to understand this project is as a rigorously critical and systematic reassessment of everything taken for granted by the often-made off-hand observation that JOB challenges or poses a crisis for traditional wisdom. Throughout, (i) I investigate the character and limits of the wisdom that JOB rejects; (ii) I consider how it could be thrown into crisis and what could challenge it; (iii) I investigate the wisdom that JOB presents[15]; (iv) I consider whether, how, and in what way JOB's wisdom opposes traditional wisdom; and (v) I explore various consequences of JOB's wisdom, of its opposition to the tradition, and of its misapprehension by interpreters.

To specify the kinds of problems that plague conventional accounts of JOB's wisdom and its meaning, consider this common notion about the relationship between Job and his friends: Job's emphasis on experience challenges the tradition's emphasis on doctrine insofar as his experience falls outside their theology. Many think that the friends impose their theology on Job and try to force his experience to accord with their thoughts about "how the world works." From this angle, the reader is bound to face numerous difficulties:

1. How should the complexities of the friends' theology be treated, especially their regular insistences on the lack of understanding that human beings can never escape?
2. What should be done about the rootedness of their theology in experience? Should this rootedness be dismissed since they treat their experiences as normative? How then can Job be treated differently for his insistence on the normativity of his experience?
3. Job's speech does much more than recount a list of symptoms, so will this angle attend adequately to the relationship between experience and theology in his discourse? And how could this angle not distance interpreters from Job's constructions of his experiences that present them as revelatory of truths about God, the world, and wisdom? How could this angle avoid overlooking the way that Job clings to these truths with dogged certitude?
4. And finally, will the theological sophistication of Job's discourse be noticed? Will it be reduced to mere reflexes of experience?

These four sets of questions suggest that the commonly held idea that the friends impose their theology on Job's experience places the interpreter at a considerable distance from the text at the outset. This example illustrates four related problems with conventional interpretations of JOB:

1. The position usually disparaged as the traditional wisdom that JOB rejects and throws into crisis—that is, the imposition of a rigid conceptual apparatus onto a particular situation whose complexity far exceeds the apparatus—does not characterize traditional wisdom as much as it does the interpreter's Procrustean bed for this wisdom;
2. Consequently, the actual position that the book of Job presents and rejects as the tradition's remains to be formulated;
3. The position usually celebrated as Job's (the character and the book)—that is, the insistence on the limits of understanding with respect to the complexities of experience—actually characterizes the tradition that JOB rejects more than the wisdom that JOB advances in opposition to it;
4. Consequently, the actual position articulated by JOB against that which it rejects remains to be formulated.

In addition to demonstrating that these four inadequacies of conventional readings apply not just to the dialogue but to the book as a whole, this project will also offer an account of those crucial aspects of the book left unexamined because of the conventional accounts' blinders.

To decouple interpretation from many currently accepted categories so as to grasp the text anew, this project strategically draws on concepts developed in disciplines beyond biblical criticism. Biblical studies has a long tradition of celebrated works that have generated insights into the text by creating "short circuits" between what is at their time considered "the field" and other approaches reckoned outside this field. Hermann Gunkel (1862–1932) can function as a figurehead for this tradition. To simplify a more complex story, Gunkel represents the strong tradition of cross-disciplinary analyses *within* biblical studies.[16] Gunkel's willingness to create "short circuits" between biblical studies and other disciplines such as folklore studies exposed the presence and function of genres in the text in a way that generated generations of work. Today one finds plenty of debates about the nature of genre, the existence and characteristics of particular genres, and the extent to which a particular text participates in a genre. However, it is more or less universally accepted that no text is genre-free, and that the relationship of a text to genre is not external, but instead affects the very nature of the text itself. That is, even though the sense in which we argue about genre today was only thematized with the rise of modern critical biblical scholarship from Herder to Gunkel to Buss, most have no problem with the critical treatment of genre as something *internal* to the ancient texts and their contexts. Similarly, I see no a priori reason why such a critical internalization could not occur with the concepts developed below such as desire, drive, enjoyment, fear, and anxiety. While a critical conversation is necessary about how and to what extent these concepts are present or represented in the text, this project demonstrates that these concepts are there, walking around throughout the texts, even if they have not yet been thematized by interpreters.

Just after the tumultuous events of May 1968 in Paris, the French psychoanalyst Jacques Lacan resumed his year-long seminar. While some student radicals were deeply informed by and close to Lacan, others attacked him. They perceived the structuralist jargon and abstract formulas Lacan kept drawing on the blackboard as yet another instance of the university's failure to address the concrete social problems that they were struggling to redress from the streets.[17] In response, Lacan insists throughout the seminar that the four constituent elements of the four discourses that he spends the year elaborating were feet. He characterizes each discourse as "quadrupedal," and he insists that they are not latent, static, or abstract but manifest, mobile, and marching around.[18] Similarly I contend that the Lacanian concepts discussed in this book are not latent, static, or abstract, but are instead dynamic and walking throughout JOB's texts.

§6 The Content of the Argument

CHAPTER 2 begins to use the concept of WISDOM as a tool for understanding how JOB critiques the transcendent theological categories of the tradition and charts a new way of understanding transcendence by narrating its emergence at the moment of an evental rupture and consequent transformation of the world.[19] The prose introduction sets the premise for the entire book by discrediting the traditional idea that God completes and coordinates what seems to humans incomplete and inconsistent. *haśśāṭān*'s[20] question—"Is it for nothing that Job fears God?" (1:9)—both sets the plot in motion and renders illegitimate any piety that is based on a sense of a transcendent order, truth, God, or principle. This premise hails unconditional piety as the only legitimate piety. As a result, the prose tale stages a kind of suicidal death of God, a kenotic emptying out of heaven/transcendence into the limits, disorder, and contingencies experienced by inhabitants on earth. The question becomes whether Job will respond to the event that has disrupted his life by appealing to or allying himself with some particular-wisdom/Wisdom, or whether he will reorient himself and persevere with respect to the WISDOM opened up to him by the events that overturn him. That he does the latter is indicated by his responses as well as the tale's explicit affirmations.

CHAPTER 3 is the first of three chapters in part 2. Each deals with some aspect or another of the speeches by Job and his three friends in the dialogue. CHAPTER 3 develops the wisdom of Job's friends by closely attending to Eliphaz's first speech in Job 4–5. This speech merits extended attention because it exemplifies both the structure of transcendence that characterizes the friends' wisdom and their perspective on Job's suffering. I develop at length the logic behind the friends' perspective and the tradition that they represent, which responds to the limits of its wisdom by appealing to transcendence. This tradition posits the existence of a separate divine domain that exists beyond the domain of human existence and integrates the various uncoordinated and inconsistent elements of human existence into a fully-functioning harmonious order. I am more sympathetic to this perspective than many interpreters since I believe that it conforms to a structure that is constitutive of many discursive realities and far more flexible and productive of knowledge than it is usually given credit for being. The remaining chapters of part 2 continue to refine CHAPTER 3's account of the friends' wisdom by considering the differences between their wisdom and Job's.

CHAPTER 4 attends to some of the deep, structural differences that distinguish Job's understanding of his experience from the friends'. These different structures inform their different ideas about how Job can best deal with his experience and are often misunderstood. For most, Job's complaints and desires arise from his *fear* that his traumatic suffering either is linked with God's absence or directly results from God's malicious presence. Both these options are available only within the structure of the friends' conception of Job's experience. I demonstrate that Job's true complaint stems from a deeper and more terrifying experience of *anxiety.* Job finds that God is not a presence of any kind, but a force that prevents any presence from establishing itself. For Job there is no presence that is not subverted by this divine agency, including himself (he is split from himself), experience (nothing remains the same, everything threatens to turn on him, against him, and into him), and God (God is nothing but this destabilizing and devastating force). God is the force that repeatedly keeps Job's self and his world from obtaining anything close to a stable presence.

CHAPTER 5 investigates the solution(s) by which Job imagines escaping his situation of anxiety. The dominant approach is to identify Job's hope with his expressions of desire in several passages for some form of a mediator beyond God and himself that could safely and meaningfully relate them to one another. Yet Job always follows such expressions of desire by proclaiming their impossibility in the light of God's character, which precludes anyone or anything from obtaining such a mediating presence. Job then subsequently expresses his resolve to persist into the adverse condition he is suffering or, as he calls it, "the bitterness of my soul." I refer to the former futile hope as a desire for guilt to distinguish it clearly from his subsequent drive into his bitter experience of shame. Although interpreters have not properly analyzed this latter drive, only in it does Job find a potential source for salvation that he does not disdain as futile. Job's experience convinces him of the impossibility of transcendence, yet he does not lose hope in the possibility of overcoming his experience since transcendence is made impossible by a divine force that keeps him undetermined and open to becoming new or different. Job hopes not in transcendence but in his immanent potential for transformation, that is, for transcending his condition. Said differently, in his confrontation with his inconsistent, self-defeating, and therefore definitively undetermined condition, Job begins to hope that he is not indefinitely determined by anything—neither his conditions nor the whims of a sovereign God.

CHAPTER 6 begins the book's third and final part with an analysis of YHWH's address to Job from the whirlwind. God initially appears to dodge, dismiss, or disparage the issues that Job has raised, but such appearances dissipate if we refuse to read the speeches solely as responses to Job's desire for guilt which, as CHAPTER 5 demonstrates, even he reckons impossible. The speeches paint the world as a montage of worlds, without harmony or overarching order. The material world is not limited with respect to an external, divine transcendence; the world's limits inhere within its plastic materiality. These immanent ("hard-wired") limits enable the world to produce monstrous, chaotic beings like Behemoth and Leviathan. The speeches are staged to teach Job that he has emerged out of the world just like such monsters. God emphasizes that Job is as alienated as they from their originary sources and surroundings. In other words, God shows Job a world that is indeed as Job thinks it is.

In the concluding CHAPTER 7 I explore some of the ethical implications of YHWH's speeches in light of my interpretation of them. I doubt that YHWH rebukes Job for failing to assume his proper place in this "multiverse" since from beginning to end YHWH's speeches describe a fundamental separation that divides the subject from the conflict-ridden forces out of which it has come into being. Instead YHWH shows Job (i) that in the beginning there was a fundamentally chaotic, less-than-unified, pulsating, and wild, asubjective multiverse, (ii) that Job has come into being out of this primordial, unbalanced antagonism of forces, and (iii) that Job remains cut off from this groundless ground of his existence. Interpreters are right to say that the divine speeches leave much unaccounted for, but they usually misidentify the issues that these speeches leave suspended, including: In what sense does Job remain tied to the imbalanced antagonism of forces that exists as the groundless ground of his existence? Correlatively, in what sense is he cut off from it/them? Finally, how does existence as such come into being out of this groundless ground?

CHAPTER 7 also offers a close analysis of Job 42, which contains Job's response in vv.1–6 followed by a prose conclusion. Several issues that the divine speeches leave suspended are at least partially addressed in the book's final chapter. Many who read God's speeches as an ethical rebuke of Job read Job's response in 42:1–6 in an ethical sense—as, for example, defiance or humility. But I doubt that Job's ambiguous response can finally sustain such an ethical interpretation. Job simultaneously rejects and affirms what he knew and now has seen and heard from God—that he exists on an ungrounded ground that is fundamentally out of joint and generative of beings that transcend it. The reasons for Job's rejection seem obvious considering the abyssal experiences he has suffered of the ground opening up and riveting him to its vorticular movement. His affirmation seems no less rooted in his speeches since he discovered in them a hope in the generative capacities of his ontological condition. God's speeches confirm that these antagonistic forces can somehow generate out of themselves beings that transcend them. In God's celebrations, creatures such as Behemoth and Leviathan not only seem to transcend their environments, Job, and even God, but are also described as God's creatures, who arose out of creation, and, in Behemoth's case, are explicitly likened to Job. In other words, in God's speech they seem to be tied to and to transcend their conditions. Job's ultimate hope is likewise that his conditions would generate a new existence in which he, his world, and God would all be transformed. As difficult and terrifying as it must have been to accept, this is in fact the only condition about which Job has led readers to think he could find consolation.

I directly relate this reading of JOB to virtue ethics, which is currently the most popular and widely accepted framework for exploring the ethical implications of biblical texts in general and wisdom literature in particular. Virtue ethics cannot account for and even reckons unethical a number of aspects of JOB that must lie at the center of any ethical considerations of it. Virtue ethics' emphases on integrity, continuity, and coherence cannot account for JOB's premise (God acts to rupture a human from his conditions so as to enable him to act ethically), Job's discovery (that his hope lies in his inherently inconsistent and antagonistic conditions and not in overcoming this internal deadlock), or God's teachings (about an acosmic, less-than-unified world[s] that generates creatures that inhabit it without fitting into it). In contrast to a communitarian and virtue-oriented framework, I demonstrate that any ethic that could account for the book of Job must have a revolutionary, transformational, and event-oriented model.

After Job's affirmation of what YHWH says, YHWH speaks again in the prose conclusion, this time affirming what Job says in the dialogue and rejecting what the friends' say. Where God's and Job's affirmations are usually read as departures from the storyline up to that point, they are more like a final plot twist in a psychological thriller that reveals what has been true all along. Job's so-called restoration at the end is far from an attempt to return Job to his pre-afflicted life (plus compensation for the pain and suffering). The "restoration" is better read as a brief glimpse into the nature of a community that is organized around a transcendent WISDOM that has emerged out of the immanent conditions of lived experience. That is, in the end JOB invites readers to contemplate the possibility that a community could be oriented around Job, bound together by the implications of his experience and of the testimonies of YHWH and Job.

§7 This Project's Point of Departure

The present project could not be introduced without considering C. Newsom's 2003 monograph, which marks a watershed in critical biblical interpretation of JOB.[21] After briefly considering the new paradigm her work inaugurates in Joban studies, I consider how the present project relates to hers as both supplement and critique. (I return to the contributions and limits of her work throughout.) While JOB has often been characterized as a staged conflict with traditional wisdom, and as a heterogeneous conjunction of different traditions or perspectives, Newsom was the first to wager that this internal differentiation was not (just) an opposition between JOB and the tradition it rejected, or (simply) a conjunction of externally opposed perspectives, but rather was an antagonism constitutive of the book's meaning. Newsom's argument allows one to read JOB's internal differentiation—what she calls its polyphonic character—as indicative neither of an inadequate redactional hand, nor of an inadequate interpretive thought, but rather as an antagonism intended to guarantee that no single, coherent account of JOB's message could be advanced:

> Read as a polyphonic work, the purpose of the book is not to advance a particular view: neither that of the prose tale, nor that of the friends, nor that of Job, nor even that of God. Rather, its purpose is to demonstrate that the idea of piety in all its "contradictory complexity" cannot in principle "be fitted within the bounds of a single consciousness." The truth about piety can only be grasped at the point of intersection of unmerged perspectives.[22]

According to Newsom, the internal antagonism of JOB's messages constitutes its dialogic truth. Newsom derives her notions of a polyphonic text and dialogic truth in large part from the work of Mikhail Bakhtin. Dialogic truth, unlike monologic truth, arises at the encounter of distinct voices, is anti-systematic, and open.

After her clear statement of the book's purpose, Newsom immediately retracts it: "dialogue cannot explain and indeed threatens to obscure important dimensions of the book."[23] Newsom identifies several obstacles JOB puts in the path of anyone who attempts to read it as a demonstration of dialogic truth. Some are particular to Bakhtin's notion of dialogic truth, for example: "Bakhtin was consistently reluctant to address the effects of power on dialogic relations."[24] One cannot ignore power relations and read JOB dialogically since unequal power relations underlie and influence its voices. But if this were the only limit of dialogic truth, one could reconceive it such that it would address the effects of power and perhaps account for JOB's truth. However, Newsom identifies other obstacles that stem from bearers of truth in JOB that no dialogic view of truth could voice. She offers various examples of these bearers of unsayable truths, including unconscious motivations, corrupted speech, the dismantled identities of a speaker and the world, and, finally, those pregnant silences that "punctuate the book . . . [and] gesture to the ultimate limits of dialogue, to the unsayable that shadows speech."[25] This statement concludes Newsom's opening chapter, thus establishing a tension between (i) the assertion that the book's point is to demonstrate a dialogic truth about piety, and (ii) the observation that the book reveals the ultimate failure of dialogue to account for its truth. In all its various modes, the unsayable presents truths that escape dialogic truth.

Newsom's argument explicates these truths—monologic, dialogic, and unsayable—their limits, and the tensions that persist between and among them throughout the book. If at one moment she explicates the truth that a particular genre or perspective presents in a monologic voice, at another she attends to the limits posed to this particular voice by another voice with a different perspective. She explores the dialogic truths that arise when two or more voices are read together as counterpoints, and how this dialogic truth exceeds and limits its constituent voices. Finally, she attends to the limits posed to monologic and dialogic truths by exploring an unsayable truth that exceeds them.

For example, Newsom's second chapter details the prose tale's monologically voiced moral imagination. Hastily put (the details are unimportant at this point), she thinks the tale proposes that unalienated piety is possible if one orients oneself with respect to contingency (and not necessity). Just as she argues at the end of her first chapter that the book presents one truth that is "said" and another "unsayable" truth for which the said truth is incapable of accounting, so too does she argue at the end of her second chapter that the prose tale presents another truth that stands in tension with its said truth. While she does not tie the unsayable to any particular thinker in her first chapter, this parallel discussion in her second chapter suggests that Emmanuel Levinas is her primary reference for an unsayable truth indicated by JOB that falls outside of what a dialogical truth can convey.[26] She refers to Adam Zachary Newton's work on narrative ethics that draws on Levinas to argue that everything that is said in a narrative (the Said) is predicated on a "Saying," which Newsom glosses as "the intersubjective relation established in narrative through its performative aspect."[27] As she indicates, the Saying is just one of Levinas's ways of demonstrating an Other on which all meaning depends.

Levinas critiques the philosophical tradition for thinking that the ethical derives from or aims for ontological notions such as unity, identity, the Same, totality, and finitude. Levinas shows how these philosophical notions try to exclude and thereby exercise violence against the absolutely Other, and he celebrates those exceptional places where he thinks Western thought includes the idea of the Other; for example, Descartes's idea of the Infinite, Plotinus's One, and Plato's Good beyond being.[28] For Levinas, all philosophy, thought, and language derive from an asymmetrical encounter with an unappropriatable Other to whom the subject is absolutely obliged. Levinas describes the Other's absoluteness in various ways; the easiest to grasp may be his description of the Other's transcendence from the differential order of signification: the "other involves a signifyingness of its own, independently of this signification received from the world. The other does not only come to us out of a context, but comes without mediation; he signifies by himself."[29] For Levinas, every Said issues from a Saying that responds to an asymmetrical relation between the Self and the immediate presence of an absolute Other that cannot be appropriated. The Self is subjected to and completely responsible for this Other whose absolute alterity keeps it unrevealed.[30] Levinas's anti-egoistic ethic of sacrificial responsibility rests on his claim that the absolute Other is Good: "To be for the Other is to be good."[31]

Newsom departs from the ethical implications that Levinas draws from his notion of the Saying as an incarnation of the trace of the Other. Like Levinas, Newsom thinks that the ethical implications of the prose tale's Saying challenge its Said by exposing its exclusion of the Other. The intersubjective relations that the Saying establishes both within the text and between the text and its readers pose problems for its ethic: "Job in the prose tale is a character who has become an instrument in the disagreement between God and haśśāṭān, a mere illustration in the thematic discourse of the didactic narrative."[32] Just as God objectifies Job into a spectacle and an instrument, a spectacular instrument with which God can settle a disagreement with haśśāṭān, so too does the discursive link between the narrative and the reader objectify Job into an illustration of piety. Even the attempt to make Job illustrate a piety that is critical of God requires one to objectify Job into an instrument wielded to settle one's own disagreement (with God). In other words, what is not said— the unethical relations established by the Said—undermines the ethic presented by what is Said. Unlike Levinas, Newsom does not privilege the approach to the Saying over the Said.[33] She acknowledges that they "are difficult to hold together" and that readers may have to suspend one to hear the other, but she exhorts her readers to attend to both the Said and the Saying for she sees neither as ethically superior and each as insufficient on its own.[34]

Having sketched the monologic ethic of the tale's Said, and the sense in which its Saying interrupts and undermines it, Newsom also considers the sense in which the Said's ethic is challenged from the perspective of Bakhtin's dialogism. Newsom seems to play on the senses in which interruption is explicitly involved in Levinas's thinking about what the Saying as a trace of the Other does to the Said, and implicitly involved in Bakhtin's thinking, since dialogism designates the co-presence of more than one voice. The tale presents its ethic with a monologic voice that is undermined by the book's insertion of "another, alien genre, that of the wisdom dialogue, the language, values, and moral perspectives of which are radically different."[35] Newsom explains that the impetus for her appeal to Levinas's idea of interruption derives from the inability of Bakhtin's dialogism to account for the ethical imperative issued by the prose tale's Saying. Dialogism cannot account for the limits "embodied in the prose tale itself" that are exposed by Levinas's notion of a Saying that opens "up the Said by continual interruption, making it acknowledge that aspect of language which is always saying something else, the possibility posed by the Other who speaks, breaking up the closure of identity and essence."[36] But she nonetheless sees Bakhtin's dialogism as functioning in tandem with Levinas's interruption insofar as the author's inclusion of a new genre in which Job gets a voice seems to respond directly to the imperative that issues from the prose tale's ethical shortcomings:

> Thus, in the prose tale, attending to the performative aspects of the story discloses an urgency already present that motivates and is answered by the structure of the book as a whole. . . . By interrupting with a wisdom dialogue, in which characters speak without significant narration, the author gives back to the character Job his subjectivity as an unfinalized presence whose last word is not yet spoken.[37]

Though Bakhtin's dialogism cannot perceive the unsayable, it provides a way to read the structure of the book as a whole as a response to the ethical demands of the unsayable.

At this point certain questions become unavoidable for this Bakhtinian–Levinasian framework. Before posing them, however, a terminological shift will be easier than sustaining the Levinasian categories. From this point on I refer to the Saying as the *Enunciation*, the Said as the

Statement, and the unsayable as the *Excess*. When appropriate, I also add subscripts to each to specify the genres to which they refer (P–prose tale, D–dialogue). The central question is whether Bakhtin's dialogic view of truth can adequately account for the dialogue and "the structure of the book as a whole" as a response to the prose tale's *Excess* (that is, $Excess_P$).

Newsom's hybrid Bakhtinian–Levinasian framework responds well to certain shortcomings of both thinkers. Bakhtin's dialogism functions as a corrective to Levinas's unsupportable relegation of the ethical to the *Enunciation* alone.[38] Levinas's *Enunciation* functions as a corrective to dialogism's inability to account for the unmasterable and internally conflicting *Excesses* that a voice generates. But there are problems with treating the dialogue's *Statement* as a response to the $Excess_P$, which Newsom exposes by attending to the $Enunciation_P$. The relationship between the *Statement* and the *Excess* fundamentally shifts when the *Statement* and the *Excess* being considered derive from two different voices. Up to this point Newsom has presented the *Excess* much like WISDOM: an *internal* limit— "embodied in the prose tale itself"—that necessarily accompanies every *Statement*. So, when she treats $Excess_P$ as something external to $Statement_D$, what gets lost is the role played by the $Excess_D$ that must necessarily be present once she transitions from one voice to another. The $Statement_D$ must be grasped with respect to its own $Excess_D$, whether or not it is read against the $Enunciation_P$ and $Excess_P$. Newsom does attend at length to various manifestations of the $Excess_D$. She even argues that Job's speech testifies to the $Excess_D$ as ontological.[39] Yet is it possible to offer a sufficient account of the response that the $Statement_D$ and "the structure of the book as a whole" are supposed to offer to the $Excess_P$ when the dialogue and book are read through a Bakhtinian lens that, she says, is unable to perceive their own *Excesses*? While Newsom's disregard of the dialogue's (and the whole book's) *Excess* in her consideration of its *Statement* occurs at a minor moment in her argument, she does not finally treat the relationship between the *Excess* and the *Statement* consistently. In her more Levinasian moments she treats the *Excess* as an internal, immanent condition of a *Statement*; in her more Bakhtinian moments she treats the *Excess* as something outside of a *Statement*. Sometimes she sees the *Statement* as a response to the *Excess*; at other times she sees the *Excess* as problematic for the *Statement* only in the sense that the *Statement* fails to say it (and not as an internal limit to what it says). But since the *Excess* is an internal limit, one cannot understand a *Statement* without attending to its *Excess*.

Contributing to these difficulties is Levinas's own failure to conceptualize alterity adequately. Levinas insists on the absolute transcendence of alterity, and he characterizes the Other as one who comes "without mediation" and "signifies by himself."[40] His emphases on immediacy and transcendence are difficult to square with the idea that the unsayable *Excess* is internal to the *Statement*. I would contend that the *Statement* is not limited because it depends upon or issues from a transcendent, unconditioned, and immediate Other; it is limited because alterity is unconditionally *immanent* to it as that which prevents it or anything else from ever transcending its mediating conditions or constituting itself. Levinas's notion of the Other is an impossible and inconsistent notion of something beyond alterity and all relations of mediation. Levinas's Other is identical to itself, signifies by itself, and is perfectly infinite and absolved of all relations with others. In short and despite himself, the Other that Levinas celebrates is indistinguishable from the Same that he denigrates.[41] His problem stems from his failure to see that what is unconditional is not an Other that limits conditions by transcending them, but the internal limit that prevents any condition from ever becoming transcendent. No condition can be constituted in itself, apart from an internal otherness that disturbs and disrupts it. Alterity is the only unconditional.

So, to say explicitly what this extended treatment of Newsom's work has been approaching all along, I define WISDOM in this sense as an immanent, unconditional limit. I analyze it in JOB apart from Levinas's deficiencies and inconsistencies. I depart from the image of a "tension" between and among monologic, dialogic, and unsayable truths, and instead investigate unsayable WISDOM as the internal and operative condition for each of the book's voiced perspectives. While I treat a number of the tensions among its voiced perspectives, I primarily focus on the fundamental and internally differentiating limit that grounds each of the book's voices. In ways that are often congruent with Newsom's analyses, I find that the book's voices are not just grounded in but preoccupied with this internal alterity that afflicts every voice. I thematize how JOB's most unifying features issue from its concern with this sense of WISDOM. The book of Job struggles to grasp and articulate how a voice can arise out of a fundamentally limited and antagonistic ground, and its voices are often illustrative of or preoccupied with how their internally inconsistent grounds continue to haunt them.

Before introducing the theoretical background to my conception of WISDOM, I can briefly indicate my sense of how WISDOM operates in JOB. JOB explicitly struggles with and/or implicitly illustrates the necessity and difficulty of voicing a perspective or a relation among perspectives, as well as the unsayable and inconsistent ground to which these voices remain tethered. In the prose tale Job is challenged to display fear that would be unconditioned by any of his circumstances, and then he is enabled to do so through the systematic removal of all the conditions of his life. The book then transitions to a dialogue in which Job tries to articulate what he knows now that he is unmoored from any of reality's conditions. The book's design thus illustrates the central issue with which it struggles: how all meaningful voices emerge out of and continue to wrestle with the monstrous, traumatic experience of an unsayable limit/excess. After the affliction in the prose tale, Job embodies and represents death—perhaps *the* unsayable condition. The unsayable abyss out of which discourses arise haunts Job's discourse in the dialogue as much as anyone else's. Throughout Job complains that he is unable to experience any consistent subjective position or stable perspective. And Job identifies God as the immanent limit that unconditionally perturbs his strivings for stability and a place in reality. Job declares that God is the ultimate ontological condition of the fundamentally limited world. Unlike the friends who think that the world is limited with respect to a transcendent God, Job thinks that his world, his language, and himself are all limited insofar as God acts as an internal condition that unconditionally breaches their integrity. The friends fail to communicate with Job for the same reason that Bakhtin's dialogism cannot perceive the unsayable: They cannot communicate with Job since they relate to the limits of their wisdom and experience as if these limits indicated the presence of a truth somewhere else (in [an]other human or divine voice[s]). They thus fail to perceive that the real WISDOM of their discourse and understanding is the decentering obstacle that keeps it limited and that Job manifests as a result of his encounter with God's abyssal "presence." Finally, nothing may be more emphasized by the divine speeches' rhetorical mode of address than the "presence" of an unsayable, immanent negativity inhering within the ontological fabric of the less-than-fully unified multiverse.

§8 The Lacanian Real

The central theoretical figures informing my work are the French psychoanalyst Jacques Lacan and various post-Lacanian thinkers such as the Slovenian philosopher Slavoj Žižek and others associated with his work. Žižek's corpus consistently reassesses the philosophical work of Kant and German idealism in light of Lacanian psychoanalytic metapsychology.[42] Both the continental philosophers and the Freudian psychoanalysts supply the conceptual coordinates of the present project. The way in which I have talked about an unsayable WISDOM that is internal to and constitutive of the discursive field of wisdom is closely related to the ways in which Lacan and various post-Lacanians describe the register of the Real and its relation to the Imaginary and the Symbolic.[43]

To introduce these three registers to which I return and develop further, I offer three different ways to understand the unsayable, one for each register. First I should distinguish these registers from other, common uses of these words. The Imaginary should be associated with images rather than make-believe; the Symbolic should be associated with signifiers—the graphemic and phonemic material that languages use to create meaning—rather than a literary trope or device; and the Real should be associated with what is impossible to symbolize into either Imaginary or Symbolic materials, rather than what is objective or actual. The registers are intentionally flexible, and Žižek has proposed that each one is refracted within the others, thus generating for the Real an Imaginary Real, Symbolic Real, and Real Real. (He does the same for the Imaginary and Symbolic)[44]:

> [T]he real Real would be the horrible Thing: the Medusa's head; the alien from the movie; the abyss; a monster . . . [The symbolic Real] is simply meaningless scientific formulae. For example, quantum physics can be understood as symbolic Real. . . . As Richard Feynman, the great quantum physicist, himself liked to emphasize, you cannot understand quantum physics, you cannot translate it into our horizon of meaning. It consists of formulae that simply function. . . . [The imaginary Real has] this totally fragile appearance: the Real can be something that transpires or shines through. For example, when you talk with another person and you are charmed by him or her. . . . It is something that is Real, but at the same time totally elusive and fragile.[45]

Although I will not consider each register refracted within the others, I think Žižek's discussion is especially helpful since it differentiates the registers on the basis of some common ground, which is also what I can do by way of the unsayable. The Symbolic unsayable refers to those elements that are not symbolized but are nonetheless structured and present within a signifying order. The dimension of the *Enunciation* developed by Newsom is one example. The *Enunciation* is not part of the *Statement*, but it is structured by the signifying elements that make up the *Statement*. At a simpler level, the Symbolic unsayable would also refer to the Qal perfect ending on the third person masculine singular verb in Hebrew. It is marked by the absence of any signifying element. The Imaginary unsayable might refer to charisma, a peaceful silence, mystical feeling, or even certain forms of racism. In all of these there is something unsayable, associated with a plenitude, which endows one's situation with a surplus of meaning. With respect to the Bible, the Imaginary unsayable would also refer to, say, a literary form or "type–scene."[46] Finally, the Real unsayable refers to a word, smell, voice, sight, or situation that cannot be spoken, smelled, heard, seen, or experienced without some eruption of anxiety or traumatic breakdown. The Real unsayable is in a sense inherent to the Imaginary–Symbolic order of what can be said, seen, and so on, since this order curves around the Real unsayable as what it is incapable of including without in some way disintegrating. The Real always exists as a limit on any discursive order—this order's condition of impossibility and its constitutive condition of possibility. Here it is hard not to think of the harrowing and perilous scene of the Israelites around the mountain, desperate for the mediating distance that the Imaginary–Symbolic law promises to provide between themselves and God's eruptive, holy, and traumatic presence (cf. Exod 19–20). Job, like others such as Nadab and Abihu, does not enjoy the privilege of such mediation.

Lacan famously likened his three registers to the three-ringed Borromean knot. The knot is such that if any of the three rings is cut, "all three are set free."[47] The knot thus illustrates that none of the registers exists apart from the others, and that none is superior to the others. It is sometimes pertinent to lump the Imaginary and the Symbolic together as they interact dialectically to constitute what speaking beings perceive as reality. There are various senses in which the Real is opposed to, or located at the interstices of, reality as it is constituted by the Imaginary–Symbolic registers of human experience. First, the Real designates our unsymbolized forces that are active in our biological/material bodies. It is crucial to remember the Borromean knot here so that the Real is not considered wholly external to reality as, for example, a material ground or "objective" reality separate from and foundational for the "subjectively" constituted Imaginary–Symbolic reality. From his first seminars in the mid-1950s Lacan consistently distinguishes the Real from a common-sense notion of objectivity.[48] Lacan claims that the "actual" or "objective" reality that seems to lie behind our distorted vision of reality is only the projected horizon produced by our distorted vision, and not some "irreducible reality."[49] In this context, Lacan's Real refers to the cause of the particular distortions we see, like an unrepresentable vanishing point that is constitutive of an artistic representation.

Despite some of Lacan's claims and the misunderstandings they have supported, Lacanian theory also rejects references to a raw, bio-material Real with no significant relation to more-than-material Imaginary–Symbolic matrices of representation.[50] Lacan decried what he saw as a naive, reductive materialism undergirding many psychoanalytic theories and practices, especially ones that rely on an impossible reference—in the sense that it exceeds what is epistemologically possible in analysis—to a bedrock of instinctual/biological needs underlying the cultural vicissitudes of the analysand's subjectivity.[51] While Lacan carried out his work largely apart from recent advances in the neurosciences, the most cutting-edge brain researchers (for example, Damasio, LeDoux, Panksepp, and Stanovich) reject both naturalism and constructivism in ways that are complementary and largely amenable to Freudian–Lacanian metapsychology.[52] These neuroscientists reject both essentialist naturalism and constructivist anti-naturalism that would reduce/divorce human subjectivity to/from bodily-biological influence. Just as Lacan rejected the idea that cognitive capacities and representational factors operate apart from bodily influence, so too do the neuroscientists recognize the significant role played by cultural, social, symbolic, representational, and other cognitive factors in inflecting emotions and mental life.[53] The Lacanian Real refers to material/biological need but only insofar as it is not a force or state in and of itself; instead, it lies at the far end of a two-way street: its presence or influence is evident in the shapings, inconsistencies, and gaps of more-than-material Imaginary and Symbolic registers; and this Real is also and to an indeterminable extent influenced by more-than-material/biological factors.[54]

Lacan himself is primarily concerned with approaching the Real through Imaginary and Symbolic representations. The Real is manifest by the boundaries and contours of Imaginary–Symbolic symbolizations, their distinctive shapings around their unsayable.

> The Lacanian real, as manifested in the patient's discourse, is that which makes the analysand come back to the same subject, event, or notion over and over, revolve around it endlessly, and feel unable to move on. The patient dwells on it and feels stuck, something essential remaining unformulated.[55]

Fink's quotation characterizes the Real in three important senses: first, the Real is causal ("that which makes . . ."); second, the Real engenders repetition ("over and over . . . endlessly"); third, the subject experiences the Real as a feeling of being "stuck." Real causality refers to a cause that exists at a different level than Imaginary and Symbolic causality. In the latter, causes and effects exist at the same level. Real causality, however, refers to unconscious causes that are lost to the level of conscious experience. One might think of famous cases in which motor paralysis, involuntary tics, and so on, result as psychosomatic symptoms in some of Freud's well-known cases of hysteria. The hysteric cathects a part of its body with libido displaced from repressed drives of which it is unaware.

This Real, lost cause should not be misread as evidence of psychoanalysis's determinism—that is, regardless of the subject's complex conscious thoughts, experiences, actions, and nature, psychoanalysis provides its own causal account of a second nature that unifies the inconsistencies of experience. Such a reading misunderstands the place and temporality of the Real. The Real is neither a transcendental condition of possibility for Imaginary and Symbolic experience, nor an objective, corporeal, or historical reality underlying it. The Real is instead the internal, unconditional, unsayable, and ahistorical condition without which Imaginary–Symbolic reality would not exist, but because of which Imaginary–Symbolic reality always contains inconsistencies/antagonisms and remains open to historical shifts/transformations. From the perspective of textual interpretation—which is similar in some important ways to psychoanalytic practice—I will refuse to treat the Real as a positive/substantial entity, and will instead insist that it is nothing but the Imaginary and Symbolic registers when they are conceived as open, incomplete, and inconsistent. Although ahistorical, the Real is not outside of history since its status and function change with the transformations undergone by Imaginary and Symbolic reality. It is ahistorical in the sense that it is the unconditional condition within history and being that keeps them open, undetermined, and unstable. Imaginary and Symbolic reality tries to keep the perturbing manifestations of this constitutive instability at bay or, if not, then fixated in displaced locations where they do not disturb reality since they seem to make no sense (as in hysterical coughing that baffles any medical or meaningful reasoning that fails to account for unconscious causation).

Thus, to return to Fink's three characterizations, the Real refers on one hand to those unsayable deadlocks in Imaginary–Symbolic representations to which they compulsively return and, on the other, to a dimension beyond Imaginary–Symbolic reality to which this reality remains open. The Real is both a conservative and transformative condition inherent to reality. The Real is both constitutive of and a limit to reality. The Real refers both to what remains beyond reality's pleasure principle and to reality when it ventures beyond its pleasure principle.

The way in which the Real functions for subjects constituted within Imaginary–Symbolic reality follows from the ways in which it functions for reality. The subject's status as Real refers to its internal inconsistency, the metaphorical bar that keeps the self from ever achieving any final identity with itself, and that ensures its interminable engagement in a movement beyond itself that prevents it from ever returning to the same self. Lacan thus strictly distinguishes the Imaginary–Symbolic self/ego from the Real subject. He writes the subject "$" to signify the constitutive lack that divides the self from itself. The split or barred subject is a negative magnitude that is a constitutive condition for any meaning/identity, and yet that keeps every meaning/identity unfinalized and open.[56] Lacan's sense of the subject thus directly opposes Levinas's idea that anything could "signify by itself." To return to the hysteric, the involuntary cough is a signifier of the hysteric's Real division from herself.[57] The particular symptom manifested depends upon the subject's conscious and unconscious Imaginary–Symbolic conceptions, but these conceptions do not cause her symptom. The Real cause or origin of the symptom is the subject's constitutive self-division that generates libidinal impulses that the subject channels through its Imaginary–Symbolic conceptions.

In the hysteric's case these conceptions can be used as outlets for repressed impulses that remain displaced from consciousness's awareness. The symptom incarnates this Real lack internal to her being and localizes outside of the conscious self a truth about the self. Phobic objects similarly incarnate the Real lack that the obsessive tries to keep at bay. The approach of the phobic object causes anxiety because it threatens to close the gap that constitutes the self as a desiring being, that is, it threatens to destroy the subject.[58] Lacan refers to these objects that incarnate the self's constitutive division as "*objet petit a*" or "object (*a*)."[59] The objects (*a*) manifest that aspect of the self that exceeds the self. I will discuss these objects in more detail in the following section. The subject always encounters them as foreign since they incarnate the lack at the core of its subjectivity and yet are not something with which the self identifies. The subject ($) and the object (*a*) are two sides of the same coin: the subject signifies the self's constitutive situation as lacking, as perpetually failing to coincide with itself; the object (*a*) signifies the self's constitutive situation as excessive, as perpetually exceeding that which it previously was (failing to be).

This conception of the Lacanian Real provides the primary framework within which this study approaches the subjective and objective aspects of unsayable WISDOM. JOB consistently reveals the subject, understood as the constitutive displacement of the self from itself, as well as the *objet petit a*, understood as the material incarnation of the subject's lack that the self encounters as a foreign object. I attend not only to the framework through which the sages locate and deal with WISDOM, but also to the libidinal economies with which they experience and grasp WISDOM.

§9 The Drive

This section introduces the psychoanalytic conception of the drive to which I return throughout the book. Lacan designates the drive as one of "the four fundamental concepts of psychoanalysis" (the others being the unconscious, repetition, and transference).[60] In Freud's 1915 metapsychology paper "Drives and Their Vicissitudes," he segments the drive (*Trieb*) into four constituent parts that, Lacan says, "cannot but appear disjointed"[61]: source (*Quelle*), pressure (*Drang*), aim (*Ziel*), and object (*Objekt*).[62] The German is important because of the unfortunate translation of *Trieb* as "instinct" in the standard English edition of Freud's works, as well as the ease with which the drive can be confused with other related concepts, such as a quantity of energy or force of pressure (*Drang*).[63] "Instinct" is a poor translation insofar as it implies a naturalistic impulse with a clear object and set parameters for its satisfaction.[64] The constituent components of the drives are internally inconsistent and incapable of being coordinated in part because of their different temporal logics. The drive's somatic *sources* issue demands for satisfaction that are affectively registered as *pressure,* which the drive *aims* to alleviate through particular *object* choices. But, as Lacan says, the four components do not fit together, and he continues, "if there is anything resembling a drive it is a montage . . . in the sense in which one speaks of montage in a surrealist collage."[65] The objects available to the temporal experience of a subject's history are unable to satisfy the timeless, constant, and reiterated demands that issue from the drive source.[66]

The drives are primarily associated with the erogenous zones identified by Freud and Lacan as privileged sites of libidinal interest in large part because they mark openings between the body and the external environment (for example, anus, genitals, eyes, ears). I will focus on the oral drive, which is centered around the mouth. To illustrate the metapsychological concept of the drive, consider the emergence of the subject–object division in an infant as illustrated in the following, mythic narration. As others have done before and after him, Freud imagined that an experience of discontent must precipitate the birth of a proto-subjective ego out of its experience of fluid indistinction (that is, pure subjectless/objectless continuity). Without discontent, Freud plausibly thinks the infant would never need to recognize the existence of the external world.[67] The nascent ego experiences the onset of dissatisfaction as some part of itself separating from itself. Since it did not previously feel this discontent, it must have possessed and enjoyed what it is now lacking. Its ability to achieve partial, temporary feelings of satisfaction from others promotes its sense that what made it "discontent-less" is outside of itself, among others. Of course, the ego neither *had* nor *lost* anything since, prior to the realization of its dissatisfaction, there was neither an ego that could have anything, nor objects that could be had. The point of this mythic account of the genesis of the subject–object division is to

illustrate Lacan's notions of the object (a)—the material incarnation of
the self's constitutive lack—and the subject-as-$—the lack that makes it
possible for a self to exist that is also what makes it impossible for a self to
exist in itself. Lacan says in this regard that the breast is the child's rather
than the mother's. The "breast" refers to the "object" that the self feels
has been detached from it and attached to the objective world. The breast
does not refer to an object in Imaginary–Symbolic reality, but rather to
the subject's (usually unconscious) libidinal investment in such objects as
potential sources for the satisfaction of its desire. The breast as *objet petit a*
is the object that propels the subject's desire and that can be delineated
as the motivating consistency or repetition that one can trace across the
subject's object choices.[68]

More needs to be said about the drive's aim and object since the
drives do not only fail. They also succeed through a process that Freud
calls "sublimation." Freud leaves an enigma, claiming both that the drives
are aim-inhibited (*zielgehemmt*) *and* capable of being sublimated, which
"is in every instance satisfaction."[69] Lacan resolves Freud's enigma by distinguishing the drives' *goal*, which they fail to attain, from their *aim*, which
succeeds through the process that fails to meet the *goal*.[70] Lacan's distinction between the thwarted goal and the attained aim of the drive renders
ambiguous the quality of the satisfaction attained through sublimation.[71]
The drive's enjoyment, which Lacan calls *jouissance*, does not (necessarily) feel pleasurable to the subject whose conscious experience (usually)
derives from the dissatisfaction of not attaining its goal.[72] The drives' internal conflict keeps them from attaining their goal, but their repeated
failures nonetheless afford the subject a sense of satisfaction.

To illustrate this dynamic, I can return to the nursing example. The
infant's demand for milk may have its *source* in the need of hunger, but
this demand cannot be reduced to the *need* to fill the stomach alone. As
soon as one is willing to imagine a subject–object distinction (according
to Lacan, usually around six months of life), the demand for milk must
be seen as a nodal point amidst a whole host of related experiences and
desires, including:

- various biological-material pressures and sensations (for example,
  hunger, warmth, satiation, hiccups, engorgement);
- material and more-than-material pleasures and sensations (for example, taste and satisfaction associated with feeding, and "the narcissistic sense of omnipotence linked to the control of the mother's behavior as a person/object supplying gratification"[73]); and
- various indications given by the mother that the activity has more
  meaning for her than it does for the child (for example, repeated pe-

culiarities such as facial expressions, acts of physical touching, or vocal inflections; and [conscious and unconscious] signs of pleasure or pain).

The infant's demand for milk involves many more concerns than mere instinct allows because of the biological facts of human beings' deficiencies— "motor impotence and nursling dependence"[74]—that cause them to live extended periods of prematurational helplessness. Once the infant's cognitive capacities develop—despite its motor incapacitation—to the point that it is to some extent aware of its reliance on an other/primary caregiver (to whom I refer as mother), it develops a protosocial bond with that other that affects its experiences. All the ways in which nursing can become a nodal point in a web of significant experiences illustrate how human activities, feelings, satisfactions, desires, and needs are from the outset more than anything for which a reductive description could account.[75]

This irreducibe intertwining of needs and desires in demands lies behind Lacan's claim that drives fail and succeed.[76] The subject's investment in an object (for example, milk) as a possible source for satisfying its desire elevates (or "sublimates") milk into something more than milk, something more than nutritional—this is why the oral drive object is not called milk but the non-nutritional and sexualized breast.[77] The drive's necessary dissatisfaction arises from the subject's (usually unconscious) investment in its object as a potential source for satisfying what no object could satisfy since such satisfaction would turn into its opposite by eliminating the constitutive lack on which the subject and object depend. However, the dissatisfaction that the subject feels at the milk's inability to fulfill its desire for the breast must mean that the subject's investment has somehow also made the breast present to the subject in order for the subject to know that the milk did not correspond to the breast. The breast is, in other words, nothing but the subject's investment in the object that enables it to present more than it is and satisfy more than it could.[78] The *objet petit a* "is in fact simply the presence of a hollow, a void . . . [It] is not introduced as the original food, it is introduced from the fact that no food will ever satisfy the oral drive, except by circumventing the eternally lacking object."[79] Lacan's image of the hollow or void allows me to clarify an important distinction between desire and drive to which I return throughout the book.

Desire corresponds to the lack felt by the subject as the objects encountered (for example, milk) fail to correspond to and satisfy the drive pressure. Explicitly following Jacques-Alain Miller, Žižek emphasizes the difference between desire's lack and drive's hole:

lack is spatial, designating a void *within* a space, while hole is more radical, it designates the point at which this spatial order itself breaks down (as in the "black hole" in physics). That is the difference between desire and drive: desire is grounded in its constitutive lack, while drive circulates around a hole, a gap in the order of being. In other words, the circular movement of drive obeys the weird logic of the curved space in which the shortest distance between the two points is not a straight line, but a curve: drive "knows" that the shortest way to attain its aim is to circulate around its goal-object.[80]

For Žižek, desire emerges from and strives to overcome the unbalanced libidinal economy by elevating ordinary objects into sublime Things that promise balance, whereas the drive is the satisfactory perpetuation of the unbalanced space of this economy. A couple of pages later, Žižek continues his discussion by saying that desire differs from drive in that desire "transcendentalizes" the imbalance that characterizes the drive by transposing it into a lack that some Thing could fill. "A drive," however,

does not bring satisfaction because its object is a stand-in for the Thing, but because a drive, as it were, turns failure into triumph—in it, the very failure to reach its goal, the repetition of this failure, the endless circulation around the object, generates a satisfaction of its own. As Lacan put it, the true aim of the drive is not to reach its goal, but to circulate endlessly around it.[81]

Much of Žižek's project entails an exploration of his wager that the "subject" of this psychoanalytic conception of the drive—conceived of as a largely unconscious satisfaction gained from the endless circulation around and repetition of failure—is equivalent to the subject as described by the German idealists as absolute self-relating negativity or, in Hegel's epigraph to this chapter, a night that becomes awful.[82] He often depicts the distance from Kant to Hegel as the same as from desire to drive.[83]

The usefulness of this extended consideration of drive may now become clear: the structure and logic of *desire* characterize traditional wisdom's treatment of its limits as indications of a transcendent Thing— God, Wisdom, Truth—that escapes them. However, the structure and logic of *drive* characterize the wisdom that the book of Job opposes to traditional wisdom. JOB treats its limits as immanent and as generative of a surplus dimension that desire mistakenly thinks escapes it—God, Wisdom, Truth.

The book of Job stages this alternative between drive and desire as one not only between different dispositions but also between different conceptions of the world. JOB explores the many implications of this alternative at both ontological and epistemological, as well as ethical and political, levels. The present project explores these dimensions of both theoretical philosophy and practical philosophy, which is to make an important step beyond Žižek's engagements with JOB (see §2).

2

Job 1–2: A Critique of Pure Fear

You have made us filth and rubbish among the peoples.
—Lamentations 3:45

We have become the rubbish of the world, the scum of all things.
—1 Corinthians 4:13

§10 Introduction

Mary-Jane Rubenstein relates a joke popular in Derridean circles in which a rabbi falls prostrate in the midst of a Yom Kippur service and proclaims, "Oh, God! Before You, I am nothing!" The Temple president is so moved that he repeats the gesture. When a simple tailor follows suit, the president nudges the rabbi and whispers, "So look who thinks he's nothing."[1] One must be something for the self-proclamation of nothingness to be effectively pious. When Lamentations complains that God has made God's people filth and rubbish, it laments the loss of such somethingness. Like the tailor, Lamentations' declaration of nullity cannot be pious because the lamenters are in an actual state of nothingness. When he says the same thing in 1 Corinthians, Paul is in a similar state—"To the present hour we are hungry and thirsty, we are poorly clothed and beaten and homeless" (4:11). But unlike Lamentations, Paul celebrates his nothingness; and unlike the tailor, Paul thinks his nothingness is something to boast about. The difference with Paul lies in the absence of any (implicit) reference to something that would exist apart from nothing. The rabbi's and president's declarations are effectively pious because they imagine that they really are somethings (unlike the tailor) who are relating to themselves *as if* they were nothing. At the end of this line lies a traditional image of God as the epitome of something apart from nothing. For Paul, when God's messiah becomes nothing and dies, Jesus negates both this idea of something positive that transcends nothingness and negates the previous, negative sense of nothingness by associating nothingness with God. Paul admonishes the Corinthians to imitate him (4:16) by realizing that they are, in their rubbishness, the holy temples of God (3:17). Similarly, the prose introduction to JOB negates any reference to transcendence untouched by nothingness *and* presents Job as the incarnation of the rubbish through which transcendence emerges.

§11 The Consensus on the Test

YHWH's initial question to *haśśāṭān* in the Joban prose tale is provocative: "Have you set your mind on my servant Job, for there is none like him on the earth, blameless and upright, one who fears God and turns from evil?" (1:8). YHWH's incitement could lead in a number of directions, and it is really *haśśāṭān*'s response in 1:9–11 that gets this narrative going.[2] *haśśāṭān* first asks, "Is it for naught that Job fears God?" He then conjectures that YHWH has blessed Job with a protective hedge surrounding his entire world such that, if YHWH were to take it away, Job would fail to act piously.[3] If Job's piety is conditioned upon the protection YHWH provides him, then it is not "for naught." The implication is that piety that is not "for naught" is inauthentic. Having primed us with its introduction to the exceedingly pious and wealthy Job in 1:1–5, the story hooks readers with *haśśāṭān*'s challenge to the story's claim about Job: will Job's piety withstand the challenges? Is authentic piety even possible? How will we know it when we see it?

The prose tale of JOB may initially read like straightforward, naive folklore, but the issues with which it deals are sophisticated and, especially in relation to mainstream biblical conceptions of piety, the ethic that it advances is radical.[4] This chapter opposes a strong scholarly consensus about the tale's central concerns and implications. This consensus can be stated concisely by enumerating its answers to three fundamental questions. This chapter critiques the consensus's responses and proposes a different set of answers. The three questions to which a representative swath of interpreters respond in concert are:

> Why does *haśśāṭān* cast doubt on Job's piety?
> On what basis could this test take place?
> How do we know whether Job has passed or failed the test, and therefore whether *haśśāṭān* or YHWH is right about Job?

The following responses represent a single starting point for critical approaches to the tale:

1. the potential self-interest of Job's piety is what gives rise to *haśśāṭān*'s suspicion;
2. Job's affliction makes a display of authentic piety possible;
3. Job's pious behavior after the affliction will prove YHWH right about Job, whereas *haśśāṭān* needs Job to reject or curse YHWH to be right.

Consider the following early and eloquent articulation of this consensus:

> The Satan disputes the inherent worth of this character: Job, he in- sinuates, had lived as he had, not simply with the result that he had become outwardly prosperous, but in order that he might prosper; he had served God not for God's sake, but to obtain the handsome price of such service: human nature is incapable of pure devotion to God, human conduct is not disinterested; if the payment for it ceases, or becomes uncertain, man's service of God will cease, man will no longer address God reverentially, or affectionately, but blasphemingly . . .
>
> Thus Job is left at last only with bare life, without which he could be no subject of testing, and his character which had been called into ques- tion, but which he had maintained intact under the last test that the Satan could suggest, by these words [2:10] proves his disinterested at- tachment to Yahweh, that he had not served him for what He gave, and thus finally and completely puts the Satan in the wrong.[5]

Dozens more could be cited, each of which would suggest that the object of *haśśāṭān*'s doubt is the self-interest of Job's piety, that the affliction makes the display of authentic piety possible, and that the outcome of the test is evident in Job's (im)piety following the affliction.[6]

§12 The Object of *haśśāṭān*'s Doubt; or, The Meaning of *ḥinnām*

According to most interpretations, it is the potential self-interest or self- ishness of Job's piety that gives rise to *haśśāṭān*'s suspicion. Not all ver- sions of the consensus are alike, of course. Most would agree with Habel: "Mortals, [Satan] proposes, . . . are righteous because they expect to be rewarded."[7] Clines, however, suggests that the test aims to discover whether "the causal link [is] not in the reverse direction, from prosperity to piety."[8] Of course, Clines's position still represents the consensus belief that *haśśāṭān* casts doubt upon Job's piety because of its connection to his prosperity, but his disagreement begins to make a problem with the consensus apparent. *haśśāṭān*'s question does not suggest that Job is pious so as to get rich, it implies that *any condition connecting piety to prosperity compromises piety.*[9]

Clines's intervention provides enough ground to reject a solely compensatory translation of *ḥinnām* ("for naught" in *haśśāṭān*'s question "Is it for naught that Job fears God?"). *ḥinnām* does have meanings associated with recompense or compensation in several contexts, for example, "wage-free" in Gen 29:15; Jer 22:13; "debt-free" in Exod 21:2, 11; "cost-free" in Num 11:5; 2 Sam 24:24. Yet more often and outside these contexts associated with compensation, it means "without purpose," "without cause," "in vain," or "for no end," often relating to random acts of violence perpetuated against innocent victims,[10] but not always.[11] Consider, for example, Ezek 14:23. Immediately after stating that even Job could not save Jerusalem from the destruction YHWH has prepared for it (Ezek 14:14, 20), YHWH promises to leave a remnant whose ways and deeds will be enough for the exiles to know that YHWH did not act "without cause" (*ḥinnām*). In other words, the mercy of YHWH will extend to a portion of those who remain in Jerusalem, sparing them from the awful destruction to come, *so that* those exiled with the prophet can observe the Jerusalemites' abominable behavior and know that the seemingly excessive violence of the events has not superceded the meaningful boundaries of YHWH's justice. YHWH takes care to communicate to the exiles that YHWH's justice lies behind the sphere of causality that they experience and perceive as Neo-Babylonian aggression, Judean expansion, and Egyptian enticements.

All these meanings of *ḥinnām* are related, so I do not mean to deny a compensatory connotation in Job 1:9. But an *exclusively* compensatory translation of *ḥinnām*, which one often finds,[12] is unsatisfactory because it effectively excludes these other connotations. For example, if *ḥinnām* is translated "without compensation," then *haśśāṭān* is not interested in Job's piety being "for *nothing*," "*without* cause," that is, in it being *un*-conditional, just in it being unconditioned by compensation. There are many conditions other than compensation that could render Job's piety inauthentic by *haśśāṭān*'s standards. Although *haśśāṭān* implies that God's blessing is a condition that renders the authenticity of Job's piety at least indeterminable and at most suspect, he does not simply question whether Job would fear God if he were not compensated for fearing God; he questions whether Job fears God "for naught," that is, unconditionally.[13]

§13 *haśśāṭān*'s "Copernican Revolution" in Wisdom

Having made a lexical case that *ḥinnām* can be and is best translated in the largest sense of "for naught," what does it mean for *haśśāṭān* to pose his question in these terms? If I am right that *haśśāṭān*'s challenge means that authentic fear of God is not about pious behavior except insofar as it is unconditional, then his notion of fear appears to be a precursor to Kant's notion of the ethical.[14] The crucial feature of Kant's "Copernican revolution" in ethics is that "the law is no longer regarded as dependent on the Good, but on the contrary, the Good itself is made to depend on the law."[15]

> Thus the moral worth of an action does not lie in the effect expected from it and so too does not lie in any principle of action that needs to borrow its motive from this expected effect. For, all these effects (agree-ableness of one's condition, indeed even promotion of others' happiness) could have been brought about by other causes . . . Hence nothing other than the *representation of the law* in itself . . . insofar as it . . . is the determining ground of the will, can constitute the preeminent good we call moral.[16]

Kant argues that nothing but the law, nothing but duty,[17] "can give [our] actions . . . unconditional and moral worth."[18] All other motives he deems "pathological"[19]—meaning they affect humans and thus oppose their freedom to act.[20] With Kant, the moral law is unconditional; it "is itself the ground for any possible definition of the good."[21]

That this is congruent with the prose tale should be obvious. Just as Kant's favorite examples of questionable morality describe philanthropists, honest merchants, those esteemed by the community as honorable, so too does *haśśāṭān* question someone whose pious behavior is sufficiently unquestionable not to distract from the true object of his challenge—authentic fear of God. The congruence between *haśśāṭān* and Kant, therefore, lies in the fact that *haśśāṭān* does not consider pious behavior as a true measure of authentic fear of God. It is irrelevant whether Job acts out of self-interest, or genuinely thinks he is doing what is in the interest of his community, or even whether or not he wants to be wise or righteous; authentic fear of God is now defined only as the fear of God "for naught."[22]

I am not suggesting that Kant has the same idea about morality as *haśśāṭān*, only that Kant's distinction between the morality and the legality of an act helps clarify the terminological confusion that *haśśāṭān*'s question creates between authentic and inauthentic piety. "The mere conformity or nonconformity of an action with law, irrespective of the incentive [*Triebfeder*] to it, is called *legality* (lawfulness); but that conformity in which the idea of duty arising from the law is also the incentive to the action is called its *morality*."[23] So, actions that are done in accordance with one's duty are legal, but not yet ethical; but if they are done exclusively for the sake of duty, then they are ethical. The ethical is "essentially a supplement,"[24] "a surplus or an excess"[25] over legality.

With Kant's distinction in mind, piety can be linked with legality; pious behavior is behavior done in accordance with sapiential norms of activity. This is what Job is already doing and not what *haśśāṭān* challenges.[26] Kant's conception of the ethical act congrues instead with *haśśāṭān*'s conception of the authentic fear of God as an act conditioned by nothing but the fear of God. In Kant's terms, *haśśāṭān* challenges the morality of Job's actions. We can refer to this as a challenge to Job's wisdom since the fear of God encapsulates and epitomizes wisdom in this tradition (cf. Job 28:28; and Proverbs' motto verses 1:7 and 9:10). Rather than challenge whether Job is faithful to some general or objective sense of wisdom or sapiential duty, *haśśāṭān*'s question constructs a new conception of what it means to be wise by grounding the fear of God in a purely subjective capacity.

With regard to my redress of the first of the consensus answers, what *haśśāṭān* challenges is whether Job's behavior is not only pious but also wise, the wise being a surplus dimension above and beyond questions of piety and impiety.[27] With *haśśāṭān*'s challenge the wise act becomes the pious act accomplished for nothing other than the act of fearing God itself, whence this chapter's title. This need not imply that the sage is unconcerned with the consequences of his fearful act, only that he is not motivated by them.

Before proceeding to the next section, I pause to make two observations to which I will return below. First, I have thus far referred to piety in a more or less formal sense as that behavior that the community judges to conform to duty and be worthy of praise and encouragement. The prose tale takes for granted that its readers will know whether or not Job's act is pious and asks instead whether this act is *not only* pious *but also* wise. That this sense of piety in the prose tale lacks content need not be seen as evidence of the tale's oversight or (illicit) assumption that pious behavior is unproblematic or ahistorical. I will argue instead that this absence stems from the book's claim that all wisdom and piety are conditioned upon a *particular* event, which thus prevents it from speaking about any *general* sense of piety.

Second, Kant provides a helpful point of access to the ethical quandary of *ḥinnām*, and Kant's notion of the "pathological" allows us to conceptualize the notion of authenticity with greater semantic precision than usual. These benefits notwithstanding, there is a problem with the attempt to transpose Kant's ethical act, which I showed to be determined by nothing other than "the *representation of the law* in itself," with a sapiential equivalent: "the fear of God for the sake of fearing God alone." The question is whether these evocations of "in itself" or "for its sake alone" meet *haśśāṭān*'s requirement of *ḥinnām*. In short, is fear for fear's sake the same as fear for nothing? As the ensuing argument demonstrates, in the end I think not, since the book does not endorse any notion of a transcendental a priori. The nothing for which one fears is not an a priori moral principle, but is instead conditioned by what is nothing or unconditioned *within* a particular situation.

§14 Rereading Job's Pre-afflicted Piety

Up to now I have argued that *haśśāṭān*'s challenge aims not merely at some particular condition(s) of Job's piety, but rather at what would be universally unconditional about it. I detail below the consequences of this argument for the rest of the consensus interpretation outlined above. Before getting to these implications I want to analyze how, if at all, this (re)interpretation of the challenge compels a different understanding of Job's pre-afflicted piety.

Recall that Job's only act of piety that the prose introduction reports prior to his afflictions are his regular sacrifices for the potential sins of his children. The text reads:

> And when the days of the feast had run their course, Job would send and sanctify them, and he would rise early in the morning and offer burnt offerings according to the number of them all; for Job said, "It may be that my sons have sinned, and cursed God in their hearts." Thus Job did continually. (1:5)

One should especially attend to this act:

> Since this is a didactic story, the words and actions of the main character are some of the most important guides to its values. Although Job's character had been briefly described in the opening words of the book, verses 4–5 provide the narrative example that gives content to the general description.[28]

When interpreters allow no shadow of *haśśāṭān*'s doubt to be cast on Job's piety, they often see in the sacrifices a display of Job's excessive piety, the way it seems "over the top" and perhaps already extends beyond any zero-sum cost-benefit analysis. Wilson writes, for example, "A single example of his almost compulsive caution and scrupulous attention to religious detail illustrates Job's piety."[29] Other interpreters grant *haśśāṭān*'s challenge some credibility and find in the sacrifices an outward expression of Job's inner conviction that he has a contract with God, that he and God are mutually subjected to a law of retribution that protects and blesses him if he remains pious.

> He gives the impression of being a believer who thinks that he must
> be in control of everything. He appears to be someone who implicitly
> knows what is right and what is wrong and what pleases or displeases
> God . . . What at first sight seemed to be clear proof of Job's piety later
> begins to look a little ambiguous and perhaps less favourable.[30]

Seen from this angle, Job tries to control with his sacrifices even what is beyond his person but what threatens his or his children's prosperity according to their contract with God.

These divergent interpretive directions share a common understanding of the subjective position from which Job offers his sacrifices. Whether it is confident piety or cocksure dogmatism, both think Job sacrifices from a position of certitude. However, one of the only details we are given about Job's piety tells us that he fears God on account of a truth that he does not know and about which he is uncertain—whether his children have somehow transgressed. Job sacrifices out of a subjective position of uncertainty. With them he tries to anticipate, capture, or satisfy the desire of God. Job performs them regularly, literally "all the days," and so one should understand Job's sacrifices not only as responses to some contingent detail that has escaped his knowledge but also as evidence of his disciplinary devotion to sustaining himself in a state of ignorance about a truth he does not know.

One of Lacan's statements on sacrifice may clarify where I think many interpretations of Job's sacrifices err. Sacrifice is made in the hope that it will capture God's desire, but it is not simply a matter of course.[31] "This is not to say that [the gods] are going to eat what is sacrificed to them, nor even that it can be of any use to them; but the important thing is that they desire it and, I would say further, that it does not make them anxious."[32] Lacan's point is that sacrifice is never a zero-sum activity, a contractual certainty. Out of his anxiety before the desire of an Other that is, by definition, finally unknowable, the sacrificer offers objects that attempt to capture the desire of this Other but, necessarily, can never do so with confident certitude. A surplus of the Other's desire always potentially exceeds or escapes the sacrifice (as in the phenomenon of rejected or inadequate sacrifices present throughout the Bible and perhaps most strikingly so at its very beginning, with the rejection of Cain's sacrifice[33]). The practice of sacrifice thus instills a lack of knowledge on the side of the sacrificer by locating true wisdom in an Other, but this practice also gives the sacrificer something to do about this lack—*ad infinitum.*

I will refer to the subjective structure that characterizes Job's practice of regular sacrifices as an obedience to a law or logic of *sacrifice.*[34] This logic of sacrifice also characterizes wisdom literature more generally. The book of Proverbs forms fearers of YHWH in relation to a universal wisdom that is the organic whole linking all creation[35]—the Cause of causes, complete understanding—but that is not finally a possible object of human knowledge.[36] Banished from the realm of human understanding, the sages can seek and incrementally advance toward wisdom, but cannot finally claim to have found it (thus the many admonitions to fear, be open to instruction, and, especially, never to be "wise in one's own eyes" for example, Prov 3:5, 7; 12:15; 16:2; 21:2; 26:5, 12, 16; 28:11).[37] The sapiential framing of life as a path and of wisdom as a search or process (for example, Prov 1:15; 2:8, 13, 20; 3:17; 4:11, 18–19; 5:21; 7:27; 8:32; 9:6; 12:28; Job 17:9; 22:3, 15; 23:11; 28:23; 31:7)[38] offers the promise of progress but requires that progress remain infinite. Wisdom is universalized by the sages' collective renunciation, their sacrifices of any universal assertions on the basis of their particular-wisdoms. Said differently, the sages form a set, become an "All," on the basis of an exception, that is, the transcendent Other who has access to wisdom. The sages pursue a wisdom that is not limited by anything within the world, and they do so by maintaining a level of contempt for their own wisdoms, ever fearfully searching for evidence that they have failed to attain what they have in mind to become.[39] Important in understanding Job's pre-afflicted piety (and the fear of God in traditional wisdom) is therefore the ignorance and uncertainty Job sustains in carrying out his perpetual sacrifices.

This description of the subjective structure of Job's pre-afflicted piety is not an isolated moment but is essential to the larger argument of this chapter and this book insofar as it defines the structure of piety that Job's post-affliction wisdom throws into crisis. As I demonstrate below, this structure of piety characterizes the piety that Job rejects when his wife tries to impose it upon him, and the piety that the consensus interpretation continues to try to impose upon him. In short, the prose tale's plot replaces piety structured as a universal constituted by means of an exception with another structure of universality that I develop below.

§15 The Consensus Account of What Makes the Test Possible

Having proposed that *haśśāṭān* incites a test aimed at discovering whether Job's piety is *unconditional* rather than *not self-interested*, and having reconsidered Job's pre-afflicted subjective position as disciplined devotion to uncertainty rather than dogged certitude, the argument turns now to the remaining two questions I defined at the outset as foundational for any understanding of the prose introduction:

- On what basis could the test take place? And,
- How can we know whether Job has passed or failed?

To which a strong consensus responds:

- Job's affliction makes a display of authentic piety possible; and
- Job's pious behavior after the affliction will prove YHWH right about Job, whereas *haśśāṭān* needs Job to reject or curse YHWH to be right.

Over the next few sections I deal with the consensus response to the second question. After offering an account of the meaning and basis for this response, I raise an issue that (ex)poses an ultimately fatal problem for it. After surveying the uncoordinated set of issues raised by the tale and made visible by the consensus's failure to coordinate them, I develop an alternative approach for understanding them.

On the one hand, the idea that Job's affliction provides the condition that makes the test of his piety possible is a truism. The logic of the story clearly requires that the reader understand the affliction as a precondition for the test. But how is it that this affliction makes this test possible? The most common answers appeal to two related reasons: first, that once Job is afflicted with the loss of everything he has, he has nothing for which he can be said to fear God and so, if he fears God, it must be for naught.[40]

The second reason involves a theological dimension of the test that I have not yet acknowledged and that requires a bit more explanation. *haśśāṭān*'s challenge—does Job fear God unconditionally? (1:9)—raises suspicions not only that Job may not truly fear God but also that God is not truly feared in-and-for-Godself. Despite the fact that God may have created the condition, or may desire to be associated with the condition, or any other apparently mitigating factor that connects God to whatever conditions Job's fear, if Job's fear is conditioned by anything other than his desire to fear God, God is not truly feared. Of course, as plenty of interpreters note, that *haśśāṭān* follows his question about Job's fear in 1:9 with another in 1:10 that is "directed at God's activity in protecting and blessing Job"[41] suggests that he is also thinking of this theological dimension. Janzen nicely articulates the necessary theological correlate of unconditional piety:

> Is the creator of the world and the divine benefactor of humankind worshipful only by virtue of what deity does for humankind? Or is God intrinsically worshipful? Is deity capable of creating a creature who, somehow, attains to such freedom and independence, such spiritual and moral maturity, as to be in a position to choose to offer God worship and service because of God's intrinsic worthiness to be loved?[42]

The way God becomes disengaged from "what deity does" in the minds and worship of humanity is by acting in such a way that cannot be construed as conditional or perceived as following a law.[43] To summarize, the act of God in afflicting Job is supposed to make the test of Job's wisdom (authentic fear of God) possible because (i) it leaves Job with nothing on account of which he can be said to fear God, and (ii) it disconnects God from any predictable, causal condition on account of which Job could be said to fear God.[44] Thus, if Job exhibits pious behavior after the affliction, one can surmise that it is for naught, that Job has passed the test, and that God has been truly worshiped.

§16 *haśśāṭān's* Wager

But, as a consideration of the figure of *haśśāṭān* shows, there is reason to doubt the apparent soundness with which this argument accounts for the conditions that make the test of Job's fear possible. In JOB, *haśśāṭān* is best described as "a particular divine being in the heavenly court, one whose specialized function was to seek out and accuse persons disloyal to God."[45] This is not the Satan who is opposed to God in a later dualistic cosmology, but "Yahweh's subordinate, presenting himself before him as one of his courtiers, responding to Yahweh's initiatives, and powerless to act without Yahweh's authorization."[46] He may be YHWH's subordinate but, in contrast to the short, direct speech of God,

> in his relatively longer speeches, [*haśśāṭān*] shows a fondness for verse-insets, clever citation of folk-sayings, argumentative positioning of syntactical members for the most persuasive effect. In short, as befits a

prosecuting attorney, he is a master of conscious rhetoric, alongside of whom God seems plainspoken.[47]

If Alter is correct, then the riches of *haśśāṭān*'s rhetoric pale in comparison to the poverty of his behavioral analysis, for it is a true gamble to bet that people suffering unfavorable circumstances lose their piety. On the contrary, such persons often exhibit the most pious behavior. Witness Daniel when faced with the lions' den (Dan 6:11, 24) or King Hezekiah surrounded by the Neo-Assyrian army (2 Kgs 19:1–4). People who suffer great loss often describe faith as the only response they considered possible in the event of their loss, as if the event itself were the cause of their turn toward faith. Such sufferers are often the most eloquent articulators of the blessing and goodness of God. Of course this is not always the case: "The baby lies gravely ill, and the father rejects God."[48] But in his wager with YHWH, is the latter really what the clever and masterful *śāṭān* bets Job will do?

Yet, does Job have to reject or curse God to fail the test? In *haśśāṭān*'s incitement there lies a well-known ambiguity. The word translated "curse" actually means "bless," a supposedly euphemistic substitution necessitated by a pious scribal aversion to write anything approximating a curse of God. Although there is not enough evidence to support the idea that this substitution is in any sense standard,[49] there is at least one other example where it is used in an ironic and/or antithetical sense,[50] and it is not used in any straightforward sense here or in most if not all of its other five occurrences in the prose tale (1:5, 10, 21; 2:5, 9). In any case, if the test is not simply a test but also a wager between YHWH—who bets that Job will remain pious—and *haśśāṭān*—who bets that Job will curse YHWH—it is peculiar that *haśśāṭān* actually bets that Job will bless YHWH.

Scholars have dealt with this interpretive oddity in several ways. Traditionally and most often, interpreters are content to substitute "curse" for "bless" in the name of the euphemism thesis and proceed as if there were no surplus of meaning created by the substitution.[51] More recently, interpreters have paid greater attention to the use of this root here and throughout the prose tale. Van Wolde, for example, decides that *brk* means bless in 1:10 and 1:21, but curse in 1:5, 11; and 2:5. The experience of having encountered the root used for both meanings forces the reader to appreciate that it could have either meaning in its final use by Job's wife (2:9).[52] In what has become the standard reference for the question of √*brk*'s meaning in the prose tale, Linafelt argues for more far-reaching consequences:

> My contention is that this semantic undecidability is an indicator of a theological faultline that runs the length of the book. Tremors associated with this faultline will no doubt be felt at various points in the

> book, but are felt most keenly on points of blessing and curse, life and
> death. That is, the book of Job functions to redefine (or at least reexam-
> ine the assumptions of) the meaning of *brk*.[53]

Linafelt thinks this ambiguity is best read as a meta-level indication that
this story and this book unsettle any straightforward meaning of blessing
and cursing.[54] This profound thesis nonetheless stops short of accounting for any sense in which Job could be said to have passed the test for
unconditional fear. My reading of 1:11 thus departs from Linafelt's in a
way that derives from my thesis that what *haśśāṭān* challenges is whether
Job fears God *unconditionally*.

What kind of a victory would it be for YHWH to win the wager because
Job exhibits piety despite suffering? In avoiding the charge that the faithful
relate to YHWH as a crude mechanism of retribution, how could YHWH
avoid the risk of being perceived as, to borrow a phrase from Freud, "a
kind of prosthetic God"[55] whose qualities support reality when and where
it fails to stand on its own? How could God's intrinsic worthiness of worship
be proven if Job worships when something bad happens? Does worship not
often follow an opposite logic to that of fair-weather-fans so that many faithful persons experience guilt about inauthenticity when, during times of
hardship, they find themselves turning to God more often and with more
earnestness? It is at such times that pious people often find themselves vow-
ing never to let their faith lapse again, or always to persist in the zeal that
they presently feel, or offering various other conditional commitments. As
the conventional wisdom goes, one rarely finds atheists in foxholes.

The nub of the argument, then: if *haśśāṭān* were really interested in
challenging God's intrinsic worthiness to be worshipped, rather than that
Job would lose his faith if he suffered, it would be much more clever for
him to suggest that suffering would make Job ever more faithful, would
make Job *bless* God. Thus the indeterminate bless/curse problem in 1:11
is the result of a test that befits the function of *haśśāṭān* in content as
much as it does in rhetorical style: from this perspective, blessing could
curse Job's worship with inauthenticity as much as cursing. If Job worships
God, such worship does not necessarily have anything to do with God's
intrinsic worthiness to be worshipped and Job's unconditional fear. Why
would *haśśāṭān* not accuse Job of looking to God as a prosthesis, hoping
for a way to overcome his failures and afflictions or to avoid losing his
soul, which is all that is left to him?

If Job's fear cannot be determined as wise because it appears to be
conditioned by his affluence, then his affliction can no less appear to condition his fear. And if one cannot be sure that God is worshipped unconditionally when Job's worship appears to be conditioned by God's bless-

ing, God's affliction cannot but lead to the same suspicion. God will seem to have scared rather than blessed Job into fearing God. Of course, if Job curses God, as all recognize, Job will seem to have only ever worshipped God for the sake of his favorable external circumstances. *haśśāṭān*'s cleverness is thus to set up a test that appears to prevent the kind of fear from being displayed that he bets Job will not exhibit.

Before asking whether *haśśāṭān* has succeeded in setting up a wager he cannot lose, it is worth noting that the consensus approach similarly frames Job's post-affliction acts such that they cannot accommodate any sense of an unconditional act. By treating the affliction as the condition for Job's act of free fear, and his post-affliction piety as proof of such an act, the consensus approach treats the empirical condition of Job's affliction as the basis on which his fear could be judged free and unconditional, and so it never even gives Job a chance to act unconditionally. The most conspicuous blind spot generated by the consensus's mistaken approach is its failure to perceive that unfavorable circumstances, hardships, and afflictions can condition piety as much as favorable ones. Job was pious before his affliction but that was not enough to prove his wisdom, and his pious behavior after his affliction is no less unable, on its own, to display wisdom. After *haśśāṭān*'s challenge, what matters is not pious behavior except insofar as it is accomplished *ḥinnām*, unconditionally. Piety conditioned by the failure to perceive a causal chain connecting historical events is as unwise as piety conditioned by the perception of causality because neither is the unconditional piety that *haśśāṭān*'s challenge defines as authentic.

Far from solving anything, this critique of the consensus has instead clarified a deeper issue facing all readings of the prose tale: how can the affliction (which creates certain conditions) be coordinated with the test (of something unconditional)? On the one hand, according to the logic of the story, the affliction is a precondition for the test. On the other, the tale is set up as a question about the possibility of unconditional fear. How can an unconditioned act be grasped as contingent upon certain preconditions? For now I leave this question suspended on the promise to return to it below.

§17 YHWH's Positive Judgment and Curious Characterization

YHWH clearly thinks that a wise act is possible and actualized by the post-afflicted Job. Here is YHWH's judgment and confession to *haśśāṭān* after the affliction: "Still [Job] perseveres in his blamelessness though you incited me against him to swallow him up for naught" (2:3b). While it may be that YHWH is as mistaken as the commentators, this could only be admitted after one had failed to discern any basis in the tale for YHWH's judgment. Neither *haśśāṭān*, the narrator, nor anyone else registers any disagreement with YHWH's judgment. So, while I have tried to give the devil his due by accounting for the complexity of *haśśāṭān*'s wager, YHWH's judgment suggests that his wager does not completely account for the situation.

This question of whether there is any basis in the tale for YHWH's judgment is not the only one raised by 2:3. What does God mean by claiming to have acted "for naught" (*ḥinnām*, discussed at length in §12)?[56] It is an odd predication of this act, and it is all the more intriguing in light of the crucial role *ḥinnām* plays in the plot's development. *ḥinnām* cannot mean "to no end" in the sense of "without consequence" since YHWH's act had clear, fatal consequences. Some read it as "in vain," as if YHWH thinks the affliction was ineffective or unnecessary.[57] But the logic of the narrative opposes this reading by presenting the affliction as necessary for creating the conditions that allow Job's wisdom to be tested. The narrative portrays the affliction as necessary since YHWH is only capable of judging whether Job's fear is free *after* it. Far from "in vain," the affliction enables the test to take place.

How then to understand *ḥinnām* in 2:3? In one of two ways: *ḥinnām* could indicate that YHWH's act was unconditioned in the sense that no conditions in Job's situation could reasonably account for the swallowing up that YHWH carries out.[58] That is, none of the conditions of Job's pre-afflicted life are sufficient to account for the affliction he suffers.

But there is another way to understand the predication of an act as "for nothing." As opposed to denying a predicate to the subject, the predication might affirm a non-predicate of the subject. For example, if I want to negate the statement "this is real," I could either say "this is not real," which would deny the predicate to the subject, or "this is unreal," which affirms a positive sense of "not-realness" of the subject. English speakers know well the difference between saying "this is not real" and "this is unreal." One can read 2:3 in similarly different senses: either "the affliction lacks some condition," or, "the affliction creates something unconditioned." Like "this is unreal," YHWH may be affirming an unconditioned condition that the affliction created within Job's conditions. Below I will explore how our reading of the prose tale is enhanced if we understand YHWH to say in 2:3 that his act creates a positive sense of "nothingness" within Job's conditions. To anticipate, such an unconditioned condition provides the only kind of condition on which the test of an unconditioned act could occur.

§18 The Affliction as Job's Symbolic Death

To understand how the affliction makes the test possible, we need a better understanding of YHWH's characterization of the affliction as *ḥinnām* in 2:3. What is different about Job after YHWH's act? Two opposed responses immediately come to mind. On the one hand, nothing seems to change. The predicates shared across 1:8, 2:3, and 2:9—"blameless and upright, fearing God and turning from evil," and "still persevering in his blamelessness"—strongly identify the pre-afflicted with the post-afflicted Job. On the other hand, everything is different. It is almost obscene to identify these subjects by their shared predicates. After the affliction Job is far from the person he was at the story's beginning. The latter Job has been devoured; it is he whom YHWH claims to have "swallowed up" (*blʿ*).[59]

The word YHWH uses to characterize the affliction, *blʿ*, is often associated with destruction and death.[60] YHWH's act essentially kills the pre-afflicted Job. YHWH severs Job from the conditions of his life, destroys his ties to the community, and unmoors him from any context.[61] Job is gone, subtracted from the world. His friends' symbolic actions in 2:11–13 confirm this interpretation: "Everything in their actions treats him as one already dead (not as one on the point of death, as Terrien thinks), and the seven days and nights fit in as a period of mourning."[62] YHWH does not *extract* Job out of his historical context, but *subtracts* from him all that he identified with and all contexts in relation to which he located himself so that only his "bare life"[63] remains. Mathewson notes that in the reports Job receives about the affliction, "The order in which Job's livestock are lost and/or killed . . . is almost the complete reversal of the order in which the introduction lists his blessings."[64] The narrative depicts the affliction as a nearly point-by-point removal of all that has been predicated of Job.[65]

Swallowed up, Job declares himself naked (1:21a), stripped, and he identifies YHWH as the agent who has given and taken away (1:21b) the objective substance to which his bare life, his naked subjectivity, had previously been related.[66] It is remarkable that, in the event of his encounter with YHWH that ends in his self-destruction, Job recognizes that a gap has always separated him from his identity and identifications. Job acknowledges that the latter were not him; they were neither external emanations from nor realizations/reflections of his subjective essence. They were instead objective substances given to him by YHWH, impositions from an Other.[67]

Job's subjectivity, then, lies in what is essentially a force of negativity, differentiation, or distance that separates himself from his imaginary traits and symbolic predicates. Job's statement implies some sense of a distinction between (i) his ego-level identity and identifications and (ii) himself as a substance-less subject.[68] In the affliction Job's ego (i) is destroyed since the affliction subtracts from him any meaningful, socio-symbolic context.

So what does YHWH's claim to have swallowed Job up and Job's statement that YHWH stripped him naked teach us about what enables an unconditional act to be carried out? *In the divine encounter that makes a wise act possible, there is not a couple, a meeting of two ones, a meeting of a one and an Other, but a splitting of the one from itself.* Every predicate reckoned to Job up to this point is devoured in the affliction that splits Job off from what or whomever one may have thought of as Job.

§19 The *nepeš* That Survives; Job's Life Between Two Deaths

What is the subject, person, or thing that survives this encounter with YHWH? On first approach, the answer is clear: YHWH demands that Job's self (1:12) and his *nepeš* (2:6) survive the affliction. However, once one tries to understand what this is—call it his *nepeš*—in light of the text's testimony about what happened to Job, one must conclude that what YHWH calls *nepeš* takes on a new, or at least a more specific, meaning.

nepeš was classically translated "soul" (for example, the KJV) but, in the interest of distinguishing it from the Greek and specifically (Neo-) Platonic conception of the soul as an (immortal) essence distinct and separable from the body (both corporeal and social), recent translations (for example, the NRSV) often use "living being."[69] The clearest basis for grasping the range of meanings *nepeš* assumes in the Hebrew Bible derives from its etymological tie to the throat. The throat is one of the privileged zones of the human body where the "inside" meets the "outside." Breath, food, and speech, all of which sustain life, pass through the zone of the throat. To include speech is to account for the sense *nepeš* has of being more than a primitive notion of the biological or "mere life." In many contexts its meaning extends to such notions as "will" (Gen 23:8), "appetite" (Prov 13:25), and "desire" (Gen 34:3).[70]

Whatever meaning one gives the "*nepeš*" that survives the affliction, he/it is something that lives, so to speak, "between two deaths,"[71] still alive despite his social/symbolic death. Here, *nepeš* cannot mean anything like a personality, an identity, the One of Job, his essence or totality, since the affliction has destroyed all such identifying traits. The affliction does not *re*center Job in the *nepeš* that remains but radically *de*centers him. What was previously thought of as Job, his ego-level identity and identifications, has been split off from him as a dispensable object, and the thing that survives—the *nepeš*—is now Job.

To say that the text divorces from Job any identifying features that were previously attributed to him is to say that the *nepeš* that remains of him, that he now is, does not reflect him at all. This is why the prose introduction ends by telling us that *his friends* looked at him from a distance, but did not recognize him (2:12).[72] This detail ensures that we readers— who look at Job from an even greater distance—do not doggedly maintain the fantasy that Job remains recognizable by some essential trait. The effect of YHWH's act can therefore be described both negatively and positively: YHWH has *subtracted* Job's personal and social context from him and *added* him back into the world as an unrecognizable *nepeš*.

§20 *ḥinnām*, Once Again

It is at this point possible to return to the question posed at the end of §16 and in §17 about the sense in which YHWH's act can be considered both *ḥinnām* and generative of the conditions that could make Job's unconditional act possible.[73] The thesis I introduced at the end of §17 can be understood now that I have shown that the affliction is simultaneously a subtraction and an addition. I showed above that *ḥinnām* in 2:3 may be read negatively—as an indication of an inability of the conditions of Job's life to account for the affliction—and positively—as an indication of a certain nothingness or unconditioned condition added to the conditions of Job's life. Whereas the notion of an unconditioned condition may have seemed abstract and amorphous above, it is now concretized in the image of Job on the ash heap scraping his discharging boils. The act of God is *ḥinnām* in the sense that it is surprising and could not have been anticipated by anyone within the conditions in which it occurs. Negatively, it disturbs the sense of causality at work in the Imaginary–Symbolic world in which it occurs. Positively, it creates an effect that appears to have come into being "out of nowhere," an effect that appears within the world as unrecognizable to it. Objects, persons, things, etc., are recognizable when they are related to other objects, persons, things, etc., within a specular field. Job is unrecognizable; he is visible only as a stain or smudge within the specular field, an excess unrelated to its surroundings. After being swallowed and digested by YHWH, Job is deposited as a *nepeš* atop a pile of dung,[74] a gratuitous, useless byproduct excreted from the Imaginary– Symbolic coordinates in which he is nonetheless "located." YHWH's act has been committed "for nothing" in the sense that it has been committed *for the sake of including a nothing* within the world—Job *qua nepeš*, an empty placeholder with no substantial link to the world. Job is included as excluded; there for the counting, Job counts for nothing.

How could such an act enable Job's unconditional fear of God? YHWH's act fractures the conditions within which it occurs. After it, certain things or persons within the world are unrecognizable; because of it, events occur within the world that cannot be anticipated. YHWH's act does not save Job from his inauthenticity, or from his folly, or from his impiety, but from himself, from determination by his own empirical conditions. YHWH's act renders these conditions internally limited, a state I refer to as "not-All."[75] YHWH's act interrupts the "natural" processes of cause and effect, generation and corruption, by cutting through the causal chains that connect the conditions of the world. YHWH's act prevents these conditions from wholly determining their subjects, in this case, Job. Job and the world are not opened up toward some place or thing "beyond" themselves; they are simply opened up. Because Job and the world are exposed as not-All, there can occur within and from them acts that could be unconditioned by them.

The following section demonstrates this thesis by considering a sense in which the logic operative in Job's post-affliction fear of God fundamentally differs from the logic operative in Job's pre-afflicted fear, which I characterized as a "logic of sacrifice" in §14. This analysis leads directly into a consideration of the third and final question defined at the outset of this chapter as fundamental to any understanding of the prose tale.

§21 Wisdom Beyond the Sacrificial Principle

The wisdom made possible by the prose tale is radically incommensurable with the law/logic of sacrifice that characterizes Job's pre-afflicted fear of God. According to this logic, Job's body, history, and wisdom remained limited because, being anchored to them, he cannot traverse the infinite distance between them and the divine locus of their truth. Wisdom is ultimately banished to a transcendent realm beyond the perceptible, finite order of time and space. No sage can finally claim the predicate wise but instead must commit to an infinite search for wisdom. The sage must accept the conditions in which he finds himself, dedicate himself to struggle with the circumstances and knowledge he inherits from those who have come before, and aim to fashion the best possible future for those who come after. In short, the sapiential life is the participation in the construction of a future that will not be without the knowledge gained in the past and the present. This external limitation thus provides the sage a sense of historical continuity and a promise of infinite progress and ever-increasing wisdom and pleasure.

Paradoxically, however, Job's actual activity showed that this limit leads to perpetual contempt and suspicion of human thought and activity, not to a celebration of progress. In this logic the fear of God is a subjective posture that maintains a respectful contempt towards one's perceptions and knowledge as penultimate or potentially foolish. The sage thus maintains a perpetual state of deferential dissatisfaction, always ready to revise her wisdom in the event of the experience of *instruction*.[76]

YHWH's activity in the prose tale contravenes this notion of the wise life as an infinite progression toward an external limit (and, I will argue below, so too does Job's). What now makes wisdom possible is an act of God, not in the sense that it is recognizably divine, but in the sense that it occurs but cannot be recognized in its state of affairs, cannot be connected to a locatable causal agent within its world. In short, wisdom's possibility is predicated on an act whose occurrence ensures that that no ultimate, transcendent Cause stands behind and promises to make sense of the historical and meaningful conditions of life. Said differently, the conditions that can serve as the preconditions for an act *for nothing* are those that have no-thing as an ultimate, transcendent referent. Wisdom is no longer considered an organic whole, the bond linking all life into a harmony that the fearer of God only partially and imperfectly perceives.[77] Instead, *wisdom is a human response that emerges out of and constitutes itself with respect to an event that happens ḥinnām*.[78] In more logically precise terms, the prose tale transforms wisdom from one logic of universalism to another, from the logic of an All constituted on a principle of exception, to the logic of a not-All made possible by an act of subtraction.[79] Job will have been wise, will have feared God ḥinnām, if his actions after the affliction conform to the logic of a not-All universality.

§22 Job's Non-Verbal Responses; ḥinnām Embodied

With this thesis in place, I can finally turn to the third question: On what basis could one judge whether or not Job passed the test? Job responds to the afflictions that create the conditions for the tests with both non-verbal and verbal actions. For each test the narrative reports Job's non-verbal responses before his verbal responses. To the first affliction Job responds with "a series of five actions. The first four are expressions of grief ('Job

rose and tore his robe and shaved his head and fell upon the ground,'
1:20)."[80] Scholars debate whether the fifth ("and he worshipped") is conventional or out of place in the context of mourning rites.[81] Regardless,
Job's "actions do not of themselves clarify the moral imagination that
would unite grief with worship rather than with curse."[82] As Newsom goes
on to put it, Job's first non-verbal response is "not self-interpreting" as a
passing or failing of the test.

Job's first non-verbal response involves acts of mourning that ritually separate mourners from the community and their (normal) lives.
Although such separation does not indicate the mourner's wise (unconditional) action, it does bring Job into the kind of interstitial social space
from which any act that could be considered unconditional would have
to arise. No fear of God that could be characterized as ḥinnām can be
directly generated out of the positive, substantial conditions in which
it is carried out; it must arise unconditionally and its purpose must be
indeterminate.[83] Job's first non-verbal responses meet these conditions.

Job's non-verbal response to the second affliction further supports
this reading: "He took a potsherd with which to scrape himself and he
was sitting amidst the ashes" (2:8). The participle translated "sitting" suggests "Job is already sitting among the ashes when the disease is inflicted
upon him."[84] Job's affliction locates him "upon the trash-heap outside the
city gate where garbage such as ashes and broken pots was dumped and
where people excluded from the community" gathered.[85] In other words,
through his non-verbal (re)actions Job positions himself in the place for
that which has no place in society. Placed out of place, he scrapes himself away from himself. It is from such an out of joint place, from such a
fractured, inhuman being, that an act could occur that would give God/
WISDOM a concrete existence. To clarify the emergence of God/WISDOM
out of this constitutively unfinalizable or not-All structure, what follows
analyzes Job's verbal responses in detail.

§23 From Life to Death?

To grasp whether and how Job passes the test for unconditional fear, it
will help to consider the rhetorical function of death in the prose tale's
plot. Death has already been important to this discussion. YHWH confesses to destroying Job, and Job's friends relate to him as one already
dead. In his non-verbal responses Job mourns, positions himself outside
the life of the social body, and even scrapes his body away from itself. In
his first verbal response, Job joins almost every other character in this

tale by acknowledging his death. Job declares that YHWH has subtracted everything from him so that only his bare life remains.

Mathewson's recent work on death in JOB argues that the prose tale's plot moves "from a scene of the coherent world of the piety/life/relationship complex to a scene of incoherent death . . . from symbolic unity and wholeness, with its related emphasis on life and liveliness, to symbolic incoherence with its connected emphasis on death."[86] This movement passes through an intermediate moment wherein Job resists, yielding three logical moments of Job's relationship to this narrative movement:

1. Job first thrives within his symbol system (that is, the "piety/life/relationship complex") to stave off the death that functions as its horizon;
2. then, when confronted with death's desymbolizing power, Job's first response is to try to resymbolize it into a coherent symbolic world;
3. in his second response Job moves beyond such death-denying resistance, but he is unable to locate himself before death in any meaningful way, and thus the tale ends with Job sitting, silent, stunned by the impotence of his symbol system before death.

Even though such an ending could hardly qualify as liberative, Mathewson's argument suggests that each moment nonetheless advances toward authenticity by confronting more directly the death he defines as the enabling condition of all life, every symbol system, every social and cultural order.[87]

Mathewson begins with Job's pre-afflicted condition: "In the lone example of Job's piety that the narrative offers (1:4–5), themes of life and liveliness predominate . . . Movement, merry-making, eating and drinking: life and liveliness to the fullest."[88] In this piety/life/relationship complex, life is what puts death in its proper place, in the after-life, not within or during life: "Death-in-life . . . is the type of death that abundant life overcomes."[89] A considerable distance thus separates Mathewson's interpretation of Job's pre-afflicted life from my own interpretation (see §14). I argued that Job's pre-afflicted life is characterized by a "logic of sacrifice" that is more intermixed with death than Mathewson allows. The life that is actually enabled by Job's subjective position is one that is bound and defined by death. When the text describes Job's only act of pre-afflicted piety as sacrifice, it presents him as one who, in trying—as Mathewson recognizes—to stave off death submits his life to it—unrecognized by Mathewson. This recognition of a dimension of death operative in Job's pre-afflicted life is implicit in those commentators who consider Job's actions as curiously obsessive. Often such interpreters use a form of the word *scrupulous*, with its dual senses of upstanding and punctilious, to describe Job.[90] The French psychoanalyst Jean Laplanche has said that the obsessive

> installs death in his life, he "plays dead," that he creates for himself a sort of shell precisely so that these excitations [of conflict or pleasure] cannot reach him directly, but only in a filtered form, completely reconstituted. Excitations are taken up into a system that aims to deaden them ("to deaden" is to put a sort of cushion in their way, so as ultimately to reach a state close to death).[91]

An obsessive perpetually seeks to secure his place in situations that are ensured of unity, coherency, connectivity, integrity, predictability. Where Mathewson takes these as characteristics of "life,"[92] with an obsessive in view they rather appear as characteristics of death, attempts to keep life at bay.

Consider also Roland Barthes's idea that, with the arrival of photography, death is found in the click of a lens, the freezing of life in photographic eternity.[93] This idea is remarkably similar to the following contention by Mathewson, part of which quotes Lifton (from whom he takes no distance on this matter): "The very core of human life is dependent upon the integrity of the image, for its absence or breakdown threatens life."[94] But the integrity of the image figures death as much as does the image's disintegration. Mathewson's one-sided description of the life that supposedly permeates the beginning of the prose tale leaves the death in the service of which this life is staged unaccounted for. Consequently, Mathewson's notion of life and death as two poles between which the prose tale moves needs to be revised.

Mathewson derives a second moment of Job's relationship to the plot's development from Job's first verbal response to his affliction:

> Naked I came out of the womb of my mother
>   and naked I shall return there.
> The Lord gives and the Lord takes away.
>   Blessed be the name of the Lord. (1:21)

For Mathewson, the servant's enunciation of *mwt* ("death") in the final report to Job (1:19) confronts Job with a "cold reality" that avoids the palliating euphemisms of the previous servants' reports (1:14–17). But,

> With one simple phrase [1:21], Job has taken all of the cold reality announced by the word *mwt*—problematic, incoherent, desymbolized death—and resymbolized it into a symbolically coherent, simple narrative of the universal human life cycle, for which Job stands as the prime

exemplar. "Death" (*mwt*), now, is . . . the return to the womb of the
mother/earth. . . . In Job's resymbolization of death, Yahweh is the very
guarantor of the coherence of death, the very one who brings about the
"return" (*šwb*) to the womb.[95]

The servant presents Job with an opportunity to stand authentically
before what Mathewson calls "desymbolized" death, by which he means
death not only as the presentation of an absence, a negative materiality
without all the cultural content that deflects it into positive meanings and
false representations, but also death as the horizon of social and cultural
existence.[96] Job turns away from this opportunity and instead subjects
death to a coherent horizon of meaning ensured by YHWH. Life over-
takes death, the womb supplants the tomb.

But Job's resymbolization does not efface death.[97] Job rethinks death
as a return to his place of birth. Job likens his nakedness at birth to his
nakedness at death; the mother's womb to which he will return is the
tomb of mother earth (cf. Ps 139:13–15) and, when he names this place
"there," he uses a reference to Sheol attested elsewhere.[98] Mathewson is
correct that the metaphorical substitutions of "there" for "womb" and
"womb" for "death" make "death" absent but, since they are metaphors,
they work by evoking death's presence. A metaphoric substitution does
not efface the latent word, but transforms it. By likening his death to his
(re)birthplace, Job actually conceives of his death as a locus from which
someone or something could be born. I will return to this point below.

In his response to the second affliction Mathewson thinks that Job
finally assumes an authentic relationship to desymbolized death—that is,
one that does not subject death's desymbolizing power to a death-denying
resymbolization but instead leaves the symbol system open such that it
could possibly "include" or sustain a relationship to death. Furthermore,
contrary to the opposition between YHWH and desymbolized death that
characterized Job's response to the first affliction, Mathewson thinks that
Job's response to the second affliction makes possible a theology of desymbolized death.

Mathewson draws a stark contrast between Job's first and second
responses.[99] A figure once again confronts Job with what Mathewson calls
"literal death." Before it was his servant; this time it is his wife. And this
time, the offer includes a lethal factor, an opportunity for Job to choose
his own death. Plus, at this point the prose tale's form, content, and style
begin to lose their coherence and become more ambiguous. The heavenly scene vanishes; the narrative integrity cracks; time and death pulver-
ize the connections that give the symbol system an appearance of immortality. "On [Job's wife's] lips, *mwt* stands far from any symbolic system that

would ground it and give it symbolic sense. Literal death is desymbolized, and paradoxically, stands for this very desymbolization."[100] Again Job rejects death. If he were to accept desymbolized death, Mathewson tells us, he would have proven *haśśāṭān* right by demonstrating that his previous resymbolization that professed that God was the cause of his experience (1:21) was false. But this time he resymbolizes with two terms that do not try to seal up the symbol system by excluding the desymbolizing power of death. Job resymbolizes by coupling *ṭwb* with *rʿ* in 2:10: "Shall we receive the good (*ṭwb*) from God, but not receive the bad (*rʿ*) from God?"

> In Job's mouth *ṭwb* and *rʿ* do not even signify in the same symbolic system . . . *ṭwb* and *rʿ* are not just a simple binary in an either/or symbolic system, but they stand for the entire system (the *ṭwb* of the life/piety/relationship complex) *and* that which calls this entire system into question (desymbolized, incoherent, unintelligible *rʿ*). . . . In Job's resymbolization, God is also responsible for *rʿ*—for that which calls the system into question including its center, namely God. . . . The implications of this resymbolization are dizzying. And so Job sits in an astounded, death-like silence.[101]

Stunned by his near encounter with the impossible "object" of experience, that is, death, Job does not try to construct a symbolic immortality into which he could escape; rather, he avails himself of the chance to articulate a symbol system that could include its internal limit.[102] But his "resymbolization" is not effective; it remains incoherent and failed. Job names a dimension "beyond good and evil" but can only sit, stunned by the impotence of the symbol system before death. Paralyzed by uncertainty about the meaning of his experience, he finds himself unable to secure any "life," unable even to speak. I argue below that Mathewson's reading locates Job in precisely the same place where Job's wife tries to put him. Mathewson's reading is thus equally implicated by Job's rebuke of his wife.

§24 Or, Life Beyond Death

In his first verbal response in 1:21 (quoted on page 62), Job reconceives of the death toward which he is heading as a locus from which someone or something could be born. As Mathewson recognizes, the symbolic social order is the locus of life, vitality, immortality, and happiness. But the symbolic order is no less a place of mortification. It alienates an individual's being into images and identificatory marks or words by which one can relate to others. Because of the rift that divides someone from the images and words that precede and persist beyond him, he must give up life (that is, die) in order to achieve life (and death, insofar as knowledge about mortality is only available vicariously). The measure of life available to human beings through the social, Symbolic order brings with it a minimal sense of mediation or alienation from their being.[103]

In order to conceive of life and death in psychoanalytically informed terms, one must say that life comes by means of a dead entity that has a life of its own—that is, the symbolic order—and one must imagine a certain form of life that persists in a real dimension outside the symbolic order and that threatens the life constituted by the symbolic order as a force of death.[104] One of Žižek's recurring points is that these two supplementary dimensions, the living dead and deadly life, constitute the two faces of what psychoanalysis infamously refers to as the death drive.

> For a human being to be "dead while alive" is to be colonized by the "dead" symbolic order; to be "alive while dead" is to give body to the remainder of Life-Substance which has escaped the symbolic colonization. What we are dealing with here is thus the split between . . . the "dead" symbolic order which mortifies the body and the non-symbolic Life-Substance of *jouissance*.[105] These two notions [of life and death] in Freud and Lacan are not what they are in our everyday standard scientific discourse: in psychoanalysis, they both designate a properly monstrous dimension. Life is the horrible palpitation of the "lamella," of the non-subjective ("acephelous") "undead" drive which persists beyond ordinary death; death is the symbolic order itself, the structure which, as a parasite, colonizes the living entity. What defines the death drive in Lacan is this double gap: not the simple opposition between life and death, but the split of life itself into "normal" life and horrifying "undead" life, and the split of the dead into "ordinary" dead and the "undead" machine.[106]

Immortality, in other words, does not only belong to the socio-symbolic order as something in which the individual is permitted a limited participation. Immortality is also experienced in the domain of the drives that compel one toward an existence without regard for and often at odds with any calculations of life and death.[107]

For psychoanalysis, therefore, life is joined with death not in the sense that the body is subjected to a transcendent finitude, but in the sense that the body has lost its connection to mere biological or organic existence. The body becomes a more-than-material substance, "the site of a *jouissance* that opens a new dimension of infinity, immortality,"[108] a dimension of life beyond death. This sense of an enjoyment "beyond the pleasure principle" and these non-literal notions of life and death are better conceptual tools for grasping what I think Job accomplishes in 1:21 through the substitution of womb for tomb, mediated by "there."

For Mathewson, Job's first verbal response refers to the womb in order to "represent a zero-sum gain: a human is born, a human dies; God gives, God takes."[109] But in the Bible the womb is only ever the site of a negation when it is negated, paradigmatically in barrenness; at all other times the womb is the site of generation. In 1:21 Job directs his experience not outward, into an immortal, social, symbol system constituted on the basis of its exclusion of desymbolized death (that is, its resymbolization of death), but backward, at a time before he found himself where he is, to a restored state as yet unaffected by temporal change. When Job says he is returning "there"—which represents "Sheol" but parallels "my mother's womb"—he gives the womb a kind of mythical status akin to Sheol. Just as he has never been to Sheol, so too must one imagine that Job is not thinking of his experience of the womb as something that was ever actual for him. Instead, it is a sort of primordial loss, a state that he had to give up—even though he was never really in it—when he received from God all life's trappings that have now been taken away from him. This experience of loss, of subtraction, has in turn prepared him to go "back to the future." Job previously related to this state as a lost, mythical state prior to his reception of all the trappings of his life that have now been taken away. Now, in the loss of all these trappings, something of this lost state has been made present to him. Of course, Job does not go all the way "there" (and he complains about this inhibition in chapter 3). But, if Job knows about this naked existence at all, it is because he has experienced some partial representative of it in God's act. Job expresses a movement beyond his reality made possible by the subtraction of his reality.

§25 God's Role in Job's Experience

Mathewson's is only one interpretation among many that reads Job's statement in 1:21 as an indication that he thinks of life as a zero-sum equation, guaranteed and carried out by a God who stands beyond it. Other readings of Job's statement according to the same structure include the contentions that Job is indifferent to the content of his experience and is only concerned with God,[110] that Job thinks his experience is woven by God's invisible hand into a great divine tapestry,[111] and that Job sees "something more," an ineffable, divine dimension behind his experience. I want to reverse this orientation. Job's statement does not position God beyond or outside experience; it infers God from the fact that his experience does not add up, that his experience makes something available to him in excess of the experience.

Job blesses God for exactly what God has done, which is not unfathomable to Job or even in question. When Job speaks of his experience as something God has done, he does not evoke a divine plan(e) beyond his experience; his experience is itself the plan(e). To be sure, insofar as he recognizes God at work in his experience at all, he shows that he does not relate to his experience as an All, that is, he recognizes a surplus dimension in his experience—"something more"—but Job gives no sign that this surplus is inaccessible or beyond his experience. On the contrary, he expresses no doubt about his experience: YHWH hath given and YHWH hath taken, pure and simple.[112] His experience is neither a means to a deeper end nor an indication of some higher truth; it is *productive* of something more than itself.

God is beyond Job's experience not in the sense that God is external to it, but only in the sense that God is that which fissures his experience from itself, the minimal difference fracturing his experience from within. *God is thus conditioned by Job's experience* as the one who makes it irreducible to his conditions, as the one who keeps Job's experience open to the transforming event he is suffering. Job's experience splits him from himself and projects him on a return curve to a place he has never really been. He has never been "there" but since he knows something about it he must have stumbled upon some partial representative of it. God is the fracturing of his experience that makes available to him such a "partial object of lack," an avatar of the void of "there." Thus, Job's doxological "Blessed be the name of YHWH" emanates from his experience of such a minimal difference that fractures his experience from within and makes a surplus dimension present to him. This means that Job, like YHWH in 2:3b, locates God in a surplus dimension vis-à-vis his experience that is nevertheless conditioned by his experience. I argued above that *ḥinnām* refers not only to a lack of conditions for the affliction, but also to a surplus, unconditioned condition produced out of the affliction. *With respect to God's act,* Job is constituted as a surplus unrelated to his conditions; *with respect to Job's experience,* God is constituted as a surplus over and above his conditions. In the structure of the story, Job and God occupy analogous, out-of-place places with respect to the affliction. From the outset, then, this story about the conditioned emergence of the unconditional narrates a radical, immanent theology.

Like a soldier whose mortal wound pushes him beyond considerations of courage and cowardice, victor and vanquished, Job is pushed beyond piety and loss of faith as he is nearly eclipsed by his experience.[113] This is no sage who remains devoted to the faith in which he has long been immersed, but *nor* does he question or doubt. Job disappears behind his experience and becomes identified with what he proclaims. He is split between the one to whom much was given and the other that remains after the taking. Out of this splitting into two, he affirms One, God, as cause. Thus the readings that speak either of a display of heroic piety or an inauthentic domestication of the traumatic encounter with death must be turned around. There is nothing on the basis of which the two involved in this encounter—God and Job—could be added together. Job does not fear God as one to another because he is overcome and made other than himself by his encounter with God. Job refuses to justify his statement, gives no reason for it, calls on no authority, no tradition, no experience, no law to sanction it. He says, simply: YHWH has done this, blessed be YHWH. This response's fear of God is not a fear of some quality of God's (acts), but neither is it indifferent to God's qualities or acts; instead this fear is what effectively renders God worshippable.[114]

§26 Job's Wife and the Deadlock of Desire

In response to his wife's provocation—"Do you still persist in your blamelessness? Curse God, and die" (2:9)—Job makes his second verbal response: "You speak like one of the fools. Shall we receive the good from God but not receive the bad from God?" (2:10). Job's wife is an ambiguous character. She appears out of nowhere, at the exact moment that the story breaks its formal pattern of alternating between scenes in heaven and on earth. Driver puts it well: "the scene in heaven dissolves into the picture" on earth.[115] After this dissolution of the heavenly realm, Job's wife is the first to speak, and in so doing she "signals the impingement of the divine world upon the human."[116]

> Her words are radical and provocative: "Do you still persist in your integrity? Curse God, and die" (2:9). What she says echoes God's assessment of Job as one who persists in his integrity (2:3b), but the course of action she urges would end the wager on the satan's terms (2:5).[117]

Job's wife represents heaven but she does not represent all of it equally. She prompts an act by Job that would decide the test and, moreover, in *haśśāṭān*'s favor since she commands what he predicts (again, literally: "*bless* God").

Her tie to *haśśāṭān* goes even further; the structure of the choice she poses to Job also locks him in a double bind by requiring that he incur guilt and/or die. The ambiguity of her words is well known, but few commentators notice how she, like *haśśāṭān*, puts Job in a dilemma whose terms prevent his escape.[118] Newsom describes the dilemma as

> one that revolves around the thematically crucial word "integrity." The term "integrity" (*tummah*) denotes a person whose conduct is in complete accord with moral and religious norms and whose character is one of utter honesty, without guile. Job's wife's disturbing question hints at a tension between these two aspects of the word. Her question could be understood in two different senses. She could be heard as saying: "Do you still persist in your integrity (=righteousness)? Look where it has gotten you. Give it up, as God has given you up. Curse God, and then die." Or she could be understood as saying: "Do you still persist in your integrity (=honesty)? If so, stand by it and say what is truly in your heart. Curse God before you die."[119]

Job's wife offers Job a choice between maintaining his honesty but sacrificing his religious innocence, or following his religious duty but sacrificing his moral integrity.[120] Righteousness implies dishonesty; honesty demands unrighteousness. In both cases he will incur guilt before one law by following the other and, no matter which he chooses, he will die. For Job's wife, then, Job's position is structurally limited and a truly "wise" act is impossible; facing certain death, he stands guilty before one law or another. Just as I argued above (on pages 51–53), what appears to be a problem with the meaning of "bless/curse" proves to be its solution at another level: both bless and curse lead Job to one and the same end.

Note the similarity between the choice Job's wife offers him and the choice with which Mathewson leaves him. Faced with two conflicting symbol systems, Mathewson argues, Job can only sit, stunned, and wait. Neither Mathewson nor Job's wife allow for the possibility of a wise act; for both, Job's ability to act wisely depends upon his relationship to a symbol system that is presently lacking. For Job's wife, there is no symbol system in which he would be innocent: he is guilty before one or the other of those between which he is torn (the moral and the religious). For Mathewson, the possibility of a symbol system that would include *ṭwb* and *r'* exists, but only as something as yet unavailable to Job. For both, Job's problem is that he lacks an adequate Third (Law/symbol system) on the basis of which the two (Job and God/death/integrity) could be meaningfully related. Job is stuck waiting and looking for an ideal that is, at least for now, impossible to attain.[121] Both Mathewson and Job's wife leave Job dangling before an impossible object of *desire*. The following section contends that Job rejects this structure to inhabit the structure of the *drive* and thereby accomplishes an unconditioned and wise act.

§27 Job's Rejection of Desire, Lodging in Drive

I discussed the difference between desire and drive at length on pages 34–39. In short, it concerns the difference between an ever-deferred *pursuit of knowledge/enjoyment*, and an always-already attained *experience of jouissance*. The drive achieves its aim of satisfaction through desire's failure to attain its goal in the process referred to as sublimation. Job's wife, Mathewson's analysis, and the logic of sacrifice informing Job's pre-afflicted piety all adhere to the structure of desire: Job stands in a fixed subjective position before a bewilderingly indeterminate objective world that lacks a mediator up to the task of relating him to the objects of his experience in a finally meaningful way. This structure fails to account for the crucial difference between Job's postures before and after the affliction. The same Job whose constant sacrifices for his children's potential sin arose out of and sustained his posture of deferential contempt toward his knowledge, this same Job responds to the events of his affliction by expressing no curiosity about how they might be connected to his activity. He does not try to sacrifice objects that may satisfy the desire of God. He does not even wonder what God's desire might be. Job's words and actions are not driven by his desire to know—by his lack of knowledge about—who or what he is for God.

If not his desire to know, then what drives Job's verbal responses? Both concern what his experience of God has made available to him: first, the removal of himself from himself; second, *r*ʿ. And yet both are also quite general, nearly asubjective. Both offer general statements about his subjective condition that express no sense of dissatisfaction. Is Job's position therefore disinterested, dispassionate, or unmotivated? (This is what so many think that the test challenges.) On the contrary, as Job's wife would attest, his passion is intense. Furthermore, nothing separates his experience from what he is passionate about. In fact, this closed circuit between his passion and his experience indicates an important difference distinguishing Job's subjective stance from the structure of desire that characterizes his wife and others. Job unequivocally rejects the "choice" with which his wife imputes guilt and death to him, but he does so by affirming his choice of *r*ʿ. What differentiates the *mwt* that Job refuses from the *r*ʿ that he affirms? Job's wife commands or represents death (*mwt*) in the abstract, as a state to which Job is heading. *r'*, however, represents a concrete sense of death that has already intersected him. Job rejects the sense of a death that opposes his conditions from the outside, and testifies instead to an experience of *r'* as a negating force within his conditions. Job's testimony to an experience of *r'* thus approximates the death drive as a force of negativity that afflicts and compels subjects beyond the life (that is, the pleasure principle) that is available through the Symbolic order (that is, the reality principle).[122] Where the structure of desire has Job paralyzed and dissatisfied before a lacking object, Job testifies to an experience of the lack itself as an object, and he expresses no dissatisfaction with it.

Job's wife attempts to get him to relate his present stance—his perseverance in blamelessness—to an external law so that he is blameless with respect to either the law of morality or the law of religion. Job rejects this, instead worshipping and then eschewing dissatisfaction by refusing recourse to anything beyond his experience. Job tries to justify neither his experience—by explaining his attribution of it to God—nor his stance—by explaining how he is innocent. The blamelessness with which he perseveres is therefore the expression of a subject who has lost the support of communal norms or the social order. Job's stance is not guided by the possibilities that the community prescribes or anything other than itself. Job does not appeal to any pre-given laws or rules, and so assumes a seemingly timeless stance. Thus located at a place where the temporal and the eternal are conjoined, Job's stance concretely materializes the timeless truth of WISDOM. Job speaks and stands as one who has lost any support in an order or an Other. That is, Job acts as an autonomous subject; he fears freely.

But we can only understand this characterization (autonomous, free) if we admit that the autonomy or freedom of the drive is not the same as the autonomy or freedom often disparaged these days as Cartesian/Liberal/Romantic. Job acts free not only of his conditions but also of himself. The autonomy of the subject/*nepeš* comes through the subversion of the ego. Job is not at one with himself; he is located in a place where "himself" meets what is not-himself, where the inside meets the outside: *on the trash heap*—where the social body externalizes the waste it produces—*with the potsherd*—with which he scrapes the pus his corporeal body excretes through his boils into the external world.[123] Job literally incarnates the excesses that are produced by and yet have no place within town and body.

According to the prose tale, the wise act of free fear is possible, but not through a feat of subjective will by which a sage could rise above her conditions to act despite them. On the contrary, free fear is possible at the moment that the distance disappears between the sage and WISDOM. At the moment God acts *ḥinnām*, at the moment of the silence of all that was previously held as wise, WISDOM achieves a voice through Job, albeit at a terrible cost.[124]

These two short chapters transform WISDOM in Israel into a product that emerges with the subject out of an event that (dis)locates the subject onto a site of potential transformation. An apparent gap normally separates the sage from God and WISDOM—the truth and ground of her being. Job's (dis)location onto the other side of this gap enables him to fear God *for-Godself* and *for-naught* by alienating him from all that he could know about God and his truth and ground. The gap between WISDOM/God and the sage disappears in Job's experience, and he knows it. WISDOM becomes indistinguishable from the sage's act—Job's concrete stance produces/ presents the universal WISDOM. Job directly produces WISDOM when he embodies the gap that normally separates the sage from WISDOM, when he incarnates the split between the *nepeš* that he is and all that he was. Job experiences the impossible and he embodies the unknown and the unrecognizable. For those such as the friends who are only capable of seeing the possibilities outlined by the previous situation, this embodiment of the unknown registers the transcendence of true Wisdom—this situation is too great to be understood and can only be responded to with ineffable silence. For Job, however, he directly presents unrepresentable WISDOM for all to see.

Before concluding this chapter, I'd like to consider how one should understand the sense of continuity implied by Job's characterization as one who *perseveres* in his blamelessness. One commentator captures the sentiments of many when he writes, "Throughout the narrative . . . an almost superhuman Job *continues to* embody sapiential virtue . . . *continues to* bless, not curse, the One who gives and takes away."[125] But understanding Job's response as a fixation, a preservation of continuity with his pre-afflicted self, violates everything this chapter has argued. On the contrary, what Job perseveres with is what is overturning him, what is swallowing him up; that is, the impossible *ḥinnām* of his experience, which makes it possible for him to act unconditionally by ceaselessly re-seizing it as the WISDOM that this event makes available to him.

§28 Looking Ahead: Guilt and Anxiety

Newson's monograph concludes that the moral imagination of the prose tale articulates a logic of piety that is unalienated, unassailable, and based on Job's heteronomous and unalienated position.[126] Does my description of Job's position as autonomous and alienated oppose her reading? On the one hand, what she means by unalienated—Job's relationship to God is not characterized by a mediating distance proper to retribution theology—is precisely what I identified as the cause of Job's alienated stance that makes his unassailable act of wisdom possible. On the other, what I have described as the autonomy of the driven (and not desiring) subject certainly comes at the cost of the autonomy of the ego *qua* the seat of reason and consciousness, which, for Newsom, is what Job lacks. So much for any simple opposition.

Just after her conclusion about the moral imagination of the tale, Newsom astutely changes her perspective on the position by which she led readers to her conclusion.[127] In a brilliant reversal, she whom we thought was beside us rustles the leaves behind us. She catches us off-guard, we who are earnestly struggling to grasp Job's moral imagination, and she holds us responsible for what we see.[128] Whereas we thought we were objectively analyzing the subject Job, she exposes us as subjects participating in the construction of Job as an objectified spectacle. The shame that this point in her chapter incites sticks to its readers.[129] It results from an encounter with our own *jouissance*, the ineradicable connection of interpretation with our bodies. If the moral imagination Newsom constructs is an unalienated and unassailable piety, the construction involves a dimension of our *jouissance* that is unassimilable. For Newsom, there is no getting beyond this dimension; noting its presence, she moves on to the book of Job's next genre.

What she thereby leaves behind, however, are the two very different ways in which we can relate to this shame that is the affective correlate to an encounter with *jouissance*. We could relate to this shame by feeling guilty, which would be to see our shame as a result of Newsom standing behind us, an external agent who represents the accumulated knowledge of the interpretive community. But the response to shame with guilt ignores the fact that, in her scenario, she is both beside and behind us, which invites us to imagine that we too are back there rustling the leaves with her. This second option is to relate to our shame as the affective correlate of an encounter with *our own* unassimilable *jouissance*. I call this feeling anxiety which, in contrast to guilt, does not approach *jouissance* as something potentially decipherable. Guilt requires ever-renewed sacrifices of this *jouissance* so as to make room for an ever-accumulating knowledge. By contrast, to feel anxiety is to treat our *jouissance* as something that remains necessarily opaque to our knowledge but that, as such, sustains our knowledge in its satisfying openness.

Part 2 takes up these and other modes of relating to *jouissance*. The difference between guilt and anxiety corresponds to what separates Job's position in the dialogue from his friends'.

Ideology, Resistance, Transformation

3

Ideology: The Wisdom of Job's Friends

§29 Cross-Word-Play

On the morning of Tuesday, November 5, 1996, election day in the United States, the *New York Times* published its crossword puzzle with the apparently presumptuous clue for 39A, a seven letter answer: "Lead story in tomorrow's newspaper (!), with 43A." 43A directly follows 39A at the center of the grid and so, together, these two answers provide one of the puzzle's "theme entries." 43A is "ELECTED." A further clue comes from the theme entry at the bottom of the grid; clue: "Title for 39A next year;" answer: "MISTER PRESIDENT." Far from presumptuous, this puzzle is set up to work if one fills in the seven letters of 39A with BOBDOLE or with CLINTON, the answers to the related down clues in 39D, 40D, 41D, 23D, 27D, 35D, 42D could each be filled in with the letter from either name. For example, 39D, "Black Halloween animal," could be either "BAT" or "CAT."

Even knowing that the puzzle has two possible answers, one can still imagine what it would be like to work it for the first time. At the outset, the naive reader would not know that the clues are ambiguous, or even that he/she is making decisions that disambiguate the ambiguous clues every time a provisional meaning is determined, for example, when the reader decides 39D is probably BAT. Filling in BOBDOLE for 39A would seem to confirm this decision and correct or confirm any other, related ambiguities that may have occurred to the reader. Once the puzzle is complete and all the evidence accounted for, any ambiguities that remain— for example, whether 27D ("Short writings") is BITS or BIOS—would appear to be resolved. However, having learned about the alternative solution to the puzzle,[1] it becomes clear that, somewhere along the way, a decision was made or a possibility failed to occur to the reader, who thus finds him/herself complicit in the meaning of the puzzle. In other words, the puzzle subverts a common assumption—reading is a passive process of uncovering a meaning that is somewhere in or behind the text—by exposing a degree of activity, whether intentional or not, on the side of the reader, thus exposing reading as a process of the production, more than of the uncovering, of meaning. The puzzle suggests that whenever a reader pulls the rabbit of meaning out of a hat, one can be sure that the reader is at least partially responsible for putting the rabbit there in the first place.

The range of reactions from those who worked the puzzle is not surprising. Will Shortz, the long-time editor of the *New York Times* crossword puzzle, has often referred to this puzzle as his favorite.

> When the puzzle appeared on Election Day, my phone at the *Times* started ringing at 9:00 and continued the whole day. Almost nobody seemed to realize that either answer fit the grid! The solvers who filled in CLINTON thought that I was being presumptuous at best, and maybe that I was inserting a political opinion into the puzzle. And the solvers who filled in BOB DOLE thought that I'd made a whopper of a mistake![2]

Those who worked the puzzle not only misrecognized their role in the production of its meaning, they also identified the intention of the editor or author (presumptuous, mistaken, ideological) with the cause of the problems or uncertainties left with them by the meaning they took to be final.

Myriad similar speculations and ambiguities plague scholarship on Eliphaz's first speech in Job 4–5. This book wagers that the essence of (the puzzle's or the speech's) WISDOM is found neither in the point of view of the editor/author nor in any other substance transcendent to the text; it is produced on the text's immanent and vibrant plane of meaning, at those lively places where one encounters the text's limits.

§30 Why Job 4–5?

This chapter focuses on Job 4–5, but opens onto larger swaths of material. *Excursus I* and CHAPTERS 4 and 5 increasingly incorporate the friends' other speeches into the analysis of their wisdom initiated by this treatment of Job 4–5. Even still, why this initial focus on Eliphaz's first address to Job? To what extent does this particular speech present a structure that inheres to the friends' speeches as a whole?

Many commentators find Job 4–5 exemplary, that it articulates the jist of the friends' message to Job. Although subtle and not so subtle differences *between* their speeches are recognized and important,[3] and although the point is rarely pushed very far or leaned on heavily, scholars often privilege Eliphaz's first speech for various reasons:

1. First—a matter of literary structure—in the narrative sequence of the book this is the first of the friends' speeches and as such defines the

initial terms of the discussion, even if the subsequent discussion cannot be reduced to these terms. This speech forms a background to
which subsequent speeches respond (or not).

2. Second—a characterological judgment—one may note the position of
Eliphaz as Job's *primary* interlocutor. He has been called the "leader of
the group,"[4] "definitely the most prominent and eloquent statesman
of the three."[5] Whether intentional (a result of editorial decisions) or,
what seems less likely, inadvertent (a contingent result of the history of
textual transmission), Eliphaz speaks the most words to Job in each
cycle of speeches.[6] In the first cycle of speeches, Eliphaz's speech is
ninety-eight lines long, whereas Bildad's and Zophar's are less than
half as long, forty-three and forty lines, respectively.[7]

3. Finally, though not isolatable from (1) and (2), some note that Job 4–5
are proleptic: "In his first speech in chaps. 4–5, Eliphaz actually presents the whole repertoire of arguments that the friends will employ in
all three cycles."[8]

This chapter gives a more adequate theoretical basis to the claim supported by this more or less empirical evidence, namely, that Eliphaz's
first speech presents the essence of the friends' wisdom to Job. In line
with the approach to wisdom worked out in CHAPTER 1, I will show *how*
the speech presents the friends' wisdom to Job, and specifically how the
transcendent essence of wisdom arises immanently from this speech.

§31 A History of Ambiguity in Interpretations of Job 4–5

As I discuss the interpretive issues that have long preoccupied the scholarly field and then offer my own exegetical deductions, readers will
benefit from consulting my text and translation of Job 4–5, which can be
found in the Appendix.

At least since Kemper Fullerton published his 1930 article on double
entendre in Job 4–5, scholarship on Eliphaz's first speech has struggled
to come to terms with its inherent ambiguity.[9] What is Eliphaz trying to
say to Job? Is he a well-intending friend who offers Job counsel that can
unfortunately be (mis)read as hostile advice when his speech is read with
excessive suspicion? Or is he a callous dogmatist whose feeble sympa-
thies hardly veil his judgmental arrogance? When he asks, "Is not your
fear your confidence? . . . Think now, what innocent person perishes?"
(4:6a, 7a), is he encouraging Job to trust in God's ultimate justice? Or is

he callously implying that Job's children and, by extension, Job himself have suffered justly because of their guilt? These questions present the battlelines around which scholarship on the speeches divides.

These debates perfectly illustrate how ideology can function to present an opposition as ultimate and exclusive that actually only involves one side of a dilemma. As soon as one accepts the terms of the debate as outlined in the previous paragraph, the war has already been lost since one has already conceded to read the speech's ambiguity as a hermeneutical problem. By hermeneutical I mean a stance that treats the limits of the speech's ability to constitute its meaning as eliminable through a proper interpretation. For example, from a hermeneutical perspective it may seem that all one needs to overcome the speech's ambiguity is some clue as to Eliphaz's attitude or mood. If we can find evidence for a friendly disposition, then we can dismiss those places where he seems to offer smug judgment as poor readings by those whose "hermeneutic of suspicion" has led them off the deep end.[10] Alternatively, if we can be sure that his disposition is one of arrogant criticism, then we can discount his apparently sympathetic consolations as pathetic condescensions and those interpreters who take them seriously as naive dupes.[11] The essentially hermeneutic nature of the problem makes the question "who is correct?" impossible to answer: one cannot make a judgment about the *particular* meaning of Eliphaz's words apart from some preconception about the *totality* of Eliphaz's mood or intention, and that preconception is based on a particular meaning.[12]

§32 The Axiology of Retribution

Given the hermeneutical nature of the problem, I want to revisit Hans-Georg Gadamer's basic conceptual distinction between the negative sense of a "prejudicial reading" and a more philosophically constructive estimation of necessary "fore-structures."[13] I propose setting aside as potentially prejudicial the question of whether Eliphaz is cocksure or consolatory, and inquire instead into the fore-structure or conceptual framework of "retribution ideology" found in almost all interpretations of the friends' speeches. Although some detractors exist, interpreters of JOB more or less agree that the friends console Job by offering him a framework of retributive justice within which he can and should locate himself and his experience so that he can begin to take control of both.

Before questioning the validity of this thesis with regard to Job 4–5, it will help to outline the passage's rhetorical movement. Chapter 4 divides neatly after v.11, at which point Eliphaz turns from the more linear argumentation of vv.2–11 to describe in detail his sensory experience of encountering the divine. This major break yields two ten-line sections (vv.2–11, 12–21), each of which may be subdivided into subsections of five lines[14]:

- Vv.2–6 are framed by Eliphaz's perhaps sarcastic rhetorical questions to Job. Much in the manner of the "lectures" in Prov 1–9, these verses position Eliphaz to Job as teacher to student.
- Vv. 7–11 present basic sapiential truisms about the fate of the righteous versus the fate of the wicked. The fate of the wicked, even of those who possess such power as the lion, is tenuous and doomed.
- Vv. 12–16 recount Eliphaz's *phenomenal* encounter with divine truth.
- And finally, vv.17–21 either explicitly or implicitly elaborate this encounter at a conceptual level, translating the overwhelming sensory experience into a message.[15]

The evidence of Eliphaz here evincing a retribution ideology is not difficult to identify. In vv.2–6 Eliphaz critiques Job's response to his encounter with suffering, which has caused Job to abandon what the sapiential tradition has had to say about the meaning of suffering, despite the fact that Job had hitherto understood and taught about ethical exigencies from within the framework of this tradition. Perceiving Job to be at a subjective brink, Eliphaz urges him to retreat.

> But now it comes upon you and you are weary.
>> It touches you and you are terrified.
> Is not your fear your confidence?
>> your hope the integrity of your ways? (4:5–6)

Momentarily setting aside the ways in which interpreters deal with Eliphaz's identification of fear with confidence, on first glance this identification seems far from intuitive. And yet Eliphaz drives it home as if it were empirical fact. Eliphaz challenges Job to find the exceptional case:

> Think now—what innocent person has perished?
>> Or where have the upright been destroyed? (4:7)

These things have not (and therefore *do* not) come to pass, a point which Eliphaz reduplicates declaratively, in one of the classic manifestations of wisdom's ethic of retribution:

> Just as I have seen, those cultivating trouble and sowing misery reap
>> the same. (4:8)

Whether intended to be encouraging or disparaging, the first part of Eliphaz's first speech appears governed by the ethical axiom of retribution.

§33 Job 4:6: A Crack in the Retributive Framework

Interpreters often note that rhetorically Eliphaz's speech recalls the prose introduction, when all in Job's world was right and subsequently removed.[16] Take for example Eliphaz's mention of Job's "fear"; in our passage Eliphaz pointedly asks, "Is not your fear your confidence?" (4:6). Compare this to JOB's opening lines: "There was once a man in the land of Uz whose name was Job. That man was blameless and upright, fearing God and turning from evil" (1:1). Eliphaz reminds Job of the subjective correlate to objective blessing—*fear* goes with *blamelessness* goes with *greatness*—or, more causatively, fear *causes* greatness.

Granted the connection between 4:6 and 1:1. But what of 4:6's odd predication identifying *fear* with *confidence*? Lexically considered, "fear" (*yr'h*) and "confidence" (*kslh*) can only be seen as strict antonyms. Interpreters almost always resolve this identification of opposites by referring to the way the wisdom tradition endows "fear" (*yr'*) with a positive ethical/epistemological value.[17] Proverbs frequently extols the posture of "fearing YHWH" as an exhortation to religious piety and the fear-of YHWH ultimately signifies the very essence of wisdom (cf. Prov 1:7; 9:10).

Apart from current disagreements about the *semantic* field of *yr'* within the wisdom tradition—does it retain the sense of "being afraid" or has it lost those affective origins?[18]—one can easily understand Eliphaz's point if fear is read within the framework of retribution as the subjective stance proper to objective blessing. The perceived contradiction of "fear" with "confidence" is alleviated since "fear" (understood as "the fear-of YHWH" that frames Job's outlook in the prose introduction) supplies the only basis for authentic sapiential confidence.

Yet, one cannot resurrect the particular, historical, sapiential permutations of certain privileged signifiers on only *one* side of the equation. "Fear" is not the *only* word that should be read within its historic, sapiential context. The sages also deploy "confidence"—*kislāh*—in particular ways that would necessarily color Eliphaz's statement. This noun and its cognates are included among Michael Fox's discussion of *words for folly*. That is, while the sages endow "fear" with a positive ethical/epistemological value, "confidence" gets a negative one. As Fox puts it, "It is an easy semantic move from confidence to overconfidence, and from there to smug obtuseness."[19] Delitzsch says the root *ksl*, to be fat, "signi-fies both the heaviness of stupidity and the boldness of confidence."[20] Fox speaks of various verses in the wisdom corpus that "assume the con-nection between (over)confidence and stupidity."[21] If we presume this connection here, then Eliphaz is suggesting that Job's stupidity, his thick-headedness, somehow follows from his fear.[22]

The problem is obvious enough; although it is undoubtedly tempt-ing to decide that the particular *sapiential* valence should be assigned to fear rather than stupidity, such a decision cannot be justified. The prob-lem is not simply a failure of our (interpretive) understanding; it runs like a crack through the retributive framework that supposedly binds Eliphaz's (and the friends') discourse together. Recall the sapiential motivation for fear: the sage must fear because of her own lack with re-spect to wisdom—she cannot be wise in her own eyes—and also because of YHWH's excessive presence that can disrupt any order, retributive or otherwise. The fear of YHWH serves to mark wisdom as incomplete and necessarily partialized but, paradoxically, this fear is the "first-part" of wisdom in the sense that it brings wisdom into existence as a thing that can be taught about and sought after.

The fool's confidence assumes a structurally symmetrical function to the sage's fear.[23] Fear and confidence are both placeholders for what falls outside of the retribution framework, and thus effect an ideal image of this framework's (possible, ultimate) completeness. Just as fear desig-nates the ignorance inherent to wisdom, confidence signals the knowl-edge at the heart of folly. That they do so from two different and opposed angles accounts for the sense of ambiguity and uncertainty generated by their juxtaposition in Job 4:6. If only one of the nouns were there, it would have served to constitute the framework by providing a place within it for that which is outside of it; and if the two were opposed, they would have together formed the boundaries of everything wise or foolish; but since they are identified, the difficulties these notions pose to the task of discerning wisdom and folly are set in stark relief. Setting side-by-side two notions that usually cover over the inability of sapiential thought ultimately to divide wisdom from folly produces a palpable sense of this framework's incompleteness.

§34 The Axiology of Total Culpability

This crack rendering the retribution framework incomplete may be sig-naled by the juxtaposition of fear and confidence in 4:6, but it is blown wide open in Eliphaz's vision in the second half of chapter 4. In v.17 Eliphaz reports the whisper of a message that stole itself into his ear (cf. v.12).[24] Although the meaning of the experience is debated, Eliphaz reports v.17's question as authoritative and significant: "Can a human be righteous before Eloah? Or a person be pure before his maker?" Similar statements implying the totality of human culpability before God are made by other interlocutors in the dialogue (for example, 9:2; 15:14; 25:4), including Job. "Thus for each of the humans still involved in the drama (Job, Eliphaz, Bildad, Zophar, Elihu) the authoritative status of Eliphaz's revelation is not in doubt."[25] A problem arises here for many because of the apparent conflict between the axioms of 4:2–11 and 4:12–21.[26] In v.7 Eliphaz implies that the innocent person does not perish (*'bd*) and in v.9 that the cultivators of trouble do perish (*'bd*), but in vv.19–21 he proclaims that those whose foundation is dirt—that is, all human beings—will perish (*'bd*) and die without wisdom. The axiom of retribution that divides the world into the wise and the foolish, the innocent and the evil, gives way to a doctrine of total culpability in which all are culpable and foolish.

Many have tried to make these two incommensurable axioms compatible within a consistent perspective. Clines argues for a modal reading of the verbs in 4:20–21, rendering these verses not "as statements of general actuality, but of particular possibility,"[27] which is to say that only some, and not all, are the subject of vv.19–21's verbs. That is, does Eliphaz say, for example, that every human will perish without being noticed (v.20), or that, for every human, the possibility exists of perishing without being noticed.[28] Eliphaz characterizes human beings by their inability to be righteous before God (v.17) and their ability to be crushed as easily, and more so, than angels (vv.18–19). So, his speech opposes the unrighteous crushed to the unrighteous uncrushed.[29]

Pace Clines, the idea that Eliphaz's speech lacks coherence need not disappoint. Another scholar might be perfectly happy with such a conclusion without thereby falling out of the critical enterprise: "Eliphaz's first speech does not in any sense consist of a fairly unified sequence of thought, but is a series of entities of very different kinds, each of which has its own structure of thought and thesis within itself. Eliphaz offers Job at least five different and slightly connected propositions to ponder."[30] What, however, are the extent and nature of the "slight connections" between these different thoughts? Can they ultimately be isolated from one another as different entities in a series? The discussion of 4:6 as a crack in the retributive framework suggests that neither of these theses is constituted as a separate or independent entity.

Earlier I suggested that the impasse about the ambivalences of Eliphaz's mood and the speech's meaning might be broken by looking to the theological framework upon which almost all interpretations agree. This theological framework now seems struck by a similar, essentially hermeneutic impasse. There is evidence for both axiologies and yet there is no ultimately satisfactory common ground for adjudicating between them insofar as they organize the ground in the first place.

§35 Job's Friends as Consolers

I am finally in a position to identify the promise of a recent article on the friends' speeches. Newsom argues that the speeches are best understood as the verbal component that likely accompanied the acts of mourning and consolation performed by family and friends for the sake of a mourner. She perceives two stages in the process. First, ritual mourning, which apparently lasted for seven days or to a point at which the mourner marked the termination of mourning through specific actions—for example, putting on clean garments—and entered into the second stage, a process of consolation, which could last much longer.[31] It was customary for mourners to receive consolers—family and friends—who encouraged mourners to advance in this process *from mourning*, in which they were ritually separated from the community and their normal lives, *to consolation*, in which normal activities could be resumed. Newsom suggests that one should not expect coherence, consistency, and non-contradiction from consolatory speeches, which aim at performing a function rather than delivering a single message.[32]

Since there is scarce evidence in the Hebrew Bible of any verbal component to such consolations—outside the book of Job—and there is abundant evidence from Greco-Roman sources, Newsom proposes to shed some light on the speeches of Job's friends by looking at the latter. She outlines five "fundamental assumptions that underlie the Greco-Roman understanding of the nature, purpose, and appropriate modes of consolation."[33] Her purpose is not to find parallels, but rather "to normalize elements of the friends' words and behavior that we are often not certain whether to treat as examples of good cultural performance of consolation or as an outrageous failure of friendship."[34] With this, Newsom positions her argument squarely within the antinomy of mood and meaning, of the subject and signification, that is at work throughout this discussion of Eliphaz's first speech. Her conclusion:

> They have, as friends, begun with sympathy, but their friendship offering would have been incomplete had they not also engaged in consolation. The rationalism of their arguments is neither inept nor inapt but

is precisely the instruction that is needed when grief disorders insight. Appropriate, too, is the eclecticism of their consolatory repertoire, for one does not know what will prove useful. Even the increasing harshness of tone and moral rebukes would have appeared appropriate from the perspective of Greco-Roman traditions.[35]

Newsom's argument frees us from the obligation to consider Eliphaz's speech as a whole. The ambivalences of mood and of meaning do not conceal an essence which, upon discovery, would allow us to separate Eliphaz's true message from those contradictory messages he simultaneously and unwittingly sends, or from Job's misinterpretations, or from the author's clever double entendres. Instead, the speech's potential meanings and the speaker's potential postures achieve a kind of semi-autonomy from other meanings and postures as so many different attempts to perform the same social function, regardless of their mutual consistency or mutual exclusivity. Consolation is not unlike a kind of talk therapy in which the law of non-contradiction exercises as little rule over the analyst's interventions as it does over the analysand's dreams. Far from something to be embarrassed about or paternalistically dismissive of as evidence of primitive irrationality, inconsistency might register the consoler's astute flexibility in responding to the (in)effectiveness of his consolation.

It is crucial to recognize why consolation works where other attempts to define a unified perspective on the speech's meaning have not. The notion of consolation does not try to envelop or account for all the ambiguities and ambivalences of the text, weaving them into a coherent whole. Taking a totally different tack, Newsom's consolatory function succeeds because it is void of content. Or rather, its content is nothing other than its function, which is to organize the speech's signifying material with respect to it. Being void of content, it avoids many of the pitfalls encountered by more essentialist proposals that necessitate an evaluation of the speech's meanings on the basis of their (dis)similarity to whatever is posited as the speaker's psychological profile.

There is a concomitant risk alongside the promise of Newsom's argument. If the designation "consolatory speech" frees us from futile attempts to grasp the speech either as a non-contradictory totality or as an authentic reflection or realization of Eliphaz the person or character, this designation nevertheless does not free us from the sense that we just cannot quite figure out what he wants to say and why he is saying it. Job 4 incites in readers a sense of intensifying uncertainty, suspicion, and desire that must not be lost with the baptism of its meanings as ultimately indeterminate and penultimate to the function of consolation. The dynamism and temporality of the reading process that produces this sense should not be exchanged for a more static and spatial model of the speech's meaning.

§36 Eliphaz's Answer

Given this irreducible sense of vexation that inheres within the meaning-effect of chapter 4, it is striking that Eliphaz begins chapter 5 by speaking about experiences of vexation and about what not to do when faced with them. In a proverb in 5:2, Eliphaz says,

> Surely vexation kills the fool, and passion slays the naive.
> *kî-le 'ᵉwîl yah°rog-kā'aś ûpōteh tāmît qināh*

Many interpreters translate *kā'aś* as "anger" and focus their interpretations on the anger of the fool as that which kills him.[36] What is important for the word in this context, and what is important about the word more generally, is its strong tie to an object with respect to which the subject is frustrated, inhibited, vexed, or provoked, as when Hannah is provoked by Peninnah about her inability to bear a child (1 Sam 1:6, 16), or when God is provoked by Israel's turning away toward other gods and sin (Deut 32:19; Ezek 20:28; Ps 85:5) or by other nations taking due credit away from God (Deut 32:27).[37] The characterization of the fool here has less to do with a particular affective response (his hotheadedness) than with his tendency to let an object frustrate or vex him (vexation also characterizes the fool in Prov 12:16; 27:3; Eccl 7:9). The parallel word to vexation, *qināh*, "jealousy, zeal, envy, animosity, enmity," also signifies an affect that is unmistakably related to an object (again, its loss, perceived loss, lack, perceived presence for another, etc.).[38] The issue is not simply the presence of an affect but the affective relationship of the fool to a (missing) object. Eliphaz's statement is more like an admonition warning Job that he is at risk of becoming vexed before the answer he cannot receive.

So, to return to my thesis, Job 5 tells readers what to think and what not to think about a sense of vexation such as subsists after reading Job 4. Below I discuss how, later in chapter 5, Eliphaz provides an alternative to vexation for dealing with uncertainty. By speaking about a force that causes vexation, he reorients the reader's perspective on vexation from an indeterminate effect of misunderstanding or opacity to an indeterminacy that is determined as an effect of God's activity in the world. Whereas vexation about the meaning of Job 4 has been considered an impediment to identifying its subject, Job 5 suggests that one particular

Subject characteristically produces gaps and uncertainties that disturb meaning.

Before trying to see how this thesis plays itself out in chapter 5, I need to outline its rhetorical movement, which is relatively uncontroversial.[39] There are three main sections:

- Vv.1–7, introduced by an imperative, give Job an negative exemplar of what not to do when faced with vexation.
- Vv.8–16, begun by a first person invocation ("As for me, I would . . ."), the effect of which (that is, "I think you should . . .") may be less direct but ultimately is not very different from the imperative. These verses teach Job about God's involvement in matters that confound the wise.[40]
- Vv.17–27, begun by an imperative, promise Job what will come to be for him should he accept that which he cannot understand. As noted by Terrien and others, vv.17 and 27, both introduced by the particle *hinnê*, are somewhat set apart from their surroundings.[41]

§37 5:1–7

Having ended his vision report in chapter 4 with the triumphant exclamation that those whose foundation is dirt die without wisdom, Eliphaz begins chapter 5 by warning Job not to think that his vexation conceals some truth which he could come to know. There is no one, Eliphaz implies in 5:1–2, no holy being to whom Job could turn to answer him. Answer what? Perhaps the questions Job surely has about Eliphaz's own speech in chapter 4, but at least those questions Job raises in chapter 3 (for example, "Why did I not die at birth? [3:11] . . . Why does he give light to the toiler? [3:20]"). Not only has Job just spoken these questions, but Eliphaz's speech also evokes them in vv.6–7, the concluding statement of this section, when it characterizes the human as born to toil (*'āmāl*), which seems to respond directly to Job's concern in 3:10 and 20. Regardless of the particular referent, the message is clear: only a fool remains vexed by these questions. They are so unanswerable that vexation by and zeal for their answers, according to the proverb in 5:2, can only lead to death. Eliphaz admonishes Job in vv.1–2 not to become fixated on resolving his vexation.

I will take Eliphaz's advice as a convenient excuse for avoiding the particulars of the vexing parable he offers in vv.3–5, concentrating instead on its images, which continue the message against fixation. In fact, "fixating" would not be a bad translation of the hiphil participle *mašrîš* in v.3,[42] which Eliphaz claims to have observed a fool doing—he is still talking about the same *°wîl* from v.2. "Fixed" captures the most common figurative meaning of the root *šrš*: riveted, immobile, stable. Second, the negative connotation of fixation in English, which is derived mainly from a vague, pop-psychological notion of an obsession, an *idée fixe*, captures the sense *šrš* receives when the sages use it of fools and the wicked to signify a maldeveloped, incompetent, and perhaps even dead root.[43] Finally, fixation includes a libidinal dynamic signifying a firm and satisfying attachment to a privileged object or a characteristic of an object.[44] Where *šrš* is not elsewhere used as the English slang *root* to denote activities such as rummaging, poking, prying, and pulling for one side/team in a competition, *mašrîš* may here receive a similar connotation since it concerns an unanswerable question and a fool's death from vexation and zeal.

Eliphaz describes the fool's tendency to root around in an unanswerable question until, fixated with zeal for its resolution, he brings about his death. Given these three connotations, what Eliphaz then describes is hardly surprising as, suddenly (v.3), the fool's "offspring are far from salvation, they are crushed at the city gate" (v.4), and his harvest goes to the hungry (v.5).[45] Eliphaz worries that Job will search so high for a holy answerer (v.1), or bore himself down so low into his questions (v.3), that he will find himself forsaking the world and the world forsaking him (vv.4–5).

Verses 6–7 reveal even more about the axioms subtending Eliphaz's concern.[46] Continuing the imagery against rooting, Eliphaz cites a proverb in v.6 proclaiming that suffering does not sprout from the ground. And in v.7 he says that all humanity (*'ādām*) is born to suffering.[47] The fool is not the sufferer *per se*. The fool is the one who entertains a particular relationship to suffering, a relationship that approaches suffering as if it were a crop whose seed could be discovered by rooting it out. The fool thinks that all the evidence simply adds up and reveals its cause; the fool is the one who reads 4:8—"those who cultivate misery (*'āmāl*) reap it"—without 4:9, where it is "from the breath of Eloah [that] they perish." In other words, there is a gap between the evidence for the cause of suffering and the suffering itself that cannot be accounted for by the evidence.[48] *This opening or gap in understanding is precisely what Eliphaz's speech consistently represents to its hearers.* In what follows Eliphaz informs Job that this gap is nothing other than the activity of God and he advises Job to seek no one other than God.

I can briefly summarize my interpretation up to now with two paradoxes. First, Eliphaz's speech in chapter 4 presents an irreducible ambiguity that incites hearers' *desire to disambiguate* as well as their *suspicion about certitude.* Second, in 5:1–7 he tells Job neither to expect an answer from a holy beyond nor to think that he can uproot the here and now of his suffering and perceive its seed. This would seem to leave Job nowhere to turn. In 5:8–27, to which I now turn, Eliphaz clarifies the option he thinks Job is left with and what effect this choice will have on him.

§38 5:8–16

After seven difficult verses teaching where and whom not to seek, v.8 finally tells Job whom to seek: God. The God of whom Eliphaz speaks, however, is not easily seekable. In fact, this God can hardly be identified by anything more or less than the trail of evidence God leaves behind. In v.9 Eliphaz characterizes God as one whose great deeds are unfathomable, incapable of being numbered (cf. 9:10), which is to say that they are incapable of being ordered or known (cf. 37:5). Eliphaz counsels against looking for an answer to suffering because the key lies instead in what remains unknown, and more specifically in failures to understand and/ or misunderstandings, in that unknown X that must be posited for a failure of understanding to be perceived as such. God is, he says, the doer of what is unfathomable and innumerable. This goes against the grain of many conceptions of the theologies of Eliphaz and the friends, which tend to imagine God as the ultimate guarantor of the system, or even the exceptional support of the rule. Instead, God is the causal agent behind the failures of the rule, the breakdowns in the system and in any totality.[49]

Eliphaz, a sage, surprisingly describes God as "frustrating the crafty" (v.12), "capturing the wise in their craftiness" (v.13), so that "daily they encounter darkness and at noon they grope as at night" (v.14).[50] Consider what fails: *maḥš⁽e⁾bôt,* the designs, plans, purposes, machinations of the crafty (*⁽a⁾rûmîm*); the craftiness of the wise; the *'ēṣāh,* the counsel, schemes, advice, plans of the crooked; and finally, sight. What fails are the attempts to plan, to anticipate, the tortuous attempts to calculate when what remains unknown is not a corner of darkness awaiting enlightenment but a force that makes enlighteners see darkness even in light. Job, Eliphaz's doxology implies, should not be trying to know more but to understand where the failure in his understanding lies and how that might instruct him, because he can be certain that, where his wisdom fails, there God has been. God cannot be anticipated, but where the unanticipatable happens, there God has been.

With this reversal whereby Eliphaz proclaims that the limits and failures of wisdom bespeak its essence, Eliphaz dares to draw some astonishing conclusions. He proclaims in v.16 that the poor have hope and in v.17 that Job has been blessed and instructed. Eliphaz does not tell Job to seek God because wisdom emanates from God's deeds, which are all perfectly harmonious and coherent, and that Job will gain understanding if he gains a perspective more like God's; instead he tells Job to seek God because God sets the lowly on high and raises the dejected (5:11). This is not the God of calculus, of a calculating retribution theology, but the one who frustrates the calculating and wise (5:12–13).[51] God is a great eclipse forcing the wise to see noontime as night (5:14), and this is the God on account of whom hope exists for the poor (5:16)—here meaning Job.

§39 5:17–27

In vv.17–27 Eliphaz turns his attention directly to Job, deploying a litany of second person subject and object pronouns and outlining what could be for Job should he accept the instruction (*mûsar*)[52] of Shadday (v.17). Accepting the instruction of Shadday is an act whose nature has gone remarkably unspecified by scholars. At the very least, it is that which Eliphaz thinks Job must do to be counted again among the set of sages, among society. With that, a question that has trailed this analysis for many pages finds its answer: what serves as the boundary between mourning and consolation for Eliphaz? One risks misunderstanding what Eliphaz promises Job by starting out with the idea that the essence of his wisdom lies in a retribution theology. Just as the interpretive key to 5:1–7 came from resisting the identification of the fool and the sufferer that Eliphaz is so often taken to assume, and insisting instead that the fool is the one who maintains a certain relationship to suffering, so too does the blessing of God's instruction come here, not from an absence of suffering, but rather from a certain relationship to suffering.

Eliphaz does not offer Job a life free of adversity,[53] as a focus on retribution may cause us to anticipate.[54] Quite the contrary: the nine prepositional phrases in vv.18–22 imagine a number of possible calamities that Job may endure, for example, injury (5:18), adversity (v.19), famine and war (v.20), devastation, starvation, and wild animals (vv.21–22). While vv.19–20 make promises of a limiting sort, "amidst seven adversities no harm will touch you" (v.19), "amidst famine, he will ransom you from death" (v.20), what these promises promise is an ultimate limit to suffering. Eliphaz is not saying that Job will suffer no more, or that he will suffer six or seven—but not seven or eight—adversities (*ṣārôt*) when he promises him that he will be spared from harm (*rā'*). The harm (*rā'*) Job will be spared is altogether different from the adversities (ṣārôt) he will suffer. Admittedly, Eliphaz's statement in v.18 creates some ambiguity insofar as the two waws joining the two dispensations of God's activity could be read temporally—God injures then binds, smites then heals. But vv.21–22 dissipate this possible confusion as Eliphaz promises not one unfortunate experience over another or a period of misfortune followed by a time of fortune, but an altogether different experience of misfortune, one which is not accompanied by an upsurge of negative affect:

> Amidst the scourge of the tongue you will be hidden;
>   you will not fear devastation when it comes;
> You will laugh at devastation and starvation;
>   and you will not fear the creatures of the earth. (5:21–22)

Here it is clear that Eliphaz thinks devastation is a sure possibility for Job's future—and how could he not—but the good news he offers is that Job will not fear it when it comes.[55] The possessive second person pronouns clustered in vv.23–25—your covenant, your tent, your habitation, your progeny, your issues—function to emphasize a subjective condition despite objective calamity such that, for example, Eliphaz promises Job that he will know peace in his tent, despite whatever storms may rage on in it; he may reckon his progeny many, despite the starvation he may endure. No matter what, Job "will enter the grave in full vigor" (v.26).

What Eliphaz promises, then, is a transformation at a second level, not an immediate transformation, that is, a transformation of his experience and not simply a different experience. This reading is strengthened when we recall how Job ends his first speech:

> Surely the fear I feared has come upon me,
>   and that which I dread encounters (bw') me
> I am not at ease, and I am not at peace, and I am not restful,
>   for anguish has come (bw'). (3:25–26)

Eliphaz acknowledges Job's complaint right away in his first speech, "But now it comes (bw') upon you and you are weary; it touches you and you are terrified" (4:5). And then Eliphaz promises at the end of his speech that, even amidst terror, Job will know no fear.

As for the content of Job's experience, Eliphaz promises Job nothing different than that which he is already suffering. As for the role of God, Eliphaz promises neither that God's good and redeeming hand will overturn the forces of death and destruction, nor that God's just hand will continue to bring death and destruction until Job accepts God's instruction. Instead, Eliphaz says, "Blessed be the person whom Eloah reproves, so do not reject the instruction of Shadday. For he injures and he binds; he smites but his hands heal" (5:17–18).[56] In the end Eliphaz offers Job a new perspective on his experience insofar as meaningfulness no longer supplies its ultimate horizon. Job is counseled against any desire to disambiguate or cohere what is ambiguous or incoherent and instead is urged to see in it the work of God. Eliphaz quarantines truth to the realm of the divine and resists identifying God with a particular meaning—injury or healing—insisting instead that God is experienced in the limitation of meaning, in the kernel of truth that distorts all meaning. Eliphaz does not offer Job a God who makes sense of it all, a God opposed to a traumatic remainder that escapes sense, but makes of God the supreme agent of senselessness, nothing other than sense's traumatic limit. Job need not be terrified by his ignorance and vexation but can instead enjoy and learn from them as privileged symptoms of a divine encounter.

On what basis does Eliphaz imagine that Job's terrifying experiences could lose their fearfulness? At the end he appeals to no other authority than Job's conscience and the force of his own argument: "hear and know for yourself" (v.27). Just as I found Eliphaz much more concerned with Job's orientation and approach to his own suffering than with any particular opinion Job may harbor about his suffering, so here does Eliphaz admonish Job to gain understanding through an orientation and not through any particular content.

But does Eliphaz not stabilize, domesticate, and thereby negate the unknowable by locating it in a structure that can instruct? Perhaps, but it seems to me that, for Eliphaz, the instruction of God is not about the unknowable per se as much as it is about the impossibility of knowing it. The inscrutable God continues to evade understanding, drifting behind and away even from the moment of instruction.

What on earth could this wisdom fail to encompass? How could Job possibly throw this infinitely flexible wisdom into crisis? In the remaining chapters of part 2, I show how Job does precisely this.

Before getting to that I want to look back at where we have been. To this point this chapter has presented the argument as a function of the text. Yet it is deeply rooted in certain notions of the individual, the subject, signification, and so on. I have not been disingenuous by neglecting direct treatment of this dimension insofar as such notions subtend every interpretation—not just my own—and I have remained silent about this dimension with respect to them all. What follows rectifies this silence by transcoding the above analysis into a set of terms that may at first appear foreign but will in the end, if I am successful, seamlessly converge upon the now familiar terms with which I read the speech. The fortunate consequence of this exercise will be a surplus of understanding.

§40 The Self and the Subject; A Theoretical Transcoding

Crucial to my interpretation is a conviction about the categorical difference between a subject and an individual. The problems I have drawn out of the confusions that plague current critical discussion of the subjects of Job 4–5—the subject matter of the speech as well as the subjective position from which it is spoken—are deeply tied to confusions about both the nature of these two subjects and the relationship between them. Some scholars operate under the premise that the speech's meaning is grounded in a pre-existent subject whose intention is transparent to itself and realized in the speech. Eliphaz's (and/or the author's) identity, intention, or mood is invested with the function of anchoring the meaning of his speech. Let us call the supposed position of mastery from which the speech's meaning is supposed to emanate S_1, and the content or meaning of the message S_2, which is constituted only on the basis of its relationship to S_1, which can be depicted like this:

$$(S_1 \rightarrow S_2)$$

Figure 1: Mastery and Meaning

The problem is that neither S_1 nor S_2 is able to ground the other, and so the barred-S ($) represents a lack of a signifying or meaningful basis that subtends every constituted relationship between S_1 and S_2:

$$\frac{(S_1 \rightarrow S_2)}{\$}$$

Figure 2: No Ground to Stand Upon

The result leaves the critic before a seemingly interminable series of interpretations, each one of which is complete and excludes the others without providing any means for evaluating among them:

$$\frac{(S_1 \rightarrow S_2)}{\$} \rightarrow (S_1 \rightarrow S_2) \text{ V } (S_1 \rightarrow S_2) \text{ V } (S_1 \rightarrow S_2)$$

Figure 3: The Interminable Effect

The lack of any ground for each determination of meaning compels the reader to circle back, imagine another sense for the passage, a sense that could only be related to the previous sense through the logical operator "or" (V) because of its independence from the previous sense.

But more needs to be said about the nature of S_1, for the idealistic notion of a pre-symbolic, self-transparent subject whose thoughts and intentions are somehow realized in his speech has been correctly attacked and rejected from many angles.[57] The point of departure for the standard critique is the priority of language and socio-symbolic structures over subjectivity and intention. The socio-symbolic field to which anyone must turn to attain the material and structures necessary for understanding and describing oneself is not the self, but something other than the self, and so what it provides cannot be understood as the self but rather as object-representations with which one identifies. Beginning with its name, the subject does not produce itself but receives from its socio-symbolic milieu the material necessary for its emergence. Following Lacan I refer to this symbolic milieu—the predominant structure of socio-symbolic space out of which any subject is produced—as the Symbolic order or the big Other. The subject is an effect of an embodied self's position with respect to its trans-individual context.

The effect of this critique on the conception of the position of mastery, intention, and desire (that is, S_1) is profound yet missed in the usual notion of a gap between intention and the alien medium of language, that is, the idea that pre-symbolic intention is more or less distorted by its forced conformity to the signifier—what one wants to say is different from what one says because no one fully possesses the medium. The true point of the subordination of the subject to the signifier is more radical; the intention to say is always already mediated by the structures and operations of signification. Intention is not an "internal" immediate force; it is always mediated through the "external" symbolic order; when we intend to say something we follow our judgment about what needs to be said because it is good, right, wise, funny, relevant, etc.

For Eliphaz and Job 4–5, this appears to be good news, for it means that no one has access to the material on the basis of which Eliphaz's intention could be identified. While this insight also lies behind Clines's attempt to solve the interpretive problems of Job 4–5 by proposing a reading that "makes a coherent interpretation of Eliphaz's speech possible and accounts best for the windings of thought,"[58] this response does not eliminate the problem. The subject continues to disappear behind, within, and from the windings of thought. Said differently, the windings of thought create the sense that the subject lies elsewhere.[59]

It is only with Newsom that the subject and S_1 are treated as two different entities; in her argument the consoler does not immediately identify with his intention(s) but instead relates to them from some other place, a place about which she does not speculate. S_1 is not the subject; S_1 is instead the phenomenal, symbolically constituted identity-construct that psychoanalysis calls the ego. The subject is the unrepresentable lack of being to which every determined, ego-level identity relates. Lacan explicitly calls the subject a "lack of being" (*manque-à-être*), a lack of substance and a lack of signification, which he designates with a barred-S: $.[60] But how does a signifier comes to occupy the place of S_1?

§41 Racine and Lacan; Fear as a Master-Signifier

To answer this question and conclude this chapter, I turn to the example on which Lacan worked out this logic of transformation in 1956: Racine's 1691 play *Athalie*, which supplements the story of Queen Athaliah from 2 Kings. Although the account in 2 Kings is not altogether clear,[61] the story behind the play can be summarized as follows. Queen Athaliah was an Omride of Israel who married J(eh)oram, king of Judah but puppet of Israel (8:27). Her son, Ahaziah, became the next king of Judah (2 Kgs 8:26). In his coup, Jehu assassinated King Ahaziah of Judah as well as King J(eh)oram of Israel, who appears to have shared a name with his brother-in-law, Ahaziah of Judah's davidic father. Following Jehu's assassination of King Ahaziah, the Queen mother Athaliah "set out to destroy all the royal family" (2 Kgs 11:1). However, Ahaziah's daughter Jehosheba took her brother Joash and hid him in the Temple, away from their grandmother's attempted genocide of the Davidic line. Jehosheba left Joash under the tutelage of the high priest Jehoiada who, faithful to the Davidic line, considered Joash the rightful king of Judah. According to the chronicler, Jehoiada was married to Jehosheba (2 Chr 22:11).

Racine's play opens with dramatic tension as Abner, the Queen's soldier, enters the Temple, house of the Judean Resistance. Lacan understandably imagines Jehoiada anxiously listening to Abner, wondering if the soldier's first line, "I come into His temple . . ." will end, ". . . to arrest the High Priest."[62] But instead Abner says, ". . . to worship the Eternal Lord," and then begins reminiscing with Jehoiada about the good old days when "masses of holy people streamed in through the gates," which has now, with the Baal-worshipping Omride on the throne, become "scarcely a handful of zealous worshippers." Having thus revealed his zeal for YHWH and, perhaps, for the Resistance, Abner goes on to express his

concern to Jehoiada: "I tremble with fear . . . that Athaliah should have
you ripped from the altar and wreak upon you her dreadful revenge." At
the moment Jehoiada is alerted to the danger by Abner, he too uses the
signifier fear, though in a way that only partly coincides:

> He who can still the raging seas
>   can also thwart the wicked in their plots.
> In respectful submission to his holy will,
>   I fear God, dear Abner, and have no other fear.

From this moment on Jehoiada has transformed Abner's fervor, zeal, uncertainty, doubt, fear, etc., into faithfulness for the cause.

> This famous fear of God completes the sleight of hand that trans-
> forms from one minute to the next, all fears into perfect courage. All
> fears—"I have no other fear"—are exchanged for what is called the
> fear of God, which, however constraining it may be, is the opposite of
> a fear. . . . Everything radiates out from and is organized around this
> signifier, similar to these little lines of force that an upholstery button
> forms on the surface of material. It's the point of convergence that
> allows everything that happens in this discourse to be situated retroac-
> tively and prospectively.[63]

Thus Lacan depicts the work of the Master-Signifier as a quilting point
(*point de capiton*). Žižek offers the following comment on this passage in
Lacan:

> Jehoiada does not simply try to convince Abner that divine forces are,
> despite everything, powerful enough to gain the upper hand over
> earthly disarray; he appeases his fears in a quite different way: by pre-
> senting their very opposite—God—as a thing more frightening than
> all earthly fears. And—that is the "miracle" of the *point de capiton*—this
> supplemental fear, fear of God, retroactively changes the character of
> all other fears.[64]

In his first speech, Eliphaz's aim for Job is no less than what Jehoida accomplishes with Abner, the sleight of hand that exchanges all his worldly
fears, his ignorance and his zeal, for the opposite, the fear of God and
the beginning of wisdom. Eliphaz takes Job's ignorant questioning in
chapter 3 and gives him God (not as an answer but) as the ultimate force
of ignorance. Thus he "magically" turns all Job's other ignorances into
their opposite, instructions (*mûsar*) of God, that is, wisdom.[65] The failure

of wisdom, in other words, is represented by the *mûsar* of God as both the proof and positive condition of wisdom's existence. With that, Eliphaz teaches Job what Gerhard von Rad and a few others have (re)learned, that the essence of wisdom is quintessentially bespoken at its limits.

§42 Conclusion

Job 4 impresses upon its hearers the sense of being one step away from grasping the true significance of the human condition or at least Eliphaz's conception of it. Eliphaz then takes this effect of his speech—the sense that the True meaning is just out of reach—and identifies this Truth in chapter 5, not as an absence from this dialogue, but as an excess internal to his speech and the world. This excess is nothing beyond the here and now, it is the effect of God's activity to keep the here and now from ever being all here or all now. Eliphaz thereby captures Job's zeal, his terror, his perplexity, his fixations, by refusing them the illusion of a possible resolution through the projection of their causes beyond themselves, on the one hand, and by transforming them into the meaningfully related effects of some meta-level object, on the other. With God and Job thus correlated around Job's failure to know, Eliphaz can promise Job all kinds of satisfaction from a God who can henceforth function as the cause but not the object of his desire.

Whereas one could hardly say that the preceding argument has been wide enough to do justice to the content of Eliphaz's first speech, not to mention the next two, I hope that it will prove preliminary for future study of the friends' speeches with respect to one matter in particular: I hope it has sketched the *essential* function of Eliphaz's confrontation with the limits of wisdom in the speech, thus cautioning future studies from relying on purely external or derivative conceptions of these limits, and encouraging future work to attend to them on a plane that is co-substantial with the essence of his wisdom. In the following excursus I indicate the presence of this structure of wisdom elsewhere in the friends' speeches and in the wisdom tradition.

Excursus

Wisdom Ideology Beyond Job 4–5

It is one thing to undercut the history of interpretation about Eliphaz, that is, to refuse the *either/or* that has framed a scholarly tradition I traced from Fullerton to the most recent commentaries. It is another thing altogether to suggest that the gap in understanding caused and carefully preserved by Eliphaz's speech is constitutive of the position of Job's friends as a whole, let alone of the wisdom tradition as a whole. Against this generalizing move weighs a more or less implicit set of assumptions:

- Eliphaz cannot be identified with Bildar and Zophar, at least not without remainder[66];
- the first cycle of speeches occupies, in some sense, a transitional moment between the friends' silence at the end of Job 2 and the narrow focus on retribution and, more specifically, the "fate of the wicked" topos in the second and third cycles of speeches[67];
- as regards the wisdom tradition as a whole, the multiple hesitations of Eliphaz do not fairly characterize the "optimistic" epistemology of Proverbs—the orthodox norm against which the wisdom tradition is measured.

§43 Bildad

The supposition that Bildad is bound to a retribution ideology is grounded on such passages as are found in Job 8.

> See, God will not reject a blameless person,
>   nor take the hand of evildoers.
> He will yet fill your mouth with laughter,
>   and your lips with a joyous cry.
> Those who hate you will be clothed with shame,
>   and the tent of the wicked will be no more. (8:20–22)

As with Eliphaz, Bildad consoles Job with the promise of an orderly universe, wherein God's favor falls upon those of integrity (*ṭom*), God's disfavor on the wicked (*mᵉrēʿîm*). Given Job's strong identification with the virtue of *ṭom* (cf. Job 1:1, 8; 2:3), Bildad apparently means to assure Job of a positive outcome—his immediate experience of suffering will be redeemed and this redemption will come into view on the basis of a broader (a "heavenly") perspective. From this perspective, experience and ethics are *immediately* linked: contrasting with the robust joy of the blameless (their irrepresible laughter—*śᵉḥôq*, their triumphant shouts—*tᵉrûʿāh*) is the puny ephemerality of the wicked, whose substance is obscured in a veil of shame (*yilbᵉšû-bōšet*) and whose security is vanished (*wᵉʾōhel rᵉšāʿîm ʾênennû*).[68] From these verses one must affirm that Bildad does indeed advocate a retribution ideology, a system in which God functions as the guarantor of a fixed order.

But, like Eliphaz, Bildad's speech cannot be reduced to an articulation of retribution. In the third cycle of speeches (in which the friends have reverted to an increasingly narrow and rigid focus on the wicked and not the righteous), Bildad says to Job:

> Dominion and fear are with God;
>> he makes peace in his high heaven.
> Is there any number to his armies?
>> Upon whom does his light not arise?
> How then can a mortal be righteous before God?
>> How can one born of woman be pure?
> If even the moon is not bright and the stars are not pure in his sight,
> how much less a mortal, who is a maggot,
>> and a human being, who is a worm. (25:2–6)

Here Bildad virtually cites, and to the same effect, Eliphaz's line of questioning from chapter 4—"Can a human be righteous before Eloah? Or a person be pure before his maker?" (cf. 15:14–16). Bildad's mounting frustration is aimed at Job's *hubris* in maintaining his innocence before God. Such stubborness is patently ridiculous, according to Bildad, when one considers the sublime distance of God from human knowledge, which is roughly as valuable as that of a maggot or of a worm when it comes to comprehending the deity.

Rather than a smooth edifice of retribution, the Bildad corpus is inhabited by the same contradiction I found in Job 4–5. On one hand, there is the *certainty* that God dispenses blessing to the righteous and woe to the wicked. On the other, any human knowledge about what God does (and why, and how) is put under the sign of *doubt*. Bildad's speeches are as marked as Eliphaz's by a vacillation between these mutually exclusive theses.

§44 Zophar

With respect to Zophar one sees the same split, though sharpened by Zophar's rhetorical flourish in condemning the "wicked" and "godless." In the first cycle of speeches, Zophar frontally criticizes Job's failure to preserve a minimal degree of *uncertainty* in his vigorous self-justification. "Is there nothing that would shame you," Zophar complains (11:3b),

> For you [Job] have said, "My conduct is pure,
>   and I am clean in God's sight."
> But oh, that God would speak,
>   and open his lips to you,
> and that he would tell you the secrets of wisdom;
>   for two sides belong to insight.
> Know then that God exacts of you less than your guilt deserves.
> Can you find out the deep things of God?
>   Can you find out the limit of the Almighty?
> It is higher than heaven—what can you do?
>   Deeper than Sheol—what can you know?
> Its measure is longer than the earth,
>   and broader than the sea. (11:4–9)

Wisdom is in its essential characteristics ungraspable by human insight:

- founded on the secret things of God,
- doubled in its character,
- split by the incalculability of divine mercy.

As to its place, Wisdom belongs to extremities inaccessible to human discovery:

- amidst the deep things of God yet at the limit of God's reach;
- higher than the heavens yet deep as the pit of hell.

From this perspective, Job's shrill cry, "I am pure! I am clean in God's sight!" represents the utmost in folly. It is a perspective, at the same time, that undercuts human certainty and thus stands in contradictory tension to Zophar's subsequent ethical insistences.

These insistences are manifest in mostly familiar terms (the wicked possess no durability, no solidity from the perspective of eternity), but Zophar's penchant for spatial imagery brings the friends' contradictory logic to a head. In his second and final speech Zophar offers this ideologically palatable though no less paradoxical "solution":

> Do you not know this from of old,
>> ever since people were placed on earth,
> that the exulting of the wicked is short,
>> and the joy of the godless is but for a moment?
> Even though their height mounts up to the heavens,
>> and their head reaches to the clouds,
> they will perish forever like their own dung;
>> those who have seen them will say, "Where are they?" (20:4–7)

The question that concerns me relates to the split between Zophar's own ethical certitude (such and such is the fate of the wicked, as has been obvious "from of old") and his demand that Job relinquish all ethical certitude (Wisdom is beyond mortal understanding, higher than heaven, deeper than hell). The solution, crisply effected by Zophar's rhetoric, is to preserve only *one* absolute tenet of wisdom: the prohibition against absolute Wisdom.

Recall that in Zophar's first response he roundly condemns Job's radical assertion of self-knowledge. Job's claims to innocence, righteousness, and purity (asserted repeatedly in chapters 9–10) are, from Zophar's perspective, epistemologically *impossible.* Job has mistaken appearances— what he has gleaned from his perceptions and memories—for the "secret things of wisdom."[69] How strange, then, that in chapter 20 Zophar recasts this *impossibility* according to the altogether different logic of *prohibition.* On one hand, the secret things of wisdom are as "high as the heavens" and therefore inaccessible (impossible); on the other, the wicked mount up "high as the heavens," and therefore they are punished (prohibited). On one hand, wisdom is removed from the sphere of what is *findable*; on the other the wicked recede from terrestrial rootage, and their old neighbors wonder, *Where are they?* In other words, Zophar quite tellingly locates Wisdom and the Wicked in the same impossible-to-find no-place, which transcends (human) limits. In a very literal sense, Zophar's teaching aims at an essence that is co-substantial with (and not beyond!) its limit.

In short, the limit that lies at the essence of the friends' wisdom and is present across all three cycles of speeches runs not along the ethical binary righteous–wicked but between

1. an insistence that God will dispose of blessing and punishment along the lines of righteous versus wicked; and
2. an insistence that human beings are constitutively ignorant of the ways of God.

§45 The Wisdom Tradition

Briefly glancing beyond the discourse of the friends, this immanent identification of wisdom's limit-essence is clearly not peculiar to their discourse, nor does it represent what some scholars have identified as a distinct, skeptical sub-tradition within the wisdom corpus. On the contrary, the folly at the heart of wisdom is hidden in plain sight in the texts that are considered the most orthodox of the tradition.

- In the Joban prose introduction, Job's pre-afflicted piety adheres to the same structure. Job's exemplary status—his uprightness and crucially his "wholeness" (*tom*)—is vouchsafed by his zealous cultivation/preservation of doubt. This is the meaning of the freighted "perhaps" that animates his piety. Job can only be "whole" as long as there remains something hidden, an unfathomable depth "in the heart" (1:5).
- In the proverbial sentences the sages dwell on *multiple* forms of human limitation.

> Do not boast about tomorrow,
>> for you do not know what a day may bring forth. (Prov 27:1)

With an almost mathematical sensibility, this proverb expresses the sages' awareness of the incalculability constituted by the passage of time. Or, in the proverb that von Rad so heavily emphasized in his discussion of wisdom's limits:

> The horse is prepared for the day of battle,
>> but victory belongs to YHWH. (Prov 21:31)

Even if time's passage were fully disclosed and each of its trajectories traced to the next day, *yet* there is an unfathomable agency that freely interrupts the ontic field of cause and effect. Here too, the disclosure of *lack* is at the heart of the sages' teaching.

- Finally, Prov 1–9 frames its instruction with the motto "The fear of YHWH is the beginning, the essence of wisdom" (Prov 1:7, 9:10). This signifier "fear," whose Joban vicissitudes I am not yet finished exploring, bestows upon wisdom's limit the dignity of a proper name.

4

Resistance: On Fear and Anxiety

This is a special way of being afraid
No trick dispels. Religion used to try,
That vast, moth-eaten musical brocade
Created to pretend we never die,
And specious stuff that says No rational being
Can fear a thing it will not feel, not seeing
That this is what we fear—no sight, no sound,
No touch or taste or smell, nothing to think with,
Nothing to love or link with,
The anaesthetic from which none come round.
 —Philip Larkin, "Aubade"[1]

§46 Introduction

In CHAPTER 2 I argued that Job's affliction in the prose introduction
made it possible for him to display WISDOM. I divided the prose tale into
two orientations—one that prevented Job from displaying that free fear
for which he was tested (offered to Job by *haśśāṭān,* Job's wife, and others)
and another that made such a display possible. The prose tale stages a
refutation of the former by presenting WISDOM as a human response
that conforms to and affirms that which the event of an encounter with
God affords. The tale places Job on the groundless void that the divine
act creates and from which WISDOM emerges, and offers Job as a model
of one who fears God *ḥinnām* by giving WISDOM his voice at the moment
of its terrible silence. But the WISDOM Job displays in the prose tale is a
performative, more declaration than articulation, there being too little
material there for it to be developed. To those who wish to understand
Job's effort to grasp that which has overturned him and the implications
of this overturning, however, the dialogue provides considerably more
material—not only in Job's responses, but also in their opposition to the
friends'.

The history of interpretation of JOB strongly cautions against the presumption that Job's response in the dialogue comes from the same position as Job's response in the prose tale.[2] For this reason, in this chapter I ask again how the book presents Job's affliction and its implications, and I introduce the range of responses imagined by the book to this affliction—these are treated further in CHAPTER 5—seeking throughout to discern those immanent limits from which a transcendent WISDOM is produced. The rest of part 2 analyzes Job's wisdom and continues CHAPTER 3's reading of the friends' wisdom, supplementing it with greater attention to the relationship between their position and Job's.

Two questions more or less respectively organize the remaining investigations in part 2: (i) What is the subjective structure of the suffering that Job experiences at God's hand? and, (ii) What are the objective solutions provided by Job to his situation? And how do they differ from those provided by his friends? CHAPTER 3 indicated the impossibility of independently investigating these questions that have so profoundly captured interpretations of JOB. The subjective and objective poles of Job's desire inevitably reverse fields so that, for instance, one can only determine Job's subjective experience in terms of the object that he desires and vice versa. It is thus a somewhat arbitrary decision (though hopefully helpful as a descriptive strategy) to approach the question of Job's subjective experience via some initial observations about the object of Job's desire. The necessarily indirect line of argumentation thus proceeds in three steps:

1. I critically take up the prevailing hypothesis as to *what* Job desires in order to
2. better determine the *subjective structure* of Job's suffering,
3. a structural knot for which Job and Job's friends provide fundamentally different *objective solutions.*

This chapter works through (1) and (2), which involves a thorough recasting of Job's subjective dilemma. CHAPTER 5 documents a gap between (1) and (3), demonstrating that what Job's friends and readers posit as the proper object of Job's desire leads them to ignore and fundamentally misinterpret Job's subjective dilemma.

§47 Theories of Job's Desire

So what does Job want from God in the dialogue? This seemingly simple question turns out to have a surprisingly complex answer with implications reaching even to some of the most important and disputed issues in Joban scholarship. Most responses suggest that Job wants: "a meeting, a response, God's presence, an explanation, a trial, a judgment, justice, etc." Such responses emphasize that Job suffers from an acute experience of God's *absence,* or at least that the acuteness of his experience is exacerbated by God's absence.

The remedy for this crippling experience of God's absence is then supposed to be an authentic experience of God's presence. While this divine "return" or "response" is couched in various discursive registers, two have especial importance for JOB. First, the idea that Job imagines his confrontation with God in a legal context informs many recent interpretations. These emphasize Job clamoring to argue his case before or against God, whom presently Job can find nowhere. Second, Job's speeches are often understood in light of the lament tradition, which has recently received abundant critical attention and which encourages the idea that the sufferer considered the presence of suffering as strictly correlative to the absence of God from the protective duties owed by a lord to his vassal. The lament petitions God to fulfill God's duties to protect the subject whose plight is taken to reflect the lord's competence.[3] In both cases, robust contemporary conversations among scholars encourage the idea that Job complains about God's absence and seeks God's presence.

While the lament and legal traditions offer compelling biblical modes for linking the movement from divine absence to presence with the movement from subjective suffering to objective redemption, the sum total of Job's testimony offers a highly ambiguous witness to the "benefits" of God's presence. Job speaks of his suffering in terms of God's *oppressive presence* as or more often than of God's *enigmatic absence.* The frequent and enthusiastic references to the lament and lawsuit genres are comprehensible insofar as they provide needed contextual cues apart from which Job's speech seems to lack sense. They set Job's speech in specific interpretative frameworks which, each for different reasons, privilege those moments in the dialogue when Job ties his suffering to his inability to perceive God's presence (or, the obverse, pins his redemption to an audience with God). Once it is established that in JOB the objective situation of divine absence-presence corresponds to the subjective situation of suffering-redemption, what remains in need of explanation is the meaning of Job's contradictory speech, specifically, why Job's expressed desire that God "leave him alone" should be subordinated to its opposite, that God "show up in court."

To put it more abstractly for the sake of clarity:

- there are *A* texts in which Job wishes to be liberated from God's overwhelming presence;

- there are *B* texts in which Job wishes to be justified via a hearing with an erstwhile absent God.

There are nearly as many ways of negotiating the abrupt juxtaposition of *A*/*B* (which is hardly the only such difficulty in JOB) as there are commentaries, which I have no interest in cataloguing. Instead, I take up the work of two scholars whose arguments are especially illustrative in that they take different paths to arrive at what is essentially the same conclusion. Claus Westermann establishes a *narrative sequence* in which *B* represents the moment of completion that corrects the starting point of *A*. Norman Habel sets them in a *logical dyad*: *B* being the primary, actual moment in relation to which *A* is derivative and virtual.

$A \rightarrow B$	$B \approx A$
Narrative Sequence	Logical Dyad
Westermann	Habel

Figure 4: Two Negotiations of Job's Desires

Westermann analyzes the book's structure according to form-critical categories, a starting point which leads him to understand the Joban dialogues as an extended lament and the book as a dramatization of a lament. One of the intrinsic features to Westermann's (that is, the standard) conception of lament is the petition or wish. The idea is simple, although perhaps not unproblematic—that anyone who laments, whether explicitly or not, simultaneously expresses a desire for something to be different.[4] Westermann arranges Job's petitions and wishes into four groups that more or less coincide with the book's sections. The first two wishes—the wish to die and the wish that God would leave him alone—correspond to *A*, and yet "terminate in the wish for a direct encounter with God (13:21–22 and 14:15) [that is, *B*]. But this latter wish gets developed only in the third cycle of discourses."[5] Westermann admits the logical incompatibility of these wishes and yet insists, "Only in the third cycle of discourse . . . does the main wish finally stand forth in clear and unhindered fashion—the wish for a direct encounter with God. *This is the real wish toward which Job has been struggling all along.* . . . In the last analysis, all Job really wants is for God to grant him a hearing."[6] Overall Westermann arranges what appears as a logical impossibility into a dynamic development. What Job desires at the outset differs from what Job *comes to desire,* and this difference can be traced along an arc of *clarification* or *resolution*: Job's incoherent and immature wishes are, at the end, resolved in his deepest, most authentic desire to gain a hearing before God.

109

This progression results in a neat resolution to the otherwise difficult to understand movement $A \rightarrow B$, that is, the culmination of Job's desire as the desire *for* God. But the two pieces of evidence Westermann cites are quite fragile, taking their support from each other in a self-sustaining circle. He claims that the optative lines of thought in the first cycle of Job's discourse have their telos in this wish, which he finds fully articulated in Job 23 and 31:35–37. However, as is almost always true of such teleological arguments, "the telos" is evident only after the fact whereas, in the moment of development, one must admit that numerous possible endings exist. Westermann at times seems to recognize this possibility that the optative lines of thought could (and, I will argue, do) end in more than one desire, yet he nonetheless claims that they find their true end in one desire.

Like Westermann, Habel gives pride of place to chapter 23 in determining the proper object of Job's desire. Also like Westermann, Habel supports his reading of chapter 23 with reference to Job's final speech in chapter 31. Furthermore, both begin their interpretations from the presupposition that Job's desire for God is split, as Habel puts it, "poised between two poles of compulsion and fear."[7] Finally, like Westermann, Habel thinks Job's *true* wish is to encounter God.

Unlike Westermann, who renders the wish that God would leave Job alone prolegomena for the wish to encounter God, Habel differentiates Job's conflicting desires in their relation to existence. Job's desire to encounter God is determined to be actual, existent, and primary, whereas Job's desire to escape God arises from his fear of a potential condition, the possibility of realizing his true wish. In the end, the threatening possibility does not succeed in deterring Job from his actual, true desire.

> He is compelled by his overwhelming desire to confront God in person and present his case in court ([23:]4–7). Yet he fears that God will continue to terrify him (see on 7:14; 21:6) and that his "face" will overwhelm Job with its terror (see on 9:34; 13:20–21), thereby preventing a fair trial. Job closes this speech with a typical cry of lament (cf. 10:20–21). This ending does not, however, negate Job's hope of finding God. For Job is now committed to meeting God face to face (cf. 31:35–37).[8]

While Job's *antipathy toward* God is logically consequent to Job's *hope in* God, the former does not finally measure up to the latter. Although Westermann associates Job's wish with the lament tradition and Habel thinks Job's wish transforms this tradition,[9] both come to the same conclusion: Job's culminating and ultimate wish is to encounter God's presence.

Westermann and Habel buttress my suspicion of the supposition that God's presence is the proper object of Job's desire by illustrating the dubious nature of arguments that:

1. posit a correct literary context by which one gains the proper reading perspective from which
2. a selection of Job's statements are elevated as sure reference points from which the remainder can be "properly" understood.

I do not think that the supposed influence of juridical or lament genres can bear the weight of the arguments that they found. The posited lament and/or legal contexts are not comprehensive enough to govern the interpretation of the whole of the book or even the speeches. Thus they should not be used to smooth out those large swaths of text that escape them. On the contrary, just as valuable as learning what one can from those places where the text fits the lament or litigious contexts are those places where the text escapes them.

While I think that my critique of Habel and Westermann can be extrapolated to form critical approaches to JOB *in general* insofar as they seem bound to draw out of their hats conclusions involving the absence of God and the theological problem of transcendence, I do not wish to downgrade the importance of the legal and/or lament genres so as to make room for some more fitting generic category. In a book whose most conspicuous feature is its generic manipulation and transformation, any triumphant assertion that *"Here Job speaks in his mother-tongue!"* is sure to reflect little more than the interpreter's preferences.[10] Granting that Job does speak in legal idiom and lament, one still cannot conclude that Job's desire is fixated on a certain object called God's presence. God's presence plays a much more ambivalent function than the object of desire, a function which I designate the object *cause* of desire and which Lacan formalizes as the *objet petit a.*

§48 There Is Fear and Then There Is . . . Fear

Job's initial lament in chapter 3 sets the stage for the friends' speeches by concluding with the following summary judgment of the terrifying and disturbing dimensions of his experience:

> Surely the fear (*phd*) I feared (*phd*) has come upon me,
> and that which I dread (*ygr*) encounters (*bw'*) me;

> I am not at ease, and I am not at peace, and I am not restful,
>   for anguish (*rgz*) has come (*bw'*). (3:25–26)

I mentioned this statement in my interpretation of Eliphaz's first speech (on page 92), which appears to respond to it directly. Eliphaz reminds Job what he has previously done for others experiencing dismay, helplessness, and inhibition:

> Look, you have instructed many,
>   and you strengthened the hands of the weary;
> Your speech supported the stumbling;
>   and you made feeble knees firm. (4:3–4)

Then Eliphaz speaks directly to Job's complaint:

> But now it comes (*bw'*) upon you and you are wearied (*l'h*);
>   it touches you and you are terrified (*bhl*). (4:5)

The "it" Eliphaz mentions is somewhat unclear but, in light of 3:25–26 and the way the speakers in the dialogue characteristically begin their speeches by referring to something said previously by another speaker,[11] "it" would seem to refer either to the terror (*phd*) and anguish (*rōgez*), or the God whose encounter with him has left him in this state (cf. 3:23). In 4:5 Eliphaz shows Job that he has understood Job's description of his experience, he acknowledges that Job's experience has brought him *bhl*, "terror" or "dismay," as well as *l'h*, "helplessness" or "weariness." In Eliphaz's next statement, however, he predicates a fear of Job that functions altogether differently:

> Is not your fear (*yr'h*) your confidence (*kslh*),[12]
>   your hope, the blamelessness of your ways? (4:6)

Eliphaz's message of hope is that, in the same way that Job's words stabilized the stumbling (4:3–4), there is a fear (*yr'h*) that is supposed to be his confidence in the face of that which is terrifying (*bhl*) him. Nearly every scholar reads "fear" here as shorthand for the "fear of God" seen elsewhere, for example, Prov 1:29; Gen 20:11; Job 28:28, and thus as meaning something like "piety."[13] The text gives us no reason to think that Eliphaz knows anything about what I described in CHAPTER 2 as the revolution *haśśāṭān* performs on the traditional, sapiential notion of the fear of God in the prose introduction. It will soon become clear that Eliphaz continues to deploy the signifier fear in ways congruent with the traditional notion.

Eliphaz refers to this other, reverential or pious fear each time he speaks. In his second speech he says,

> But you annul (*prr*) fear (*yr'h*), and belittle meditation before El. (15:4)

In his third speech he poses the following question, which smacks of sarcasm.

> Is it because of your fear (*yr'h*) that he reproves you,
>   and enters into judgment with you? (22:4)

In each of these three uses of the word *yr'h* Eliphaz evokes the semantic domain of a positive power that contrasts sharply with the negative force that words for fear (including *yr'h*; cf. 11:15) otherwise signify. In the positive instances, fear is an attribute of the pious and its affective avatar is attractive—a sense of stability, security, confidence—whereas elsewhere fear characterizes the wicked or foolish (for example, 15:20–21, 24; 20:25) or what Job could avoid if he turned to God (for example, 5:21; 11:15–16; 22:10). In these negative cases fear is experienced as surprising (for example, 22:10), terrifying (15:24), inhibiting (for example, 11:15–16), and alienating (18:14).

I refer to *semantic domains* of words for fear because the distinction between the types of fear lies not at the lexical level. The words for fear are not exclusively technical terms in the speeches or elsewhere in the Hebrew Bible. To take the most prominent example, *yr'h* is both that which is supposed to be Job's confidence against the terrifying events that have happened to him (4:6) as well as that which Job will not suffer when violence strikes him (5:21)—as long as he does not reject the instruction of Shadday (5:17). Alternatively, the positive, pious fear of God is elsewhere signified with *phd* (cf. Ps 36:2; 2 Chr 20:29) whereas Eliphaz names it as that which afflicts the wicked (Job 15:21; 22:10).[14]

Stated succinctly, at the end of his first speech Eliphaz promises Job that, if he does not reject the instruction (*mûsar*)[15] of Shadday (5:17b), terrifying things will come upon him but he will not fear them—"You will not fear (*yr'*) devastation when it comes (*bw'*)" (5:21b)—and, in contrast to his present state, he will know that his tent is at peace (5:24a). Even amidst terror, Job will know no fear.

Eliphaz's first speech thus operates on the basis of two distinctions. The first distinguishes *a knowledge* about one's experience—according to which one knows oneself to be suffering a terrifying experience—from *a belief* about which one can be certain regardless of one's experientially based knowledge. The second distinguishes *a* (negative) *terror* with which Job is presently afflicted, from *a* (positive) *fear* that can save him from it by giving him a place from which his terrifying experience could be safely viewed.

§49 The Friends' Fears; Ethics and Agency

The wicked are distinguishable from the righteous not by the presence or absence of the terrifying experience, but rather by the ultimacy or penultimacy of their experience of terror, the negative fear. Terror does not afflict the wicked alone. In 4:13–14 Eliphaz describes an experience of facing anxieties (*śʻpym*) when dread and trembling (*pḥd wrʻdh*) encountered him such that all of his bones were in dread (*pḥd*). From the friends' perspective, terror lacks a properly ethical status. The question of righteousness or wickedness arises only in relation to the presence or absence of the positive sense of fear.

While the friends may consider terror to be in a certain sense beyond—or better, below—ethics proper, descriptions of terror do regularly occur in their accounts both of the fate of the wicked (for example, 18:11, 14) and of what Job would avoid were he to adopt a righteous stance. That the wicked are more strongly associated with terror than the righteous has less to do with (the presence of) terror and more if not everything to do with (the absence of) the positive fear. Fear is the antidote to terror and this antidote is exclusively available to the sage. The sage *is* the one who fears when afflicted with a terrifying experience.

This is to distinguish an active fear from a passive or, better yet, middle terror. Terror happens; it befalls the individual who can escape it by fear.[16] Fear is something one can sustain, forsake, relate to, have confidence in, and it is always the proper reaction to the conditions of the sage's life. Terror stands for the pre-discursive reality, so to speak, what the sapiential framework calls what came before it was sublimated into fear. Sages always speak of terror from within the safe confines of fear, as when Eliphaz describes the terror he (previously) suffered.

Terror therefore does not really precede fear. Terror emerges simultaneously with fear as the name for the experience prior to the present fear. Insofar as terror is constituted within the framework of fear, it is something altogether different and cut off from the actual prior experience. Fear transubstantiates a certain kind of amorphous experience into terror *qua* the seed from which fear grew. So what about those who suffer an experience that the sages understand from the perspective of fear as terror, but who do not do so from within the discursive framework of traditional wisdom? For anyone unwilling or unable to relate to their experience with fear, the experience is not of terror such as Eliphaz describes in chapter 4, but rather of what I call *anxiety*. Anxiety may become fear (then it would be counted retroactively as terror), but as such it stands for an alternative way of relating to a terrifying experience apart from the discursive framework of fear/traditional wisdom.

For the friends who stand within this sapiential framework of fear before a sufferer, what is important is that Job should respond to his terrible experience with fear. This approach is incompatible with the common conception that the friends attempt to get Job to suppress *his experience* in favor of *their knowledge*. On the contrary, they encourage him to fear so as to find security from the anxious terror he suffers and to understand something about what his experience is making available to him. When the friends exhort Job to fear in the face of terror, they clearly assume the agency required for the exercise of fear is available to Job, who is suffering anxiety because he is failing either to assume this agency or to do something that would enable him to assume it. From the perspective of the fearer, anxiety, unlike terror, risks bringing guilt upon the one who suffers it. If the sufferer of a terrifying experience is not relating to it fearfully, then she is doomed (and dooming herself) to the prison-house of anxiety. Thus one should understand the friends' tendency to think that Job is denying or ignoring some folly/guilt as, at least in part, a result of Job's resistance to fear after his experience and not only as a causal condition for his experience.

This relationship between righteousness and wickedness as regards fear and anxiety is even more complex. For the friends, wickedness affords an *ontological* insecurity despite any hope, confidence, or thought that says otherwise.

> The hope of the godless shall perish. For his confidence is broken,[17]
>> and his security (*mbth*) is a spider's house.
> If his house is leaned against, it will not stand;
>> if one seizes it, it will not hold up. (8:13b-15)

The anxiety of the wicked is but a signal of this insecurity.

> Terrors (*blhwt*) terrify (*b't*) him on every side;
>> and cause his feet to scatter . . .
> [The wicked one] is torn from his tent, from his security (*mbth*),
>> and terrors (*blhwt*)[18] march him off to the king. (18:11, 14)

For now, the wicked may lie comfortably in their tents, but soon terrors will tear them away and leave them totally insecure.

If the wicked are insecure as a rule, hounded by their anxieties and dread, whereas the righteous are certain, secure in their hope, this is more an ontological truth than an empirical condition. The states of terror or peace do not correspond empirically to righteousness or wickedness. This non-correspondence is negotiated in various ways, but fundamentally the terror of the wicked is thought to impinge upon them even if they are (temporarily) at peace.[19] So, Eliphaz says,

> The wicked one writhes all his days;
>> and the number of years are stored up for the ruthless one.
> The sound of terrors (*pḥdym*) is in his ears;
>> and *when he is at peace* (*šlwm*), devastation comes.
> He cannot be sure (*'mn*) about returning from darkness . . .
> Distress terrifies (*b't*) him, and anxiety (*mṣwqh*) overpowers him.
>> (15:20–22a, 24a)

Eliphaz can say that writhing occupies *all* the days of the wicked, *even* those days in which he is at peace, because the wicked one's peace is not a peace he can be sure of. Zophar says,

> In the fullness of his [v.5: the impious or wicked] sufficiency,
>> distress will be his; all kinds of misery[20] will come to him.
> Heaven will expose his iniquity, and earth will rise up against him . . .
> This is the wicked one's portion from Elohim,
>> and the inheritance appointed for him from El. (20:22, 27, 29)

Even when *full* of all they want, room exists for the misery that is to come; their distress is sure. Responsibility for this misery that will come to the wicked, whether in heaven or on earth, is given to God (cf. 20:15: "He will vomit the wealth that he swallowed; God will empty out his stomach"). But so are the states that stand in need of such restoration. Bildad admits, "Dominion and terror [*pḥd*] are with him, he makes peace in his heights" (25:2). Dominion, terror, and peace are all with God, which bestows upon God a high degree of plasticity. Recall that the God in whom Zophar commands Job to have such confidence resides in the virtual heights, beyond knowledge and calculation: "higher than heaven . . . deeper than Sheol; what do you know?" (11:8).

The non-empirical, ontological nature of the insecurity, suffering, and anxiety that befalls the wicked means that the anxiety and suffering Job endures need not register Job's wickedness, but can function as a terror on account of which Job could fear God. If he fears, they exclaim, "You will be without anguish, and you will not fear" (11:15b; cf. 5:21b). Fear promises certainty (11:15a; cf. 5:24a), security (11:18a); pleasure (5:22a), and virility (5:24b; cf. 11:19a) in the face of the evils suffered in anxiety.

How should one understand the friends' exhortations to Job to fear God alongside their implications and accusations that he is wicked, that he harbors some iniquity that he is denying or ignoring? How is it that the security, stability, confidence, and hope that are the fundamental attributes available to the righteous are simultaneously those that are available to Job if he turns to God and admits his iniquity? Why is it that admitting to the presence of wickedness in him would save him from (and not destine him to) the fate of the wicked?

Those who fear God do not exclude themselves from their belief about a real, ontological condition of the righteous and the wicked that is separate from but more true than what can be perceived and understood from phenomenal, empirical reality. Counting themselves among the righteous gives them, on one hand, a certain confidence or hope despite their experience but, on the other, requires some humility before the possibility that this unknown dimension tells not of their righteousness and wisdom but of their wickedness and folly. Job is promised a certain confidence and hope for his future—but only on the basis of his prior humility, his readiness to reject any aspect of his condition that may be iniquitous, *his remaining uncertain about his present*. He must forsake a part of himself in order to view his condition from the safe confines of fear.

Consider Zophar's conclusion to his first speech with its promise predicated upon two conditional statements:

> If you establish (*hkynwt*) your attention (*libbekā*),
>   and spread out your hands to him,[21]
> If iniquity is in your hand, distance yourself from it,
>   and do not let wickedness reside in your tents,
> Surely then will you lift your face without blemish,
>   you will be without anguish,[22] and you will not fear (*yr'*).
> Surely will you forget misery . . .
> And you will be secure, for there is hope (*tqwh*).
>   You will search[23] and you will rest securely (*bṭḥ*).
> And you will lie down, without trembling (*w'yn mḥryd*). (11:13–16a, 18–19a)

Zophar's promise includes a spatial image that accords with a simple way of understanding (self)consciousness. From within the flux of lived experience, consciousness is not yet present. It is only on the basis of some distance from myself that the reflexive awareness that I am a being submitted to the flux of lived experience can arise. This reflexivity is often thought of as consciousness. For self-consciousness to exist, there must appear to be some place "above" or external to oneself from which one can relate to oneself. Zophar promises Job relief from his present terror in the elevation of his perceptive capacities (*libbekā*) above himself. Being externalized from himself will give him the distance required to reject any part of himself that may harbor iniquity or wickedness.[24] With this Job can secure himself even against those dimensions of himself that he is uncertain about. Zophar tries to break Job out of the immanent flux of his experience so that he can view himself as one about whom he does not know everything and relate to himself as one about whom some truth remains unknown.

The ironic aspects of Zophar's rebuke should not be missed, in that his teaching would return Job precisely to his pristine, pre-afflicted state. Recall my specification of Job's "wholeness" (*tom*) as it is represented in the prose introduction (on pages 46–48). Such ethical perfection is not attested by Job's substance, that is, his considerable progeny or wealth. Instead, the story cites Job's punctilious ritual of sacrifice, which he carries out saying, "It may be that my sons have sinned, and cursed God in their hearts" (1:5). The unfathomability of the human heart is, from Zophar's orthodox point of view, the basis of Job's guilt before God. And Job's blameworthy action is not some particular sin that Zophar feels Job is hiding. On the contrary, Job's sin is the blatant, overt one of suspending his properly human doubt before God ("*It may be . . .*").

On the face of it, the friends' counsel sounds paradoxical: the exclusion of truth to the divine realm yields the production of (limited) knowledge about his experience and his trust and hope in something beyond his miserable experience. How can Job's uncertainty about his situation be the key to gaining a safe perspective on it? How can his eagerness to admit the possibility that he has overlooked some iniquity engender his trust? How can his willingness to see himself as alienated from himself make him more comfortable with himself? The friends' promises are not rooted in any additional, positive knowledge that fear will give Job about his experience, but in the clarity that comes from (i) setting up a locus of truth, being, God, and certainty as unattainable, and (ii) defining the ideal subject as the one who pursues this unattainable truth nonetheless. By negating this dimension of truth and the Real from what is accessible, the ideology of sapiential fear installs it in a beyond. Saying it is not here or now gives it a positive existence elsewhere.[25]

It is therefore wrong if we only say that this locus of truth is excluded from the discursive framework of wisdom since wisdom's framework constitutes itself by means of reference to this dimension. Though negated, a crucial role remains inside the system for what is said to be outside. Though the system excludes it, this very act of exclusion gives it a way of being included. Furthermore, this inclusion of what is excluded is what makes possible intelligibility within the system. If Job agrees (or submits) to this prohibition against knowledgeably accessing the truth and the Real, then he can judge his perceptions against this missing dimension. That is, Job can glean some knowledge from the consistency or inconsistency with which his perceptions correspond to this missing dimension.[26] Fear will allow Job to escape his anxiety not because it tells him something he does not know but because it locates the unknown dimension of his experience at a safe distance from himself. Thus (dis)located, the unspeakable can be held in place by a structure and so no longer threaten to overtake Job. Job's energies can then be transformed from his concern with fleeing its cause to understanding what it may mean. The difference is between distancing himself from something and closing the gap between it and himself. This is why God must be located in a beyond that is out of reach to Job; Zophar says in this speech, "higher than heaven . . . deeper than Sheol; what do you know?" (11:8), and he speaks of the mystery and limit of God (11:7). In contrast to this virtuality in which Job can have the utmost confidence and highest hopes for his material reality, Zophar concludes by telling Job that the wicked have no such escape, their hope being restricted to the material world of breathing bodies.

> The eyes of the wicked will fail, and refuge will be lost to them;
> since their hope is a breathing body. (11:20)

CHAPTER 5 argues that Job locates his hope in his corporeal experience alone.

§50 The Friends' Sublime Hope, Strong Superego

I briefly mentioned the sublime on page 16, a concept that has been of some help to biblical scholars of JOB.[27] I want to broaden the scope of these recent studies by connecting the sublime to psychoanalysis. In German Idealism and Freudian Psychoanalysis, there exists a structure similar to what I ascribed to the positive dimension of the friends' fear. The friends proffer an experience of *fear* that affords confidence, security, and hope from an elevated position above the fray of the *anxiety* that threatens to overwhelm and overtake the individual's subjectivity in an experience of terror. In Kant's famous description of the experience of the sublime, it is crucial that the subject see herself subjected to or confronted with a power that is greater than herself. For Kant the sublime is far from what is often designated as such in popular discourse. The sublime is not the beautiful. Instead, it is what we feel when we witness our own powerlessness and mortality as if elevated above ourselves. Zupančič has noted and analyzed at length the link between the Kantian sublime and the Freudian superego.[28] The elevation inherent to the words sublime (*das Erhabene*, "the raised") and superego (*das Überich*, "the over-I") makes an initial connection. But the conceptual link becomes apparent when we recall Freud's discussion of the superego as that psychic apparatus that, when invested with the subject's accent, looks down upon the ego as something tiny and trivial.[29] The superego, in other words, can be thought of as Freud's account of that psychic apparatus on which the feeling of the sublime is based.

I cannot do better than Zupančič when she draws from Monty Python to illustrate this connection between the superego and the feeling of the sublime, so I here paraphrase her account.[30] In the *Meaning of Life* there is a scene in which two men enter the apartment of a married couple in order to harvest the liver he agreed to donate in his will. When he protests that he is still alive, they respond by informing him that he will not likely survive the operation, and so one of them goes to work butchering the man's body. The other accompanies the wife to the kitchen and asks if she too is willing to donate her liver. She says no and shrinks in fear. But then,

> A tuxedo-clad man emerges from the refrigerator and proceeds to escort her out of the kitchen of her everyday life, on a promenade across the universe. While they are strolling across the starry heavens, he sings about the "millions of billions" of stars and planets, about their "intelligent" arrangement, etc., etc. Thanks to the cosmic (and for her undoubtedly sublime) experience, the woman comes, of course, to the desired conclusion: how small and insignificant I am in this amazing and unthinkable space! As a result, when she is asked once again to donate her liver, she no longer hesitates.[31]

This caricature illustrates the way we can get caught up in something that is bigger than ourselves, even to the point that we are ready to sacrifice our well-being for it, and it illustrates also the way this sacrifice can seem ridiculous to the observer who is not caught up in the same, sublime experience. So, the friends' thesis is that Job's experience metonymically represents an excess that may have something to do with a hidden sin or injustice that could be intelligible but that, in any case, cannot be explained except by reference to a God that is beyond intelligibility, above and below the field of representation, and correspondent to every place representation fails. The friends approach the senseless eruption of an inexplicable excess in the world by affirming a prohibition that installs the truth of this excess elsewhere. By managing the otherwise inexplicable, they achieve a feeling of the sublime.

§51 Why Job Cannot Assume the Friends' Fear

Why is Job unable to do as the friends counsel and look upon his condition from the heights of sublimity? For a start, his anxiety keeps him riveted to his body and prevents him from attaining the safe place that Kant recognized as necessary for sublime experience.[32] The terror Job experiences before God's presence and the anxiety he suffers are not reported from a safe place. Job does not relate to his affliction as something he has gotten beyond or could rise above. The horrifying events continue to overtake him. The moment an experience is reported may stand at an irreducible temporal distance from the experience itself, but that does not mean that the future always puts the past behind it. In his speech in chapter 16 Job reports that neither his speech nor his silence provides him any relief:

> If I speak, my pain (k^e'$\bar{e}b\hat{\imath}$, cf. 2:13) is not alleviated;
>   and if I do not, what of it goes away?
> Surely now [God] has wearied me ($l'h$). (16:6–7a)

Along with most translations I render the hiphil perfect verb with a perfect sense: "he has wearied." But this should not suggest that the text reports a state resulting from an action completed in the past. Job is not only speaking of a past time when God wore him out. He uses the adverb "now" ('th) with the hiphil stem and perfect conjugation to accuse God of actions that previously brought him into a state of weariness and that even now keep him in that state (which Eliphaz recognizes in 4:5), no matter what he does, no matter whether he speaks or stops speaking.

The merismus Job creates with the contrary terms—speech and silence (hdl)—indicates a totality of ineffective actions. Nothing he has done has been able to erect a wall or set a boundary between himself and what he is undergoing. Job is unable to invest himself in a position from which he could look upon his affliction because the line that would delimit the ground on which he must stand in order to assume such a viewpoint keeps moving. The terrain of his experience is shifting and unsettled and leaves him no place to stand.[33] The next section closely examines one experience of loss, which Job cites so repeatedly that it approaches apparent inevitability.

§52 Job's Experience of Anxiety

In this experience of loss Job either expresses or imagines expressing a desire that is immediately not only inhibited, so that he is unable to attain his goal, but reversed, so that the aim he achieves is precisely opposed to his intended goal. Speaking his desire brings upon him a situation where this desire could not possibly be realized because whatever he identifies as the condition for the possibility of realizing his desire—sleep, a divine response, righteous speech, a cleansing bath—turns into the condition that makes his desire impossible. It is as if his speech were inherently antagonistic to him, each utterance necessarily leaving his lips and turning on him, betraying and opposing his desire. Job identifies the necessitating condition, the condition that necessitates the reversal of his desire and even of his being, with God.

> When I say my bed will comfort me, my couch will ease my complaint,
> You terrify (*bḥl*) me with dreams,
>   and frighten (*b't*) me with visions,
> So that my throat (spirit) (*napšî*) chooses strangulation,
>   Death, to my bones.
> I reject.[34] I will not live forever.
>   Let me be for my days are a breath (*hebel*). (7:13–16)

If Job wants comfort through sleep, God is there with nightmares. This ends in an autoimmune experience in which Job's very being attacks him; his *nepeš* turns on him and chooses death by strangulation. Job links his asphyxiating experience to a suffocatingly overproximate God who invades his body and mind.

> If I summoned and [Eloah] answered me,
>   I do not believe that he would hear my voice.
> Because he crushes me with a storm;
>   and he multiplies my wounds without cause.
> He will not let me catch my breath (*rûḥî*),
>   because he fills me with bitterness. (9:16–18)

Here Job considers summoning God and receiving a response and concludes that God will be unable to hear his voice. Why? Because the effect of getting a response from God is not the ability to speak with God, to ask God "What are you doing?"—a possibility he dismisses in 9:12[35]—but rather the loss of this ability. So busy stuffing him with bitterness, God's response would withhold from Job his breath. No one can speak without breath. The image is simultaneously one of *shattering*—Job is crushed and multiplied—and *saturation*—filled with bitterness. As before, Job describes his experience of God's presence as suffocating, a hindrance to his desire and a dis-integration of his being.

> If I am righteous, my mouth condemns me;
>> I am blameless, but it/he [mouth/God] perverts ('*qš*) me.
> I am blameless. I do not know myself (*napšî*).[36] I reject my life. (9:20–21)

Scholars debate the referent of the third-person masculine singular subject of the verb '*qš*, "to pervert." Those who identify it with "God" are supported by the context in which God is the one distorting Job throughout chapter 9 and elsewhere (for example, 19:6).[37] Others prefer the closest nominal antecedent: "mouth."[38] In the ambiguity, one might say, lies this verse's precise truth. If Job were to testify to his righteousness, his mouth would condemn him. In the same kind of reversal that he associates with God's presence elsewhere, Job confronts himself as implicated in his destruction and thus leaves the subject ambiguous, concluding that he is both blameless *and yet* perverted, innocent *and yet* guilty. His mouth is his own *and yet* is set against him, on the side of God. Job is not himself; his identity has exploded into difference, not because he is now different than he was, but because he is not what he is. Job repeatedly confronts his world, his bed, his breath, his mouth, his *nepeš*—himself—as other than he expects.

The interpretation to avoid here is the one that would conclude that these texts display the deconstruction of the subject (Job) in the experience of self-obliteration or self-difference.[39] The antagonism Job suffers is not a tension between himself and purely external elements but an inner tension that defines his sense of self. Job is not simply obliterated or deconstructed; he experiences himself as obliterated/deconstructed. That is, Job is constituted in this experience as the subject of obliteration/deconstruction. In his own words, "I do not know myself. I reject my life."

Given such experiences, one can understand why Job begins to relate to his desire as something foreign, as something which is not simply his but can itself be desired or not. Job's experience confirms what some have suggested about desire being accessible to the will only as a second-order and not as a first-order phenomenon.[40] I can desire to desire X, say, a drug, or I can desire not to desire that drug, but it is questionable how much control, if any, I have over whether or not I do in fact desire that drug. This kernel of ourselves that we do not have control over is not, Job's experience suggests, uncontrolled; it is controlled by another— by God.

> If I say, I will forget my complaint,
>> I will abandon my face and I will smile,
> I fear all my pain; I know that you will not acquit me;
>> I will be guilty. Why then should I strive in vain? (9:27–29)

Job's attempts to abandon and forget reward him with fear and worry; even his *passive* wish not to think of his concerns is transformed into *active* labor done gratuitously. God remains an obstacle for Job. God is the disrupter of Job's desire and the impediment to justice.

In these texts, Job (i) expresses a wish, (ii) suffers an inexplicable experience directly opposed to this wish, (iii) attributes this reversal to God's presence, and (iv) describes an attendant experience of confronting himself as other than himself. Freud names such an event an experience of the uncanny (*das Unheimliche*).[41] In the first section of his essay on the uncanny, Freud focuses on its linguistic usage which, literally, means the opposite of *heimlich*, un-homely, the opposite of "familiar, agreeable, not strange, intimate, belonging to the house, what is kept concealed." Freud argues that the uncanny is not simply the unfamiliar but rather the familiar or intimate when its familiarity has been stripped from it such that it is experienced as unfamiliar and frightening, *das Heimliche* as *unheimlich*.[42]

Job offers a striking illustration of this uncanny experience:

> If I wash with soap, and cleanse my hands with lye,
>> then you dip me in the pit so that my clothes abhor me. (9:30–31)

As Habel writes, "The repulsive feeling an individual experiences when putrid wet clothes cling to the body is brilliantly reversed here (v.31b) and portrayed as a feeling of the clothes themselves."[43] And Newsom adds, "Personifying the clothes makes Job himself into the object of disgust (cf. 30:19)."[44] In other words, Job encounters himself not only as different from himself but also as disgusting and abhorrent, as an *unheimliches Heim*.

It is time to take stock. Job's conscious experience of himself as a desiring subject, as seeking out that which he lacks, stumbles repeatedly when this desire goes lacking, when God excessively disorients him or thwarts him with various obstructions.[45] Job experiences his being as *essentially* displaced, as estranged from himself to such an extent that he identifies his encounter with his displaced self as an encounter with the presence of God. Job's experience of himself, in other words, is an experience of being fundamentally out-of-joint with the corporeal being with which he identifies. This is important because it keeps us from locating Job's sense of self in a purely Imaginary register. Job's experience of God and self cannot be accounted for in the phenomenological terms of reflection or identification. Job confronts God's presence as a force *within* his world that keeps him from feeling integrated, that keeps him anxious in his own skin. Thus, I need to modify an earlier suggestion (on pages 120–21); Job feels anxiety not so much because the ground on which he stood was shaken out from under him, but rather because the normal drift of his life and desire are halted by his collision with a ground that will neither budge nor allow him to peel himself away.[46] Psychoanalysis teaches "that the subject's inability to coincide with herself stems from the fact that (her) libido or *jouissance* appears more like something that attaches itself to her than something she is."[47] Job tells us that he is unable to coincide with himself because God lives (in) him as an Other.[48] Where Job expects to find himself but instead finds himself unfamiliar and frightening, where Job expects justice and instead finds only unanticipated obstacles to justice (for example, 9:14–24), in such displacements or gaps, Job tells us, is God's presence. God is the wall Job runs up against when he tries to articulate his desire and express himself.[49]

This discussion's focus on the disintegrating character of Job's experiences risks underemphasizing a crucial aspect of his experience of God's presence. I want to avoid giving the impression that in describing these experiences in which he is somehow cut off from himself Job is echoing what his friends said. The analysis in §49 claimed that, on account of their fear, the friends relate to the experience of terror from a position that is in a sense outside, cut off, or separate from themselves. Although Job experiences his being as something from which he is alienated, it is also something to which he is riveted.[50] Job's experience of God has led him to conclude that he does not coincide with himself, that he is not a container for all that he is, yet his experience of God has not made him think he can or has stepped outside of his self. He might not feel fully himself, but he is also not something or someone else.[51]

Consider Job's statement to God in 16:8, which repeats a sentiment expressed in several quotations above:

> You have seized (shriveled) me (up) to be a witness,
> my leanness rises up against me; it testifies to my face.

The first verb (*qmt*) can either mean "to seize/snatch" or "to shrivel." Again, Job could not have chosen a more apt ambiguity. God has *seized* Job by the neck (16:12) and *shriveled* him up so that even the little that remains of him testifies against him. Job does not speak outside of his shriveled body; his testimony for himself simultaneously testifies against himself.[52] So, I can now nuance my initial suggestion (in §51) that Job is unable to adopt the friends' position of fear because his anxiety keeps him riveted to his body and prevents him from attaining a safe place. Job's anxiety prevents him from assuming the friends' fear because his anxiety indicates to him the immanent presence of the dimension that fear treats as transcendent (that is, the locus of God, truth, etc.). The sage's fear is made possible because he locates this dimension on an infinitely receding horizon excluded from himself. However, Job's anxiety registers the immanent presence of this transcendent otherness to himself. Not that the truth of his experience is any clearer to Job, but rather that he assumes a different relationship to it than do his friends.

§53 Job's Refutation of the Friends

What is the nature of the relationship between how the friends understand the subjective structure of Job's experience (§§48–50) and Job's testimony about his experience (§§51–52). The friends think Job is suffering an experience of anxiety because his experience is one out of which he is unable or unwilling to climb, despite the fact that he knows that it is inexplicable on its own terms. Unlike the wicked, the righteous have a notion of fear akin to piety that they can use to gain some distance from the horrifying experience of anxiety and so be instructed in wisdom. While this funds the friends' tendency to think that there is some hidden folly that Job is denying or ignoring, they do not think that his situation lacks hope. So how does their take on the situation relate to Job's own description of his experience as one of an anxiety from which he cannot break free?

In my argument that the friends' statements about the fate of the righteous and wicked are made on an ontological and not an empirical basis, I cited numerous texts in which they spoke of empirical conditions of the righteous and the wicked that directly contradicted their claims about the conditions of each at an ontological level. The friends' speech about the *future destruction* of the wicked is unconcerned with the *present peace* of the wicked (cf. 15:21b). Job answers their lack of concern with a great deal of his own. In chapter 21 Job is particularly consumed with refuting the friends.

Job describes the wicked with images and metaphors that are the opposite of those in the friends' descriptions. Where the friends described the enfeeblement of the wicked (15:29–34; 18:5–7; 20:6–11), Job speaks of their strength (21:7). In contrast to their extinguished line and devastated household (18:14–15, 19; 20:10, 28), Job notes their secure households and well established offspring (21:8–9, 11). Their wealth does not dissipate (15:29; 20:10, 15) but multiplies (21:10). Instead of being subject to terrors, violence, and premature death (15:21, 30; 18:13–14; 20:23–25), they enjoy a happy and secure life, culminating in a peaceful death (21:9, 11–13). Each image reverses one claimed by the friends to characterize the wicked.[53]

Throughout chapter 21, he cites and questions several of their admissions, for example,

> Why do the wicked live, grow old and gain wealth? . . .
> Their homes are at peace (*šlwm*), without terror (*pḥd*),
>   and the rod of Eloah falls not upon them . . .
> But their thriving is not in their hands. (21:7, 9, 16a)

"Not in their hands" implies that God not only spares the rod but is also responsible for creating situations that contradict those on account of which the friends have hope. Job mocks the actual occurrence of what the friends trust:

> How often is the light of the wicked extinguished,
>   Or does calamity come upon them,
>   Or are destructions apportioned by [God's] anger? (21:17)

Whereas the friends may object,[54]

> God stores up a human's iniquity for his sons;[55] (21:19a)

Job replies,

> Let [God] repay [the human] so that he will know;
> let his eyes see according to his hands . . .
> For what delight does he have in his house that comes after him?
>   (21:19b–20a, 21a)

Job's response to the following sentiment espoused by the friends is somewhat less straightforward than the previous two, though it is not completely unclear.

> Can one teach knowledge to God; he who judges [from[56]] heights?
>   (21:22)

Job questions whether the category of judgment can be applied to God, since it relies on distinctions presumably applicable only to humans. The evidence for the category error seems to be that

> One person dies with total integrity,
>   completely tranquil (*šl'nn*) and at ease (*šlw*) . . .
> Yet another person dies with an embittered spirit,
>   without tasting any goodness.
> Together they lie upon the dust, and worms cover them. (21:23, 25–26)

So, while the friends admit the (empirical) existence but subordinate the (ontological) significance of circumstances that oppose their hopes for judgment against the wicked and for the constitution of a righteous community, Job grants such circumstances ontological significance.

Chapter 21 recalls two similar sentiments expressed earlier in the dialogue:

> It is one; therefore I say: blameless and wicked he annihilates.
> If a scourge brings sudden death, he mocks the trial of the innocent.
> If land falls into the hand of a wicked person,
>   he covers the face of its judges.
> If not [he], then who? (9:22–24)

Just as he depicts God as the antagonist of the just in chapter 9, so too does he place the security of the provocateurs of God in God's hand in chapter 12.

> The tents of marauders are at ease (*šlh*),
>   and those who provoke (*rgz*) El are secure (*bṭh*),
>   those whom Eloah brings into his hand.[57] (12:6)

At times Job refutes the friends by claiming that God actually does the opposite of what provides the basis for their hope, security, and trust. If this constituted the extent of the difference between their accounts of God's activity in the world, then Job would appear to be *a skeptic* who offers no new constellation of wisdom, or perhaps *a reformer*—not a revolutionary—who sheds light on the limits of the system, bringing into view aspects of itself that it did not recognize.[58] I once saw such a conclusion figured as follows:

If A, then B   If A, then not-B

vs.

Traditional Wisdom   Job's Skepticism

Figure 5: Job as Skeptical Wisdom

In light of chapter 21 there is ample evidence that the book proposes an either/or. Either, with the friends, God brings terror to the repose of the wicked and security to the terror of the righteous; or, with Job, God makes the wicked secure and terrorizes the righteous.[59] Yet some of Job's other statements compel one to reject the idea that Job is a mere reformer or skeptic operating within the tradition, and to regard him instead as a revolutionary offering a truly new framework for sapiential understanding.

§54 God: The Surprising Limit of Wisdom

Job 12 illustrates this new framework for wisdom. Job tells the friends, "wisdom will die with you" (v.2b), and yet in the very next line claims to have a mind like theirs (v.3a). To what extent does his understanding really resemble theirs? At the outset Job makes statements that sound like those of chapter 21. He claims that those who provoke God are secure (v.6) whereas God's actions characteristically render that which they touch insecure, contradicting Zophar's promise that security will come to him by turning to God in prayer and repentance (11:13, 18). The rest of the chapter characterizes God as the one who upsets what appears to be settled. This perspective he shares with the friends; they are of a mind about God being one who acts outside of knowledge, from beyond what appears possible to a given situation. Job then cites a knowledge they share with the animals and the earth, namely, that all life and breath (12:10), wisdom and courage (v.13), and strength and prudence (v.16) are in God's hand, and that what it is impossible to undo, God has done (vv.14–15). The examples he lists tie the two points of agreement together in a way that can be approached via the culminating characterization of God's proprietary relationship to creation, the last of the "things" that belong to God[60]:

> In whose hand is the soul of every creature,
>> and the breath of all humans . . .
> With him is wisdom and strength,
>> he has counsel and understanding . . .

> With him is strength and cunning,
>> he has the deceived and the deceiver alike. (12:10, 13, 16)

"Deceived and deceiver" (*šōgēg ûmašgeh*) is a particularly instructive pair, for before its inclusion what is "proper" to God sounds unsurprising— wisdom, strength, and understanding derive their character from an a priori proximity to God's own character. Then the text surprises. First because "good universals" such as wisdom and strength enjoy no privileged status over what is deceiving or deceived. Second, because *all these states of being* are bound up in and subordinated to *the singular experience of reversal*, which is held up as the one sure sign of God's activity in the world:

> He leads counselors away, stripped, and of judges he makes fools.
> The bonds of kings he opens, and ties a waistcloth on their loins.
> He leads priests away, stripped, and the mighty he overthrows.
> He steals the speech of the trusted, and the judgment of elders he takes.
> He pours out contempt on the nobles,
>> and loosens the belt of the mighty.
> He discloses the depths of the darkness,
>> and brings to light the deep darkness. (12:17–22)

In short, God is the non-deceiving root of deception and honesty, a rootage whose absolute ground is not honesty but the deceptive essence of everything that appears to be.

This apparently abstruse way of putting things allows an important distinction, for Eliphaz similarly supports his promise of hope to Job in chapter 5 by affirming God as the agent of surprising reversals: "But as for me, I would seek El . . . [who] sets the lowly on high . . . so hope exists for the poor" (5:8a, 11a, 16a).[61] Unlike Eliphaz, however, Job refuses to postulate any sort of ideal to which such reversals refer. He attacks transcendence, making "reversals as such" the defining attribute of God's work in the world. "At no point in these verses is any moral purpose served by the upheavals. Job's concentration is wholly upon the upsetting of expectations."[62] So, those who are supposed to be cornerstones of the social order and impervious to vulnerability—judges, counselors, kings, priests, those who are trusted, elders, the great and the mighty—these are the ones whom God defeats, makes fools of, humiliates, disgraces, and perverts (12:17–21). Just as nations are exalted *and* exterminated, expanded *and* exiled (v.23) by God, so too are mysteries brought to light and leaders made to walk in darkness (vv.22, 24–25).

I fully admit the difficulties of understanding any reference to God as an attack on transcendence. But, as Gerhard von Rad quipped in response to Henning Graf Reventlow's claim that YHWH is the focal point of the Old Testament, one must ask, "What kind of a Jahweh?"[63] for they are not all the same. When Job speaks about God he is, I believe, first of all critical of every claim to speak of something transcendent in the name of God. The work Job attributes to God is purely immanent to the world.

The point becomes clear if we reformulate Job 12 to highlight Job's rejection of the friends' position. The friends think God acts from a position of remote transcendence in ways that oppose the world and upset reality as it is known. Job's position on God's activity, however, is that the upsetting of the world is the manifestation of divine presence. The difference between Job and the friends appears as something like a reversal of subject and predicate. *Where the friends claim* that God's hand causes all kinds of surprising events, *Job counters* that surprising events are God's handiwork. The two positions share some important aspects. *In both,* God exceeds knowledge as the agent responsible for something that could not be anticipated within the situation in which it occurs. But each locates this excess differently. *Both* begin with the affirmation of God as that which opens up and operates in a gap that separates some situation from itself. *For the friends,* God transcends phenomena and can be identified as the agent "behind" various phenomena that cannot be explained or understood through recourse to other phenomena. That is, God is a dense presence that can disturb causal connections within reality, a Real virtuality behind/above/below the constructed reality that is the product of human knowledge. *For Job,* God is not the external reference for phenomena that do not fit, not their synthesis or their background, not a third term transcending the difference between the reality in which some event could not have been anticipated and the event itself. Instead, *for Job* God is something immanent to reality, something that is perceptible in those moments when reality does not coincide with itself or transforms into something else. *For the friends,* God exists at some distance from reality, in the virtuality that is higher than heaven, deeper than Sheol (11:8). *For Job,* God is not distanced from reality but is that which distances reality from itself. God is something much more like an edge that separates and holds different realities together. *The friends* think of God as that which can limit reality; *Job* thinks of God as that which decompletes reality, that which keeps reality's inherent limitation from closing.

Neither thinks reality is complete. *Both* agree that the incompleteness is not always perceptible. Their difference emerges in their opposing accounts of how God is related to those moments when reality appears limited, when the appearance that reality is unlimited stumbles. *For the friends*, the excess that is perceptible at such moments registers humans' inability to construct a reality that is adequate to the Real of God. *For Job*, such moments directly register God's presence. *The friends* counsel fear, and thus keep God at a distance from the world whose limitation is taken to be evidence of God's distance from it. *Job* insists on God's proximity to himself and the world as that which splits them from themselves. In the instrumentalization of reality's non-coincidence with itself, *the friends* exclude the truth of events that disrupt reality from the reality that they disrupt, and thereby (inconsistently) sustain the (false) appearance of reality's wholeness. *For Job*, God is the force that limits reality and prevents any whole from being formed of it.

Job reckons his anxiety an affective avatar of God's presence.[64] At the beginning of chapter 13 Job scolds the friends for arguing for God, for being partial to God's side, a partiality that even God opposes (v.10). Job asks them if it will go well with them when God examines them (v.9), and then says, "Is it not that his arousal would terrify you; and terror of him would fall upon you?" (v.11). *The friends think* anxiety must be fled in favor of a fear that assures them that they may be deceived about God, that God is too big and too wonderful for their knowledge. *Job, however, says* that anxiety is a sign that God is close by. Job recognizes the dimension of certainty that must be present for one to understand that a deception has occurred; that is, one can only be surprised if one knows that the surprise is something that was not previously anticipated. That Job's experience comes as a surprise indicates that God has been at work in it. The events that have afflicted Job are events whose cause, although unknown, is not uncertain; the events could only have been caused by God, which is the proof that they were caused by no one or nothing other than God. Job's anxiety is aroused by an experience of God's presence.

§55 Fear and Anxiety in Other Fields

So far I have differentiated Job's position from the friends' on God's activity in the world by locating this difference in the affects each attributes to the manifestation of God's presence. God's presence elevates the friends' fear but arouses Job's anxiety. Anyone familiar with the long and robust philosophical and psychological, structural and phenomenological discussion of the difference between fear and anxiety knows that it has hovered like a spectral accompaniment over this discussion of what I have, up to now, distinguished only on the basis of the use of words for fear in the dialogue.

The psychological or phenomenological argument locates the difference between fear and anxiety in the presence or absence of an object. In his article on fear, anxiety, and reverence, Gruber quotes and relies upon a couple of psychologists who can represent this conventional position.[65] Gaylin explains the difference as follows: "Fear . . . is the anticipation of a painful . . . experience . . . [Moreover], fear tends to be direct, object or event oriented, specific, and conscious . . . When we feel anxious, it is usually vague and indirect, with no particular source, and more unconsciously oriented."[66] Similarly, Kielholz writes,

> [F]ear is always distinguished from anxiety by the fact that it is invariably objective and reflects the magnitude of the threatening danger. Those affected can therefore meet the threat by rational and appropriate action. Let us take fear of examinations as an example. It is a spur to work, and the better the student is prepared the more readily he can master his fear, and even acquire a feeling of security through the acquisition of a sufficient stock of knowledge. The position is quite different with examination anxiety. In spite of the most assiduous study, the anxiety grows more acute as the examination approaches and, on the examination day, turns into an examination stupor with total failure as the outcome.[67]

Fear, he claims, is objective; it is fear of something when that something is an object constituted within the symbolic world as something explainable, identifiable, specifiable, orientable, and, finally, dispellable through rational thought. Anxiety, on the other hand, lacks any specific object, it is unjustifiable, unreasonable, and impervious to the conscious attempts by the subject to combat it.

I can use Kielholz's example to reveal the pitfalls of his own account and to better identify the source of the difference between fear and anxiety. In the example, the first student is supposed to feel fear before an object—the examination—because the feeling is dissipated with the accumulation of knowledge about this object. The second student's feeling is supposed to be anxiety because, although triggered by the test and amplified by its proximity, no amount of knowledge about it reduces the feeling. In other words, the second student feels anxiety because no object corresponds to his feeling; the object—the examination—is not the source of the feeling if the feeling does not change when he gains knowledge about it.

Yet the opposite argument makes as much or even better sense of the two students. The first student is not first afraid of the exam and then unafraid of the exam. The two objects are not at all the same. He is first afraid of an unknown dimension, some indeterminate X that the exam represents, and he then accumulates knowledge about the exam so as to build up his defenses against this unspecified nothing of which he is afraid. By accumulating knowledge he hopes to ensure that this nothing—of which he desires not to know anything and which he, in this case, successfully defended himself against through the exercise of his desire to know about the exam—remains "out there," "beyond his defenses." Of course, it is likely to manifest itself on another front in the future and, in any case, it is not as absent as he may imagine, for it is precisely what conditions his desire for knowledge about the test and it must remain "absent" for the knowledge that he desires to sustain its value/desirability. What, then, of the second student? What is the examination for him if not that which arouses his anxiety? Contrary to the psychologists, I do not think the examination is without a sense of objectivity, even if this objectivity is not to be equated with whether it can be known and distinguished from other objects. The *examination* that is the object of his anxiety is not the same as the *test* he actually takes, not because it is another object but rather because there is some added value in the test that simply results from the student having elected it and invested it with his libido.[68] His anxiety is triggered by the test and nothing else, and the "examination" designates the way in which the test does not correspond to itself, the way in which his anxiety sticks to the test regardless even of its content. Any interpretation of the test's content or significance is irrelevant to anxiety. Unlike the test, the examination is not an isolatable object; but it is objective in the sense that it must be posited as the object that gives rise to the student's anxiety. This object does not exist apart from the test, but no knowledge of the test can integrate it.

It is for this reason that Lacan warns, "It is wrongly said that anxiety is without an object. Anxiety has a completely different sort of object to any apprehension that has been prepared, structured."[69] Based on his analytic experience, Lacan felt compelled to develop a concept of this unique object of anxiety, which he called the *objet petit a.*[70] He corrects what is commonly transmitted about anxiety (that is, "it is without an object") by saying, "'it is not without an object'. . . . This relationship of 'not being without having' does not mean that one knows what object is involved."[71] So, anxiety's object is one that is not known objectively, cannot be expected, but whose presence is unmistakably signaled by anxiety. Seven years later Lacan reiterates that this is a non-objective object by calling it unnameable and yet translatable, which he does, by way of Marx's "surplus value," as "surplus *jouissance* [*plus-de-jouir*]." The "surplus" designates the unique ontological status of this object, the sense in which it is produced as that which the subject has lost by its forced alienation into the symbolic order and yet which, when approached, disintegrates rather than unifies its sense of self. Anxiety serves the subject as a signal of the potential dangers from this impending disintegration. Lacan tries to capture this unique ontological status with the litotes "not without."[72] "*Jouissance*" designates this object as an embodiment of libido, which appears to the subject as a foreignness that sticks to it rather than as the objective embodiment of its being. To be sure, Lacan did not depart from the psychological tradition on his own; he was anticipated in important ways in the philosophical and psychoanalytic tradition by Kierkegaard,[73] Freud,[74] and especially Heidegger.[75] But Lacan surely did the most to specify the nature of this object and referred to that as his unique contribution to psychoanalysis.[76]

To summarize: the object of fear can be present or absent, but it has a Symbolic place; whereas the object of anxiety is a unique object, without a place in the Symbolic order and in a privileged relationship to the Real. Job's paradoxical experience of God is his experience of being in relation to something from which he is excluded but to which he is attached and with which he is even identified. In anxiety, Job suffers a heightened sense of himself as an inalienable alienness to which he is stuck.[77] Job's experience of God consists of an experience of uncanny confrontation with himself as other than himself, as a self with which he is not integrated, a self that even opposes him, that testifies against him and yet gives him no message about himself. God makes Job who he is and prevents him from knowing himself.[78] Job describes God as a surplus within the world whose presence splits the world from itself so that objects or experiences are surprising and unanticipatable. God is thus transcendent to the world, not in the sense that God is the formal condition for the world's existence nor in the sense that God is located in some beyond of the world, but rather in the sense that God is somehow a surplus within the world over itself. Thus God is also immanent to the world, a presence on account of which the world stumbles, the one who, even the animals know, has encountered Job. In other words, God is immanent to the world and manifested in connection with a sensible form. What, then, accounts for the transcendent dimension of this immanent transcendence? The sensible manifestation of God's presence neither has any determinate referent nor does it deliver any meaning or message to Job. So Job locates God precisely in the position that Lacan will call the *objet petit a*, that unique object that is a product of and surplus beyond the Symbolic order, a reference to the Real whose proximity gives rise to anxiety.

5

Transformation: On Guilt and Shame

§56 Introduction

I have described Job's subjective structure in terms of the affect *anxiety*, and I have strictly opposed his situation to the one of *fear*. From all parties implicated in these dialogues—Job and the friends, but also a host of subsequent interpreters—it is clear that anxiety is not a sustainable subjective position. On all accounts anxiety is something that must be escaped. In connection with the rough scheme introduced at the outset of CHAPTER 4—the successive determinations of (i) the object of desire, (ii) Job's subjective dilemma, and (iii) various solutions proposed in the name of liberation—it now seems clear that any solution to Job's subjective dilemma must somehow manage or flee from anxiety. In this chapter I first specify a limit that renders unsatisfactory the conventional idea that Job's expressions of desire to flee are finally or paradigmatically structured by the legal metaphor. While all advancements of this idea are limited, not all are equally valuable. So, I discuss not only the Limit that afflicts the legal metaphor as such as an approach to Job's desire, but also various limits that render certain articulations of this idea less successful than others. The second task of the chapter is to articulate those aspects of Job's position that the dominant approach has failed to see. Whereas the dominant approach accounts for Job's desire within a structure of transcendence that I call guilt, I uncover a very different structure—shame—in which Job locates his ultimate desire and salvation.[1]

§57 Job's Initial, Subtractive Desire

In chapter 3, at the outset of the poetry, Job initially responds to his anxiety with a subtractive desire. Job wishes to be subtracted from God's presence and God's world, and the various responses to this desire (of the friends, of interpreters, and of Job himself in his subsequent speeches) are at least partly motivated by a dissatisfaction with it. Job's subtractive desire is thus a point of departure for understanding his desire and hope.

Job's initial speech repeatedly expresses his desire to be subtracted from God and God's world in a litany of volitives and interrogatives:

> Let the day on which I was born perish . . .
>> May Eloah above not seek (*drš*) it . . .
> Why did I not die at birth? . . .
> Why does he give light to the laborer? And life to the bitter in spirit?
> Those who wait for death, but there is none,
>> Who seek (*ḥpr*) it more than[2] treasures,
> Who are gladly rejoicing, they exult when they find a grave;
> To the one whose way is hidden, whom God has overshadowed? (3:3a, 4b, 11a, 20–23)

In contrast to this desire for *his* bare life to be subtracted, Job elsewhere wishes for *God* to be subtracted from him and his world so that he could live a decent life.

> My days are faster than a loom . . .
> Remember that my life is a breath . . .
>> Your eye will be with me but there will be no me . . .
> I reject. I will not live forever.
> Let me be (*ḥdl*) for my days are a breath . . .
>> Leave me alone (*rph*) until I could swallow my spittle . . .
>> You would seek (*šḥr*) me, but there would be no me. (7:6a, 7a, 8b, 16, 19b, 21d)

In Job's third speech he says,

> Are my days not few? So cease (*ḥdl*);
>> Turn away from me (*wᵉšît mimmennî*) so that I may smile a little. (10:20)

Finally, in his fourth speech Job says,

> A human is born of woman, short in days and filled with turmoil . . .
> If his days are determined, the number of his months are with you,
>> you make a limit (*ḥq*) he cannot transgress.
> Look away from him and stop (*šᵉʿê mēʿālāyw wᵉyeḥdāl*),
>> until he could enjoy his day like a hireling. (14:1, 5–6)

In each of his first four speeches, Job experiences his anxiety as a signal to flee God's overproximity, which prevents him from enjoying himself and from feeling integrated with himself (cf. 9:34–35; 13:20–21). Job then utters various imperatives expressing his unattained desire for God's subtraction from himself—*leave me alone, let me be, cease, stop, turn away, look away.*

As noted in CHAPTER 4, the interpretative community has tended to respond to these insistent and despairing, nearly suicidal or theocidal sentiments by subordinating them to other texts in which Job supposedly expresses his desire for God's presence. Job's desire for *presence* is thought to represent a more mature position (so Westermann), or one having priority as regards Job's real situation (so Habel). One can find numerous examples, such as the following conclusion to a discussion of the second cycle of speeches:

> Whilst being sceptical of God's ways and the possibility of a relationship with him, Job clings to the hope that, after all, God is just and listens to man. Occasionally his hope resurfaces and his scepticism disappears—but these sentiments are only momentary. His desire to find God becomes for Job the only way out of his predicament.[3]

In other words, while Job's disposition toward his desire for God's presence vacillates between optimism and pessimism, this desire finally "becomes for Job the only way out." Balentine similarly splits the God whose presence causes Job's suffering from a God whose absence permits his suffering to continue. Balentine's analysis begins with the incoherent claim that Job "petitions an absent God to let him be," and ends with a complete inversion of Job's desire from a desire for God to let him be to a "clamor[ing] for God to be present."[4] Such interpretive gymnastics pepper the secondary literature.[5] Scholars routinely sublimate Job's desire for divine absence into hope for a different sort of presence.

I have chosen some of the best interpreters to exemplify a general tendency. Despite the universal acknowledgment of Job's expressions of subtractive desire and the pervasive comments on the radicality of such language, interpreters overwhelmingly subordinate these expressions to others.

§58 The Antinomy of Job's Desire

Job's subtractive desire is enframed almost as often by the *general* notion that Job desires God's presence as it is by the supposition of Job's *specific* desire for a legal encounter. I have already shown the privileged role given to the trial motif in arranging the apparent disorder in JOB.[6]

The confusion that pervades scholarship on Job's desire stems from the difficulty of coordinating texts in which Job expresses a desire for God's presence with texts in which Job complains about God's over-proximity and expresses his desire for God's absence.[7] One does not need CHAPTER 4's extensive analysis to identify problems with the many unsuccessful attempts to subordinate Job's subtractive desire to another framework. Yet CHAPTER 4's analysis of the unique presence that Job associates with God allows one to take a step further to see that the issue is not an either/or that poses a contradiction, and that its presentation as such inevitably yields interpretive confusion. Job's expressions of desire for God's presence and God's absence are two sides of the same coin; absence and presence are perceptible only from a fixed position *within* an operative Symbolic order. Whether Job complains that God is all over him or laments that he cannot find God, Job's fundamental problem is that he lacks a mediating distance from God by which he could differentiate himself from God and relate to God as a present or absent other. Job's anxiety arises not from the presence or the lack of an object/God, but from the disappearance of a more fundamental lack, the lack that serves as the basis for meaningfully distinguishing presences and absences.[8] Such differentiations are always founded on the efficacy of Symbolic mediation, which presupposes the existence of a constitutive lack that would allow for its operations of making sense.[9] In negative terms, apart from an established Symbolic network, the experiences of the subject are undifferentiable, "without zones, subdivisions, localized highs and lows, or gaps in plentitudes . . . unrent, undifferentiated fabric."[10]

Read from this perspective, Job's seemingly exclusive desires—for God's absence and for God's presence—are not contradictory. In Kant's "Transcendental Dialectic," the largest section of his first *Critique*,[11] Kant deals with the antinomies that plague reason when it approaches concepts—for example, God, the world, the soul—that transcend the bounds of any possible sensible experience. These antinomies present problems because valid arguments can be constructed in favor of two opposite conclusions, each side demonstrating the falsity of the other. For example, one can conclusively demonstrate that the world is both finite and infinite, and there is no way for reason to adjudicate between the two. Although both cannot be correct, Kant resists the temptation to think that one or the other is correct. He refuses the choice and wants instead to propose an alternative to both. Kant's strategy for dissolving and resolving such debates is now known as Ramsey's maxim:

> [I]t is a heuristic maxim that the truth lies not in one of the two disputed views but in some third possibility which has not yet been thought

of, which we can only discover by rejecting something assumed as obvious by the disputants.[12]

By negating the premise Kant can move beyond both and assert a
third view.[13]

The problem plaguing interpretations of Job's desire is similarly
antinomic. One should resist the compulsion to decide in favor of one
or the other option: either Job suffers God's absence and desires God's
presence, or Job suffers God's presence and desires God's absence. Instead, one should ask whether there is a false assumption that both share.

The false assumption shared by the thesis—Job suffers God's absence and desires God's presence—and antithesis—Job suffers God's
presence and desires God's absence—is that God is for Job an object of
experience, something or someone that could be considered present or
absent. This assumption is false because Job experiences God neither as
a presence nor an absence but in the elimination of his ability to delimit
presences from absences, subject from object, himself from an other, etc.
Might Job's desire then be read at a second order? Job's hope for God's
presence does not simply want God's presence, it wants the presence of
the presence of God, a God who could be present, in contrast to his experience of God in the disruption of presence. Correlatively, Job's desire
for God's absence hopes for the presence of the absence of God, for a
God who could be absent, in contrast to his experience of God as one
from whom no absence can be found. In short, Job's two desires are not
contradictory when they are understood as two sides of the same desire
for the presence of both presence and absence.

So we approach Job's desire in structural terms as a desire for Symbolic mediation. Job's desire is not simply about the dyadic relationship
between himself and God but about the possibility of a triadic relationship in which he and God would be related on the basis of a third. The
trial scene is one stage on which Job *imagines* this desire's fulfillment but
it is not the only or the necessary one. It is in fact a defining characteristic
of those interpretive confusions mentioned above that they (mis)take the
imaginary resolution (the courtroom scene) as the truth of Job's desire.
All kinds of problems stem from this conflation: (i) Job's expressions of
desire are overdetermined by the kind of reasoning that the courtroom
scene inevitably conjures; (ii) Job's expressions of desire get transmuted
into grievances about particular offenses; (iii) Job's statements to the contrary of this resolution are misread as articulations of a different desire;
(iv) finally, interpreters become blind to the possibility, explored in the
second half of this chapter, that Job's desire might be read otherwise than
in relation to the desire for the constitution of a Law.

In the following section I evaluate the prevailing conception of Job's desire for a Symbolic order largely with reference to its presentation in Newsom's monograph because it exemplifies proper restraint before the temptation to take the Imaginary resolution of Job's desire as the direct referent of its articulation, thereby avoiding many prevalent problems.[14] She correctly sees that Job's complaint against God has less to do with particular offenses than with the offensive nature of God's relationship to human beings. Before moving forward a comment is in order to allay any confusion that might arise from the persistence of the terms Imaginary, Symbolic, and Real in what follows. *On the one hand*, in the preceeding paragraphs I have referred to certain shortcomings in scholarship on Job that arise from the tendency to "imaginarize" the Symbolic, to take Job's desire for the triadic structure of Symbolic mediation and conflate it with a dyadic image of Job in God's presence. The fact that the image by which the Symbolic is reduced to a dyadic, Imaginary structure is an image of the Law, a legal image, may cause confusion insofar as the Law regularly serves as a model for the triadic, Symbolic order. Despite this common usage, descriptions of Job's desire in the terms of the legal metaphor are not necessarily triadic, Symbolic descriptions. In fact, I have suggested that these descriptions are regularly made in dyadic terms. This is not universally the case, however, as shown by Newsom's Symbolic account of Job's desire. *On the other hand*, in what follows my object of study shifts from the interpretive community's approach to Job's account of his suffering to the accounts offered within the book by Job and the friends. Thus the Imaginary, Symbolic, and Real registers of Job's experience are deployed below somewhat differently than they were above. At this point it will suffice to prevent the possibility of confusion to keep the fact of this difference in mind.

§59 Job's Desire for Symbolic Mediation

This section draws upon Lacan's registers of the Imaginary, Symbolic, and Real to argue that the friends offer Job an Imaginary solution to his experience. While he accepts some of their presuppositions, Job rejects their solution as ineffective against God who encounters him outside the Imaginary, in the Real. In contrast to their Imaginary solution, Job sometimes desires a Symbolic solution to his encounter with the Real. After considering some ethical implications of this Symbolic account of Job's desire, I demonstrate that its characterization of Job's desire as a desire to escape the Real cannot account for Job's ultimate articulation of a subjective position from which the imperative to flee the Real has disappeared. In the end the Real's proximity to Job no longer threatens him with annihilation and, instead, affords him an appearance or experience of a transformation of his condition without transcendence.[15]

§59.1 The Imaginary

It is conventional to approach the Imaginary through what Lacan defined as the mirror stage. Between the ages of six and eighteen months, a human child experiences a moment of (mis)recognition in which she alienates her being into in an image of herself usually found on some reflective surface such as a mirror. Given the extended period of prematurational helplessness endured by human beings, the image of a whole body, functioning together and apparently in control of itself, gives rise to a sense of jubilation. At the same time, however, the child's ongoing confrontations with the difficult task of managing her actual body give rise to her aggression before and against this false image that she fails to live up to. This involves humans in a struggle that will stick with them for life, instigating their attempts to emulate those images that they are not but desire to be, and their aggression against both the less-than-ideal selves they actually are, as well as others whose difference from them reveals to them their inadequacies.[16]

The strictly dyadic opposition characteristic of Imaginary thought informs Job's as well as the friends' characterizations of Job's situation. Both see Job's situation as a particularly strong register of God's alterity. On one hand, the friends articulate a theology in which God occupies the position of the ideal, Imaginary other, the perfect image of which reveals to humans their imperfection. Newsom explains "the logic of the argument":

> What supports [the friends'] claim about the inferiority of human moral nature (4:17) is simply the human propensity to perish. . . . [The breakable human body's] mortality is associated with moral corruptness and impurity and contrasted with that which is other—immortal, incorruptible, and holy.[17]

The friends base their conception of the relationship between God and humans on the Imaginary identification of God's similarity and difference from themselves. The friends console Job with what Newsom calls a masochistic theodicy that does not acknowledge the similarity or continuity uniting God to humans and emphasizes the difference so as to "locate being and meaning in God, that is, safely beyond the reach of all powers of destruction and meaninglessness."[18] (For illustrative purposes, one could imagine an infant for whom the apparent wholeness of its *imago* was such an experience of triumph that the ongoing discombobulation of infantile life is paid no heed.) The upshot of this theodicy is masochistic pleasure. Job could gain pleasure from pursuing an existence as the object of God's desire.[19]

Job also puts the theological function of the Imaginary to work. In contrast to the friends, he seems "determined to bring to light what their formulation tacitly assumes but represses, namely, the continuity between God and himself."[20] He agrees that God and humans are incomparable (9:2) and he identifies his suffering with God's aggressive attempts to destroy that which is different, but he shows how this aggression (and the perception of difference from which it arises) are grounded in God's connection to human beings. Job locates this connection in the relationship of creator to creation.[21] In chapter 10 "Job investigates the paradoxes and perversities to which this relationship is subject."[22] Newsom elaborates these "paradoxes and perversities" as follows:

> The psychology of creation is inherently ambivalent. That which I make is an object over against me but also in some sense part of me. I may take pride in it, love it, be pleased with it. But insofar as it is, or as I perceive it to be, defective or inadequate, I may despise it, loathe it. In some way it is my defect or my inability to exercise power that is displayed therein.[23]

Throughout the beginning of chapter 10 Job refers to God's hand as a metonym for God's creative activity. Job accuses God in v.3: "You reject the work of your hands (kp)," and in v.8: "Your hands (yd) shaped me and made me, and afterward you swallowed me up on every side."[24] Newsom comments, "the thing that has been made is destroyed by its creator, the pot crushed back into dust (10:8–9). What generates the destructive impulse is the presence of a flaw. Since the human is a moral agent, the flaw sought out is not a physical one but a disfiguring 'iniquity' or 'sin' (10:6)."[25] Just as the friends disavow their *similarity* with God despite their theology's dependence on it, so too does God want to destroy Job's *otherness* despite the dependence of the notion of creation on it (that is, when one creates something, it is necessarily something other than oneself).

§59.2 The Real

Although Job responds to the friends through recourse to the Imaginary dimension that largely informs their position, he finally locates the cause of God's drive toward his destruction in a dimension beyond the dialectic of the Imaginary, beyond God's recognition of some *particular* difference Job represents, in the Real difference that separates humans from God. Newsom draws extensively on Levinas for categories to identify and explain this dimension in Job's speeches. For Levinas, my ego comes to be through its constitution in and construction of a world in which it can dwell and on which it can rely. At some moment I encounter an Other that eludes me and my world.[26] Being addressed by this Other destroys the egotism by which I previously lived as if the world were my own. The Other's address summons me to renounce my egotism and my world and to assume an infinite responsibility to and for this Other.[27] My relationship with this Other is radically asymmetrical and nonreciprocal because I am always-already responsible to its unconditional command but have no right to claim this Other's responsibility to or for me.[28] "Subjectivity as such is primordially a hostage, responsible to the extent that it becomes the sacrifice for others."[29] The ethical is the domain of an a priori, asymmetrical disturbance that "happens" prior to the constitution of the political world of universality and symmetrical relations, prior to the constitution of the subject. The subject does not exist prior to the ethical moment (when there was only the ego) but comes to be in it. Levinas famously claims ethics is first philosophy. Prior to the establishment of the political, prior to the existence of the subject, is nothing less than "the ethical moment in all its terrible freedom."[30]

For Newsom this sense of absolute or Real Otherness in/of Job, that which makes Job as human/creature other than God as divine/creator, is the best way to account for God's completely insatiable search for something in Job that escapes him and escapes God, "the quality of frustrated obsession Job attributes to God . . . an incessant surveilance [*sic*], a sort of stalking (7:12, 14, 17–19, 21b; 10:4–7, 14–17; 14:13)."[31] Job "can account for [God's behavior] neither with respect to the nature of his own being ('Am I the Sea, or the sea monster, that you set a guard over me?' 7:12) nor the nature of God's being ('Do you have eyes of flesh? Do you see as humans see? . . .' 10:4–7)."[32] Explanation comes up short, something escapes.

> Through no intentional act of his own, Job remains to some degree
> opaque to God. Similarly, despite what Job describes as God's rage to
> annihilate, Job, like some hideously resilient monster from a horror
> movie, cannot be disposed of. Although one may kill concrete others,
> one cannot kill otherness, *the* Other. And this is what Job intuitively un-
> derstands himself to represent—God's Other, in a Levinasian sense.[33]

Newsom's point is even more clear if we modify her language at the end of this quotation—"what Job intuitively understands himself to represent." Job does not understand himself to *represent* the absolute or Real Other, if only because such an Other is precisely what cannot be represented. I draw on the notion of the Real precisely so as to name the sense in which Job is something for God that falls outside the field of representation. For this reason one could say that Job's speech traces two different modes of his existence, one that can be represented and another that is unrepresentable and about which all one can say is that it exists.[34] There is another Job that Job understands himself to be for God but there is nothing one can say about it/him because it/he is outside (his or our or anyone's) knowledge or representation. It is not outside in the sense that it is another being, external to the represented one, but in the sense that it is found at the limit of his representation. It is structurally unknowable but makes its presence "intuitable" at the limit of representation.[35]

Above I cited Newsom's contention that in 10:6 Job explicitly identifies the object of God's tormenting pursuit of himself with some stain of his guilt (see page 142), which would seem to be in tension with the idea that God is obsessed with a dimension of Job that escapes knowledge. While Job does think God's gaze searches for his transgression, he concludes that God knows that the object of God's search is nonexistent, thereby further supporting the idea that God does not relate to Job within an Imaginary or Symbolic circuit:

> I say to Eloah: Do not condemn me. Inform me of what you charge me.
> Is it good to you that you oppress,
> > that you reject the work of your hands,
> > and favor[36] the counsel of the wicked?
> Do you have eyes of flesh? Or do you see like a human sees?
> Are your days like a human's days?
> > Or are your years like the years of a person?
> For you search for my sin and you seek out my iniquity.
> As you know, however, I am not guilty,
> > though there is no deliverance from your hand. (10:2–7)

Although Job demands that God make known (yd') to him God's case or cause for investigation, he concludes that God knows (yd') Job is not guilty, that is, that God knows that there is no case against him, that there is nothing to be made known. What we learn from this is that no correlation exists between the presence of God's gaze on Job, the pressure of God's hand on Job, and Job's status before the Law. Even though God's gaze is interested in Job's status before the Law and, specifically, his transgression, this gaze persists regardless of the Law. Thus, Job does not fear God's presence because it represents the Law or exposes his guilt. These instruments of God's presence—God's eye and God's hand—affect Job despite his status before the Law. This is another reason why the affect they arouse—anxiety, *not* fear—signals the Real.

§59.3 The Symbolic

For Levinas the subject that is held hostage to the Other after the encounter with the Other shatters the solipsistic world created by the ego. This situation can be responded to in one of two ways: "One possible response to the Other is the attempt to reduce its alterity, to absorb it into the Same, either by means of knowledge or power. This is in fact a futile gesture . . . [the] point is not so much that this is bad as that it is impossible. It fails . . . the Other resists appropriation . . . simply because it is Other."[37] In addition to the futile pursuit of destruction, another, ethical response involves the surrender of oneself in a posture of vulnerable receptivity, an endangering openness toward the Other. The receptivity is total in that one might be called on to sacrifice oneself for the Other, to take the place of the Other.[38] Out of this response one can appeal to a Third that would mediate the disjunctive encounter between the Self and the Other. Levinas thinks universality and symmetrical relations through mediatory discourses such as politics are born out of this asymmetrical encounter.

Job uses the legal metaphor to try to establish such a Third that would limit the absoluteness of his face-to-face encounter with God, enable them to relate nonviolently, and on whose ground they could start to cohabitate an objective space of reasoned argument without the inequality inherent to their asymmetrical and non-reciprocal encounter.[39] Job's call for justice aims to provoke God's response/ibility and to interrupt God's murderous refusal of the Third in God's encounter with God's Other, that is, Job.[40] One can draw a structural homology between the symbolic Third evoked by Job's use of legal discourse and the personified figure of justice—the arbiter, umpire, witness, mediator—Job wishes for in several oft-analyzed passages (9:32–35; 13:18–23; 16:18–22; 19:23–27). In the case of both—the symbolic Third and the personified Third—Job articulates his desire for a universal. To summarize the argument according to the Lacanian registers: Job counters the Imaginary basis for the friends' theology by appealing to the Real nature of God's encounter with human beings and then expresses his desire for the Symbolic.

Furthermore, Newsom rightly claims that the basis for Job's articulation of the Third lies in a conviction that he shares with the friends despite their disavowal of it, namely, that humans share a dimension of continuity with God. The friends' statements on divine alterity insist on the radical difference separating God from humans, which protects God's Otherness from any continuity or contamination with themselves, the domain of Sameness. But even though their comparison of divine to human justice is made to manifest the qualitative incomparability of God to human beings as regards justice, it "points to a fundamental continuity between the divine and the human . . . [H]umans share with the deity the capacity to make moral decisions."[41] Job then capitalizes on this continuity by using the legal metaphor as a map on which he can chart his experience differently than the map of traditional piety available to the friends' discourse of prayer:

> [T]he immense alterity between God and humans, which is lifted up by Eliphaz and which is a reassuring feature in the divine warrior hymns, appears as disturbing and morally troubling when reframed in a forensic context. . . . For legal procedure to have any meaning, the outcome must be genuinely open, not preempted by violent power. . . . Yet if what is affirmed of God in Eliphaz's teaching and in these traditions of hymnic praise is true, the possibility of justice between God and a human is put in question.[42]

Job's explorations of his experience within the framework of the legal metaphor and his responses to the friends that evoke legal discourse all seem to find their basis in and gain their polemical edge from the continuity between God and humans that undergirds the friends' discourse: "What Job eventually does . . . is to make use of this extensive conceptualization of divine justice to organize an aspect of experience where it did not traditionally function—the right of a person before God."[43] The courtroom promises to accomplish the initial subtractive gesture Job longs for by giving his experience meaning in relation to, and a verdict on the basis of, transcendent norms of justice.

The legal metaphor enables Job to imagine a framework grounded by a truth whose value derives from its universal recognition by all its subjects. Since this truth would be found "out there," Job could measure himself and others against it, pay a penalty or dole out debts on its terms, be found guilty or not.[44] The guilt gained through such symbolic mediation would be a welcome relief to his burdenous anxiety. Job desires a Third so that guilt can be determined, calculations made, and judgment rendered. Job wants his day in court, *commanding the deity*:

> Do not condemn me. Inform me of what you charge me. (10:2)

and demanding of his friends:

> Listen to my arguments
>> and pay attention to the contentions of my lips . . .
> Listen attentively to my words
>> and let my declarations come into your ears.
> Look, I have arranged a case. I know that I am righteous . . .
> How many are my iniquities and sins?
>> Inform me of my transgression and my sin. (13:6, 17–18, 23)

Guilt can be argued about, calculated; it is something one has or has done, something one can talk about, judge, acknowledge, confess; it is a part of oneself. The Symbolic order is the promised land for the partitioning of the self, the space of determination and calculation.

§60 The Ethics of Job's Desire

A number of commentators celebrate the ethical implications of Job's resolve to pursue his desire for a Third despite God's silence and the friends' counsel.[45] The model that supports the legal framework and compels a theological structure of transcendence may be at least partially responsible. This model tends to imagine Job a citizen, indivisible and claiming his rights before/from God, who resides above/beyond the plane of Job's experiences. Job's testimony, of course, says much to the contrary (see §52, for example). Job does not turn his face toward an empty seat of justice, enlightened by the pure foundation of his conviction, to condemn and rouse God to take the seat. God does not stop unsettling the ground under his feet or shrouding his position in darkness (cf. 23:13–17).

Levinas's thought leads to a more radical conclusion about the ethical implications of Job's pursuit of relief from anxiety through Symbolic (re)mediation. Far from an ethical celebration of Job as a hero of theological doggedness, from Levinas's perspective, Job's assertion of his right to exist apart from the immediate presence of God's terrorizing Otherness can only be construed as *unethical*. Levinas's ethic is grounded in human finitude, the primordial lack of autonomy suffered by the subject who is thrown into a situation that exceeds him and is unassumbale by him.[46] Measuring any ethical action against a norm is impossible in that no one is capable of mastering their situatedness so as to formulate a norm that could attain universality. But the key twist is that this impossibility and fundamental heteronomy of human beings is not to be lamented and is not the end of ethics; it conditions a new kind of ethics, an ethics of solidarity based on mutual vulnerability. Levinas's ethical stance can be summed up as a radical openness to the Other as to a Good beyond being, even to the point of sacrifice.

The insinuation may seem absurd—Job is a perpetrator of ethical violence and not a victim seeking symmetrical relations!? Such absurdity is the heart and soul of Levinasian ethics. Politics and ethics remain fundamentally separate; to desire symmetrical relations is to desire a Third that could be impervious to the Otherness of the Other, a Third that would annihilate the Other as Other by giving it an identity, a place within its order.[47] Any assertion of one's right to exist threatens the social order.

The essence of Derrida's critique/specification of Levinas's ethic is that the openness to the Other is always possibly unethical insofar as its turn toward one other inherently involves turning away from an other other.[48] The Third is always "present" in its "absence" from the face-to-face encounter, in a presence that challenges the claim that the encounter could ground ethics.[49] Any ethical decision is therefore finally indeterminate, it being always possible that the decision to open oneself to the face of an Other turns away from a Third to/for whom one is also responsible. There is thus an "initial perjury" of the immediacy involved in the encounter with the other.[50]

In my own critique of Levinas—that is, in what I perceive as the challenge Job's testimony issues to Levinas's ethic—something else will be at stake, even if Job does not abandon the most radical insights of Levinas and Derrida. Job's testimony witnesses to a conception of the subject that does not square with theirs, according to which the subject threatens the social order by asserting itself as a positive presence within it—either by submitting to the demand of the Second in the face-to-face encounter, which makes one always possibly at fault for neglecting the faceless Third (Derrida), or by usurping some other in the assertion of the rights of the Self/Same (Levinas).[51]

Even if these philosophers become unhelpful to readers of JOB at some point, they agree upon one important matter that the celebrants of Job's desire for a Third fail to endorse. The latter esteem Job's resolve to exist in harmonious, symmetrical relations with God, and to indict God for impeding these relations through either omission (refusing to submit to a Third) or commission (acting to prevent the constitution of a Third through some contingent, obstructive interventions). Job's testimony, however, testifies to a God whose presence necessarily prevents the constitution of any Third, not to a God whose presence transcends a Third. In this case Job's testimony is closer to Levinas and Derrida than these Joban scholars who stand proximate to Job's friends. The friends also conceive of Job's experience according to a structure in which God acts from a place beyond what God's activity makes impossible (cf. 11:8).

For Job, on the other hand, God is immanent to the impossibility as much as the impossibility is to Job.

Newsom's argument that Job brings to light what remains tacit and repressed in the friends' discourse now needs nuancing. She convincingly shows how Job's use of legal language assumes more continuity between God and human beings than the friends admit, and thereby exposes the continuity that the friends' position disavows. But are there any differences between the actual sense or degree of continuity present in Job's and in the friends' positions, or are any differences between them solely a result of the friends' silence or misunderstanding about this continuity? The friends encourage Job to acknowledge and explore the limits of his understanding as limits vis-à-vis a transcendent realm to which they banish being and meaning.[52] Job does not banish God from the represented world; he includes God in it as the cause of its limits, the force behind its failures. Because Job "includes" God in the world as that which exceeds it, it seems best to conclude that Job's position articulates both a greater continuity and a greater alterity with God than the friends'—greater continuity in the sense that God is immanent to Job and to his world, but greater alterity in the sense that God is what prevents Job's and the world's constitution as entities in and of themselves. God is a force that prevents the establishment of any Third with respect to which Job could be located vis-à-vis an other. In Job's immanent theology, God is an inherent cause of otherness and incompleteness.

Newsom agrees that Job deems the establishment of a Third impossible, which is one reason why her work exceeds so many analyses that treat Job's statements on impossibility as claims about a mere contingency or epistemological limit. Many interpreters err by sapping these statements of the ontological weight I think they compel. Consider 9:32–35:

> Truly [God is] not a man like me that I could answer him;
> that we could enter a case together.
> There is no arbiter between us
> who would set his hand on the two of us;
> he would divert his rod from upon me,
> and let not his terror frighten me;
> I would speak and I would not fear him;
> Truly I am not with myself.[53]

Newsom comments:

> [I]t is at the end of the chapter, as Job considers the conditions that render an acutal trial with God an impossibility . . . that he simultane-

> ously envisions the conditions of possibility. . . . Following this cluster
> of legal terminology, one can readily hear the opening of chapter 10 as
> what Job would like to say if such a trial were possible.[54]

So, Job accomplishes something like a Utopian imagining of a present unlike his own, in which the impossible could be possible.

While Newsom acknowledges the fundamentally impossible character of the Third,[55] her conclusion does not fully account for the challenges this impossibility poses to her position that Job identifies his right to a just relationship with God by bringing to light the friends' disavowed presupposition of universal justice. Despite Newsom's consistent warnings and reticence to treat the legal metaphor as if it accounted for too much of Job's speeches,[56] when it comes to accounting for his desire and disposition toward his experience, she makes room for little else. The first problem that is obfuscated by her complementary formula in which the condition of impossibility becomes the condition of possibility is that the two conditions are not complementary; the impossibility of any Third undercuts every imagining of a possible Third. Consequently, every imagined Third is marked from the outset as a deceptive escape, and any hope in a Third comes across as false since it is invested in a possibility that is destined to fail. Job may procure some satisfaction from such cruel optimism, but it seems a sham satisfaction since it depends upon disavowing the impossibility of escaping God's presence.[57] Newsom never turns back to her formulation to ask what the impossibility does to the possibility. She leaves the impossibility behind as a formal a priori for the imagined possibility of a Third, which she spends most of her work productively analyzing. But she never wonders whether there may be another way in which Job relates to his anxiety-provoking encounter with God's presence.

If Job finally reckons the constitution of any Third impossible, then what function do his expressions of desire for a Third play (other than enabling him to procure some sham satisfaction)? At the least they register what is unavailable to him. Accordingly, I am less interested in characterizing Job's desire for a Third as an unethical (in the Levinasian sense) wish to annihilate an Other, and am more inclined to see it as an indication of Job's recognition of the groundlessness upon which Levinas's ethic is based, namely, the impossibility that any Third could ever be constituted such that the assymetrical force of the encounter with an Other could be escaped.

By simultaneously articulating his desire for a Third and its impossibility, Job's speeches should prevent readers from believing that

1. he thinks of his situation as a limit situation that could or would return to normalcy,

2. God would ever fail to act as a force of asymmetry, or

3. he would function as a part in a harmonious order.

According to certain theorists of sovereignty, when the appearance of a Third that normally functions to structure social relations is suspended, one enters into a "state of exception."[58] According to Job, there is no other state; the normal situation is the state of exception. Job testifies to an experience of the exceptional as normal, eternal, infinite.

As I argue in the following section, while Job simultaneously articulates a desire and its impossibility, he does not do so to express either

1. *defiant hope* in the possibility of a Third that could actually send him a satisfactory message about his identity, about his guilt or innocence; or

2. *tragic resignation* before the unattainability of a satisfaction that could come from a Third that will never be.

Instead, Job ultimately finds a sense of himself in the transformational experience of God that his articulation of his desire affords. My term for the sentiment of this experience is shame.[59]

§61 Desire and Impossibility

Several texts show why I find a concept of shame necessary for understanding Job's stance toward his experience. These texts relate Job's experience of the Third's impossibility, moments when Job's desire for a Third falters and he gets hung up, not on an obstruction issuing from an other or an impeding foreign object, but on *a foreignness within* himself. In chapter 13, Job initially articulates his desire and the conditions needed to meet God in court:

> Listen carefully to my words; and let my declaration come into your ears.
> Look, I have arranged a case. I know that I am righteous.
> Who would argue with me? For then I would be silent and die.
> But two things do not do to me, then I will not be hidden from your face.
> Distance your hand from me, and do not let your terror frighten me.
> Then summon[60] and I will respond; or I will speak and you reply to me.
> How many are my transgressions and sins?
> > Inform me of my transgression and my sin. (13:17–23)

To the one before whom Job has suggested that no one can be in the right (9:2), Job stands ready to testify. He subsequently concludes, however, that God prevents such conditions by rendering the very premise of such an encounter—that is, the bridgeable *difference* between God and Job—impossible:

> Why do you hide your face and reckon me your enemy?
> Will you frighten a windblown leaf, and pursue dry chaff?
> For you inscribe bitter things against me,
> > and bequeath to me the iniquities of my youth.
> You set my feet in stocks and watch all my paths;
> > you carve out my footprints. (13:24–27)

God does not simply prevent the trial as an external force; God inscribes bitter things against Job, including the iniquity of his youth. So, after Job boasts, "Who would argue with me? . . . Summon and I will respond. . . . How many are my transgressions and sins?" (13:19a, 22a, 23a), he then falters, "Surely you inscribe bitter things against/upon me; and bequeath to me the iniquities of my youth" (13:26). Job may ascribe to God the agency both to inscribe and to bequeath, but what he "receives" from God are *his own* iniquities.

In chapter 14 Job expresses his desire for some hiding place away from God's presence, a place where he would be concealed from exposure:

> If only you would treasure me up in Sheol,
> > you would hide me until your anger turns . . .
> For then you would count my steps;
> > you would not watch over my sin. (14:13ab, 16)

And subsequently he concludes,

> Water wears down stones, its torrents wash away the earth's soil,
> > so you destroy a human's hope.
> You overpower him forever;
> > he goes where you send him with a changed face. (14:19–20)

Job's initial hope, for a place where he would be veiled from God who watches over his sin, falters, and he concludes that he goes where God sends him.

In chapter 19 Job issues his definitive pronouncement on the impossibility of justice:

> Know then, that Eloah has wronged me,
> > and caused his net to surround me.

> Look, I cry out "Violence" but I am not answered,
>> I shout but there is no justice.
> He has immured my path so that I cannot pass,
>> and upon my ways he has laid darkness.
> He has stripped my honor from me,
>> and removed the crown from my head.
> He disintegrates me all-around so that I am gone[61];
>> he uproots my hope like a tree.[62] (19:6–10)

Job is depersonalized, disintegrated, and his hope is uprooted. In his dissolution, he finds no space he can call his own. Being disintegrated means he can locate no private space for himself not exposed by his experience. Job's is an odd predicament; he is fully exposed and yet receives no recognition. He calls out but receives no answer from the Other, no recognition of himself or his desire. He stands not on his dignity, but confesses, "He has stripped my honor from me, and removed the crown from my head" (19:9). Just after this passage, in 19:13–19, he will describe the totality of public and private relations from which he is alienated through his exposure.

Paradigmatically, in a passage discussed in §52, Job says, "Though I am righteous, my mouth condemns me. . . . If I wash myself with soap . . . then you dip me in the pit so that my clothes abhor me" (9:20a, 30a, 31). Reducing such statements to grievances ignores the extent to which the line between the aggrievor and the aggrieved disappears in them.

Finally, in chapter 23, after imagining a place where a just contention with God might be possible, Job concludes that such a place for contention cannot be found:

> Were I to go east, then he would not be there;
>> and west, then I would not perceive him;
> north, by his doing I would have no vision;
>> he would conceal himself south so that I would not see. (23:8–9)

Job then relates the result: anxiety (v.15) and enfeeblement (v.16).

As such texts pile up in which Job's resolute march to contend with God is halted, it becomes inconceivable to read Job's subsequent resolve to speak "in the face of darkness" (23:17), or "in the bitterness of my soul" (10:1), or "in the adversity of my spirit" (7:11), as new expressions of the same desire. Job's speech about his sin (13:23; 14:16), iniquity (13:26), and dishonor (19:9) frustrates the ideas that his newfound resolve issues from his convictions about his innocence, honor, decency, and dignity, and that his resolve aims to determine innocence and guilt. Yet Job does not exactly or simply admit guilt or assume responsibility. Quite the contrary: each of these texts sits uneasily beside insistences on his innocence. This uneasy juxtaposition signals Job's encounter with something he has not mastered, something beyond guilt and innonence, beyond good and evil, which interrupts Job's demands for a Third and saps them of their libidinal investment. Job stumbles upon something that turns his attention away from the (absent, impossible) object of his desire so that he is no longer captivated by its promised determinations of guilt and innocence. Job is instead turned toward something else—darkness, bitterness, adversity. It seems his dignity has become useless as the Third no longer appears "out there." At these moments, innocence and guilt, dignity and conviction, certainty and decency, are all stripped from Job. Absent is any neat division of himself from God, which invalidates any idea of a guilty Other and innocent subject, much less a guilty subject and innocent Other.

To better understand Job's experience of interruption and subsequent resolve, consider Job's third speech once again. Job says,

> My spirit loathes my life;
>> I will abandon (*'e'ezbâ*) my complaint against myself
>> I will speak in the bitterness of my soul (*b*^e*mar napšî*). (10:1)

Here Job clearly returns to the wish he expressed a few lines before,

> If I say, I will forget my complaint,
>> I will abandon my face and I will smile,
>> I fear all my pain; I know that you will not acquit me;
>> I will be guilty. Why then should I strive in vain? (9:27–29)

Job 10:1, however, adds a twist registering an important difference. The sense of 10:1b is uncertain at first. It literally reads, "I will abandon my complaint against/concerning myself," which seems counter to the sentiment Job expresses a few verses earlier in 9:27–29, that is, that the hope of abandon is impossible amidst anxiety. But 10:1c, "I will speak in/against the bitterness of my spirit," suggests that the verb *'zb* ("to abandon") in 10:1b should be read in its other sense, not "forsake" but "let loose," "give free reign to."[63] In other words, the lesson of 10:1 is that the resolve Job expresses after his desire stumbles does not emanate from the same sense of pressure to flee his condition. What changes from 9:27–29 to 10:1 is that *the imperative to flee* (to somewhere he could smile) *has disappeared*, being replaced by his resolve to speak in the bitterness of his soul.

In sum, at times Job's pursuit of his desire (to flee) stumbles, a surprising arrest that he attributes to God's efforts to dissolve the position from which he uttered his desire. In this experience God exposes the bitterness of his soul, the adversity of his spirit, which is a dimension beyond dignity, guilt, and innocence, a darkness or non-place where such categories do not apply. God gives Job an experience of himself that survives himself, an excess of life beyond dignity, beyond himself.

In order to bestow more precision upon this excess of darkness or bitterness that his experience affords him, consider the section of chapter 19 mentioned on page 153:

> [God] has alienated my kin from me;
>   and my acquaintances are estranged from me.
> My relatives are gone; my friends have forgotten me.
> My houseguests and my maidservants reckon me a stranger;
>   I am an alien in their eyes.
> I summon my servant but he does not respond;
>   I must entreat (*ḥnn*) him with my mouth.
> My breath[64] (*rûaḥ*) estranges my wife;
>   my body is loathesome (*ḥnn*) to my children.
> Even youths reject me; when[65] I arise they speak against me.
> All my intimate friends abhor me; and those I love turn against me.
>   (19:13–19)

Translations often correct the unbalanced metric pattern in vv.14–15 by moving "houseguests" up from 15a to be the subject of 14b, thus making both "relatives" and "friends" the subject of 14a.[66] The dispute about this correction involves a question about whether the *gry byty* (literally "guests in my house"; its precise meaning is uncertain) belongs to the group of terms clustered in vv.13–14 and 18–19 that are concerned with broader social relations, or with those in vv.15–17 that belong to the more intimate sphere of the household. *Houseguests*' isolation in the chapter's stichometry thus corresponds to its unique semantic position in vv.13–19, for it brings the two spheres together, marking their permeability and openness toward one another even as it solidifies the sense that the two spheres are (normally) separable. This term's isolation is even more interesting because it constitutes a topologically precise correlate to Job's position. Job's position is the exact opposite of the houseguest's, a place to which both private and public worlds have closed themselves off in the very act of his exposure to them. Job inhabits a space that belongs neither to the public nor the private, but that simultaneously unites the two worlds around this exclusion that they share in common. This is the space of the bitterness and darkness that God exposes; this is the space of the excessive dimension beyond/between guilt and innocence that Job experiences. This dimension can be depicted with overlapping circles, a Venn diagram, so long as the space of "overlap" is understood *not* as a space of conjunction but of disjunction. (To capture this visually I have erased the points of intersection so that the circles appear turned in on themselves, limited from within.) Job is what the public and private have in common, but Job is part neither of the public nor of the private.[67] Belonging neither to the public nor to the private, Job is nonetheless that (lack) which they both share.[68]

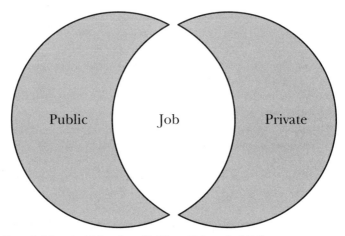

Figure 6: Job at the *Dis*junction of Public and Private Social Life

Not unlike the dunghill on which Job sits in the prose tale (discussed on page 57), Job experiences himself in a place from which the world has shifted away by opening up. In this case, it has shifted away from him on two sides that together are supposed to constitute the totality of social life but here fail to contain the same object that exceeds them both.

§62 Shame versus Guilt

Having discussed numerous texts in which Job's desire for a Third is arrested and he subsequently assumes a different resolve toward his experience, I can now differerntiate these two resolute postures more clearly. My use of the notion of shame in what follows differs from its use in other contexts. First, my use differs from those that use it, along with honor, to describe cultures in which one's reputation or status is drawn primarily from social recognition.[69] To quote Julian Pitt-Rivers, honor is one's "*claim* to pride, but it is also the acknowledgement of that claim, his excellence recognized by society, his *right* to pride," whereas shame "is what makes a person sensitive to the pressure exerted by public opinion."[70] "Shame cultures" can then be opposed to "guilt cultures," such as my own, Western culture, whose members have developed an internal morality that no longer relies on the recognition of others. Such typologizing deployments of guilt and shame have a well-known, unfortunate, and problematic history—up to and including the United States' attacks on "the Arab mind" in recent wars, shamelessly documented by the Abu Ghraib photographs.[71]

When I designate some of Job's experiences as experiences of shame, I follow Copjec's "curt and contrary thesis":

> *The affects of guilt and shame are improperly used to define kinds of cultures; what they define, rather, are different relations to one's culture.* I use *culture* here to refer to the form of life we inherit at birth (not our biological birth, but our birth into language), all those things—family, race, ethnicity, sex—we do not choose, but which choose us, the entire past that precedes us and marks our belatedness. The manner in which we assume this inheritance, and the way we understand what it means to keep faith with it, are . . . what distinguish shame from guilt.[72]

Shame and guilt do not refer to kinds of cultures, but to different modes of relating to culture. Guilt and shame are affects that can organize the experience of one and the same member of a society.

In what follows guilt and shame designate two modes of relating to Job's experience. Much of the first half of this chapter is occupied with guilt. The judicial context establishes an initial correlation between guilt and Job's desire for a Third, the Law, the legal metaphor, etc. Shame designates that aspect of Job's relationship to his experience for which guilt fails to account. Just after recounting his creation at God's hand, Job mentions both guilt and shame in this passage:

> And these things you treasured up in your heart,
> 　I know that this was with you:
> If I sinned, then you would watch me,
> 　and from my iniquity you would not acquit me.
> If I am guilty, woe to me; but I am righteous.
> 　I cannot lift my head, sated with shame (*qālôn*) and look,[73] my misery.
> 　　(10:13–15)

According to Job, God created him so as to watch him sin and then judge him guilty (vv.13–14). But, he protests, he is righteous; he presents no guilt visible to the scrutinizing gaze of God (v.15a). At this point, mid-verse even, something happens that is similar to that which occurred in those many texts surveyed in §61. Job's resolute movement toward God halts; his fearless desire to make God see that there is no sinful part of him to be seen gets choked up on shame. He bends his head low as he senses his exposure. What is exposed of him is not some part of him that is guilty, but a malaise that fills all of him.

Shame, Job testifies, is an experience of saturation. Shame draws Job's being entirely onto a single exposed plane, unlike guilt, which thrives on divisions between planes, such as hidden/seen, private/public, surface/depth. Those engaged in a trial are forever piercing the superficies, penetrating into depths in search of the facts that would ground the true story. I have cited several texts in which Job desires to symbolize his experience, to divide it up and undertake to determine of what, if anything, he may be guilty (see especially 10:2; 13:6, 17–18, and 23, discussed at the end of §59.3). Shame, however, leaves nowhere to go. Shame cannot be symbolized like guilt; it cannot be calculated, objectified. Shame does not partition the self; it consumes and satiates the whole self. One says *I am guilty of something*, but *I am ashamed of myself*.[74] As Copjec writes, even this is somewhat misleading:

> Strictly speaking, the syntagm "shame for" is a solecism; one feels shame neither for oneself nor for others. Shame is intransitive; it has no object in the ordinary sense. To experience it is to experience oneself as subject, not as a degraded or despised object. *I am not ashamed of myself, I am the shame I feel.* . . . It is a sentiment that sharpens the sense of who one is but also, and this is crucial, consists of a feeling of not being integrated with who we are.[75]

In 10:15 Job gives the impression of being caught unawares, stopped mid-verse by an on-rushing of shame as he suddenly switches from a certainty of his righteousness, a resolve to face any accuser, to the inability to face anything, the impossibility of lifting his head.[76] Job lowers his head, loses face, and all partitions or stratifications of his being under the saturating flood of shame.[77] Being unable to lift his head is akin to being unable to keep the warm blood from reddening your cheeks and ears when embarrassed. Shame cannot be stopped. If Job's lowered head hides a rush of red into his cheeks, he becomes nothing but what is exposed of him, his lowered head. The same goes for Jerusalem and Nineveh in Jer 13:26 and Nah 3:5, where YHWH lifts their skirts to cover their faces. Such covering conceals nothing because there is no deeper plane of their being; their being is fully exposed by their denuded genitalia, which is why both texts deem their experience shameful (*qālôn*).

Shame as a saturating experience other than the differentiating quest of guilt is evident in other texts, such as Job's complaint in 10:15 that *he is so filled (śb') with shame that he is unable to lift his head*, which recalls his earlier accusation in 9:18 that *God so fills (śb') him with bitterness that he is unable to catch his breath*. These texts evoke the many texts discussed in §§52 and 61 where Job describes his body as an inalienable alienness and relates his experiences of the halted movement of his desire. For example, in 7:4 Job associates his inability to arise and his sense of the yawning abyss of night with an experience of saturated restlessness:

> When (*'im*) I lie down I say, "When will I arise?"
> But the night stretches out;
> I am sated (*śb'*) with restlessness (*nddym*) until dawn.

Time stretches out and engulfs the sufferer just as trauma snatches its victim out of the flow of history. In 14:1 Job claims that his experience is indicative of a human condition—being sated (*śb'*) with *rōgez* ("anguish").[78]

The shift of Job's subjective position, which I am refering to as a shift from guilt to shame, has to do with his posture toward the limit of his experience, not with any change in the certainty or uncertainty of his disposition. This point is crucial for understanding the difference between shame and guilt. The posture of guilt seeks to push beyond this limit, and I have cited several places where Job desires to penetrate below surfaces and enlighten dark corners. This is the posture of Nietzsche's contemporaries before whom Nietzsche felt such repugnance when he wrote, "Nothing is so nauseating in . . . the believers in 'modern ideas' as their lack of shame, their complaisant impudence of eye and hand with which they touch, lick, and finger everything."[79] Every limit beckons the one in guilt to transgress it.

But in Job's experience of shame, the darkness does not conceal a separate essence; it is itself a presence. The opacity of what he encounters bears an ontological weight that does not impel him to transgress into it with his torch of reason. Job is constituted in his experience of shame not by an urge to go beyond his experience but by the absence of anywhere to go and his consequent inhabitation of the surface level of his experience, a world of pure immanence.[80]

Shame therefore differs from guilt in that it requires a limit to be recognized, honored. Guilt leads to the pointing of fingers, and has everyone looking at Job, searching for truth, justice, or reason, and want-

ing to calculate a possible cause. Such searching is sure to persist indefinitely and beyond any apparent limit because it operates on the basis of a
reference to God as ultimately incalculable. When Job suffers the inalienable alienness at the root of his anxiety, guilt treats it as though it signaled
something located somewhere else, as though it were alien, which is why
those pursuant of guilt are willing to "touch, lick, and finger" any aspect
of his experience.[81]

If the posture of guilt has everyone looking at him from entrenched
positions, shame names what infects everyone's posture with pressure to
look away. In 19:13–19 (quoted on page 155) Job is estranged from and
loathesomely inapproachable to his kin, acquaintances, friends, guests,
servants, wife, children, youths, intimate friends, and those he loves. It is
Job's shame that has everyone looking away from him or looking at him in
disgust. Again Job credits (or, rather, *charges*) God as the cause of his condition, the one on account of which he and others encounter his being as
an inalienable alienness, an abhorent display of excessive *jouissance*. Job
19 opposes the shame-full responses in vv.13–19 to his three interlocutors
who, he says in v.3, humiliate and wrong him *shamelessly* (*l'-bwš*).

§63 Visible Darkness

There are no better images for what Job thinks his experience exposes
than darkness and invisibility. Job complains in several places of being
unable to see God, the source of his disjunctive experience.

> He passes by me but I do not *see* (*r'h*);
> he goes by but I do not *perceive* (*byn*) him. (9:11)

In 13:24 he asks God, "Why do you hide (*str*) your face?" (cf. 13:20). In
23:8–9 he speaks of being unable to find God despite traveling in every
direction. It is worth noting that JOB, whose anthropomorphic tendencies are well known (especially evident in the prose tale), never lifts this
veil. God resists the imaginary; Job in no way images God. Instead, Job
fundamentally relates to God through his body, specifically, through his
nonrapport with his body.

This may initially seem unsurprising. Many have depicted God as
one who sees without being seen—even God in Deut 31:18. So what differentiates Job's blindness from mystical reverie about God's ineffable
presence? Job's God is not beyond the visible but its inner limit.[82] God
causes Job's blindness. Job complains that, because of God,

My *eyes* (*'yny*) fail from vexation; my limbs[83] are all like a shadow. (17:7)

In 16:16 he complains of a deep darkness on his eyes:

My face is red from weeping,
and deep darkness (*ṣlmwt*) is on my *eyelids* (*'p'ppy*).

In 23:8–9, Job says that he cannot see God by God's own doing:

Were I to go east, then he would not be there;
and west, then I would not *perceive* (*byn*) him;
north, by his doing I would have no *vision* (*ḥz*);
he would conceal himself (*'ṭp*) south so that I would not *see* (*r'h*).

In 19:8 he says,

[God] has immured my path so that I cannot pass,
and upon my ways has laid darkness (*ḥšk*).

In 12:22 Job characterizes God's work in the world as follows:

He uncovers the depths of darkness (*ḥšk*),
and brings to light deep darkness (*ṣlmwt*).

The cause of Job's anxiety-provoking alienation from himself—that is, God—is a blind spot in his field of view. This is not just any blind spot; it's a visible smudge that God brings to light. God is not located outside the sensible realm of vision but within it, in the non-phenomenal manifestation of invisibility.[84] As argued in CHAPTER 4, anxiety is often the affect of this manifestation,[85] as in 23:15–16:

Therefore, before his face I am terrified;
I consider well and I fear before him;
El has enfeebled my heart, and Shadday has terrified me.

Job just told us that God is invisible, so we know that God's face is not something that exists or happens, something Job sees that cannot be seen by the friends. Instead, like the Gorgon, being before God's face means perceiving the invisible, seeing what cannot be seen.[86] God's face represents to Job what cannot be seen, what cannot be represented. The proximity of God's face is indicated by the arousal of Job's anxiety. Just as I found in several places above (for example, §52), God's presence arouses

Job's anxiety, which he describes as an impossibility of being at one with himself. God's presence makes Job other than himself and exposes to him the impossibility of being at one with himself. Once again what Job describes is an immanent theism: God's face and Job's blindness are one and the same impossibility of seeing, of representation.

In addition to texts where Job associates God with the exposure and visibility of the invisible, in others he relates his experience of the exposure of phenomena upon which no one can look. Consider these examples of what his experience makes visible:

> Let the day on which I was born perish . . .
> For it did not shut the doors of my womb,
>   and hide (*str*) trouble (*'ml*) from my *eyes* (*m'yny*). (3:3a, 10)

The next time he speaks he says to his friends:

> You *see* (*r'h*) terror (*ḥtt*) and you fear (*yr'*). (6:21b)

And then to God:

> Remember that my life is a breath,
>   my *eye* (*'yny*) will never again *see* (*r'h*) good (*ṭwb*).[87]
> You terrify me (*ḥtt*) with dreams,
>   and frighten me (*b't*) with *visions* (*mḥzynwt*). (7:7, 14)

Later he complains,

> I cannot lift my head, sated with shame and *look* (*r'h*), my misery (*'ny*).
> (10:15b)

Job's experience makes visible to him trouble, terror, nothing good, frightening visions, and misery. The primary characteristic of these phenomena is the impossibility of sustaining one's gaze upon them.[88] In 6:20–21 Job suggests that his friends are shamed, disgraced, and fearful of the terror they see. In chapter 3 Job curses the day of his birth because it did not keep hidden the trouble that should have remained out of his sight, and he longs there and elsewhere (for example, chapter 7) for some distance from the terrible sights he sees.

In sum, God is responsible for two different modes whereby the limit of the visual field appears as something internal to this field itself. God's presence makes visible a non-phenomenal darkness, an invisibility uncaptured by the specular field. Second, God's presence makes visible phenomena of inhuman misery upon which it is impossible to gaze, phenomena that extend beyond what is recognizable in the specular field. In neither case does the appearance of the limit suggest the presence of something that lies outside of the specular field, some substance that has an external relationship to this field. What appears is an immanent limit, something that cannot be captured by speaking simply of visibility or invisibility, and that requires one to speak of a visible invisibility and an invisible visibility. In both cases the appearance of the immanent limit is accompanied by an onset of shame.[89]

The non-phenomenal character of the darkness afforded Job by his experience is why I suggested that it could be figured by an unconventional Venn diagram of the sort that figure 6 on page 156 used to depict chapter 19's positioning of Job with respect to social relations. The specular field, consisting of visible and invisible phenomena, is limited by the manifestation in the phenomenal field of a non-phenomenal darkness:

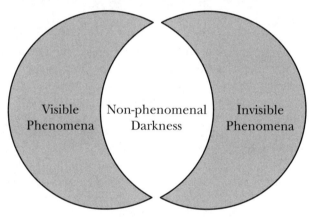

Figure 7: Darkness, Limiting the Specular Field from Within

Job experiences the boundary between the visible and the invisible not as a limit that separates the specular field from something that escapes or lies outside it, but as what divides it from within, its immanent limit.

We can easily grasp the importance of this insistence on immanence by noting how the scholarly celebrations of the legal metaphor (mentioned at the outset of §60) fail to satisfy insofar as they do not come to terms with it. Such celebrations often accompany more or less explicit critiques of God's absence from the courtroom. Job is presented as some sort of early exemplar of *Ideologiekritik* who harangues God for failing to show up. The invisible silence of God being placed in the courtroom as a register of God's absence, that is, a register of God's presence on another stage, in another place, forces the interpreter to conclude that God could be there were it not for some contingency/ies and that any possible encounter with God's presence could only happen in some future moment. What is presented as an ideology-critique of theology turns out to perform the most ideological of theological moves, safely installing God in a realm transcendent to the Bible and to experience, and thus safely protecting the Bible and experience from God's presence. What is avoided is the traumatic presence of God to which Job's testimony testifies, a presence that is not transcendent to the courtroom but is the courtroom's immanent limit, that which keeps it from ever constituting itself. In short, the celebrants of the legal metaphor fail to apprehend the text because they transpose Job's testimony about the non-phenomenal character of God into testimony about a God that resides beyond phenomena.

§64 Exposure and Concealment

To say, for example, that in guilt all eyes fixate on Job whereas shame leads to the aversion of gazes clearly ties shame to exposure. The question is, in what sense and how, if at all, is social censure involved in this relationship? Shame is commonly thought of as a product of social censure, something close to embarrassment or conscience. This is another common conception from which Job's experience departs. Job's shame arises from his encounter with a dimension beyond the reach of the categories of social censure, such as dignity, guilt, and innocence. Numerous psychoanalytic and philosophical investigations come to a similar conclusion—shame is experienced beyond the superego pressure to calculate, beyond good and evil. The close affinity of this conclusion to Job's experience should already be apparent, but it merits further exploration since it may clarify this question about the relationship between shame and exposure.

In Levinas's brief but brilliant early essay "On Escape," he writes,

> On first analysis, shame appears to be reserved for phenomena of a
> moral order: one feels ashamed for having acted badly, for having devi-
> ated from the norm. . . . Yet shame's whole intensity . . . consists precisely
> in our inability not to identify with this being who is already foreign to
> us and whose motives for acting we can no longer comprehend.[90]

Shame is not an affect that arises when one senses oneself under the censorious scrutiny of an other; it is what arises when one is confronted with the impossibility of escape from one's being.[91] This being may be our own but, as Levinas says, it is "foreign to us," a being "we can no longer comprehend." In other words, this being is that inalienable alienness that CHAPTER 4 tied to the onset of anxiety.

But, again, I worry that this linkage of shame to a confrontation with the impossibility of escape may suggest a tie between shame and social censure insofar as it sounds similar to the feeling of being caught. In Jean-Paul Sartre's deservedly famous commentary on *le regard*[92] ("the look"; following Lacan's translators I refer to it as "the gaze"), a voyeur who peers through a keyhole or hunts for something outdoors vanishes in his intense investment into the scene upon which he looks. His absorption into his act gets interrupted when he encounters a sensible manifestation that signals the presence of others for whom he exists—for example, a foot in the corridor, the rustling of leaves. It is only at this moment that the voyeur exists as a subject, at the moment "a gaze surprises him . . . disturbs him, overwhelms him and reduces him to a feeling of shame."[93] As with Levinas, Sartre does not think that shame arises because the voyeur has been caught doing something wrong; the rustled leaves do not represent the Law and make him feel guilty or embarrassed. The shame has not to do with the perversity of the look. Instead, shame is "the feeling that attends the insertion of the subject into society, his sudden immersion in a world of others. This insertion into the social precedes all measure and every rule by which a subject might find himself judged."[94] The subject whose body and being were absorbed into his act moments before is reminded of his vulnerably embodied, finite existence through his sense of the presence of others.

Contrary to how it may sound, Sartre does not think of this experience as one of enlightenment. Sartre repeatedly states that the self that is experienced in shame as well as the other from whom the gaze is supposed to emanate is "unrevealed" and must remain indeterminate. Under the gaze, I do not see the eye that looks at me and if I determine which eye sees me, the gaze disappears. In short, for Sartre, exposure and concealment (being and nothingness) occur simultaneously in the experience of shame.

Sartre's account accords well with Job's experience. As I saw in numerous texts in §61, Job testifies to a similar experience of shameful exposure that occurs beyond judgment and that makes apparent something that remains "unrevealed." Job is fully exposed to the totality of public and private relations but, by this, finds himself in a place from which they have turned away (cf. 19:13–19). And he himself turns away from the object of his desire, toward darkness, bitterness, adversity (cf. 23:17; 10:1; 7:11), that is, toward the excess of life beyond his dignity that his experience has exposed. As Sartre said, what is made apparent is unrevealed. There is a concealment simultaneous to the exposure and consequent dissolution of Job's being. Job's subsequent resolve aims to explore the unrevealed darkness that his experience makes apparent.

Following Levinas and Sartre, it might seem that what is exposed of Job is his limitation, his inability to displace into a structure of guilt the alienness that sticks to him and causes his anxiety.[95] The absence of the imperative of flight, of Job's subtractive desire, would therefore be a function of the passivity of the experience of shame, that is, the exposure of Job's complete subjection to his finite, bodily existence. It is already clear, however, that this fails to account for Job's experience of shame. Job's shame arises when his investment in his desire to flee what causes his anxiety falters, whereupon not only is his active submission to an impossible desire put on display, but he also appears slightly detached from himself and from visibility.[96] Job's appearance as one who is perishing simultaneously betrays a place where he is hiding from every eye. Furthermore, Job's experience of shame does not destroy or weaken his desire but redirects it onto that which his experience makes available to him (darkness, misery, bitterness, adversity).

The next section takes up in greater detail this dark, bitter, adverse dimension to which Job's attention turns when he expresses his resolve to speak, not of something of which his experience deprives him, but of something his experience affords him.

§65 Uncontained Exposure

Job makes it clear from several angles that the darkness his experience presents to him, the deep darkness that falls on his eyes (16:16) and is laid upon his path (19:8), is no mere light deprivation. Neither is it only something he is currently suffering or has recently suffered. In 10:20–22 Job speaks of a void of darkness, a deep darkness that extends beyond himself, his world, and beyond God, as a land he expects to enter:

> Are my days not few?
> So cease; turn away from me so that I may smile a little.
> Before I go and never return,
> to a land of darkness (ḥšk) and deep darkness (ṣlmwt),
> a land of gloom ('ypth), like thick, deep darkness ('pl ṣlmwt),
> and without order, where it shines like blackness ('pl).

When Job admonishes his friends for thinking that darkness and light, night and day, are continuous, it is again clear that this darkness is something more than light deprivation:

> Come back and I shall not find a wise one among you.
> My days have passed; my plans, my heart's desire[97] is broken off.
> They assign night to day (*lylh lywm yśymw*),[98]
>   light, near the presence of darkness (*'wr qrwb mppny-ḥšk*).
> If I must await (*qwh*) Sheol as my home,
>   Spread my couch in darkness (*ḥšk*),
> Proclaim to the pit, "You are my father,"
>   To the worm, "My mother, my sister,"
> Where, then,[99] is my hope (*tqwty*)?
>   Who, then, can see my hope (*tqwty*)?
> Will it descend with me[100] to Sheol?
>   Shall we go down together into the dust? (17:10b–16)

Job initially complains about a historical rupture created by his experience, the way it has disabled any projection of himself into the future ("my plans are broken off").[101] He complains that his opponents, whom he finds unwise, think night belongs to day and light is near darkness. Job does not think that his experience of the night is dark because it is located at the other end of a continuum with the light of day. Job thinks that the darkness is the origin of something new[102]; Job proclaims the pit his father and the worm his mother and sister.[103] His rejection of hope continues his rejection of his unwise opponents (his friends and scholars alike) who exhort him with cruel optimism about possibly escaping his condition. It is absurd to think that hope goes down to Sheol with him, for there what shines is like blackness (10:22). The dark place where he is going may have been made visible by his experience, but it is not transparent to him or anyone else; its opacity remains. Since nothing about this place can be known (confirming again its non-phenomenal character), Job finds it absurd to speak of hope in it.

In chapter 7 Job says that his experience is carrying him to a place no eye can follow. The eye watching him will not be able to see him because he will no longer be, and the one whom he will become will be unrecognizable. This is a place about which nothing can be foreseen except that it is the site of the creation of something new, something that will not even be recognizable by its own home. Instead of hope, Job expresses resolve and persistence about the possibilities he anticipates from the direction his experience carries him in.

> Remember that my life is a breath,
>> my eye will never again see good.
> The eye that watches me will not observe me;
>> your eye will be with me but there will be no me.
> As a cloud ends and vanishes,
>> so do those who go down to Sheol not come up.
> He will never return to his home;
>> his place will no longer recognize him.
> As for me, I will not restrain my mouth;
>> I will speak in the adversity of my spirit,
>> I will meditate on the bitterness of my soul. (7:7–11)

Job is sure that nothing and no one, not even God, will be able to follow him where his experience is carrying him, and he resolves in v.11 to persist in this direction.

In chapter 13 Job locates the source of his salvation in his resolve to contend with God:

> Be silent before me that I may speak,
>> whatever may come over me.
> Why do I place my flesh in my teeth,
>> and take my life in my hand?
> If he kills me, I will not wait;
>> but I will argue my path to his face.
> And this shall be my salvation. (13:13–16a)

In light of all that I have said, salvation here cannot mean justification. Job believes that justification is impossible and, moreover, he refuses expectations—"whatever may come . . ." His salvation comes not because he now thinks that the Other will recognize his irrefutable case, but because he takes his life in his hand, regardless of the consequences. Job does not succumb to the temptation to seek some eye of the storm, some inner chamber into which he could withdraw, above or below the fray of his thought or his body. Job knows his speech places him in the face of God, as well as the problems and violence inherent to this encounter, which has defaced him by alienating him from himself and dislocating him into a space that is unbreachable by any gaze (cf. 10:18). He refuses mystical silence and insists on speaking. Job views the stakes of his speech as no less than the material and ontological dimension of his being—he likens the speech from his mouth to his flesh in his teeth and he names death as a possible consequence of his speech. Finally Job locates his salvation in the corporeal experience of himself in God's presence that speaking his case affords him.[104]

Consider the conclusion to chapter 23 once again, Job's statement on the terrifying darkness God's presence makes present to him[105]:

> Therefore I am terrified before his face; I consider and I fear before him;
> El has enfeebled my heart; Shadday has terrified me;
> Yet I am not silenced in the face of darkness (*ḥšk*);
>   though blackness (*ʾpl*) covers my face. (23:15–17)

Here again Job speaks of the darkness as a progenitor of something new, not something that is "out there," awaiting him. His present speech rises into and traces the contours of this black void that God has hollowed out of himself and his world, and that now covers his face, opening it to an unforeseeable metamorphosis. In this moment Job becomes bat-like; guided by his speech he flies not from but into the plastic surface of his being,[106] into the thick darkness that falls over him in folds that efface his face. He no longer tries in vain to distance himself from his traumatic experience of God's plastically explosive face and finds himself differently related to it. In this dark void Job finds himself in a place distanced from any eye; so distanced from himself, his world, and from God, that all three may be transformed.

Excursus

The Final Speeches

§66 Utter Dissonance

Although I claimed to be going beyond Newsom, it seems I have done so only to catch up to her at the point at which she too ventures beyond the point at which I left her. In the final section of her chapter, Newsom turns from the analysis of the ways in which Job uses the legal metaphor to oppose the friends' discourse of traditional piety, to the final cycle of speeches, in which the friends oddly fall silent and Job oddly articulates their arguments about the fate of the wicked; even more oddly, he does so as refutations of their perspective. The conventional approach she relates as follows:

> The presence of these words in Job's mouth seems to many commentators so out of place that they propose that the third cycle of speeches has been disturbed. . . . According to many versions of this theory, the material in 24:18–25 and 27:12–23 originally formed part of the speeches of Bildad and Zophar. The difficulty, however, is that no textual evidence exists to support such a theory. It is simply a desparate gesture in response to an interpretive embarrassment.[107]

Of those who appear to depart from convention by interpreting the words as Job's, some have recourse to a notion of the sarcastic tonality with which Job is supposed to speak them. But, Newsom says, such interpretations offer no real alternative, since they still understand the speech as Bildad's and Zophar's, albeit with a sarcastic tone, whereas Job presents it as his own (24:25). The straightforward reading of the words as evidence that Job has changed his mind and accepted the friends' arguments also fails because it ignores the way in which Job presents the arguments as refutations of theirs (see 24:25 and 27:12).

As is characteristic of her work as a whole, Newsom is more interested in the discursive effect of Job's speech than in hammering down a stable meaning. She understands both passages in question as Job's attempts to speak about his experience of what Buber calls "the rent in the heart of the world," but she considers each independently because they "do not present identical interpretive problems."[108] Chapter 24 opposes what are present injustices (vv.1–17) to a justice that should be (vv.18–24). Newsom suggests that Job's use of the fate of the wicked topos can be read analogously to his use of the legal metaphor:

> Job's exploration of the legal metaphor enabled him to envision as a real possibility both God's recognition of the claims of justice and God's violent repudiation of them. Analogously, Job can imagine the working out of justice against evildoers, even as he knows the realities of injustice.[109]

But she is not finally happy with this reading, complaining that its logical coordination of the two claims of the chapter into "what is versus what could be" improperly reduces the dissonance that she sees as a reflection of Job's experience. Speaking dissonantly, she says, effects on its hearers "a painful cognitive dissonance, a loss of mastery, that is an echo, however faint, of what Job has experienced of the world."[110] Job's speech, in other words, makes sensible (however faintly) the void that he has experienced.

In chapter 27, Job expresses his desire that his enemies be as the wicked to whom, he says, God apportions a fate that cannot but sound like his own. Most notably for my purposes, he says that the wicked are those whom "terrors (*blhwt*) overtake like the waters [and] a whirlwind carries off at night" (v.20). Newsom once again entertains the temptation to see the dissonance between Job's position and his speech according to the logical relation between *what is* and *what could be but is not,* but she rejects this reading because it risks reducing the effect of the inverted coherency of Job's speech, that is, the way in which it manifests incoherency. She concludes with a comment on the discursive effect:

> No wonder the friends have nothing to say. They speak a language of sanity in a presumably sane world. Job speaks a language bordering on madness in a world turned upside down. Job's language, however, has the quality of a dare or provocation. He has mastered one of the possible languages of subversive resistance in a totalitarian world. When the one whose existence contradicts the dominant ideology that he nevertheless speaks, while his body silently witnesses to the truth, he lays out the scandal for all to see.[111]

The connection with the above interpretation should be clear. In Job's earlier speeches too, I argued, Job's body silently witnesses to the truth despite, and yet only by means of, his speech. Job's corporeal experience of himself in God's presence is not something he could fully relate through his speech, which always says too much or too little. But it is his speech that affords him this experience, into which we are also drawn by his testimony. And it is in his speech that, Job tells us, salvation lies, in the void in which it traces and offers a glimpse of a space of newness, the space from which the limits of dominant ideologies burgeon. From these limits, Job gives voice to WISDOM.

Part 3

Ontology, Aesthetics, Ethics

6

Ontology, Aesthetics, and the Divine Speeches

§67 Brief Orientations

In chapter 38 YHWH appears triumphantly in a whirlwind. But what YHWH speaks about initially appears alien to the book's previous concerns.[1] Even though one knows what God is saying in the speeches, it takes some time to grasp what it might mean for God to say what is said in the context of the book.[2] Like hearing a new word composed of previously known words, the reader suffers a sense of dissonance and must pause for some time to try to coordinate God's highly aesthetic speeches and Job's largely political demands for justice (treated at length in §59).[3] The proposals for such a coordination have varied widely—all the way from exclusion[4] to embrace[5]—and are discussed in a spate of recent works.[6] *Mutatis mutandis*, previous interpretations treated the aesthetic and the political either as two dimensions separated by an abyss that might be bridged by some mediating explanation, or by collapsing one (usually the aesthetic) into the other (the political). Several recent turns to aesthetics, which I treat below, inaugurate a shift in our interpretive perspective and stem from the need for a more critical conception of the politics of aesthetics.[7] Before assessing this aesthetic turn, some brief orientations are needed; first, to the speeches; second, to the contemporary critical discussion out of which these interpretations arise; and third, to the aesthetic categories on which they draw.

The speeches clearly divide in half, though there are two ways of drawing the boundary line.[8] On the one hand, there are two speeches. The first ends with Job's brief response at the beginning of chapter 40 and the second concludes with Job's second response at the beginning of chapter 42. Each speech is introduced with the same formula—"Then YHWH answered Job from the whirlwind and said . . ." (38:1 // 40:6)—and each starts out with the same demands of Job (38:3 // 40:7). YHWH begins both by speaking directly to Job but then turns to aspects of creation that may at first appear to be mere vehicles for the message but subsequently, as they extend in elaborate detail, seem to assume a more central role as to the message itself. The initial moment of direct address to Job is longer in the second speech than the first (38:2–3; 40:6–14), but the weight of both speeches undoubtedly shifts to those aspects of creation that are subsequently described. Both speeches initially seem aimed at communicating a message from the first person grammatical subject to the second via references to third person objects; these objects, however, ultimately become the principal subjects of the speeches. In both speeches, the sections following the initial direct address to Job have two main subsections. The first divides thematically, focusing initially on inanimate creation in 38:4–38, and then on animate creation in 38:39–39:30. The second divides according to the two particular inhabitants of creation it describes: Behemoth in 40:15–24 and Leviathan in 40:25–41:26 (Eng: 41:1–34). The second way of dividing the speeches in half, therefore, draws the line within the first speech, at the moment God shifts focus from inanimate creation to pairs of animate creatures. The shift in the speeches from inanimate to animate creation is commonly characterized as a movement from cosmos to chaos. Before turning to the aesthetic categories and the three interpreters, I need to consider this characterization in more detail.

§68 Cosmos and Chaos

The biblical and ancient Near Eastern mythos of creation is largely cast as a struggle to wrest order out of chaos. Creation is the emergence of a structured cosmos out of an unstructured chaos.[9] Van Leeuwen's recently published study details the strong, inherent link in creation stories between the order created by the construction of the world and the order maintained by constructions within the world that are formed so as to sustain life within their bounds. He also details a number of important motifs in these stories, including (i) the role of sacred places such as temples as mediators between these two spheres of construction, (ii) the predominance of references to the builder's wisdom (be it the god or king), and (iii) the patterned combination of these constructions with the filling or provisioning of that which is constructed.[10]

YHWH's initial focus on inanimate creation draws heavily on these motifs. Job 38:36–37 includes a reference to the builder's wisdom. In 38:4–7 YHWH describes creation in terms primarily associated with construction. YHWH speaks of the earth's "foundations" and "cornerstone" (cf. Jer 51:26), its "dimensions" and "measurements" (cf. Ezek 47:3). Some of the terms are particularly associated with the construction of a sacred building. For example, "bases" (*'eden*) in v.6a almost exclusively refers to the footings of the tabernacle in Priestly texts. Thus, Balentine writes, "God is both the architect and the hands-on builder. . . . God's

world is structured not simply as a *safe house* in which one may live without fear of its collapse; it is also envisioned as a *sacred temple* in which one
all [sic] may seek refuge from hostile forces (for example, Pss 23:5–6;
46:4–5; 48:1–4)."[11] Such "hostile forces" are paradigmatically represented
in creation texts by the primordial waters/chaos that are the focus of
vv.8–11:

> Who shut in the sea with doors when it burst forth from the womb? . . .
>   When I set bars and doors and said,
> "Thus far shall you come and no further,
>   and here shall your proud waves stop." (Job 38:8, 10b–11)

> When he set his limit for the sea,
>   so that the waters would not transgress his command. (Prov 8:29ab)

> [The bolt], the bar of the sea,
> [They had given] to Enki, the prince (*Atra-ḥasis* 1.15–16)[12]

Janzen describes the role of the sea in other ancient Near Eastern and
biblical creation accounts as follows: "the Sea appears as a chaotic energy
threatening destruction; and cosmic order with its life-giving and meaningful forms presupposes the effective limitation of this energy."[13]

In this traditional mythos, not only does the created order emerge
originally out of primordial chaos—call it chaos$_1$—it continues to constitute itself by defining itself against and excluding from itself figures
of chaos that, in the terms made famous by Levenson's classic study,[14]
persist in the form (or formlessness) of evil—call these chaos$_2$. Thus,
while the mention of the wicked in vv.13 and 15 may seem out of place
in speeches that otherwise focus their attention almost exclusively on
domains in which humans play no role, the link these speeches have to
the ancient mythos of creation hardly makes their presence surprising,
especially after the mention of the primordial sea in vv.8–11. That which
fills the newly constructed world, as Van Leeuwen shows, continues the
creative work of the construction of the world. In vv.12–15 YHWH refers
to the "place" of the morning whence "it seizes the hems of the earth
and shakes the wicked from it" (v.13). The word I translate "hems" functions elsewhere as an idiom for the ends or edges of the earth (see Job
37:3; Isa 11:12) but the image of "shaking" here nicely draws also on its
literal meaning of "skirts" (see Ruth 3:9). Every day, as it was in the beginning, the world is at odds with itself. "Like the hedging in of the sea
with bars and doors, the light of day contains and limits but does not
eliminate the wicked from the world."[15] In this creation tradition, the

nonhuman world's struggle against chaos$_1$ spills over into chaos$_2$, regardless of the fact that the wicked can be distinguished only in a human social order.

In sum, the connections with temple building and constructions within the world, the presence of the sea at the origin of the world, and the transition from the sea to the wicked, all suggest that the traditional mythos of creation informs chapter 38's description of the cosmos and associates the cosmos with the emergence and constant re-emergence of order over and against chaos. But is this accurate?

§69 From Cosmos to Chaos?

According to a number of interpreters, the speeches share the tradition's perspective on the relationships between order and chaos. For Habel, "Yahweh's design for the cosmos is a meticulously controlled network of structures and processes."[16] About the place of the wicked in vv.12–15, he writes, "The alien forces in the structure of society are also in Yahweh's design and under his control."[17] Habel thinks the speeches begin with a securely bound and ordered cosmos that is duly separated into parts that are synthesized into a fully functioning, inter-connected system. That the speeches mention the sea or the wicked in their account of the cosmos and that they go on to detail a number of figures traditionally associated with chaos are taken as evidence that the latter only exists within the ordered, firm, and secure structure maintained by YHWH's control. Habel is not alone; he is representative of a strong reading that views God's message to Job as an assurance that wickedness, freedom, or chaos in the world is measured, limited, or bound by the cosmos.[18] According to this view, the figures of chaos and wickedness that are present within and following the description of the cosmos in chapter 38 are either parallel to the role of chaos$_2$ in traditional creation accounts—meaning that they are external and opposed to the cosmic order—or they are sapped of their chaotic or wicked character since they too are given a place at the table of God's cosmic design. This interpretation tends to grant chaos two possible roles, both of which have textual support; chaos is either ordered and thus negated by, for example, God's bars and doors, or it is externally opposed to the ordered cosmos that negates it by, for example, shaking it out.

While Habel represents the view that downplays the figures of chaos in favor of a strongly unified cosmos, there is also a "weaker" version that grants the forces of chaos a more prominent role and depicts the cosmos as a more complex synthesis. Schifferdecker offers a recent representative:

> The world is not a safe place, but it is indeed an ordered one. Forces of chaos and wildness are given a place in the world, but they are also given boundaries so that they cannot overwhelm it. . . . Job must acknowledge God's sovereignty; but he must also live with the knowledge that God's sovereignty does not exclude forces indifferent toward, and even dangerous to, humanity. Job must submit to God and learn to live in the untamed, dangerous, but stunningly beautiful world that is God's creation.[19]

Although this argument appears to be a "weaker" version of Habel's, one should not be fooled; the apparent privileging of chaos finally serves a more extreme sovereignty. The secure boundaries and synthesizing force of the cosmos are never in doubt. The cosmos is simply more complex, which testifies all the more to God's mastery. Ending as it does in an affirmation of mastery, this view cannot help but see God's message as an insistence on submission.[20]

One might raise a number of questions to this view, the most embarrassing of which involves Job's place vis-à-vis this cosmos. If the cosmos is so ordered, firm, and secure, then how could Job (or any figures of chaos) have gotten out of line? Is God's ability to master and synthesize such a complex system somehow threatened by Job? Pursuing such questions long enough, one will end with the sense that the speeches actually present the empty braggings of a "master" caught in a moment of impotence.[21] One need not pursue such a direction, however, if one thinks that these speeches fail to support such a strong tie between creation and order. Not only do I think that they do not, I think the larger tradition is profoundly ambiguous about it as well.

The relationship in the tradition between order and chaos, violence and creation, is much more complicated than a simple external opposition would suggest. This complication does not only involve a postmodern, deconstructive point about how the conditions for the impossibility of order and the cosmos—that is, chaos and violence—are simultaneously their conditions of possibility, even though this point is valid and pronounced in the tradition even if it often goes unacknowledged among interpreters.[22] Instead, in a vein that one could call Hegelian in light of the difference narrated above (on pages 14–15) between Hegel and Kant, order and creation pass directly into chaos and violence. In more concrete social terms, one need think only of how sovereign powers control subjects not only and often not mainly through violence but by the practices of division and assignment, tactical partitions and distributions.[23] The order of creation is and must be recognized as a force of violence and a source of disorder. Creation is plastic in the senses elaborated by Catherine Malabou: it involves the reception of form like plastic arts, the bestowal of form like plastic surgery, and the destruction of form like plastic explosives.[24] So long as those (for example, Habel) who offer strong readings of order in these speeches and those (for example, Schifferdecker) who offer weak readings of disorder fail to acknowledge this fundamentally plastic character of matter and form, the elemental role of God's speeches in creation traditions will remain unappreciated. These traditions may at times portray order and chaos as mutually exclusive, but on the whole and especially in God's speeches, creation narratives overwhelmingly betray a violent origin of creation.

§70 A Weak or Less-than-fully Unified Cosmos

As several recent interpretations argue, God's speeches are actually uninterested in conjuring an image of the cosmos as an ordered whole. What YHWH describes in the opening sections of this speech is not a closed totality but a dynamic genesis, not foundations but a founding (v.4a), not a measured whole but the stretching out of a measuring line (v.5b), not a secure basis but the sinking of bases (v.6a). The earth YHWH details is not a bound, eternally secure structure but an active production. And, as Balentine explains, "to the extent that there are *boundaries* or borders in God's canopied world, they are . . . *porous* and *permeable*."[25] Brown's characterization is even better: "Creation is polycentric. It has its various centers or domains, each accommodating different forms of life. . . . Earth itself is a multiverse!"[26] As for the figures of chaos and wildness YHWH goes on to describe, consider O'Connor's claim, which is far more satisfying than the idea that the speeches aim to assure Job that all the cosmos is under control:

> [C]ontrol is not the primary issue behind God's questioning. . . . What makes it even less clear that we are to see God as saying "I can do this, but you cannot," is that each of these animals is unbounded, fearless, and beautiful. Each follows its own way that Job (and God) can neither know nor control. And the only mention of divine control concerns the ostrich whom God created without giving it wisdom, yet even it is wild, fearless, and laughing (39:13–18). When God does claim to act using "I"

language ("when I laid the foundation of the earth, I made the clouds for a garment, hail I have reserved for time of trouble"; 38:4, 9, 23), the speech accentuates divine creativity more than control. The poem celebrates abundant, fecund life that needs no control.[27]

These speeches tender a different image of a creator God than do their (weak or strong) interpretations discussed above. The latter may note that YHWH delights in beautiful creatures, but the idea that YHWH intends to put Job in his place conditions this delight upon these creatures' submission to YHWH's order rather than upon their beautifully free and unbound lives.[28]

I want to return to the figure of the sea that appears in vv.8–11. I already noted that it is followed immediately by the presence of the wicked in vv.12–15. The sea reappears in vv.16–18, thus poetically flanking the wicked on both sides. The sea's reappearance in v.16 occurs at the outset of a subsection that deals with the "deep" (*thwm*), "the gates of death" (*š'ry–mwt*), and "the gates of deep darkness" (*š'ry–ṣlmwt*). Above I referred to the co-presence of the sea and the wicked as indicative of the tradition's tedency to identify them as "figures of chaos." Parallels between the sea, the wicked, the deeps, darkness, and death can be found elsewhere,[29] and so one may think that this poem, which clearly draws on traditions about creation, analogizes these over and against figures such as order, the righteous, life, and light. But even though the sea and the wicked both represent an internal conflict that persists within material reality, the sea is depicted quite differently from the wicked. Verses 8–11 locate the sea, darkness, and depth not with the wicked and what the dawn shakes out, but rather—and no less than the dawn—at the ontological ground of the cosmos, as figures coddled by the creator. YHWH asks,

> Who shut in the sea with doors when it burst forth from the womb?
> When I made clouds its clothes,
>   and deep darkness its swaddling band? (38:8–9)

Commentators often note the surprising terms with which YHWH describes the sea. Not only is the sea clothed in the "clouds" (*'nn*) and the "deep darkness" (*'rpl*), figures that are deeply associated in ancient Israel with the appearance of YHWH (cf. Job 22:12–14; Ps 97:1–2; Exod 20:21; Deut 4:11; 5:22; 1 Kgs 8:12; Zeph 1:15), but the traditional mythos is upended so that the sea is not subdued or killed but birthed at the moment of creation. The creative act does not oppose the sea in Job 38, it generates it. Keller's characteristically eloquent prose describes the scene:

"the ocean here bursts forth in amniotic liquidity, caught like a baby by the midwife and wrapped in the soft darkness. A 'frigid mastery of the chaos'? Or an intimate tehomophilia? YHWH does not dilute the mythic danger of the sea and the darkness of origins but liberates them from the mood and meaning of evil."[30] Keller then suggests that this womb "that precedes all creatures" is God's, a kinship which their strong resemblance may also indicate.[31]

The expanses of the sea (e.g., v.16), earth (e.g. v.18), and sky (e.g. v.22) from which Job is cut off, and the cosmological (e.g., vv.31–33) and meteorological (e.g., vv.28–30) elements of which Job cannot know, are all staged to depict not some unified design interconnecting all material and immaterial reality, but rather a heterogeneous jumble of cosmic worlds. The sea that gushes forth does not externally oppose these worlds; it supplies an internal condition for their existence. It is as if God hard-wires the world with chaotic forces whose presence guarantees that the cosmos's constituents will always be open to re-wiring and will never achieve harmonious interconnections with one another.[32]

Even when the speeches seem to imply connections among the cosmos's constituents, such "connections" mostly illustrate the opposite: disconnection and alienation. Consider the waters that rain upon the wilderness and cause the grass to sprout in vv.26–27. Some connection is clearly implied among these elements—water, wilderness, grass—but the description emphasizes the disconnection and alienation that inheres to the "relationship" between soaking waters and scorched wasteland. The "connection" between the rain and the ground is far less connective than it is a tensive encounter between two alien elements. As if to prove the point beyond reproach, YHWH adds that the fecund grass that sprouts out of this alien encounter is located in a place that is cut off from the reach of human beings. This final detail unambiguously indicates that the earths inhabited by both human beings and the inherently heterogeneous "fecund wasteland" form no unified or interconnected space.

Any relationships at all are a rare find in these speeches. Forces are named, beings are described, but hardly is anything said to depend upon or even be affected by another. Again the exceptions appear designed to prove the rule. Within a few verses of one another the ostrich and the horse are described interacting with something human and each are led to laughter. That is, their "relationships" with humans are closer to a collision of aliens than an interdependent collusion. Brown puts it well: "creation teems with life characterized by fierce strength, inalienable freedom, and wild beauty. . . . God's world is filled with scavengers and predators, even monsters (cf. Gen 1:21), all coexisting, though never peacefully. The lions eat their prey; the vultures feast on the slain. This world is God's wild kingdom."[33] The elements and beings of these worlds are neither harmoniously interconnected nor utterly unaffected by one another. And yet what is most natural about nature in these speeches seems to be its belief in its independence, the way each inhabitant carries on *as if* it were alienated from and independent of others. When dependency is predicated of an animal—such as the raven's young who cry to El (38:41)—it is always on God. This is neither a homeostatic, integrated system of fully-functioning harmonious parts, nor an atomistic set of isolated elements, even if they carry on as if the latter were the case.

On this reading God's speeches are a far cry from a revelation to Job of the cosmic horizon of his existence so as to rebuke him for his particularly human sin of pride. The content of the speeches would prove disastrously ineffective to such a message since the nature that God describes is all too "human" in its vivid and palpable belief in itself, its independence, and its self-sufficiency. This is not a world where everything knows its place and no one takes another's. The raven's young is starving (38:41), the goat's young leaves and does not return (*šwb* 39:4), the ox cannot be trusted to return (*šwb* 39:12), the horse is so sure of itself that it laughs at fear and does not turn back (*šwb*) before the sword (39:22). The ostrich is an imbecile that fearlessly abandons its egg on the ground, which does not offer a warm embrace or provide a protective womb, but rather holds the egg until some other animal comes along and tramples it (39:13–17). While Behemoth finds food (40:20) and a shade tree (40:22), the river does not wash it, bring it food, or sustain it, it rather rushes against it just as Behemoth's strength and independence are established by withstanding its onrushing force (40:23). Nature in these speeches is fearless, untameable, coursing in directions from which it is not deterred until it collides with another unrelenting creature.

Neither the cosmos nor the earth is described as a solid or safe place. The message is not that Job inhabits a world that provides him with safe refuge, nor is it that the world is unsafe but synthesized in YHWH's great design. The message is rather that Job inhabits a world from whose foundations he is fundamentally disconnected and with which no solid connection is possible because it is not fully connected with itself.

§71 From Hermeneutics to Aesthetics

How are we to understand what this message means when we consider its addressee? What do God's speeches communicate in light of Job's condition and speeches? A hermeneutical approach to these questions would take some positive/substantial meaning as the ultimate horizon of any gaps or disconnects that make them difficult to answer. For the hermeneut, discord can be overcome by the discovery of a more essential or ultimate message. In this sense the dominant interpretations are hermeneutical since they grasp the disjunctions that God narrates within the world against a more substantial or meaningful background, such as a notion of God's great design or complex synthesis. My argument should thus be considered anti-hermeneutical since I think the speeches present nothing but an un-unified ground, shot through with tensions, cracks, and splits between and within an array of material and immaterial substances. As I now turn to the question of the disjunctions between the content of God's speeches and the content of Job's, once again the hermeneutical tendency prevails: the predominant interpretive response is to seek some deeper, more true level at which the disconnect disappears.

For example, consider the following questions:

> Have you penetrated the sources of the sea?
> Or walked around in the fathoms of the deep?
> Have the gates of death been exposed to you?
> Have you seen the gates of deep darkness?
> Have you comprehended the expanses of the earth?
> Declare if you know all this. (38:16–18)

Discord arises when one reads these questions because, while they occur within a series of questions to which the implied answer is clearly "no," in a number of places Job has testified to his experience of the deep, death, and deep darkness. Keller puts it this way: "Yet these rhetorical questions give one pause: in some sense Job could answer 'Yes'—he of all people had seen the gates of deep darkness; it swallowed his children."[34] Balentine similarly asks, "Who else can speak about death with a conviction that equals the pained experience of Job (e.g., 3:20–22; 7:20–21; 10:18–22; 16:15–17; 17:1–2, 11–16)?"[35] The hermeneut treats such discord as what interpretation must resolve in order to conclude. Thus Balentine suggests, "Perhaps, now at long last, when God says, 'Declare, if you know all this' (v.18), the invitation signals that God is indeed willing to listen to what Job has to say about suffering and death."[36] But few are so eager to see in God's command an openness to dialogue and, in any case, there is no indication that YHWH pauses for a response.[37] Indeed no good reason exists for reading these questions outside of the series of rhetorical questions in which they occur, a series that marches steadily toward YHWH's facetious comment in v.21, "You know, for you were born then, and the number of your days is myriad." Others, therefore, find it more likely that God thinks Job knows as much about suffering and death as he does about commanding the morning or laying the foundations of the earth.[38] From this hermeneutical angle, YHWH's message to Job is something like: "You may think you want or have seen deep darkness, but you are mistaken." I think that the turn to aesthetics made by several scholars at the beginning of the millennium stems in large part from their refusal to take the hermeneutical step toward such a deeper level of understanding.

Hans Urs von Balthasar describes the apparently independent and contemporaneous publications on "the dialogue principle" by Martin Buber, Franz Rosenzweig, Ferdinand Ebner, and Gabriel Marcel as "one of the strangest phenomena of 'acausal contemporaneity' in the history of the intellect."[39] While not as far-reaching, another instance of intellectual "acausal contemporaneity" occurred in and around 2003 in multiple interpretations of JOB's divine speeches. None explicitly mentions the others, though one may take account of another author's previous work, and yet they create among them a number of intriguing lines of convergence. They are, in order of appearance, Carol Newsom's chapter from her 2003 monograph, Kathleen O'Connor's 2003 article, and Catherine Keller's chapter from her 2004 monograph.[40] It is as if history demanded a shift of interpretive perspective on the divine speeches and each of these scholars responded.

Each of these readings, while immersed in biblical scholarship, interprets the speeches by means of aesthetic categories. O'Connor draws on E. Scarry's reconsideration of the notion of beauty; Newsom develops what she calls the tragic sublime; and Keller reads the speeches through a comic paradigm. The beautiful, the sublime, tragedy, and comedy are all major and inter-related categories in aesthetics, as is obvious in the common hybrids "tragic sublime," "tragicomic," "sublime beauty," and so forth. It is difficult not to take this strange, simultaneous convergence of readings as symptomatic and worthy of further exploration. Is there some dimension to these speeches that previous interpretations could not grasp and that these interpreters could only grasp by turning to aesthetics? Much of the rest of this chapter explores, explicates, and coordinates relations among these interpretations, whose impact has not yet been felt or comprehended.

These interpreters depart from the hermeneutical approach by analyzing the conflict, the contradiction, the discord, as essential to the message. While they differ as to how it is best understood, I think they all correctly view the move toward resolution at a deeper level as a step in the wrong direction. Rather than searching for some essential connection that merely appears as a disconnect, one should discern what the disconnect means and how it is structured. No interpretation will be satisfactory that leaves behind the discord that inheres in the cosmos or the incongruencies that divide the registers in which Job and YHWH speak.

§72 The Beautiful and the Sublime

I now turn to the different aesthetic categories that each of these three interpreters uses to help them deal with the disconnects that God's speeches present, that is, the less-than-unified, conflict-ridden cosmos, and the discrepencies between YHWH's and Job's perspectives. In this section I discuss the beautiful and the sublime, which are, respectively, the primary categories for Newsom and O'Connor. The beautiful and the sublime have a long, complicated history that far exceeds my particular interests, and so remains largely unexplored (this is also true in my treatments of tragedy and comedy). Though Kant is not the first to consider them together, I take as my starting point his third *Critique* since the analyses of both O'Connor and Newsom are rooted in it.[41]

A brief overview is in order to situate these aesthetic categories within Kant's larger system. Kant thought our minds worked through the deployments and interactions among various faculties, which might be simplified into the following figure of nested relations:

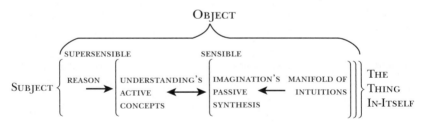

Figure 8: Kant's Theory of the Relations among Cognitive Faculties

The imagination can be thought of as that faculty that presents to the mind intuitions drawn from a sensibly given manifold, that is, from experience. With our imagination we *apprehend*, according to certain rules, whatever intuitions come to mind about our experience. The imagination directly engages our intuitions through a kind of passive synthesis. The imagination looks for patternings, relations, movement; it seeks formal coherence amidst a manifold of intuitions. Then the understanding works with concepts to organize and *comprehend* the object that has been imaginatively apprehended. Reason is then the faculty by which one can reflect on the success or failure of the concepts and categories of the understanding.

One way Kant distinguishes aesthetic judgments such as "X is beautiful" from, say, rational judgments is that the former do not use concepts. The imagination goes about its business without the understanding pressing in on its apprehensions so as to cognize them conceptually. The imagination continues to do the same kinds of activities it normally does at the behest of the understanding, that is, the imagination continues to try to apprehend the manifold it perceives in a way that is amenable to the conceptualizing activity of the understanding even though, in this case, the understanding does not try to conceptualize. This is why Kant calls the experience of beauty free and playful—before the beautiful object the imagination operates without being determined by any of the understanding's concepts—and yet purposive and harmonious—the object apprehended seems suited for the work of the understanding and one's powers of judgment in general. The beautiful, he writes, "directly brings with it a feeling of the promotion of life, and hence is compatible with charms and an imagination at play. . . . [Beauty] carries with it a purposiveness in its form . . . [that] seems as it were to be predetermined for our power of judgment."[42] When we feel pleasure before a piece of art, Kant thinks that we are feeling a sense of harmony between the imagination and the understanding because the imagination has discerned in the object a form that is suitable for the work of the understanding in general, even though the understanding does not in this case go to work on it. Beauty only pertains to an object that seems as if it were purposive or designed, without any definite purpose or telos actually fitting this purposiveness. For Kant, neither beauty nor the sublime are teleological; "both please for themselves," they are both liked for their own sake, disinterestedly.[43]

If there is a sense of harmony behind the pleasure that arises with beauty, the experience of the sublime arises in the face of an unpleasurable discord between what the imagination tries to apprehend and that which the understanding could comprehend. That which "excites in us the feeling of the sublime, may to be sure appear in its form to be contrapurposive [*zweckwidrig*] for our power of judgment, unsuitable for our faculty of presentation [*Darstellung*], and as it were doing violence to our imagination, but is nevertheless judged all the more sublime for that."[44] Where the beautiful is *zweckmäßig*, purposive, the sublime is *zweckwidrig*, contrapurposive. The imagination's attempt to unify the manifold into a coherent form is frustrated by the disharmony of the sublime object before which the subject stands. The object is too irregular or idiosyncratic for conceptualization, in short, too formless with respect to the thought of totality. If the idea of a totality is driving one's cognizing activity which is, in this case, failing to apprehend the sensorily derived manifold of intuitions as formally coherent, then the idea of a totality must be supersensible—in Kant's somewhat archaic terms, above what can be perceived through the senses. Kant then posits a faculty of reason as the source of this supersensible idea of a totality.

The experience of the sublime is, therefore, the experience of something that occasions the feeling that there is a vocation within us that is not governed by and does not derive from anything sensible. In the experience of the sublime we look down upon our sensible nature and its limited capacities from the supersensible and unconditioned heights of pure reason. The sublime thus brings

> a pleasure that arises only indirectly, being generated, namely, by the feeling of a momentary inhibition of the vital powers and the immediately following and all the more powerful outpouring of them; hence as an emotion it seems to be not play but something serious in the activity of the imagination . . . the mind is not merely attracted by the object [as it is in the beautiful], but is also always reciprocally repelled by it, the satisfaction in the sublime does not so much contain positive pleasure as it does admiration or respect, i.e., it deserves to be called negative pleasure.[45]

The subject experiencing the sublime is both audience and hero of a tragic drama, lured into viewing something that will expose and overwhelm the limits and capacities of her sensible being, and yet will thereby also reaffirm her heroic transcendence beyond the sensible. Sublime pleasure thus arrives not only through a negative pleasure, it also arises in a negative way, not through some representation one has of the actual object encountered, but rather through a dimension that one's imagination fails to represent and which comes not from the object but from the subject, from reason.[46]

For Kant there are two basic modes or structures through which this failure appears and gives rise to the feeling of the sublime. The first he calls mathematical and associates with quantity or magnitude; the second he calls dynamical and associates with quality. The primary object of the mathematical sublime is infinity, which he illustrates by reference to the stars. When the imagination looks up at the stars, reason wants to totalize the starry sky into a whole, and so demands that the imagination start counting. But there is a moment when the imagination fails, fails to keep in mind, in a single intuition, a single whole, the beginning of the counting and where it is in its counting at a later moment, and so the counter is confronted with the failure of her imagination before reason's requirement to totalize the infinity of stars over her head. With that, reason appears as a supersensible power within us, a power that demands what one cannot even imagine, and so surpasses any standard of sense.[47] The dynamically sublime, however, is felt before figures of power and might, violence and destruction; threatening cliffs, a lofty waterfall on a mighty river, volcanoes and hurricanes trailing destruction, thunder clouds towering to the heavens. Before them, "as long as we find ourselves in safety,"[48] we recognize our physical impotence, but nonetheless confront within ourselves a capacity for judging ourselves that remains independent of such sublime objects.[49]

§73 Job's Sublime Experience

According to Newsom, "Chapter 38 is largely concerned with what Kant would call the 'mathematical sublime,' which engenders sublimity by overwhelming the mind with what it cannot comprehend in the categories available to it . . . [whereas] chapters 39–41 are more concerned with the 'dynamically sublime.'"[50] My discussion of chapter 38 would seem to agree fully with her former point since I found that the speech consistently describes material reality in ways that fail to represent it as a totalized whole. Since the cosmos fails to form a unified whole, Job's imagination is unable to apprehend it as a unified whole, which is what the interrogative mood through which God presents the cosmos to Job implies by emphasizing the cosmos's incomprehensibility. Many readers, I argued above, misapprehend this connection, believing that the interrogatives imply a merely human, epistemological limitation. I argued instead that the cosmos is less-than-fully unified at an *ontological* level. This cosmos is not some thing that could be comprehended were it not for humans' epistemological limitations, even though the inadequacy of subjective comprehension is unquestionably on display in these speeches.

The animals provide wonderful illustrations of dynamically sublime objects. They are "the wild and fierce denizens of inaccessible mountains and desert wastelands."[51] Newsom describes them as "liminal beings who belong to the boundaries of the symbolic world . . . they manifest the alien Other, with the terror of the chaotic present in their very being."[52] Just as Kant describes a sublime object as absolute, in every respect beyond all comparison since "we do not allow a suitable standard for it to be sought outside of it, but merely within it,"[53] so too does God limn Behemoth: "the first/chief of the acts of God" (40:19a). "Like Behemoth," Newsom adds, "Leviathan will also be described as a creature 'without equal,' a king over all the proud (41:25–26)."[54] Although she thinks the speeches begin with more attention than I have allowed to the order of the cosmos,[55] throughout her analysis Newsom draws attention to the properly sublime character of the objects of God's focus, be it in their alien habitat and/or terrifying strength and violence (dynamic), or in their vast expansiveness (mathematical).

The objects God represents to Job in these speeches may provide prime candidates for affording an experience of the sublime, but one does not necessarily have a sublime experience when faced with such objects. Thus far I have only suggested one side of the experience of the sublime that these speeches seem to be aimed at arousing in Job— that is, feelings of impotence, nullity, and inhibition—but where in these speeches is there evidence of the sublime's feelings of supremacy, independence, and respect? Echoing an earlier interpretation by Gordis, Newsom argues that Job's experience can be seen to be doubled or indirect in the same way as the experience of the sublime when he cites in his second response what God previously said (42:3a // 38:2; 42:4b // 38:3b; 40:7b).[56] In his citations, Job testifies to an experience of "ex-static transport" in which God's words become his own and he experiences himself as though he were the source of their creative power,

> as though he had created what he heard. . . . It is a profound loss of unity, a recognition of the deeply fractured nature of reality. The experience of sublime transport resolves nothing substantively. It does, however, provide a means by which the loss of unity is itself experientially displaced, as Job feels the words of the divine speech as though he himself were speaking them.[57]

To ask, apropos Job's ambiguous response in 42:1–6, whether Job has accepted or defied God's rebuke, is to miss the sense in which the line between Job's and God's positions is transgressed in the moment of sublime transport. Job not only assumes God's words about his inadequacy ("Who is this who darkens counsel without knowledge" 42:3a), but also stands victorious in his defeat, having now gained an idea of what is too wonderful for him to know (42:3c). I return to Newsom's interpretation below.

§74 Job's Experience of Beauty

In her brief but provocative essay, O'Connor argues that the divine speeches afford Job an experience of beauty in the specific sense defined by Scarry.[58] Scarry tries to rehabilitate beauty despite its detractors across the humanities.[59] Beauty's opposition to the sublime has been strongly operative in earning it this bad reputation.[60] Kant's work is certainly influenced by this opposition but he is more guilty of the particular offenses Scarry rejects in an earlier, pre-critical text than he is in the third *Critique.*[61] In the traditional opposition, the beautiful "was almost always the diminutive member, [so] it was also the dismissible member."[62] Scarry attempts a thorough redefinition of the beautiful that would restore to it the potent and perturbing aspects that have been cut off from it by dint of their attribution to the sublime, beauty's so-called opposite. Scarry thinks the experience of beauty is potent and perturbing because it is decentering and "unselfing." Beauty forces us to surrender our imaginary position at the center of the world and incites in us an ethical will to share and replicate for the sake of others what we have experienced.[63]

Scarry's understanding of beauty specifies but does not wholly depart from Kant's. Scarry's framework is no more limited to beauty's agitating force than Kant's is to its symmetry. Scarry adopts John Rawls's definition of fairness as a "symmetry of everyone's relation to each other,"[64] which serves as the referent for her claim that beauty heightens our awareness of justice, awakens us to injustice, and begets in us a will toward ethical fairness. Kant thinks there must be in judgments of beauty a moment of excess or indeterminateness in which form emerges out of or breaks away from conceptuality. This excess beyond conceptuality is what allows the purposiveness of form or mere form to be experienced.[65]

So, for Scarry, beholding a beautiful object displaces us from the inertia plaguing our ego-driven pursuits and into a posture that believes that symmetrical relations with all are possible; and it prompts in us a positive pleasure. In light of Scarry's redefinition of the experience of beauty, it may be helpful to reformulate the difference between beauty and the sublime. The sublime affords a negative pleasure, a pleasure which arises from a displeasure, as well as from a discontinuity with the world and with ourselves. Both the beautiful and the sublime tear us from our narcissistic complacency, the unity of an imaginary one, but they do so in two different ways and to two different ends. Beauty divides us in half, cuts us off from ourselves, but instills in us a belief that we can create a world in and with which we could be unified. The sublime cleaves us in two, but pleases us by locating us in a seemingly impossible place wherefrom our split self can be perceived.[66] Beauty appears at first to be a more or less unified and harmonious experience of satisfaction that actually constitutes us as desiring, less-than-unified subjects. The sublime, on the other hand, appears at first an unpleasurable experience of a profound loss of unity that actually turns out to please by placing us in an impossible confrontation with the (split) essence of our being. In short, beauty promises us unity by cutting us off from it, and the sublime gives us unity that we can only perceive as two. The senses of "unity" involved at the end of both experiences are far from the imaginary "one" in which we previously lived.

A number of prominent interpretations prior to O'Connor's describe what the speeches convey to Job as beautiful.[67] The aspects of the poem that she finds beautiful are often aligned with these prior studies. I must agree that in these speeches nature's mysteries seem to convey a particularly vivid beauty. The speeches describe the overflowing glory of the cosmos and its inhabitants, and accompanying these descriptions are statements of God's pride, detailed attention, and exuberant delight in creation and its creatures.

But, like sublime objects, beautiful objects do not necessarily afford an experience of beauty. Like Newsom, O'Connor demonstrates that Job has enjoyed and been transformed by beauty as she understands it by drawing heavily on Job's second response and the prose conclusion:

> There is language of sight: "But now my eyes see you" (42:5); there is Job's unselfing: "I put my hand over my mouth, I am of small account," "I repent in/of/concerning dust and ashes" (42:6). There is evidence that his focus turns outward as he repairs injuries, interceding for his friends (42:7–9) and extending extraordinary care to his daughters (42:13–15).[68]

Linafelt's similar point more clearly states how Job's care for his daughters aligns with Scarry's argument that beauty begets in the beholder a will toward justice:

> Job also, we are told in an understated aside, gives his daughters an inheritance along with their brothers—an act that would seem to more or less directly subvert the gendered basis of ancient inheritance laws, which allowed daughters to inherit only if there were no living male relatives . . . In the social structure that Job has just subverted, a daughter did not inherit because she was essentially sold off for a brideprice to a suitor, whose responsibility she would now be, and the value of beauty lay in its ability to bring a heftier brideprice. But by giving his daughters an inheritance, Job has provided them a way out of this economic system; their beauty is not defined by its use-value.[69]

The pressure exerted by the speeches' beauty also extends to present readers:

The speeches invite us to participate in God's wild, raging creativity, to replicate beauty, to create new beauty, to generate harmony and wild freedom in our work and relationships, to extend our realm of care from our families to the whole cosmos and its denizens, to make a world where creative flourishing is available to all beings.[70]

O'Connor's move from JOB to reader is not simply another iteration of the "So what?" question that pervades the end of theologico-ethical readings. Her move arises immanently from her interpretation, according to which an experience of beauty in itself compels an ethical will toward universal symmetry. Such universality is not the postulate that there is or should be a symmetry among all that X is beautiful, nor even that the beauty that one experiences as a symmetry among her faculties can or should be taken as an analogy for political equality, but rather that the concrete, aesthetic symmetry one experiences from beauty compels and helps her to actualize just symmetrical relations for all.[71]

§75 Beautiful or Sublime?

The largest obstacles to describing the experience that the divine speeches afford as one of beauty may initially seem to stem from the discordances that plague the speeches (described in §70). However, Scarry's redefinition predicates the experience of beauty on just such discordances.[72] The un-unified, conflict-ridden nature of the cosmos, as well as the incongruencies dividing YHWH from Job and Job from the world, can all be taken as the instigating forces behind beauty's perturbing effects. O'Connor denies that the speeches attempt to bully Job into humiliation and instead thinks that the speeches' antagonistic features participate in the same sort of disruption of one's general narcissism that an encounter with something beautiful effects when it draws one's attention away from oneself, out of one's unmindfulness.

Beauty is quite helpful for grasping those moments in the speeches when God gets absorbed in the intricacies of a creature such that Job recedes into irrelevance. But the problem is that God does not remain there, which strains a reader's ability to remain within the paradigm of beauty. In the experience of beauty the decentering moment is preliminary; once accomplished, the self falls away as one's regard shifts laterally. Job may recede, but he never falls away. In the end, these speeches remain staged for Job. Well into the speeches, just before turning to Behemoth and Leviathan, God again focuses squarely on Job (40:1–14). And

Job's concern in both verbal responses is less with the beauty or even the existence of creation and its creatures, and more with himself and what God has said about him. Thus, beauty may be most helpful at particular moments within and after the speeches, for example, when he gives his daughters such sensuous and aesthetic names and shows his concern for justice, but beauty does not supply a paradigm with which one can approach the speeches more broadly.

The sublime seems particularly well-suited for grasping those aspects of the speeches for which beauty seems ill-suited, namely, the uses to which God puts creation. The speeches emphasize Job's powerlessness and inabilities (what Kant calls *Unvermögen*) and certainly seem intended to evoke his deep displeasure. They present so many attempts at humiliation and violence in the experience of limitation. All these—humiliation, limitation, violence, impotence, etc.—are precisely the terms with which Kant refers to the displeasure that characterizes one half of the sublime.

So, both the sublime and the beautiful are productive paradigms for grasping particular moments in the speeches but, like the beautiful, the sublime is not without its problems. The most troubling issue for both is the sense in which Job fails to meet the conditions they require of the one who will experience their feelings. Both frameworks need the speeches to address and perturb a man who finds himself in a state of imaginary unity. Whether it is the vertical image of sublime humiliation (looking down on oneself), or the horizontal image of beauty's decentering (lateral regard toward others), both rely on a reference to Job's self-regard or self-absorption. Textual support can be found for such a reference; Job's speeches in chapters 3 and 29–31 often perform this task. But it is inadequate, if not obscene to refer to Job—considered across his speeches—as arrogant, self-absorbed, or one with too high a sense of entitlement. I think in particular of all those texts that I drew on in CHAPTER 4 to describe Job's anxiety, and in CHAPTER 5 to describe Job's shame. The image they depict cannot be called self-absorption since in them Job repeatedly asserts that he is not at one with himself.

The friends, I argued in §50, relate to Job through the experience of the sublime and they encourage Job to adopt a similar relationship to his experience. But, I argued in §§51–52, Job is incapable of assuming the sublime standpoint on his experience because of his profound sense of a lack of unity and self-identity. Does YHWH here repeat the friends' offer? Does YHWH operate with the same ethic?[73] I said Job is unable to assume a sublime stance toward his condition in the dialogue since he lacks the ground from which he could get beyond or rise above his condition. Even if one were to argue that chapters 29–31 show that Job has attained what he previously lacked, would this be enough to annul or render irrelevant Job's previous condition? To read the divine speeches as if they responded only to Job's speech in chapters 29–31 would certainly sap them of much of their force. In either case, if YHWH's solution seeks to afford Job a sublime experience, then YHWH would seem, no less than the friends, to offer a solution that is at least ineffective and at most ignorant with respect to that dimension of his experience which, I argued above, the sublime is unable to account for.

In sum, in response to this section's question "Beautiful or sublime?" I offer the Leninist answer: "No thanks, both are worse." The unselfing involved in the experience of beauty misses the sense in which Job remains a focal point for these speeches, and the sublime's focus on the demotion of the self misses the already abundantly demoted condition of the speeches' addressee.

§76 The Sublimes and Tragedy

At this point it is necessary to revisit the notion of the sublime if we are to keep from throwing out the proverbial baby with the bath water. There are two modes or structures through which one can come to an experience of the sublime—the mathematical and the dynamical—and these two structures involve not only different kinds of objects but also a different subjective experience. In what follows I argue that the problems with ascribing to Job an experience of the sublime concern the dynamical and not the mathematical sublime.

The mathematical sublime is felt before phenomena *within* the phenomenal realm that one's imagination is incapable of thinking together. But to be aware of this failure "requires a faculty in the human mind that is itself supersensible."[74] The supersensible of which one is aware in the experience of the mathematical sublime involves a split within oneself, a gap between one's imagination, which fails to synthesize one's sensible intuitions into a single intuition, and one's reason, which can nonetheless "think the given infinite without contradiction."[75] The dynamical sublime is felt before a phenomenon that is exceptional to the phenomenal realm, in moments when one is transported beyond one's sensible experience and cognitive capacities into the supersensible faculty of reason from which one can judge oneself independently of nature.[76] The dynamical sublime arises when one is elevated above phenomena such that one is capable of conceptualizing an exceptional and inconceivable phenomenon. Thus the supersensible of which one is aware in the dynamical sublime involves a capacity to transcend oneself. In short, whereas in the mathematical sublime two thoughts whose co-presence seems impossible are somehow held together in one divided experience, in the dynamical sublime one is transported above oneself.

One can see that Newsom's reading of Job's experience as sublime primarily involves the dynamical sublime rather than the mathematical in her argument that Job's sublime experience has a tragic structure. Newsom associates the tragic not with the chaotic or the evil that destroys human plans and desires, but rather with "the inevitable clash of two necessities,"[77] by which she means a clash between Job's passion in chapters 29–31 for a rationally transparent world and the intrinsic and unmasterable violence of existence. Confronted with this clash, Job's aim is no longer to preserve the possibility of emancipation, but to testify with his mourning to the irremediable catastrophe, and with his silence to his subjection to an unrepresentable otherness. Job testifies to a catastrophe and an otherness, a catastrophic and sublime otherness that lies at the origin and essence of cosmic and human being.

Because of his experience of sublime transport, Job is not simply subjected to this tragic structure, he is also allowed to grasp it as such. In his assumption of YHWH's words as his own he freely assumes the necessity of his tragic existence. Job's embrace of tragic existence in his experience of sublime transport allows him a modicum of pleasure that can be indexed in Job's decision in the prose conclusion to bring children into the world once again, to endow them with inheritances and names that conjure various forms of beauty. "Such playful names," Newsom writes, "are a form of laughter—not heedless or anarchic laughter—but human and therefore tragic laughter."[78] Tragic existence consists in this clash between two heterogeneous dimensions. The experience of this clash brings not only pain and violence but can also inspire respect for the unrepresentable and unconditional dimension in which the subject can recognize, and freely assume, its destiny. From this complex experience emerges the subject that can be seen laughing and enjoying, in all its tragically sublime splendor.

Tragedy is often characterized by a certain disconnect between the subjective views of the hero and the objective circumstances in which he finds himself. Tragedies create suspense by building toward the clash of two contradictory elements.[79] The hero will embody this clash at the moment she is brought down and simultaneously elevated. Think of Oedipus in Sophocles's plays. One element is the Oracle's prediction of what will happen; the other is the characters' actions that aim to prevent the fulfillment of this prediction, along with the events consequent to these actions. Suspense is thus created, sustained, and escalated as readers progress toward the moment these two elements clash. When they do, they take Oedipus down, but nonetheless elevate him in tragic dignity at the moment of his assumption of guilt. In other words, tragedies often afford their heroes dynamically sublime experiences. By contrast, in what follows I argue that Job's experience is not of this tragic, dynamically sublime sort; it is instead a mathematically sublime experience.

§77 Job's Mathematically Sublime Experience

Both the mathematical and the dynamical structures of the sublime manage an impossible relationship between (at least) two non-relational elements, but they do so in different ways. That is, both designate structures that relate multiple elements that for some reason exclude one another. *In the dynamical sublime* two heterogeneous elements clash so that, in the end, certain figures (e.g., the hero's body in *Antigone*) are brought down only to have others (e.g., the idea of fidelity) elevated in sublime splendor. *In the mathematical sublime*, however, the heterogeneous elements are immanent to one another in an impossible co-presence. The dynamic involved in the mathematical sublime does not derive principally from unifying or connecting the two elements, but from maintaining their manifest disconnection. The mathematical sublime does not move toward a synthesis or an overcoming of one by the other (as in the tragic or dynamical structure), but instead oscillates in a mode that is neither conclusive nor fluid. The road on which the mathematical sublime travels is generated by the disconnect between two entities whose (impossible) coexistence it spans.

There is no question that the divine speeches present a coexistent encounter of two excluding realities. They bring a sudden intrusion of the heavens into the earth in the form of a storm or whirlwind (*hasseʿārâ*). This theophany does not provide instructions on how to live, as was the case for Moses and Aaron in Exod 19:16–20:18, deliverence from enemies, as for David in 2 Sam 22:8–18 (// Ps 18:8–18), clarity regarding the historical situation and what should be done in it, as for Elijah in 1 Kings 19:11–18. Instead, in JOB God indulges in a speech that is truly heterogeneous to the situation into which it has intruded. The situation and the speech therefore coexist alongside each other and become articulated in one and the same scene.

The question is whether this co-existence of two heterogeneous realities is better read according to the dynamical or the mathematical paradigm. As is clear from my above discussions of the sublime and tragedy, some favor the former, thinking that the book suspends the confrontation between two non-relational elements—God and Job, covenantal fidelity and sovereign freedom, etc.—until the divine speeches.[80] But, following my thoughts from the end of §75, if one were to take seriously Job's comments throughout the dialogue about God's presence and Job's failure to be at one with himself, then one would have to say that the co-presence of two excluding elements has taken place from the beginning and continues to take place throughout the book. In other words, the appearance of YHWH in the whirlwind does not restructure the situation into which it arrives, it presents what is better described as a variation or new development of the same structure that has animated the book throughout.

The beautiful and the dynamical sublime can be thought of as two opposing manifestations of the tragic paradigm. I defined tragedy around a point from which two clashing elements can be perceived. I argued on page 191 that beauty splits us from ourselves but instills in us a belief that we can create a world in and with which we could be unified, whereas the sublime cleaves us in two, but pleases us by locating us in a place wherefrom our split self can be perceived. In both there is a fundamental duality that achieves an impossible unity, which is how I described tragedy. The tragic perspective consists in exposing the impasses that arise from the clash of non-intersecting elements as well as the effects that these impasses have on the individuals caught within the structures in which the impasses inhere. Where a tragic reading focuses on how Job is caught within the impasses of his world, a victim of a clash with his world, Job actually appears to incarnate the impasses of the world. The tragic structure treats Job as distanced from the world and God's speeches as "putting him in his place" or, in the dynamically sublime reading, God's speeches transport Job out of his place and to the sublime heights of God's place. But if read according to the structure of the mathematical sublime, Job's distance from himself and the world does not oppose him to the world but makes him continuous with it since this distance also inheres within the world.

Consider Job 9:16–20, in which Job imagines summoning God and God granting him a response, the outcome of which Job fears: "God will crush me with a tempest (*biś'ārâ*) . . . he is the strong one . . . my own mouth will condemn me . . . [and] will prove me perverse." When YHWH does show up, it is indeed in a tempest (*hasse'ārâ*) and with speech that celebrates YHWH's strength, declares that Job's mouth has condemned him, and proves Job perverse (esp. 38:1–3; 40:6–8).[81]

Similar exercises could be performed on much of what YHWH says. Let me take a few verses from chapter 40 as examples. YHWH asks Job,

> Have you an arm like God,
>> and can you thunder with a voice like his? (40:9)

As far as Job is concerned, there is no question of comparing his strength to God's because the contest is continuously being carried out. Each time he loses, losses for which he repeatedly suffers:

> If it is about strength, look at [his] might. (9:19a)

> Water wears down stones, its torrents wash away the earth's soil,
> so you destroy a human's hope.
>> You overpower him forever. (14:19–20a)

> Pity me, pity me. You are my friends.
>> For the hand of Eloah has struck me. (19:21)

In the next verse YHWH demands,

> Deck yourself with majesty and dignity;
>> clothe yourself with glory and splendor. (40:10)

But Job has no delusions about his own majesty, glory, or splendor:

> He has stripped my honor from me,
>> and removed the crown from my head. (19:9)

I argued in §61 that, at their most extreme, Job's experiences dislocated him into a place where the categories of dignity, glory, innocence, and guilt became irrelevant. But YHWH seems unaware of these parts of Job's speeches when YHWH concludes that, if Job answers the questions and complies with the demands,

> Then I will also acknowledge you
>> that your own right hand can give you victory. (40:14)

Now recall what Job has said about his hand:

> Why do I place my flesh in my teeth, and take my life in my hand?
> If he kills me, I will not wait; but I will argue my path to his face.
>> (13:14–15)

> My own hand weighs heavily upon my groaning.[82] (23:2b)

Far from the tool with which he thinks he can gain victory, Job speaks of his hand as that which weighs heavily on him but with which he will nevertheless grasp what is left of his life and hurl it before God, come what may. This is a final gesture of desperation, not triumph. Furthermore, Job has had much more to say about the power and authority of God's hand than his own, as in this echo of certain statements in the Psalms (e.g., 104:27–30; 145:15–16):

> In his hand is the life of every living being,
>> and the breath of every human being. (12:10)

Similarly, in 38:21 YHWH sarcastically quips, following a set of questions challenging Job's knowledge and experience of the dwelling places of light and darkness, "You know, for you were born then, and the number of your days is many." Job, however, has not said that he has lived many days, but that the days he lives stretch out in indefinite suffering (7:1). Far from a claim to eternal being, Job has rather longed for a finite ending to days that pose infinitely more than he can bear. Later, Job speaks about the number of days humans live, but he calls them "short (q^eṣar yāmîm) and replete with anguish" (14:1). He likens humans not to eternal stalwarts, but to rotting waste and moth-eaten garments (13:28), withering flowers and fleeing shadows (14:2). Job speaks not of many days but of few, very long ones. Thus one could imagine Job responding to YHWH's quip in 38:21 by saying, "Well, no, I was not born then but, thanks to you, it certainly feels like it!"

YHWH not only challenges Job's capabilities and knowledge, but also seems to think Job has failed to acknolwedge YHWH's own capabilities and sovereignty. Right after saying that Job lacks knowledge in 38:2b, YHWH asks if Job knows who laid out the dimensions of the cosmos (38:4–6), who shut in the sea with doors (38:8), who has the wisdom to count the clouds (38:37), if Job has ever commanded the dawn so that it seizes and shakes the earth (38:12–13), or if he can orchestrate the constellations (38:31–33). One cannot help but think of Job's earlier citation of the following hymn fragment:

> Truly I know this is so . . . [El is] wise-hearted and mightily strong . . .
> Who shakes the earth from its place so that its pillars tremble.
> Who commands the sun and it does not shine, and who seals up the stars.
> Who spread out the heavens by himself,
>> and who trod upon the back of the sea.
> Who made Ash, Kesil, and Kimah, and the chambers of the south.
> Who does greatness unfathomable
>> and wonders innumerable. (9:2a, 4a, 6–10)

If one turns what they say into propositions, YHWH and Job appear to say the same thing, but they clearly speak as if their statements challenge the other. Again, the mathematically sublime structure seems better because there are two heterogeneous but co-present elements, bound together by the appearance that they say the same thing. Job acknowledges YHWH's principal role in creation; YHWH responds by asking Job if he knows who holds or if he has ever held the principal role in creation—all the while suggesting that it is YHWH himself who holds this role. Despite the apparent agreement, each speaks as if his statement disagrees with or even opposes the other's position.

In the mathematically sublime structure that I am uncovering, some point must exist from which two elements are resonantly diverging or dissonantly converging, it does not matter which. Thus the same structure is present whether Job and YHWH appear to disagree, despite making the same basic point, or whether they make contradictory statements that actually agree. Consider this question from YHWH:

> Have you commanded the morning since your days began,
>   and caused the dawn to know its place? (38:12)

The implication is clearly "no," that Job has not done such things. But in Job's opening speech he actually does issue such commands:

> Let the stars of its dawn be dark;
>   let it hope for light, but have none;
>   may it not see the eyelids of the morning. (3:9)

A similar dynamic lies behind many interpreters' responses to YHWH's questions:

> Have you penetrated the sources of the sea?
>   Or walked around in the fathoms of the deep?
> Have the gates of death been exposed to you?
>   Have you seen the gates of deep darkness? (38:16–17)

As many scholars recognize (see §71), much of Job's testimony suggests that he could indeed answer "yes."[83] In other words, in some texts YHWH and Job appear to make contradictory statements that actually agree, and in other texts YHWH and Job appear to say the same thing and yet oppose one another. In neither is there a clash of two necessities. There is rather an oscillation between two identical statements that are opposed to one another, or between two opposed perspectives that actually agree.

In neither is there a movement toward resolution or toward an overcoming of one statement/perspective by another. There is rather a dissolute drift from one figure to another that are never co-present and yet never separate. The utterly heterogeneous figures of YHWH and Job are united and divided around a point that remains missing, as if they each stood on the opposite side of the same piece of paper that both united them and divided them from one another.

This crucial "missing" point of "unification" can be seen in YHWH's description of the closing in of the sea with doors in 38:8, which evokes some of Job's earlier accusations in the dialogue that YHWH is treating him like a chaos monster which, he concludes, he cannot endure.

- In 7:12 Job complains, "Am I the Sea or the Dragon that you have set watch over me?" Job laments that God's gaze oppresses him as if he were a chaos monster. In 10:8–11 Job pleas with God to remember that he is God's creature and not an enemy. And in 13:27 he complains that God has shackled and bound him which, in 14:5, he broadens to a general condition of humanity.
- Then, in chapter 38, YHWH waxes about the creation of the sea . . . how she burst forth in her amniotic liquidity . . . how YHWH swaddled her with clouds and gave her glory a place to thrive. In the second speech YHWH rapturously asks Job if he knows how powerful the chaos monsters are . . . how large is the one's member . . . how exquisite the other's armor . . . and then YHWH astoundingly expresses great delight in gazing upon them.

This is precisely the kind of divine attention and "enjoyment" (*jouissance*) that Job complained about receiving. Job, apparently thinking of the Sea as God's uncreated enemy that warrants God's gaze, tries to get God to cease treating him like the Sea by reminding God that he is God's creature. YHWH's response speaks about how he created and then nurtured the sea and takes great delight in gazing upon figures of chaos. YHWH and Job both speak about God's excessive and libidinally charged attention to figures of chaos. This point of unification, however, remains missing in that they each speak about it in totally different registers, like two sides of a single plane. The same is true of the un-coordinated relationships between Job and the figures of chaos and Job and the world.

The structure here is key. Job's complaint likens himself to a chaos monster because of the excessive divine attention and overbearing scrutiny with which he felt oppressed by YHWH; YHWH responds with an excessive amount of attention and scrutiny to the chaos monsters, although in a mode that is delightful and enraptured rather than heavy and abusive. The crucial "missing link"—excessive divine attention—remains missing since YHWH and Job do not in any sense share it, it being so different for each. The "presence" of this missing link is what animates the dynamic relationship between the heterogeneous figures of Job and YHWH. Unlike the tragic sublime reading, therefore, one's interest does not derive from suspense as to the outcome of a clash between two externally related and conflicting necessities, but rather from the missing link that keeps the various figures co-present to each other and yet suspends any direct relationship between them.

In short, in the relationship between what Job says and what YHWH says, there are not two—Job and the world—that are brought together; there is but one substance—Job-and-the-world alike—that is internally divided against itself. The mathematically sublime reading does not eliminate the opposition between Job and the world, it just insists that the opposition is internal to and thus shared by both Job and the world. Job and the world resonate with each other because they share this inherent distance.

§78 Conclusion: The Mathematical Sublime

Even if YHWH is unaware of it, the kind of world YHWH describes is clearly one in which Job could come to be as he is. Job is the truth of the "multiverse" YHWH describes in the sense that the kind of existence Job has suffered could only have occurred within a less-than-fully unified multiverse. By suggesting that one is the truth of the other I do not mean that one determines or undermines the other. Instead I think that the truth of both is half-said by each. Both YHWH and Job speak as if their speech implies that the other is wrong. However, what each describes is merely one side of a double-sided entity whose other side is that which the other describes. The topological model here is a Möbius band and not a sheet of paper. If you persist on the side of Job long enough, you will have to end up imagining the kind of world YHWH describes; if you persist on the side of the world YHWH describes long enough, you will end up coming to terms with the kinds of monsters it can produce—not just the beautiful ones God describes, but the horrid, rancid ones atop the trash heap like Job. The truth of Job's situation as well as God's cosmos is constituted only at the moment they are brought together and read coterminously.

What does my argument that the relationship between God's speeches and Job's has the structure of the mathematical and not the dynamical sublime do to Newsom's argument that the speeches move from the mathematical to the dynamical sublime?[84] I do not think that the mathematical gives way to the dynamical since the mathematical sublime insists even within the animals that conclude the speeches and are supposed to exemplify the dynamical sublime. To be sure, both Behemoth and Leviathan are described as qualitatively singular (40:19a; 41:25–26) and celebrated for their power and prowess, but YHWH's speech about them "engages Job in a tightly focused exercise of close and rigorous comtemplation."[85] As much as YHWH celebrates Behemoth and Leviathan for standing out against their environment, they are nonetheless pulled under YHWH's gaze and become objects of YHWH's fascination at the most detailed, minute level.

This "mathematicalization" of the dynamically sublime objects is especially evident in Brown's recent interpretation. He claims that the speeches transport Job to the very places its questions imply that he has not been, seen, known. In itself, this paradox is not new, but his description alerted me to the sense in which the standard reading is misleading—according to it, God's speeches are dilatatic; they intend to broaden Job's vision beyond himself and toward the vast and variegated cosmos. All the broadening will be misread if one remains within the logic of extension, imagining something external to the cosmos on account of which it extends beyond the borders of some previous consideration. Within this misleading logic, the limits displayed by the speeches—the limits of Job's knowledge of the world, of Job's power and capabilities, of the world's coherence, its denizens, environs, and so on—remain external to the world, defining it as if from beyond it (as in the tragic structure). Instead, the speeches' excessive inclusion of all that appears to stand out stems from God's primary fascination and concern with an internal limit to the cosmos, an inherent limit that defines the cosmos's very nature, a limit that divides even one scale from another on the underside of the king of all the proud:

> [Job] is flung far off to "the gates of death" and dragged next to Leviathan's underbelly, zooming in close enough to view the infinitesimal space that separates one scaly shield from another. Vast disparities of scale are dramatically covered as Job is taken across incalculable distances and depths.[86]

In the end, I believe that the speeches are principally concerned more with this internal incalculability that characterizes the mathematical sublime than they are with the transcendent, unaccounted for spaces that characterize the dynamical sublime. Furthermore, it is just such an immanent limit that serves as the "missing link" tying God's speeches to Job's in an alliance between two enduringly separate perspectives that together outline the emerging contours of a new wisdom.

7

Ethics and the Ending

Must one smash their ears before they learn to listen with their eyes?
—F. Nietzsche, *Thus Spoke Zarathustra*

§79 Introduction

This chapter first considers a recent trend in biblical studies to embrace
character ethics as the privileged discourse for articulating the ethical
implications of biblical texts and, in particular, of wisdom literature. After
introducing this trend I make explicit numerous fatal problems that my
approach to JOB poses to any attempt to privilege character in one's approach to the book. For character ethics, as practiced by certain key figures in biblical studies, the fundamental framework and inevitable condition of all ethical formation is a process of character development, a
dialogical negotiation of communal standards and values in light of the
community's ongoing experiences and developing knowledge. Job, however, emerges as an ethical subject at the moment of a traumatic experience of rupture from his past and himself. He struggles not to negotiate
his experience with communal standards, but to discern and articulate
how the truth revealed to him by his experience exposes the distance that
separates him and his burgeoning knowledge from the previous situation's misconceptions. The second part of this chapter turns to JOB's final
chapter. My treatments of Job's (in)famous second response to YHWH
(42:1–6) and the subsequent prose conclusion (42:7–17) continue to develop this book's previous analyses which, in their light, appear anew.

§80 The (Re)Turn to Virtue Ethics

Aristotle is usually credited as the progenitor of character ethics, if not
ethics in general, with his founding document, the *Nicomachean Ethics*.[1]

Virtue ethics thrived in medieval thought influenced by Thomas Aquinas, suffered attack from some Reformers, including Luther,[2] and from "natural law" philosophers such as Grotius, was eclipsed by moral systems of modernity such as Kantian and utilitarian consequentialist, but notably returned to prominence in the second half of the twentieth century, especially in the work of ethicists such as Alasdair MacIntyre and theologians such as Stanley Hauerwas.[3]

The reclamation of virtue ethics is no simple repetition of Aristotle or Aquinas, but instead adopts many of the paradigmatic changes brought about in modernity.[4] Scholars most often define the ethic ushered in by modernity as a transition away from the premodern Western practice of grounding ethics in life, in being, in an order that is the natural and right form of society. Premodern, hierarchical societies are often rooted in ontological ideas about the goodness of their arrangement (in the well-known medieval arrangement, there are those who pray, those who fight, and those who work). The arrangement of functions is not perceived as contingent but natural, cosmological, and divine. The result is a complementarity of the social body—the body being an important metaphor throughout this tradition—such that it can, when arranged in right relation, function as a cosmological whole enabling the flourishing and excellence of all its parts. The ethic, therefore, asks how one should live and it strives for virtuous excellence according to the extent possible and to one's allotted role. So, while deep mutuality and a strong sense of co-dependence are present, these mutual and codependent relations are rooted in a normative, hierarchical order that permeates the substance of all creation.

Modern thought's departure from this virtue ethic is fundamentally related to its view of every distribution of social functions as contingent, and its axiom of universal human equality. With the rise of universal humanity, no structure of social organization or differentiation could define the good, and every such structure could only be justified or judged instrumentally. This is not to say that there are no normative principles, no sense of order, and no complementarity. On the contrary, the new order aims to ensure for each of its members certain minimal rights and freedoms. Each of society's members is obliged to respect one another and participate actively and productively in the social order that secures their rights and freedoms. No longer is one a moral agent only within the social order, judged according to one's virtuous participation in a hierarchical complementarity; now citizens are judged as free agents, ultimately responsible to God and the moral law. Rather than trying to play a rightful role, individuals must now decide what the right thing to do is. In short, in premodern thought, the order is considered primary, real, and effective; the lives within it are responsible to it; and it aims to further human flourishing. In modern thought, the individual is considered primary, the order contingent and instrumental, and the individual responsible for reforming and reinventing this order so as to improve its ability to secure the basic rights of its subjects. Thus it is often wrongly said that individualism arises at the cost of a social ethic and communal bond. On the contrary, individualism brings a different social ethic and communal bond.[5]

The recent reclamation of virtue ethics returns to the premodern question *How should one live?* out of frustration with several characteristics of modern moral systems, not all of which are equally well founded. First, virtue ethics rejects the way the modern question *How should one act?* separates persons from their actions. "If a person is forced to ask about how to act without at the same time seeing the answer to that question as being related to one's particular life, then one's relation to morality becomes fissured."[6] Virtue ethics also rejects modernist ethics' tendencies to be hostile to emotions and to rely on various false conceptions of a transcendental, a priori, autonomous, and/or rational ethical agent. In other words, the return to virtue ethics is in large part motivated by a rejection of a perception of modern ethics' false premises concerning what is possible for human beings.

The new virtue ethics thinks modern thought makes two big mistakes. The first is to treat individuals as too autonomous, too capable of making unconditioned decisions about actions. Virtue ethicists reject the idea that moral agents or their ideas about morality could exist prior to or beyond the conditions of their socially contextualized lives. Second, modern moral thought treats the Symbolic order as too disconnected from the Real when it prohibits moral reflection beyond action to lives. Despite modernity's apparent intentions to protect certain freedoms and to protect ethics from being reduced to an effect of the existing social order, virtue ethics rejects the prohibition against asking how people should live because virtue ethics denies that actions can be divorced from life conditions. If actions necessarily stem from and in turn affect a person's life and character, then life, experience, desire, and actions are ethical through and through. The ethicist therefore cannot avoid investigating the relationship that links actions to life, and exploring the ethical conclusions that could be drawn from this relationship.

In light of the renewed interest in wisdom literature in the second half of the twentieth century, as well as the concurrent return to classical forms of ethical inquiry, it is no surprise that scholars have recently mined wisdom literature for ethical insight from the perspective of neo-Aristotelian virtue ethics. At the center of the recent embrace of virtue ethics as the privileged hermeneutic for ethical explorations of biblical and wisdom literature stands W. Brown, on whose work my reflections focus.[7] Brown draws on the shared use of the term "character" in literary and ethical discourses to explain the way his approach joins ethical inquiry with literary analysis. After the previous section, it should be clear that this aligns with what I characterized as the postmodern return to the premodern ethical question *How should one live?*[8] Brown's approach seeks the ethical character of a person and community in their perception,[9] intention (evident in the thread that unites their decisions and actions), and virtues. Virtues are normative dispositions—habits, attitudes, thoughts, emotions—"that dispose one to a consistency of certain action and expression"[10] that "makes good he who has it and renders good his work."[11] While virtues resemble and consist of habits, skills, abilities, and moral standards, virtue ethicists insist on their distinctiveness: *unlike habits*, virtues are not automatic but instead elevate one's rational and volitional capacities;[12] *unlike skills*, virtues do not guarantee success; *unlike abilities*, virtues are not potential but exercised and used; *unlike moral principles*, virtues take into account intentions, motivations, and the exigencies of situations.

The aim of virtue ethics remains as it was at the beginning: to cultivate and enable human flourishing or happiness, a chief end that each virtue supposedly serves. But exactly what such happiness and flourishing look like is unclear and must be continually renegotiated by the community. Thus the new virtue ethicists ultimately define virtue in ways that are close to the Kantian terms they often decry: on one hand, I must adjudicate the virtuous dimension of what I do, say, or think by relating it to some transcendent rules or values; on the other, virtue is declared an end in itself, an immanent or intrinsic judge of what one says, does, thinks, or feels.[13]

§81 Character Ethics, Wisdom Literature, and the Joban Prose Tale

According to Brown, what Proverbs, Job, and Qohelet share "from a character standpoint is that all three chart the self as it starts from a central, familiar locale that provides expected security and identity. But the moral subject does not remain in this position for long; it moves into certain realms of liminality, to the frontiers of community, creation, and knowledge."[14] In each case different characters, virtues, and dispositions are (re)formed:

- in Proverbs the son learns to associate all that maintains and strengthens the communal bond with wisdom, and all that threatens that bond with folly, as he steps out of the family and into the larger community;

- Job suffers the destruction of all communal bonds and the undermining of every norm. By Job's grievances, protests, and sense of entitlement he comes to understand his solidarity with the dynamic, strange, free, insecure, and incalculable. YHWH's speech from the whirlwind then compels him to "return home in humble gratitude and service to his community" and to those at its margins;[15] and
- Qohelet is catapulted by despair out of the monotonous repetition of his miserable life, only to find that there is no telos and existence is meaningless. Yet he thereby achieves a new perspective on the fleeting pleasures that alone can be enjoyed.

Brown has his favorite—Proverbs[16]—and yet insists that they cannot be synthesized and that none emerges as normative:

> [T]hese portraits of character are part of a larger canvas: the inclusive, empathetic community of God's good creation, one filled with enjoyment and potency as well as suffering and consolation. Such wisdom calls for a greater humility regarding humanity's place in the cosmos and, concomitantly, a greater sense of responsibility toward all of life.[17]

In what follows I argue that most of what I have said thus far about the book of Job is excluded from or even extinguished by Brown's liberal-humanist ethical canvas.[18] In the dialogue Job does not try to include or respect those with whom he differs; he either opposes or is indifferent toward them. From YHWH's speeches Job does not learn to assume his place in the cosmos, but that those (dis)placed in the cosmos exceed its bounds and relate to one another as aliens. And in the prose conclusion, Job does not gain a greater sense of responsibility toward all life; he compiles a community on the basis of the particular truth of his experience. All of these points merit elaboration.

First, consider the "critique of pure fear" that *haśśāṭān* issues to traditional wisdom in 1:9. His question defines the truly wise act as unconditional by abstracting it from the conditions that may influence piety, and then he asks whether such an unconditional act is possible. The tale's resounding "yes" utterly opposes virtue ethics' unequivocal "no" since virtue ethics does not allow for an unconditioned act. The subjective position of unconditional fear falls outside the bounds of an ethic conceived in terms of character and community or virtue and duty. The fear of God for naught disallows that any appeal to virtue or duty, or that any reliance on historical experience or communal goods, could serve as incentives for an authentically wise act. The prose introduction divorces WISDOM from any sort of humanistic concern for others and instead founds it on an event that subtracts the subject from its conditions, even reducing it to abject destitution. The wise subject becomes the one who perseveres with the burden and trajectory of this event that breaks her out of a past situation. In a sense I agree with virtue ethics: WISDOM's genesis in a particular event renders it specific and immanent to a situation. WISDOM cannot be grasped as an *ethic in general* or as a Kantian *transcendental a priori*. What virtue ethics cannot allow is that the WISDOM that Job must display could be both *particular* to his situation and *universal* for his situation. Job's particular experience renders him non-particular, the incarnation of *nepeš* as such, the limit of experience for all in his situation.[19] The prose introduction clearly intends to depict the event out of which these limits emerge as a quintessentially unanticipatable incident, something to which the situation's internal logic renders it blind. Thus, while these limits are produced by a situation, their appearance within the situation nonetheless breaks the one who follows them out of that situation. The universal appeal of Job's experience is evident in the generality and anonymity of his responses in the prose tale, in his linkage of his experience to the universal ways of God, as well as in his rejection of his wife's attempt to reduce his experience to a particular, contingent anomaly that could only be escaped through death. Realizing that the limits that Job embodies are immanent to the situation from which he is torn is especially crucial because it requires one to explore the logical reasons why these limits are universal for this situation and so hopefully resists any facile veneration of Job's abjection. That is, his abjection alone does not cause him to embody the universal truth of his situation.

Virtue-based interpretations predominately frame ethical conduct within a notion of character that includes, restricts, and/or eliminates any idea of excess. The focus falls both on characters located within a stream of history and tradition whose identities are in flux—but never absent[20]—and on virtues that must be recontextualized, reapplied, and revised—but never decontextualized. In the end, character ethics is framed and led by its interest in "coherence," "consistency," "normativity," "wholeness," and "identity":

> [C]haracter is more than the sum of its contituent parts. The shape of character entails an organized, harmonious unity. . . . From Aristotle's perspective, the exercise of the virtues requires a unity of the soul in its three elements—perception, intelligence, and desire. Cast another way, there is an *integrity* to the person of character, a wholeness or completeness regarding the exercise of virtue. Such a holistic notion of integrity is crucial to biblical wisdom, particularly in the character of Job.[21]

While virtue ethics does not imagine any simple (that is, non-complex) integrity, identity, or consistency, a degree of complexity or even a transformation of content bears not on the integral, identical, and consistent frame within which ethical conduct occurs.

Unlike character ethics' consistent frame, my reading repeatedly uncovers and analyzes numerous excessive elements that the prose tale presents as necessary components at the heart of the ethical act. By "excessive" I mean those crucial elements in the prose tale that exceed a mutually exclusive alternative. First, the subjective stance of unconditional fear is a surplus beyond the alternative between pious and impious activity. Second, in the first affliction it is clear—and it is confirmed by YH-WH's description of it—that everything readers have been told about Job is systematically "swallowed up." YHWH claims to have destroyed Job and then leaves behind an unrecognizable *nepeš* of what once was Job. This *nepeš* that "Job" now is exceeds the mutually exclusive alternative between Job's pre-afflicted and post-afflicted character since nothing about Job's character supplies any continuity. Through numerous devices the narrative forecloses any sense of continuity. Just consider how inappropriate it sounds to refer to Job's experience as a "transformation." In the end Job becomes a *nepeš* completely discontinuous with what we previously thought of as Job. Third, Job performs several mourning rites and sits outside the social body, amidst its excesses, atop a trash heap or, in the Greek tradition, dunghill (see page 57). There he scrapes himself with a potsherd. The details are crucial. Job is not just outside the social body, excluded from it as an animal, foreigner, or unclean person; Job is positioned in a particular place reserved for that which the social body excretes from itself. The excesses pushed out of the pores of town and body define Job's position, which exceeds the mutually exclusive alternatives of inside and outside the social body (on the trash heap), and inside and outside his own body (his excreting boils). Fourth, Job's friends do not recognize him and relate to him as if he were already dead. Here again Job occupies an excessive position, an unrecognizable, undead monster removed from the mutually exclusive alternatives of life and death.

In these four examples the prose tale unequivocally displays an excessive component at the core of its ethic—an excess that I have identified throughout with Lacan's *objet petit a*. There is a lack of unity or an incoherence, a dislocated or excessive element that must be present within a situation in order for ethical conduct to occur. Like Job to his friends, this component can never be visible to those who read through the lens of character ethics.

Furthermore, the character of God in the prose tale acts in ways that directly oppose the sense of character on which virtue ethics relies. Character ethics rightly points out and rejects some mistakes of the previous generation's focus on "God's mighty acts in history."[22] Such efforts were plagued by the vestiges of a supernaturalist, transcendent God who intervenes into history and creation from some place beyond them. Instead, character ethics embraces notions of creation and community as foundational and singular planes on which all characters work themselves out—divine and human alike.[23] While character ethics commendably investigates God in the texts as variously characterized and operative with desires, interests, guilt, enjoyment, laudable virtues, and deplorable vices, all the weight of transcendence that character ethics thinks it has unloaded remains present in this notion of a foundational and singular plane. This foundation often comes in the form of a divinely willed, ahistorical, and transcendent notion of creation or community. The prose tale destroys just such a foundation by identifying it as the very thing that renders imperceptible what the tale defines as an ethical act. YHWH's activity not only fails to adhere to the notion of a singular plane within which human experience and history unfold, YHWH acts precisely so as to ensure that no such foundation exists. God may be a developing character but this development is not a comprehensible background for all character development. Instead, God acts (at the ethical moment!) as the force that keeps character, community, and creation from ever establishing any foundation or background.

Granted that the prose tale establishes that any Joban ethic will be anti-foundational, does this mean that it is akin to some sort of poststructural, anti-essentialist celebration of difference, multiplicity, and fragmentation? I think not, as the following section demonstrates by drawing on Job's testimony in the dialogue, which may seem an unlikely source given Job's focus on his shattering experience of anxiety.

§82 The Dialogue and Character-Based Readings

In the dialogue Job testifies to an experience that challenges the idea that the prose tale's clearly anti-foundationalist ethic ends in a celebration of difference and multiplicity. Job repeatedly cites a disruptive experience that I discussed at length in §52. In this experience Job describes himself as a desiring subject whose pursuits are repeatedly frustrated when he stumbles against an impediment that is a part of himself and yet displaced from himself such that he experiences it as a foreign obstruction. Job links this experience of self-estrangement and autoimmunity to the work of God. God is the one who prevents any foundation from settling, but this is not because God fragments, multiplies, or differentiates a foundation; it is rather because God appears in the splitting of an entity from itself. Job is not impeded because he pursues or crashes into an infinite difference, a transcendent Other, or a countless multitude, but because he runs into himself. In short and at the risk of unfairly reducing complex figures in contemporary ethics, an ethic that takes Job's testimony in the dialogue into account will neither sound like a Levinasian concern with responsibility to the unfathomable abyss of the Other, nor a Deleuzian concern with celebrating new and proliferating subjectivities. It will instead be concerned primarily with a subject that is capable of operating independently of itself and others.

While Job's testimony in the dialogue departs from a postmodern ethic that celebrates otherness, difference, and multiplicity, it comes no closer to an ethic based on character. Job's testimony in the dialogue challenges the attempt to treat character ethics as the proper horizon for wisdom hermeneutics from a different angle than that of the prose tale. While the tale displays an *objective* excess that disrupts every background to character formation, the dialogue shifts the lens to the *subject* and yet no less problematizes recourse to character as ethical. Job is not primarily concerned with identity. Job does not struggle with integrating disparate or foreign elements into his sense of self, because Job lacks any framework within which such incorporating activity could take place.[24] Job repeatedly insists that he does not coincide with himself, and yet he never achieves any sort of perspective on his split selves. Job is fundamentally alienated from *and* essentially attached to himself. Job's primary concern is not with fusing his sense of self with that part of himself that he confronts as foreign, but rather with understanding the cause that produces his difference from himself. He struggles to grasp his uncanny experience and he ultimately locates his salvation not in a future fusion of himself or in a strong and secure self, but in his willingness to betray his sense of self so as to explore his current condition as the venue that opens onto a transformed and unknown future. I cannot imagine a character-based approach that could explore this sense of salvation.

Brown strongly differentiates the characters and virtues that each of the three main wisdom books depicts, and yet he sees them as "part of a larger canvas"[25] whose internal differences illustrate "the *developmental* nature of wisdom as one rooted in the *continuum* of character."[26] For Brown, each book begins with a character that is firmly rooted in a context that is subsequently altered. Each character then develops and adapts in various ways to its new environment such that each book "does not conclude with the self in limbo, severed from its point of departure. . . . All three main characters in the wisdom books end with a full profile of character formed or reformed."[27] Each character returns to its transformed context as a more full and virtuous character. Character and context develop on a continuum.

Brown treats the developments within each book as a model for reading the three books on a continuum. Their differences illustrate different moments within the ethical life of an ever fluctuating and developing character and community. Characters are always formed against the background of their community, and thus the community's different contexts require it to tolerate different moral characters.[28] The differences within and between the books result from the different contexts they describe. Brown takes the canon's inclusion of all three as a model for the proper ethical community, which is "more than pedagogical" since it provides "established structures of interdependence and support" within which different characters are free to form.[29] The ideal sagacious community tolerates differences and freedoms so long as they do not engender moral fascists or sectarian divisions, "for both roads cut off the possibility of genuine, informed dialogue as well as new frontiers of empathy and fellowship."[30]

From the perspective of Job's testimony, Brown's ideal ethical community is problematic because it fails to account for many of his speeches' ethical implications. This ideal community could only see Job's split subjectivity as a problem in need of overcoming. Recall that Brown repeatedly emphasizes the importance to the ethical subject of integrity, consistency, wholeness, and identity, whereas Job insists that he is stricken with division through and through. Moreover, Job ultimately places his hope nowhere other than in his experience of division. Job's perseverance with respect to what overturns him in the prose tale is just like the resolve he expresses in the dialogue that is precipitated by his experience of shame. His perseverance and his resolve are adopted after experiences of rupture and both carry Job into situations whose consequences he cannot comprehend since they are fundamentally discontinuous with the preceding situation. One cannot accept the book's presentation of these acts as models of truly ethical behavior and Brown's description of perpetual character development as the inevitable condition of ethical formation. Brown's description preserves what the book's presentation destroys—the sense of a single subjective continuity and a continuum of ethical formation. Job "favors models of, as it were, punctuated as opposed to gradual evolution."[31] Job's ethical subjectivity is not generated out of the unfolding, dialogical interactions between his present experiences, past history, personal convictions, and community's values. Instead, Job emerges as an ethical subject at the moment of a traumatic experience of rupture from his present and his past. His subjectivity is incommensurable with his past self and the community with which he sits and speaks. Job's struggle in the dialogue to grasp the ethical implications of his experience is not a result of his community's failure to provide him with interdependency and mutual support, but of a unique subjectifying event that ushers in a new reality.

§83 42:1–6: Text, Translation, and Structure

JOB's final chapter contains Job's (in)famous second response to YHWH's speeches (42:1–6), followed by an equally (in)famous prose conclusion (42:7–17). Translating and, a fortiori, understanding Job's second response is notoriously difficult. The following supplies a provisional starting point:

Job 42:1–6: Text and Translation

wayya'an 'iôb 'et-YHWH wayyō'mar	1	Then Job answered YHWH and said,
yāda 'tî kî–kōl tûkāl	2a	I know[1] that you can do all things,
uˀlō'–yibbāṣēr mimmˀkā mˀzimmāh	2b	and no purpose is beyond you.
mî zeh ma'lîm 'ēṣâ bˀlîdā'at	3a	Who is this obscuring counsel without knowledge?[2]
lākēn higgadtî 'ābîn	3b	Thus I spoke and I did not understand,
niplā'ôt mimmennî uˀlō' 'ēdā'	3c	wonders beyond me that I knew not.
šˀma'–nā' uˀ'ānōkî 'ˀdabbēr	4a	Hear, and I will speak;
'eš'ālkā uˀhôdî'ēnî	4b	I will ask you and you inform me.[3]
lˀšēma'–'ōzen šˀma'tîkā	5a	By the hearing of the ear I heard you,[4]
uˀ'attâ 'ênî rā'ātkā	5b	and now my eye sees you.[5]
'al–kēn 'em'as	6a	Therefore I reject and I am consoled
uˀniḥamtî 'al–'āpār wā'ēper	6b	concerning dust and ashes.[6]

1. While I read with the Qere, the Kethib ("you know") is also possible. There is no reason to think that Job means to imply that he knows something that YHWH does not. As for Job's knowledge, even if Job says "You know that you can do all things . . ." the fact that Job is the speaker requires us to understand an implicit "I know," as in, "[I know that] You know that you can . . ."

2. Job's question nearly quotes God's in 38:2: "Who is this darkening (*maḥšîk*) counsel with words without knowledge?"

3. Again Job quotes God, who spoke these words in 38:3b and 40:7b.

4. While this wooden translation lacks elegance, I render it literally so as to preserve the continuation of hearing from the imperative in v.4 through its two occurrences in this line.

5. Here I follow the argument of Edwin M. Good, *In Turns of Tempest: A Reading of Job, with a Translation* (Stanford, Calif.: Stanford University Press, 1990), 373-75; see also Carol A. Newsom, "The Book of Job," vol. 4 of *The New Interpreter's Bible*, ed. L. Keck (Nashville: Abingdon, 1996), 628. In contrast to most interpreters—e.g., E. Dhorme, *A Commentary on the Book of Job* (Nashville: T. Nelson, 1984), 646; Marvin H. Pope, *Job*, 3rd ed. (Garden City, N.Y.: Doubleday, 1973), 347; John E. Hartley, *The Book of Job* (Grand Rapids: Eerdmans, 1988), 536—I doubt that the "now" that begins this line distinguishes present, firsthand seeing from past, secondhand hearing (see also Ps 18:44[45] and Isa 11:3). Instead, since Job has been listening to YHWH for nearly four chapters, and since Job alludes in v.4 to YHWH's command to "hear" in 40:7b, Job's response in v.5 assures YHWH that he has heard and even now sees YHWH.

6. I discuss the translation and meaning of this difficult line below. Thorough philological and grammatical analyses have been provided by Ellen Van Wolde, "Job 42,1–6: The Reversal of Job" in *The Book of Job*, ed. W. A. M. Beuken (Leuven: Leuven University Press, 1994), 223–50; and William Morrow, "Consolation, Rejection, and Repentance in Job 42:6," *Journal of Biblical Literature* 105 (1986): 211–25; see also Newsom *Job*, 627–29.

Interpretive difficulties extend from v.2 to v.6. The *translation* of each word in vv.2–5 is rarely a problem, yet the *meaning* of these verses is deeply disputed. Far from clarifying matters, v.6 brings a host of translational difficulties and occupies the lion's share of critical attention on the passage.[32] The passage is structured with one enveloping and two enframed parallelisms; each concerns the relationship between YHWH and Job, divinity and humanity:

A	Job's second-order reflections about YHWH	v.2
B	Job quotes YHWH's statement about him	v.3a
C	Job's testimony in response to YHWH's statement	v.3bc
B'	Job quotes YHWH's statement about him	v.4
C'	Job's testimony in response to YHWH's statement	v.5
A'	Job's second-order reflections about YHWH	v.6

Figure 9: Job 42:2–6—Enframing and Enframed Parallelisms

Job's opening statement in v.2 presents two theological judgments: the first affirms that YHWH can do all things; the second denies that any purpose is impossible for YHWH. Job quotes two of YHWH's statements about and to him in vv.3a and 4, to which he responds in vv.3bc and 5. In v.3 Job first cites one of YHWH's rhetorical questions that positions Job as one who "darkens counsel," then Job admits that he spoke without understanding.[33] Job cites YHWH again in v.4, though this time he cites YHWH's commands that he hear what YHWH says and asks, and that he respond by informing YHWH.[34] Job's response in v.5 claims that he has heard and now sees God. The "therefore" (*'al–kēn*) that introduces v.6 marks it as his concluding statement.

The final verse of Job's response requires an extended discussion because it brings a host of interpretive difficulties and conflicting proposals from scholars. While I limit this discussion to a few central issues, "Almost every word in this verse raises questions."[35] The first issues arise from the first verb, *'m's*. There are two roots for the three consonants *m's*, one means "to despise, reject, or [perhaps] feel loathing," and the other, which is likely a byform of *mss*, means "to waste away, to flow out or flow away."[36] The first occurs frequently, the second rarely. The Septuagint includes both, but most interpreters choose the first.[37] The lack of any object that would be rejected or despised poses problems for this choice. The verb is usually transitive, but in five notable instances—notable because four occur in Job—it lacks a clear object, which may suggest that it also has an intransitive form (Ps 89:38[39]; Job 7:16; 34:33; 36:5; 42:6). Many reject the intransitive reading and offer various explanations for each case—textual corruption, another object serves double duty, etc.—

but no argument carries the day for which object one should choose when reading the verb transitively.[38] As in my translation of 7:16 on page 121, in light of the larger function this verb assumes throughout the dialogue (as in 5:17; 8:20; 9:21; 10:3), I deliberately leave it on its own and without an object since I find the indeterminacies this may produce more palatable than limiting Job's rejection to a particular object.

I want to raise a second set of questions about the second verb: *nhmty*. Numerous translations could be justified.[39] Though there is only one root, again there are two basic semantic domains to choose from (unless one reads a double entendre). *nhm* can have a range of meanings such as "to regret, be sorry, be moved to pity, repent (of), or relent," or it can have a range of meanings such as "to comfort or console oneself, to be comforted or consoled, to observe a time of mourning, or to find consolation about something." The most important data for my translation are the other occurrences of *nhm* with the preposition *'al*, and the other occurrences of *nhm* within the book of Job. When the preposition *'al* governs the object of the verb *nhm*, that object is often *r'h* ("bad, evil, wicked") or, in one instance, its regular pair *tbh* ("good, pleasing, delightful")—in this case *r'h* is present earlier in the verse.[40] This strongly suggests that *nhm* + *'al* + *r'h* is a conventional way of saying that a subject repents or relents over an evil, wicked, or bad thing. In other verses, such as Job 42:6, where *nhm* is followed by *'al* but not *r'h* or *tbh*, *nhm* predominately has the consolatory sense (Ps 90:13; Jer 31:15; Ezek 32:31; 2 Sam 13:39).

The other occurrences of *nhm* in JOB, when considered in their contexts, buttress the case to read the consolatory sense in 42:6:

- In the prose conclusion, just after 42:6 and his restoration, Job's brothers, sisters, and friends "console" him in 42:11.
- In the prose tale Job's friends come to "console" him after his affliction in 2:11.
- In the dialogue, Job imagines that his bed will "comfort" him in 7:13.
- Job refers to the friends as "labored comforters" (*mnhmy 'ml*) in 16:2.
- Job asks his friends how they can "comfort" him with nothingness (*hebel*) in 21:34.
- In Job's final speech he remembers living like one who "comforts" mourners in 29:25.

Because *nhm* with *'al* but without *r'h* or *tbh* predominately has the consolatory sense, and because *nhm* clearly has a consolatory sense in *all* six of its other occurrences in JOB, I translate it with this sense in its seventh occurrence in 42:6.

§84 From Recognizing a Transcendent Limit . . .

Across all kinds of different interpretations, the predominate sense is that in 42:1–6 Job recognizes a limit to his situation with respect to something that transcends it and defines it.[41] Perhaps Job submits because he accepts his insignificance, or because he is comforted about his insignificance.[42] Perhaps Job remains defiant but finally accepts that God is a brutal sovereign.[43] Or perhaps Job accepts the limits of his condition by means of God's perspective on it.[44] In these and many other interpretations, Job's response acknowledges the limits of his finite knowledge (v.3bc) and his mortal body (v.6b) with respect to wonders (v.3c) and a God (v.5) that transcend them. On this reading, which I also discuss on page 190, Job's response testifies to his experience of momentarily and miraculously transcending the limits of his condition so that he could perceive his condition as limited with respect to a transcendent realm that escapes and remains untouched by his condition's limitations of finitude and mortality.

This standard interpretation fundamentally errs by treating mortality ("dust and ashes" in v.6b) and finitude (ignorance in v.3bc) as negative limitations that prevent Job from accessing wonders (v.3c) and God (v.5), which lie beyond him. I have consistently argued that Job rejects and critiques this idea that a negative limit constrains the subject with respect to figures of transcendence. Because this reading defines Job's limitations with respect to entities in a realm that transcends him, it requires one to imagine that YHWH's speeches somehow allow or enable Job to escape the limitations of his human condition and come to know (about) something that one who is subject to these limitations could not know. Balentine puts this position well when he claims that Job finally accepts his destiny "to live at the dangerous intersection between the merely human and the supremely divine."[45]

But why should one accept that Job's (human) conditions place him outside a (divine) realm of wonders and God that he somehow exceptionally experiences? No good reason exists, and Job's second response actually refutes the idea that the limits of knowledge and mortality are opposed to God and to wonders. That is, we need a complete shift of perspective on Job's statements so that they can be correctly seen as an affirmation of his finite and mortal conditions as the conditions within which God and wonders appear and can be perceived. Job does not say that God miraculously and momentarily excludes him from his limited conditions such that his eye sees God. On the contrary, Job approvingly cites God's statements about him that imply that the limits of his conditions are unlimited.

§85 . . . to Affirming an
Immanent Condition

The alternative reading I am proposing adheres to the same logical opposition to which I have returned repeatedly in this book. Transcendence
is not the only structure by which something can be limited. One thing
can be limited not only by something that transcends it, but also by its
own immanent condition. Since Job says nothing to suggest that he has
been excluded from the limits of his conditions, and since he says that
the divine and wondrous have appeared to him, then we should enter-
tain the idea that the divine and the wondrous appear to him *within* his
conditions of limitation, and thus that Job's body and mind are contaminated not only by ignorance and death, but also by the divine and the
wondrous. Job's response opposes the idea that his limits are limits with
respect to something external or transcendent, and it suggests instead
that it is precisely through such limited conditions that anything divine
and wondrous appears. Recalling Nietzsche's quotation in this chapter's
epigraph, perhaps the divine and the wondrous are heard through the
eyes, after one's ears are smashed, and seen through the ears, after one's
eyes are crushed. In any case, things wondrous and divine can be seen
and heard at the zones of the ear and eye.

On this interpretation, v.6 is consistent with certain features of the
dialogue, especially the subjective position that I defined in CHAPTER 5
as shame, and of the prose introduction, especially Job's verbal responses
discussed in CHAPTER 2. The initial and final statements of Job's verbal
responses in the prose introduction are notably similar.

- In Job's first response in the prose tale: "the noun (Adonai) or predicate complement (naked; mother's womb/there) remains the same in
  each half, whereas the verbs are binary opposites (come forth/return;
  give/take)."[46]
- In Job's second response in the prose tale: "the verb ('receive') is the
  repeated term, whereas the contrast comes with the object, 'good' and
  'trouble'."[47]

So, in the prose introduction Job first declares that YHWH gives and takes,
and second he characterizes that which is given and taken as both good
and bad. In 42:6 Job again uses verbs that appear opposed with two objects that remain the same: he "rejects" and "is consoled" about the same
condition—"dust and ashes." Most interpreters think that by "dust and
ashes" Job characterizes his condition in a way that is either rejectable or
consolatory. But along the lines of his affirmations of apparent opposites

in the prose introduction, we should rethink the relationship between rejection and consolation as non-oppositional. Verses 6a and 6b would then present two balanced lines in which the first *waw* is a conjunction (not a disjunction) and the *atnach* indicates the balanced division between two strongly parallel lines (not the separation of the verb[s] from the objects):

therefore	I reject	and	I am consoled
'l–kn	*'m's*	*w–*	*nḥmty*
particle	verb 1	conjunction	verb 2
↕	↕	↕	↕
particle	object 1	conjunction	object 2
'l	*'pr*	*w–*	*'pr*
concerning	dust	and	ashes

Figure 10: Job 42:6—Syntactic Parallels

In short, Job rejects and is consoled about one and the same condition—dust and ashes. It is not difficult to understand Job's rejection of his condition, but why would he simultaneously claim to be consoled by it? Job has just indicated that God and things too wonderful for him are not beyond but are experienced within his mortal and finite conditions. That is, they are temporal, experienced in the passing of dust and ashes. If God and wonders are temporal, then the temporality of his condition is consolable because it means that God and wonders remain as open as he to transformation. This interpretation accords well with what I discovered about Job's subjective position of shame. In CHAPTER 5 I argued that Job's ultimate consolation in the dialogue derives from his realization that the unlimited openness of his condition is not lamentable but constitutes the only ground in which he can invest his hope. Thus in the dialogue as well as in his final response Job asserts that the ultimate groundlessness of his condition has not only opened him to rejectable conditions, it also keeps his conditions open to transformations in which he can hope.

In sum, in his final response to YHWH's whirlwind speeches, Job testifies that the limits of his knowledge and experience do not prevent but enable him to experience the divine and wonders that are beyond them. This beyond is not an outside, but a surplus that appears within his knowledge and experience as that which keeps them open to transformation and capable of exceeding themselves. Job's final testimony is consistent with his discovery in the dialogue that God is immanent to his conditions as that which keeps them from coinciding with themselves, and thus indefinitely open to transformation. Since God is immanent to his conditions, God is also subject to the unconditional openness of his conditions that has exposed him to radical transformation. Job can therefore both reject his particular conditions *and* find consoling hope that their unconditional groundlessness keeps them as well as God open to potential future transformation.

§86 42:7–17: JOB's Turn to Collectivity

JOB's prose conclusion narrates a scene that has elicited rejection *and* consolation from the most ethically naive to the most sophisticated readers.[48] Before considering the features of the narrative that most often instigate such reactions, it is worth reflecting on the ethical implications of the paltry space and detail that JOB devotes to this situation. While the conclusion is important, it is on the periphery of the book's ethical concerns. JOB's primary ethical concern is to depict the difficulty of experiencing, discerning, and articulating the WISDOM that derives from a particular event that forces a break with a past situation. The book stands as a witness to the great endurance required of one who seeks to articulate the consequences and truth of an unanticipated event for the situation in which it occurs.

JOB also devotes considerable attention to different opposition figures and their tactics for inhibiting ethical attempts to discern and articulate WISDOM. Representatives of the previous situation—from his wife in chapter 2 through Elihu in chapter 37 to many contemporary interpreters—bombard Job with various attempts to refer his experience to a realm that transcends the situation in which it occurs. When faced with an event that exceeds what a framework is capable of knowing, such appeals to a realm that transcends the situation may appear humble or even critical of that situation's framework. Even though they may serve one or another progressive cause at any moment, such appeals risk being conservative insofar as their exclusion of the event from the situation forecloses any attempt to hold the situation responsible for the event's consequences. In other words, humility before an unanticipated event can function to protect the framework that delimits what is (un)knowable from the event's unsettling implications. JOB depicts other opposition tactics as well, such as the appeal to a particular or contingent aspect of the situation that would explain an event from within what the situation is capable of understanding. In Job's case, this primarily takes the form of appeals to Job's guilt.[49] In short, the chief concerns of the materials that JOB offers for ethical reflection involve the importance, difficulty, and opposition that one may face in the ethical attempt to discern and articulate how an unanticipatable event can present the limits that define what a situation can and cannot know.

When compared to these larger issues, JOB's prose conclusion is meager in size and detail, and yet its ethical significance has not been and should not be overlooked. The conclusion illustrates several concrete practices of a community constituted with respect to the truth or WISDOM of an event. The first thing that the prose conclusion reports is that the community is constituted with respect to the truth of Job's words (42:7). This ethic is not respectful of all differences and opinions; it implies the falsity of the words of Eliphaz and his two friends. Reparations must be made for the friends' distorting falsities (v.8). YHWH commands the friends to take animals to "my servant Job" so that he can sacrifice them on their behalf, and so that "my servant Job" can pray over them, all so that YHWH's anger will subside and YHWH will not act against them since, we are told once again, they did not speak the truth like "my servant Job." The friends obey YHWH's command and YHWH looks favorably upon Job (v.9). YHWH returns to Job twice as much as Job previously had (v.10).

Several aspects of the scene recounted in vv.7–10 seem awkward. YHWH shifts perspective on Job's words—from "without knowledge" (cf. 38:2) to "true"—and on Job himself—from one who is excessively limited (who has not seen, does not know, has not been, etc.) to one who is excessively lauded as "my servant" (four times in two verses!). Second, there is the "restoration." Is this a retributive reward?[50] Is it "hush money"? Does Job "sell out"? Does this doubling double right back over the difficult issues raised by the book? Some may think so, but others read YHWH's command to the friends to get Job to sacrifice for them as a chance for Job to overcome any antagonism that remains after the dialogue between him and the friends, and to reconstitute the community as a place that sanctions the truth of his experience.[51]

In v.11, after over thirty-nine chapters, the scene returns to the intimate community of Job's brothers and sisters and "all who previously knew him." They bring him symbolic gifts: money—which will enable him to re-enter communal life—and jewelry—a signifier of value in excess of use-value. YHWH also gives Job great wealth (v.12). The gifts he receives from his family are homologous with the gifts he gives his daughters (vv.13–15). Job gives them very useful inheritances along with their brothers as well as aesthetically charged names that signify their value beyond their use-value. Their beauty, greater than that of any women in all the land, is enough to grab the attention even of this terse narrative. Job's gifts to his daughters are unusual and ethically charged since, according to ancient inheritance laws, daughters inherit only when there are no living male relatives. Their inheritances may free them from relying on their beauty and other means to secure their financial futures by procuring a hefty brideprice.[52] The community in vv.7–17 is beautiful and aesthetically charged, extensive in horizontal and vertical relations, and enduring over four generations and 140 years.

From my perspective, the most significant ethical aspect of the prose conclusion is its shift of focus from a subject-centered concern with Job's understanding, activities, and obedience, to Job's role in what constitutes and maintains the cultural, legal, and religious institutions of the community. From the outset the book focuses on the individual character of Job, and it often isolates and/or reveals Job's isolation from the community. Furthermore, much of the book's content suggests that one's neighbors in the community and the traditions that one inherits function as obstacles to ethical thought and activity, blinders to any attempt to discern an event and persevere in its truth. In other words, the book initially seems to offer little to help someone think about ethical matters beyond the individual and with respect to the community. The prose conclusion, however, shifts the focus toward the community and toward Job's role in what constitutes and maintains the collective.

§87 The Double Affirmations of Job and YHWH

Many readers feel surprised that, in the final chapter, both YHWH and Job seem to affirm one another. But recall my argument in CHAPTER 6 that, while Job and YHWH both speak as if their speech implies that the other is wrong, one should not treat them as externally opposed to one another. Instead of two different and clashing positions, on page 203 I evoked the figure of a Möbius strip to illustrate my sense that each stands on two sides of the same surface and mistakenly thinks that the other's stance on the other side implies that there is an edge between them. The Möbius strip is key because in it one need only persist on one side and not cross an edge in order to arrive at the other side—one surface, two sides. If we take the ontological implications of Job's testimony seriously, the kind of world it implies must be like the one YHWH describes: structurally incomplete and generative of wild, monstrous creatures. Alternatively, if we persist in thinking through the implications of the world YHWH describes, we will have to account not only for the beautiful and majestic monsters it relates, but also horrid and rancid ones like Job. The truth of YHWH's cosmos and of Job's experience is constituted only when they are read coterminously, such that one does not determine or oppose the other, and both are seen as two sides of the same truth.

CHAPTER 6's argument receives a further twist in Job 42's mutual affirmations. After so many chapters railing against God, Job says, "I know that you can do all things, and no purpose is beyond you. . . . I spoke and I did not understand, wonders beyond me that I did not know. . . . I heard you, and now my eye sees you" (42:2, 3, 5). After four chapters attacking Job, YHWH can hardly get a phrase out without refering to "my servant Job," and twice YHWH says to Eliphaz, "You did not speak truth to me like my servant Job" (vv.7, 8). Many read these two affirmations as strikingly incongruous with, if not vapid abandonments of, the previous speeches. After CHAPTER 6, however, the full weight of truth behind these affirmations can be recognized. Both YHWH and Job finally assume the truth of the other's speech as the truth of their own.

Therefore, rather than departures from the previous chapters, I propose that the affirmations in chapter 42 be read like a final twist in the plot of a psychological thriller that reveals what has been true all along. Throughout JOB these two main characters oppose one another at many levels until, at the end, each realizes that he has misapprehended his position in the opposition. At the end, YHWH and Job remain two different figures, and one does not require the other's destruction.[53] Instead, the truth of each of their positions is ultimately found on the side of the other. I could easily be misunderstood here. I do not mean that they could be added together to create one truth, or that the truth of each is outside of its position, or that the sense of opposition no longer holds between them. Thinking again of the Möbius strip, they complete each other's position in the sense that each one is always on the other side of the single-sided surface that their positions articulate. Each one occupies the place of the blind spot produced by the other's position; the other is positioned for each in the blind spot that his own position inherently produces. Neither is the completion or transcendental truth of the other. It only becomes clear that each occupies the place of the truth of the other's position once we change our perspective on that position. That is, the truth of one position that the other articulates or embodies is not evident from within that position, but only after we shift our perspective out of it. It is only after Job and YHWH encounter one another that they and we can shift perspective and grasp the truth about them from what the other says.

§88 The Coherent and Consistent Wisdom of JOB

This study has found that JOB clearly and consistently presents a single conception of WISDOM in opposition to the two-tiered conception of wisdom-and-Wisdom. My argument differs both from the older critical quest to discern a single, overarching message that brings the book's different voices to speak in one accord, as well as from the recent scholarly trend, at the forefront of which stands Newsom's work, to deny the possibility of such efforts at homogenization, and to articulate instead, on one hand, JOB's messages as multiple and ultimately heterogeneous and, on the other, the significance of the (lack of) relationship among them. My work breaks out of these apparently exhaustive possibilities—either unity or multiplicity—by accepting the recent arguments against abstract unity, and yet articulating the single, coherent issue that underlies and generates the book's multitude of voices. Ultimately the book of Job is fragmented and heterogeneous; it lacks an overarching or general message and it even includes messages that directly oppose attempts to read it through a unifying perspective. However, the multitude of messages in JOB all issue from a single, consistent struggle: to articulate and endorse a WISDOM theology that is immanent to a single though un-unified plane of existence in opposition to the tradition's two-tiered conception—one for what is available to human, finite, limited subjects, and another for theological ideas such as God and Wisdom that transcend and yet are indicated by the limits of human knowledge. JOB's struggle is, in other words, similar to the scholar's struggle to articulate JOB's own WISDOM. Just as I accept that JOB offers a series of heterogeneous messages, so too do I deny that the book consistently presents its WISDOM in opposition to Wisdom. On the contrary, it sometimes fails to persevere in its explorations of the immanent consequences of the presence of WISDOM (as when Job posits and desires such a transcendent realm in his use of the legal metaphor). However, these moments return to a realization of the ontological priority of WISDOM with respect to wisdom-and-Wisdom. So, while I have not suggested that the book presents a single, consistent position, I believe that I have demonstrated that a single, consistent issue informs its positions from beginning to end.

This book is therefore closely aligned with Adrian Johnston's monograph on Slavoj Žižek and Martin Hägglund's monograph on Jacques

Derrida.[54] Both Johnston and Hägglund argue that a single logic unifies and informs these two prolific philosophers whose wide-ranging works seem in many ways to resist systematization. So, for example, neither Žižek's "dizzying rampage through any and every disciplinary area and level of conceptual analysis,"[55] nor Derrida's so-called ethical or religious "turn," show evidence of inconsistencies or qualitative differences in the conceptual and theoretical apparatuses of these two thinkers. What they show instead are the deployments of the same apparatus into a plurality of areas that add to and do not detract from the persuasiveness of these apparatuses.[56] So too have I demonstrated that the plurality of Job's messages are best read as persuasive deployments of a consistent logic. I articulated this singular logic and these multiple messages by developing and organizing my arguments with respect to multiple oppositions—desire and drive, sacrifice and satisfaction, fear and anxiety, guilt and shame, and the dynamical and mathematical sublimes. Each has, on one side, a two-tiered structure in which an immanent plane is limited with respect to a transcendence that lies beyond it and, on the other, a transcendence that refers to the immanent plane's non-coincidence with itself on account of which it remains ever capable of generating beings that exceed it. The latter, immanent transcendence provides Job the only hope he maintains for moving beyond his conditions.

The book of Job's concluding moment follows and encourages Job's hope with its brief glimpse into a possible outcome of his experience. The ethical implications of YHWH's affirmation thus go much further than a celebration of Job's ethical triumph. YHWH does not only ordain Job's speech, YHWH's affirmation enables Job to reorient himself out of an individual and toward a collective struggle. The prose conclusion affords a glimpse of what could occur after a wise subject barges through the open space revealed by his conditions and constitutes a collective with respect to the truth that resounds within its gaping hole. There is perhaps no better way to end a book on Job than by evoking the political possibility that this singular book conjures through its final glimpse of a collective life that could be oriented around and find its vibrancy in no less, but also no more, than the figure—or rather, the event—of Job.

Appendix

Job 4–5: Text and Translation

wayya'an *ᵉlîpaz hattêmānî* *wayyō'mar*	4:1	Then Eliphaz the Temanite answered and said:
hᵃnissāh dābār 'ēlêkā til'eh	2a	If one tries a word with you, will you be wearied?
wa'ᵉṣōr bᵉmillîn mî yûkāl	2b	but who is able to restrain speech?
hinnê yissartā rabbîm	3a	Look, you have instructed many;
wᵉyādayim rāpôt tᵉḥazzēq	3b	and you strengthened the hands of the weary;
kôšēl yᵉqîmûn millêkā	4a	Your speech supported the stumbling;
ûbirkayim kōrᵉ'ôt tᵉ'ammēṣ	4b	and you made feeble knees firm.
kî 'attâ tābô' 'ēlêkā wattēle'	5a	But now it comes upon you and you are wearied;
tigga' 'ādêkā wattibbāhēl	5b	it touches you and you are terrified.
hᵃlō' yir'ātᵉkā kislātekā	6a	Is not your fear your confidence,[1]
tiqᵉwātᵉkā wᵉtōm dᵉrākêkā	6b	your hope the blamelessness of your ways?[2]
. . .		
zᵉkār-nā' mî hû' nāqî 'ābād	7a	Think now, what innocent person perishes;
wᵉ'êpō yᵉšārîm nikḥādû	7b	and where are the upright effaced?
ka'ᵃšer rā'îtî ḥōršê 'āwen	8a	Just as I have seen, those cultivating trouble
wᵉzōrᵉ'ê 'āmāl yiqṣᵉruhû	8b	and sowing misery reap the same
minnišmat ᵉlôah yō'bēdû	9a	From the breath of Eloah they perish;
ûmērûaḥ 'appô yiklû	9b	and from the spirit of his anger they are finished.
ša'ᵃgat 'aryê	10a	The roar of the *aryeh*-lion
wᵉqôl šāḥal	10b	and the voice of the *shaxal*-lion
wᵉšinnê kᵉpîrîm nittā'û	10c	and the teeth of the *kephir*-lion are removed.[3]
layiš 'ōbēd mibbᵉlî-ṭārep	11a	The *layish*-lion perishes from lack of prey,
ûbnê lābî' yitpārādû	11b	and the *labi'*-lions are scattered.[4]
. . .		
wᵉ'ēlay dābār yᵉgunnāb	12a	A word came to me furtively;
wattiqqaḥ 'oznî šēmeṣ menhû	12b	and my ear took a whisper from it;
biś'ippîm mēḥezyōnôt lāylâ	13a	amid anxieties from nightime visions,[5]
binpōl tardēmâ 'al-'ᵃnāšîm	13b	when deep sleep falls upon people;
paḥad qᵉrā'anî ûr'ādâ	14a	Dread befell me, and trembling,
wᵉrōb 'aṣmôtay hipḥîd	14b	so that the mass of my bones were in dread.
wᵉrûaḥ 'al-pānay yaḥᵃlōp	15a	Then a wind passed over my face,
tᵉsammēr śa'ᵃrat bᵉśārî	15b	a storm[6] made my flesh prickle.
ya'ᵃmōd wᵉlō'-'akkîr mar'ēhû	16a	It stood still, but I did not recognize its appearance;
tᵉmûnâ lᵉneged 'ēynāy	16b	a form was before my eyes;

APPENDIX

dᵉmāmâ wāqôl 'ešmā'	16c	silent, and then I heard a voice,[7]
	...	
haᵉᵛnôš mē'ᵛlôah yiṣdāq	17a	"Can a human be righteous before Eloah?
'im mē'ōśēhû yithar-gāber	17b	Or a person be pure before his maker?"
hēn ba'ᵃbādāyw lō' ya'ᵃmîn	18a	If[8] he does not trust his servants,
ûbᵉmal'ākāyw yāśîm tohᵒlāh	18b	and charges his messengers with folly,[9]
'ap šōknê bāttê-ḥōmer	19a	how much more will those dwelling in houses of clay,
'ᵃšer-be'āpār yᵉsôdām	19b	whose foundation is of clay,
yᵉdakkᵉ'ûm lipnê-'āš	19c	be crushed before a moth;[10]
mibbōqer lā'ereb yukkatû	20a	from morning to evening they may be shattered;
mibbᵉlî mēśîm lāneṣaḥ yō'bēdû	20b	they may perish forever without anyone understanding.[11]
hᵃlō'-nissa' yitrām bām	21a	Will their remnant[12] not be plucked up with them?
yāmûtû wᵉlō'bᵉḥākmāh	21b	They will die, without wisdom.
	...	
qᵉrā'-nā hᵃyēš 'ônekkā	5:1a	Call now! Is there anyone who will answer you?
wᵉ'el-mî miqqᵉdošîm tipneh	1b	To whom among the holy beings will you turn?
kî-le'ᵛwîl yahᵃrog-kā'aś	2a	Surely vexation[13] kills the fool,
ûpōteh tāmît qināh	2b	and passion slays the naive.[14]
'ᵃnî-rā'îtî 'ᵛwîl mašrîš	3a	I myself have seen a fool fixating,[15]
wā'eqqôb nāwēhû pit'ōm	3b	and I noted his habitation; suddenly,[16]
yirḥᵃqû bānāyw mîeša'	4a	His children are far from salvation,
wᵉyiddakkᵉ'û baššaᵅar wᵉ'ên maṣṣîl	4b	they are crushed at the city gate, with no one to help;
'ᵃšer qᵉṣîrô rā'ēb yō'kēl	5a	whose harvest the hungry will eat,
wᵉ'el-miṣṣinnîm yiqqāḥēhû	5b	and take it in baskets;
wᵉšā'ap ṣammîm ḥêlām	5c	trapped ones will pant after their wealth.[17]
kî lō'-yēṣē' mē'āpār 'āwen	6a	Surely trouble does not grow from the dirt,
ûmē'ᵃdāmā lō'-yiṣmaḥ 'āmāl	6b	nor does misery sprout from the ground.
kî-'ādām lᵉ'āmāl yûllād	7a	However, a human is born[18] to misery,
ûbnê-rešep yagbîhû 'ûp	7b	as sparks[19] fly high.
	...	
'ûlām 'ᵃnî 'edrōš 'el-'ēl	8a	But as for me I would seek El;
wᵉ'el-'ᵛlōhîm 'āśîm dibrātî	8b	and to Elohim I would present my word;
'ōśeh gᵉdōlôt wᵉ'ên ḥēqer	9a	who does marvels unfathomable,
niplā'ôt 'ad-'ên mispār	9b	wonders innumerable,
hannōtēn māṭār 'al-pᵉnê-'āreṣ	10a	who gives rain on the earth;
wᵉšōkēaḥ mayim 'al-pᵉnê ḥûṣôt	10b	and sends water on fields;
lāśûm šᵉpālîm lᵉmārôm	11a	sets[20] the lowly on high,
wᵉqōdᵉrîm śāgbû yeša'	11b	and the abject are elevated salvifically;[21]
mēpēr maḥšᵉbôt 'ᵃrûmîm	12a	who frustrates the machinations of the crafty,
wᵉlō'-ta'ᵃśênâ yᵉdêhem tûšîāh	12b	so that their hands do not achieve success;
lōkēd ḥᵃkāmîm bᵉ'ormām	13a	who captures the wise in their craftiness,
wa'ᵃṣat niptālîm nimhārāh	13b	and the plans of the crooked are precipitated.
yômām yᵉpagg'šû-ḥōšek	14a	Daily they encounter darkness,
wᵉkallaylâ yᵉmaš'šû baṣṣohᵃrāyim	14b	and at noon they grope as at night.
wayyōša' mēḥereb mippîhem	15a	But he saves from their sharp mouth,[22]

ûmîad ḥāzāq 'ebyôn	15b	and the needy from the hand of the strong;
watt^ehî laddal tiqwâ	16a	so hope exists for the poor,
w^e'ōlātâ qāpṣâ pîhā	16b	and wrongdoing shuts its mouth.
	. . .	
hinnê 'ašrê ^xnôš yôkiḥennû ^xlôah	17a	Look, blessed be the one whom Eloah reproves,
ûmûsar šadday 'al-tim'ās	17b	so do not reject the instruction of Shadday.
kî hû' yak'îb w^eyeḥbāš	18a	For he injures and he binds;
yimḥaṣ w^eyādô tirpênāh	18b	he smites but his hands heal.
b^ešēš ṣārôt yaṣṣîlekā	19a	Amidst six adversities, he will deliver you,
ûb^ešeba' lô'-yigga' b^ekā rā'	19b	amidst seven, no harm will touch you;
b^erā'āb pādkā mimmāwet	20a	Amidst famine, he will ransom you from death,
ûbmilḥāmâ mîdê ḥāreb	20b	amidst war, from the hands of the sword;
b^ešôṭ lāšôn tēḥābē'	21a	You shall be hidden amidst the scourge of the tongue,
w^elô'-tîrā' miššōd kî yābô'	21b	and you will not fear devastation when it comes;
l^ešōd ûkkāpān tiśḥāq	22a	You will laugh at devastation and starvation,
ûmēḥayyat hā'āreṣ 'al-tîrā'	22b	and you will not fear the creatures of the earth.
kî 'im-'abnê haśśādeh b^erîtekā	23a	For your covenant will be with the stones of the field,
w^eḥayyat haśśādeh hāšl^emâ-lāk	23b	and the creatures of the field will be peaceable with you.
w^eyāda'tā kî-šālôm 'oh^olekā	24a	You will know that your tent is at peace,
ûpāqadtā nāwkā w^elô' teḥ^eṭā'	24b	you will visit your habitation and will not fail.
w^eyāda'tā kî-rab zar'ekā	25a	And you will know that your progeny will be great,
w^eṣe'^xṣā'êkā k^e'ēśeb hā'āreṣ	25b	and your issue like the grass of the earth.
tābô' b^ekelaḥ ^xlê-qāber	26a	You will enter the grave in full-vigor,[23]
ka'^alôt gādîš b^e'ittô	26b	like the stacking of grain in its season;
	. . .	
hinnê-zō't ḥ^aqarnûhā ken-hî'	27a	See, this is what we have searched out;
šmā'ennā w^e'attâ da'-lāk	27b	thus you can hear it[24] and know it for yourself.

1. This word means confidence in its other two occurrences (Ps 85:9; 143:9), but the masculine form of the substantive means both confidence (Job 8:14; 31:24; Ps 78:7) and folly, stupidity (Qoh 7:25; Ps 49:11, 14).

2. Taking *wtm drkyk* as *casus pendens* with the *w*– of apodosis. See C. L Seow, *Job 1–21: Interpretation and Commentary* (Illuminations; Grand Rapids: Eerdmans, 2013), 396.

3. A hapax; Seow, *Job 1–21*, 397, plausibly suggests the verb *nt'w* belongs with the "Hebrew roots beginning with *nt*– that suggest elimination or removal"; e.g., *ntḥ*; *ntk*; *nts*; *ntṣ*; *ntq*; *ntr*, *ntš*.

4. The five words for lions in vv.10-11 appear to carry indeterminate differences.

5. Cf. 20:8; 33:15; Dan 2:19; 7:2, 7, 13; Gen 46:2; Num 12:6.

6. Most versions read this as the construct of the word "hair" ("a hair of my flesh"), despite several problems detailed by Seow, *Job 1–21*, 401–2. Tg. takes it as "whirlwind." While a play between "storm" and "hair" should be admitted, I read this as an absolute form of *ś^e'ārāh* ("storm"; cf. 9:17). Compare *naḥ^alat* in 27:13.

7. I follow Seow, *Job 1–21*, 403. who departs from many who read a hendiadys ("a silent/hushed voice"), though I have no stake in his argument that Eliphaz may be evoking a tradition of receiving a revelatory word amidst the calm of a storm. The reading of a hendiadys fails to account for the verse's use of *casus pendens*, emphasizing "it stood," "a form," and "silent."

8. Among others, David W. Cotter, *A Study of Job 4–5 in the Light of Contemporary Literary Theory* (Atlanta: Scholars Press, 1992), 191, has "Look," which is certainly possible, especially considering the frequency with which JOB uses *hēn* (instead of *hinnê*) to form presentative exclamations (see Bruce K. Waltke and M. O'Connor, *An Introduction to Biblical Hebrew Syntax* [Winona Lake, Indiana: Eisenbrauns, 1990], §40.2.1). However, *hēn* means "if" and states a premise when followed by *'p* or *'p ky* in the friends' speeches in Job (15:15–16; 25:5–6), but also elsewhere (Deut 31:27; Prov 11:31). Cf. F. Brown, S. Driver and C. Briggs, *The Brown-Driver-Briggs Hebrew and English Lexicon* (Peabody, Mass.: Hendrickson, 1906), 243b.

9. A hapax; some read *hll*, "to be deceived, a fool, mad," but the *t–* preformative occurs nowhere else (cf. the *m–* in Qoh 2:2). Others cite the Ethiopic and Arabic root meaning "to wander," and so translate something close to "error." *tᵉhillâ* is a common word meaning praise so some read the *lō'* doing double duty and cite the parallel of *'mn* and *thlh* in Ps 106:12. The wisdom-folly motif throughout the speech makes "folly" the most likely meaning here. Cf. Cotter, *Job 4-5*, 192.

10. A very difficult verse. I offer this translation tentatively; it matters little to my larger argument. For discussions, see Seow, *Job 1–21*, 406–7; and Cotter, *Job 4–5*, 187, 194.

11. It is difficult to make sense of the text as it stands. One expects an object of the verb *mēśîm*, and so at least since Rashi many have taken it as elliptical for *mibbᵉlî mēśîm lēb*, "without anyone noticing." For a similar problem see 23:6b. Others (e.g., Habel), following Dahood's proposal to read an enclitic *mem*, vocalize *mbly-m šm*, "without a name." I chose to follow a reading present in the Vulgate ("and because no one understands"), which probably reflects the former, elliptical reading, but gives the idiom a sense more like a verb of perception as, for example, in Isa 41:22. I choose this reading in light of its accord with the v.21b.

12. Or "tent-peg," which accords nicely with the focus on housing.

13. I discuss the meaning of this word on page 87.

14. E. Dhorme, *A Commentary on the Book of Job* (Nashville: T. Nelson, 1984), 57, suggests that *k's* refers to inward irritation or annoyance and *qn'h* to outward indignation.

15. I discuss this translation on pages 88–89.

16. This line affords a number of different translations. The verb is often read as the geminate *qbb* or *nqb*, both meaning "to curse," i.e., "I cursed his habitation," but *nqb* also means "to note" (e.g., Num 1:17; Amos 6:1; 1 Chr 16:41; cf. HALOT, 718-19), which would be a close parallel of *r'h* ("to see") in the second line (Seow, *Job 1–21*, 429–30). Secondly, it is unclear what the adverb *pit'ōm*, "suddenly," is supposed to modify. Gordis repoints it to the abstract noun *pᵉtā'im*, an unattested form of the root *pth*, which appears in the previous verse as a parallel to *'wyl*. The noun, however, always contains the *y*. See *ptym* in Prov 1:22, 32; *ptyym* in Ps 119:130; or *pt'ym* in Ps 116:6; Prov 8:5; 9:6. There are several ways to read the adverb here without amending the consonantal text or denying a possible allusion to the *pty*, "simpleton." Options include "I noted/cursed his sudden habitation"; "Suddenly, I noted/cursed his habitation" (NRSV, JPSV); "I noted/cursed his habitation; suddenly . . ." I opted for the last because the adverb is regularly used to characterize the fate of the fool or wicked person which the speech goes on to detail. The sages regularly oppose the staying power of the righteous to the sudden downfall of the wicked (e.g., Prov 3:25; 6:15; 7:22).

17. This is the most difficult verse and the only triplet in this difficult section (vv.1–7). I discuss it on page 252n45 but do not provide a definitive interpretation. The point seems to be that a precarious ephemerality plagues any wealth that a fool may (temporarily) accumulate. For discussions, see Seow, *Job 1–21*, 432–36; and David J. A. Clines, *Job 1–20* (Dallas: Word, 1989), 115–16.

18. Out of their concern with the coherence of vv.6–7, many repoint this verb to give it an active sense (e.g., Duhm, Dhorme, Clines, Gordis, Terrien). The relationship between vv.6 and 7, and my decision to render the verb as a passive, are discussed on page 252n47.

19. Given the mythological associations of *rešep* (cf. Deut 32:24), many transliterate rather than translate this word: "as sons of Resheph fly high" (e.g., Gordis, Habel). The allusion is possible but not necessary, which is why I elected to translate the word. See the discussion in Clines, *Job 1–20*, 141–42.

20. Many discuss the awkwardness of the infinitive here. Its relationship to v.10 is unclear (that God sends rain *in order to* set the lowly on high is far-fetched; cf. Gordis), and so the best solution may be to take it as equivalent to a finite verb. Alternatively, one could read it in close succession to v.8, where the same verb (*śym*) is present, yielding something like, "I would present (*śym*) my word to Elohim—*who does all kinds of mighty deeds*—(in order for him) to set (*lśwm*) the lowly on high"; cf. Cotter, *Job 4–5*, 215–16.

21. Reading *yešaʿ* as an adverbial accusative.

22. This awkward line has two major issues. First, "from the sword" and "from their mouth" present a redundancy that I eliminate (following Gordis) with a hendiadys combining these commonly associated words: "from their sharp mouth." Second, there is no object, which some (e.g., Dhorme, Rowley) resolve by repointing *mēḥereb* to *mohᵒrāb*, a hophal participle meaning "the desolated one." See the discussion in Clines, *Job 1–20*, 117.

23. This word, which appears elsewhere only in 30:2, has no convincing Semitic cognate. I am inclined toward the proposal of Seow, *Job 1–21*, 447–48, that the word is a conflation of *kl* and *lḥ* (see also Deut 34:7), with the assimilation of the shared consonant, so that it functions like a composite noun, "full-vigor," both here and in 30:2.

24. All other versions have the 1cp rather than the imperative, and so read: "thus it is we have heard, so you should know it yourself." See Seow, *Job 1–21*, 448.

Notes

Introduction

1. To avoid confusion between the book of Job and the character, I use small capitals to refer to the book where this would otherwise be ambiguous, because of a lack of chapter or verse reference or an overt reference to "the book."

2. The idea of a dappled world is developed at length by Nancy Cartwright, *The Dappled World: A Study of the Boundaries of Science* (Cambridge: Cambridge University Press, 1999), which takes the word "dappled" from the Gerard Manley Hopkins poem "Pied Beauty." Cartwright's work is developed in important ways that overcome various limitations in Adrian Johnston, *Prolegomena to Any Future Materialism: Volume 2, A Weak Nature Alone* (forthcoming from Northwestern University Press).

3. See, for example, Clayton Crockett, *Radical Political Theology* (New York: Columbia University Press, 2011); Anthony Paul Smith and Daniel Whistler, eds., *After the Postsecular and the Postmodern: New Essays in Continental Philosophy of Religion* (Cambridge, Eng.: Cambridge Scholars Press, 2010); and Jeffrey W. Robbins, *Radical Democracy and Political Theology* (New York: Columbia University Press, 2011).

4. This deconstruction has been carried out by Talal Asad in, for example, *Genealogies of Religion: Discipline and Reasons of Power in Christianity and Islam* (Baltimore: The Johns Hopkins University Press, 1993), and Tomoko Masuzawa, *The Invention of World Religions: Or, How European Universalism Was Preserved in the Language of Pluralism* (Chicago and London: The University of Chicago Press, 2005).

5. For a perspective from biblical studies in particular, see Stephen D. Moore and Yvonne Sherwood, *The Invention of the Biblical Scholar: A Critical Manifesto* (Minneapolis, Minn.: Fortress, 2011).

6. There are notable exceptions such as Moore and Sherwood, *Invention*. However, they and other biblical scholars they discuss (e.g., Ward Blanton) often engage biblical studies more than the biblical text. Biblical scholars who primarily engage the biblical text are even fewer.

7. For a set of different perspectives that illustrate the continued concern with and the difficulty of maintaining this boundary, see Roland Boer, ed., *Secularism and Biblical Studies* (London and Oakland, Conn.: Equinox, 2010), especially the essay by Ward Blanton, "Neither Religious nor Secular: On Saving the Critic in Biblical-Criticism," 141–62.

8. Exceptions exist, such as Jean-Luc Nancy's turn away from Paul and toward "The Epistle of Saint James" in *Dis-Closure: The Deconstruction of Christianity*, trans. B. Bergo et al. (New York: Fordham University Press, 2008). Plus, Slavoj Žižek's

significant voice in these discussions is more influenced by Jacques Lacan's engagements with religion, belief, and biblical literature, which do not share this primary focus on Paul and Christianity.

9. Slavoj Žižek, *For They Know Not What They Do: Enjoyment as a Political Factor*, 2nd ed. (London: Verso, 2002), lii.

10. Žižek, *For They*, li. See also Slavoj Žižek and Glyn Daly, *Conversations with Žižek* (Cambridge, Eng.: Polity, 2004), 162.

11. Slavoj Žižek, *The Puppet and the Dwarf: The Perverse Core of Christianity* (Cambridge, Mass.: MIT Press, 2003), 126.

12. G. K. Chesterton, *Introduction to The Book of Job* (London: S. Wellwood, 1907). See also Slavoj Žižek, "The Fear of Four Words: A Modest Plea for the Hegelian Reading of Christianity" in Slavoj Žižek and John Milbank, *The Monstrosity of Christ: Paradox or Dialectic*, ed. Creston Davis (Cambridge, Mass.: MIT Press, 2009), 52–57.

13. Žižek, *Monstrosity*, 53.

14. Žižek, *Monstrosity*, 54–55.

15. Žižek, *Monstrosity*, 55–56.

16. Jacques Lacan, "Le triomphe de la religion" in *Le Triomphe de la religion, précédé de Discours aux catholiques*, ed. J.-A. Miller (Paris: Éditions du Seuil, 2005), 67–102. Sigmund Freud, *The Future of an Illusion* in *SE XXI* (1961 [1927]), 1–56.

17. Adrian Johnston, *Prolegomena to Any Future Materialism, Volume One: the Outcome of Contemporary French Philosophy* (Evanston, Ill.: Northwestern University Press, 2013).

18. See Davis Hankins, introduction to *Ice Axes for Frozen Seas: A Biblical Theology of Provocation*, by Walter Brueggemann, ed. Davis Hankins (Waco, Tex.: Baylor University Press, 2014), where I further develop this notion of an immanent theology by discussing the centrality of Walter Brueggemann's biblical theology for my understanding of it.

Chapter 1

1. Most include within the wisdom tradition Proverbs, Job, Qohelet (and often certain Psalms, e.g., 37); within the Greek Old Testament, Sirach and Wisdom of Solomon. For a discussion of the lexical group of words for wisdom and of the ideas of wisdom that they convey, see Michael V. Fox, *Proverbs 1–9: A New Translation with Introduction and Commentary* (Garden City, N.Y.: Doubleday, 2000), 28–43; see also Michael V. Fox, "The Epistemology of the Book of Proverbs," *Journal of Biblical Literature* 126 (2007): 669n.1.

2. Others have also used the typographical distinction between Wisdom and wisdom; e.g., Carole R. Fontaine, *Smooth Words: Women, Proverbs, and Performance in Biblical Wisdom* (Sheffield: Sheffield Academic, 2002), 2.

3. Michael V. Fox, "Ideas of Wisdom in Proverbs 1–9," *Journal of Biblical Literature* 116 (1997): 630.

4. "Proverbs emphatically assigns the transcendental wisdom to the mun-

dane as well as the divine realm and does not distinguish degrees of purity or excellence." Fox, "Ideas," 632n.39.

5. Fox, "Ideas," 631.

6. Fox, "Ideas," 633. For the former claim, see p. 632: "The book of Proverbs is one precipitate of the primeval, universal wisdom, as this is transmitted by and filtered through individual sages."

7. So, Fox, "Ideas," 632, 633: "Wisdom, in its essence rather than in its infinite particulars, is God's gift to humanity. . . . [W]isdom embraces such [particular] teachings but is greater than their sum total."

8. In the classroom, scholars often refer to the qualitative distinction between sapiential wisdom and divine Wisdom as a simple way to characterize wisdom's distinctiveness from, say, priestly law, where human and divine codes of conduct are identified.

9. Kathleen M. O'Connor, *The Wisdom Literature* (Collegeville, Minn.: The Liturgical Press, 1990), 19–20.

10. Georg Wilhelm Friedrich Hegel, *The Encyclopædia Logic: Part 1 of the Encylopædia of Philosophical Sciences with the Zusätze*, trans. T. F. Geraets, W. A. Suchting, and H. S. Harris (Indianapolis: Hackett, 1991), §60.

11. Slavoj Žižek, *Organs Without Bodies: On Deleuze and Consequences* (New York: Routledge, 2004), 60, 61, 65. See the discussion of the relationship between Kant and Hegel and of Žižek's interest in and conception of this relationship in Adrian Johnston, *Žižek's Ontology: A Transcendental Materialist Theory of Subjectivity* (Evanston, Ill. Northwestern University Press, 2008), especially ch. 11.

12. For a closely related investigation of WISDOM in the book of Proverbs, see David Cromwell Knauert, "The Limits of Wisdom and the Dialectic of Desire" (PhD diss., Duke University, 2009). See also Davis Hankins and David Knauert, "Desire and Ideology in Wisdom's Inaugural Address: Proverbs 1:22–33" in *Imagination, Ideology, and Inspiration: Exploring Walter Brueggemann's Influence in Biblical Studies*, ed. R. Williamson and J. Kaplan (Sheffield: Sheffield Phoenix, forthcoming).

13. See Fredric Jameson, "The Vanishing Mediator; or, Max Weber as Storyteller" in *The Ideologies of Theory* (London: Verso, 2008).

14. Not to mention Qohelet, whose proximity to Hegel in the consideration of a limit's relationship to the whole will have to await further work. To give a indication, where the tradition sees what is ephemeral, fleeting, and unclear (*hebel*) as a limitation with respect to the sage's ability to be wise about everything, Qohelet responds by admitting these limits and affirming his knowledge through his assertion that everything is *hebel*. For Hegel's part, consider his rejection of the Kantian tradition's perception of limitation: "With respect to the form of the limitation . . . great stress is laid on the limitations of thought, of reason, and so on, and it is asserted that the limitation cannot be transcended. To make such an assertion is to be unaware that the very fact that something is determined as a limitation implies that the limitation is already transcended." Georg Wilhelm Friedrich Hegel, *Hegel's Science of Logic* (Atlantic Highlands, N.J.: Humanities Press International, 1989), 134.

15. I have chosen to exclude from this book's analysis of JOB the wisdom poem in Job 28 and Elihu's speeches in Job 32–37. On the former, see Davis Han-

kins, "Wisdom as an Immanent Event in Job 28, Not a Transcendent Ideal," *Vetus Testamentum* 63/2 (2013): 210–35. The latter choice is not arbitrary since JOB itself indicates the secondary status of these speeches in numerous ways; see Davis Hankins and Brennan Breed, "The Book of Job" in *The Oxford Encyclopedia of the Books of the Bible, Vol. 1*, ed. M. Coogan (New York: Oxford University Press, 2011), 434–50.

16. For the more complex version of the story that highlights the deeply interdisciplinary character of Gunkel's work, see Martin J. Buss, *Biblical Form Criticism in Its Context* (Sheffield: Sheffield Academic, 1999).

17. Here is a sampling of a few interruptions to a lecture Lacan gave at Vincennes, a newly created experimental university: "While this little class is purring along peacefully there are 150 comrades at Beaux-Arts who are being arrested by the cops . . . they are not giving classes on the object *a* like this Mandarin here in our presence, and who no one could care less about. . . . So I think that the smooth running of this magisterial lecture is a fairly good translation of the current state of decay in the university." . . . "If we think that by listening to Lacan's discourse, or Foucault's, or someone else's we will obtain the means to criticize the ideology that they are making us swallow, we're making a big mistake. I claim that we have to look outside to find the means to overthrow the university." Jacques Lacan, *The Seminar of Jacques Lacan, Book XVII: The Other Side of Psychoanalysis, 1969–1970*, ed. Jacques-Alain Miller; trans. Russell Grigg (New York: W. W. Norton & Company, 2007), 204, 205.

18. See Lacan, *Seminar XVII*, 20, 105, 187, 188.

19. I refer to this book's CHAPTERS in small capitals to avoid confusion with JOB's chapter divisions.

20. I discuss the figure of "the-satan" in more detail in CHAPTER 2. Here it will suffice to say that I transliterate it because the definite article marks it as a function and not a name. The figure is inherently ambiguous. He is on God's team if not simply on God's side; that is, more devil's advocate than devil. The Devil will not appear for some time in Jewish and Christian literature.

21. Carol A. Newsom, *The Book of Job: A Contest of Moral Imaginations* (Oxford: Oxford University Press, 2003).

22. Newsom, *Contest*, 30.

23. Newsom, *Contest*, 30.

24. Newsom, *Contest*, 30.

25. Newsom, *Contest*, 31.

26. Linking the unsayable to Levinas finds further support in Newsom's continued references to Levinas (e.g., *Contest*, 92) and to others closely associated with Levinas's work such as Philippe Nemo (e.g., *Contest*, 128, 148–49). Levinas himself says as much: "the inexpressible [i.e., unsayable] is not separated from this saying . . . [which] hides while uncovering, says and silences the inexpressible." *Totality and Infinity: An Essay on Exteriority*, trans. A. Lingis (Pittsburgh: Duquesne University Press, 1969), 260.

27. Newsom, *Contest*, 65.

28. See Emmanuel Levinas, "The Trace of the Other" in *Deconstruction in Context: Literature and Philosophy*, ed. M. C. Taylor; trans. A. Lingis (Chicago: The University of Chicago Press, 1986), 347.

29. Levinas, "Trace," 351. Elsewhere he says that the Other manifests itself "καθ᾽ αὑτό. It *expresses itself.*" Levinas, *Totality,* 51.

30. See Levinas, "Trace," 347.

31. Levinas, *Totality,* 261.

32. Newsom, *Contest,* 71; see also 68.

33. Emmanuel Levinas, *Otherwise than Being or Beyond Essence,* trans. A. Lingis (Pittsburgh: Duquesne University Press, 1998), 143–45, 199.

34. Newsom, *Contest,* 70.

35. Newsom, *Contest,* 70.

36. Newsom, *Contest,* 71.

37. Newsom, *Contest,* 71.

38. Although Newsom neither acknowledges nor explains her departure from Levinas on this matter, I think she is correct to depart from him in this way. For an amenable critique on which I draw in the critical reflections on Levinas below, see Martin Hägglund, *Radical Atheism: Derrida and the Time of Life* (Stanford, Calif.: Stanford University Press, 2008), ch. 3.

39. Newsom, *Contest,* 96, refers to the ontological nature of the $Excess_D$ (*rôgez*) in Job's first speech. Elsewhere she discusses "the limits of language itself" that are revealed when "Job speaks a language bordering on madness in a world turned upside down." *Contest,* 161, 168.

40. So, Levinas, "Trace," 358: "Only a being that transcends the world can leave a trace."

41. See also the discussion in Hägglund, *Radical,* ch. 3.

42. The most productive critical account of Žižek's work is by Johnston, *Žižek's Ontology.*

43. In what follows I largely disregard the complexity, variation, and development of Lacan's work, which spans many decades and resists systematization in numerous ways.

44. See also Slavoj Žižek, *On Belief* (London: Routledge, 2001), 82–83.

45. Slavoj Žižek and Glyn Daly, *Conversations with Žižek* (Cambridge, Eng.: Polity, 2004), 68–69.

46. The "type-scene" is a concept originally developed in Homer scholarship but then used in biblical studies by many following Robert Alter, *The Art of Biblical Narrative* (New York: Basic, 1981), 50.

47. Jacques Lacan, *The Seminar of Jacques Lacan, Book XX: Encore, 1972–1973,* ed. Jacques-Alain Miller; trans. Bruce Fink (New York: W. W. Norton & Company, 1998), 124.

48. So, "the real in question is no doubt not to be taken in the sense in which we normally understand it, which implies objectivity." Jacques Lacan, *The Seminar of Jacques Lacan, Book III: The Psychoses, 1955–1956,* ed. Jacques-Alain Miller; trans. Russell Grigg (New York: W. W. Norton & Co., 1993), 186.

49. Lacan (*Seminar III,* 118) insists that "we abandon the idea, implicit in many systems, that what the subject puts into words is an improper and always distorted enunciation of a lived experience that would be some irreducible reality."

50. On the one hand this means that there is no biological foundation for concepts such as the ego, drive, and unconscious. "To put it succinctly, the in-

stinctual stages are already organized in subjectivity when they are being lived."
Jacques Lacan, "The Function and Field of Speech and Language in Psychoanalysis," in *Écrits*, trans. Bruce Fink (New York: W. W. Norton & Company, 2006),
217. But Lacanian theory also does not endorse a social constructivist claim that
metapsychology gives biology its proper place.

51. In response to the excessive reductionism of his colleague's naturalistic
references, Lacan offered his own reductive interpretation that "reference to the
organic foundations is dictated by nothing but a need to be reassured." Jacques
Lacan, *Le Séminaire de Jacques Lacan, Livre IV: La relation d'objet, 1956–1957*, ed.
Jacques-Alain Miller (Paris: Éditions du Seuil, 1994), 32 (as quoted by Lorenzo
Chiesa, *Subjectivity and Otherness: A Philosophical Reading of Lacan* [Cambridge, Mass.:
MIT Press, 2007], 127). In other contexts, however, he tries to dispel the sense that
he denied that the Real, biological body influences the Imaginarily and Symbolically constituted subject: "I do not mean for all that, that if we do not know [the
real], we have no relations to [it]," *The Seminar of Jacques Lacan, Book XII: Crucial
Problems for Psychoanalysis, 1964–1965*, 12/2/64. See also Adrian Johnston, *Time
Driven: Metapsychology and the Splitting of the Drive* (Evanston, Ill.: Northwestern University Press, 2005), ch. 9; and especially Johnston's contribution to his book with
Catherine Malabou, "Misfelt Feelings: Unconscious Affect Between Psychoanalysis,
Neuroscience, and Philosophy" in *Self and Emotional Life: Philosophy, Psychoanalysis,
and Neuroscience* (New York: Columbia University Press, 2013), 73–210.

52. Several notable Lacanian theorists have begun to engage recent neuroscientific findings with Freudian–Lacanian metapsychology in ways that promise
to be productive for both fields. See especially several well-referenced works by
Adrian Johnston: "Misfelt Feelings," in *Self and Emotional Life*, 73–210; "Ghosts of
Substance Past: Schelling, Lacan, and the Denaturalization of Nature," in *Lacan:
The Silent Partners*, ed. S. Žižek (London: Verso, 2006), 34–55; "Conflicted Matter:
Jacques Lacan and the Challenge of Secularizing Materialism," *Pli: The Warwick
Journal of Philosophy* 19 (2008), 166–88; "The Weakness of Nature: Hegel, Freud,
Lacan, and Negativity Materialized," in *Hegel and the Infinite: Religion, Politics, and
Dialectic*, ed. S. Žižek, C. Crockett, and C. Davis (New York: Columbia University
Press, 2011), 159–80; and Slavoj Žižek, *The Parallax View* (Cambridge, Mass.: MIT
Press, 2006).

53. So, Jaak Panksepp, *Affective Neuroscience: The Foundations of Human and
Animal Emotions* (Oxford: Oxford University Press, 1998), 26 (see also 122): "one
can never capture innate emotional dynamics in their pure form, except perhaps
when they are aroused artificially by direct stimulation of brain areas where those
operating systems are most concentrated."

54. Compare this with the dialectical materialism exemplified by neuralplasticity as discussed by Catherine Malabou, *What Should We Do with Our Brain?*,
trans. S. Rand (New York: Fordham University Press, 2008).

55. Bruce Fink, *A Clinical Introduction to Lacanian Psychoanalysis: Theory and
Technique* (Cambridge: Harvard University Press, 1997), 47–48.

56. Compare with Lacan's often-cited definition: "a signifier is what represents the subject to another signifier." "The Subversion of the Subject and the
Dialectic of Desire in the Freudian Unconscious," in *Écrits*, 694.

57. For Lacan, the hysteric's manifestation of the split inherent to subjectivity makes her representative of subjectivity in general.

58. Compare with *The Seminar of Jacques Lacan, Book X: Anxiety, 1962–1963*.

59. Lacan says that the *objet petit a* "is in fact simply the presence of a hollow, a void . . . [an] eternally lacking object." *The Seminar of Jacques Lacan, Book XI: The Four Fundamental Concepts of Psycho-Analysis, 1964*, ed. Jacques-Alain Miller; trans. Alan Sheridan (New York: W. W. Norton & Co., 1977), 180.

60. See also Lacan, *Seminar XI*, 12 and the book-length study of the drive by Johnston, *Time Driven*.

61. Lacan, *Seminar XI*, 163.

62. Sigmund Freud, "Instincts and Their Vicissitudes" in *SE XIV* (1955 [1915]), 109–40.

63. Lacan ("Subversion," 680) notes that "drive" is a fine translation in English, and he says *"dérive"* [drift] would be his last resort in French if he "were unable to give the bastardized term *pulsion* [drive or urge] its point of impact."

64. "Instinct has a natural object or state of affairs that it strives to obtain. In the case of the need to eat . . . the appropriate nutritional materials as objects and, consequently, the sating of hunger as the resulting state of affairs." Johnston, *Time Driven*, 158.

65. Lacan, *Seminar XI*, 169.

66. This is the central argument of Johnston, *Time Driven*, especially chs. 6–7.

67. Compare Sigmund Freud, "Civilization and Its Discontents" in *SE XXI* (1961 [1929]), 66–67, and "A Metapsychological Supplement to the Theory of Dreams" in *SE XIV* (1955 [1917]), 231.

68. Jacques Lacan, *The Seminar of Jacques Lacan, Book XIV: The Logic of Fantasy, 1966–1967*, 6/14/67. More interesting than Lacan's discussion of the mother or the breast is his idea of the placenta as the "lost object." The placenta is an organ that mediates between child and mother without confusing them or allowing either to be seen as autonomous; "Position of the Unconscious" in *Écrits*, 719.

69. Freud, "Instincts," 122.

70. "When you entrust someone with a mission, the *aim* is not what he brings back, but the itinerary he must take. The *aim* is the way taken." Lacan, *Seminar XI*, 179. For the reference to sublimation, see *Seminar XI*, 165, and the extensive engagement with sublimation throughout *The Seminar of Jacques Lacan, Book VII: The Ethics of Psychoanalysis, 1959–1960*, ed. Jacques-Alain Miller; trans. Dennis Porter (New York: W. W. Norton & Co., 1992). Later, in *Seminar XI*, 243, he calls the drive's object "the object around which the drive turns."

71. "The function of the drive has for me no other purpose than to put in question what is meant by satisfaction." Lacan, *Seminar XI*, 166.

72. *Jouissance* is often left untranslated because English lacks an appropriate word to capture the uses to which it is put in Lacan's reworking of the Freudian notion of libido, including, as Žižek has put it, "the paradoxical satisfaction procured by a painful encounter with a Thing that perturbs the equilibrium of the 'pleasure principle'," *Tarrying with the Negative: Kant, Hegel, and the Critique of Ideology* (Durham: Duke University Press, 1993), 280. *Jouissance*, in other words, can often mean something quite contrary to what is commonly considered pleas-

antness or enjoyability. It is worth recalling here that psychoanalysis refers to all drives as, in the end, death drives; see also Johnston, *Time Driven*, 175–83.

73. Johnston, *Time Driven*, 131.

74. Jacques Lacan, "The Mirror Stage as Formative of the *I* Function as Revealed in Psychoanalytic Experience," in *Écrits*, 76.

75. See Johnston's account of the neuroscientific findings that the human brain is genetically pre-programmed to be open to epigenetic/non-genetic influences of a Symbolic/linguistic sort; as he puts it: "hardwired to be rewired"; "Misfelt Feelings," 197; see also "Conflicted Matter," 177–81.

76. Lacan, "Subversion," 689.

77. Compare Johnston, *Time Driven*, 206–7.

78. Compare Joan Copjec, *Imagine There's No Woman: Ethics and Sublimation* (Cambridge, Mass.: MIT Press, 2002), 60, "The milk fills more than the stomach, it fills the gullet of the drive."

79. Lacan, *Seminar XI*, 180.

80. Žižek, *Parallax*, 60–61. For a nearly identical discussion that nonetheless advances toward a different conclusion, see Žižek, *In Defense of Lost Causes* (London: Verso, 2008), 327–29.

81. Žižek, *Parallax*, 63–64.

82. Žižek and Daly, *Conversations*, 61–63. See also Žižek, *The Indivisible Remainder: An Essay on Schelling and Related Matters* (London: Verso, 1996), 121–22, and Johnston, *Žižek's Ontology*, especially ch. 13.

83. I discuss the difference between Kant and Hegel on pages 14–15. See, for example, Žižek, *Indivisible*, 95–99.

Chapter 2

1. Mary-Jane Rubenstein, "Dionysius, Derrida, and the Critique of Ontotheology" (2008). *Division I Faculty Publications*. Paper 98. http://wesscholar .wesleyan.edu/div1facpubs/98.

2. Commentators often recognize the import of these verses. For example, Marvin H. Pope, *Job*, 3rd ed. (Garden City, N.Y.: Doubleday, 1973), 12: "Here is the crux of the issue, the question which provoked the cruel experiment."

3. Literally, *haśśāṭān* says, "But stretch out your hand and touch all that is his . . ." The hand, which often symbolizes power (cf. Gen 9:2; 16:6; Exod 3:8, 20), is elsewhere stretched out by God in order to smite (cf. Exod 3:20; 9:15), but also to touch (cf. Jer 1:9). At the least, here it means more than "touch"; see David J. A. Clines, *Job 1–20* (Dallas: Word, 1989), 28.

4. A different but related point is made in Clines's classical article, "False Naivety in the Prologue to Job," *Hebrew Annual Review* 9 (1985): 127–36. J. Crenshaw also recognizes the radical nature of *haśśāṭān*'s charge, which, he claims, "struck at the heart of ancient religion," *Old Testament Wisdom: An Introduction*, rev. and enl. ed. (Louisville: Westminster John Knox, 1998), 92.

5. Samuel R. Driver and George Buchanan Gray, *A Critical and Exegetical Commentary on the Book of Job* (Edinburgh: T. & T. Clark, 1921), lii, liii.

6. Various articulations of part or all of this consensus can also be found in: Crenshaw, *Introduction*, 92; Katharine J. Dell, *The Book of Job as Sceptical Literature* (Berlin: Walter de Gruyter, 1991), 30; E. Dhorme, *A Commentary on the Book of Job* (Nashville: T. Nelson, 1984), 7; Norman C. Habel, *The Book of Job* (Philadelphia: Westminster, 1985), 61; John E. Hartley, *The Book of Job* (Grand Rapids: Eerdmans, 1988), 43; Dan Mathewson, *Death and Survival in the Book of Job: Desymbolization and Traumatic Experience* (New York: T. & T. Clark, 2006), 36; Pope, *Job*, xvi; H. H. Rowley, *Job* (London: Nelson, 1970), 32; Meir Weiss, *The Story of Job's Beginning: Job 1–2: A Literary Analysis* (Jerusalem: Magness Press, Hebrew University, 1983), 45, 46; Gerald H. Wilson, *Job* (Peabody, Mass.: Hendrickson, 2007), 12.

7. Habel, *Job*, 61.

8. Clines, *Job 1–20*, 25.

9. Compare the following, similar statement: "In my view, Satan is not questioning the direction of causality, but raising it as an issue in the first place." Alan Cooper, "Reading and Misreading the Prologue to Job," *Journal for the Study of the Old Testament* 46 (1990): 70.

10. 1 Sam 19:5, 25:31; 1 Kgs 2:31; Job 9:17; Ps 35:7, 69:4, 109:3, 119:161; Prov 1:11; Lam 3:52.

11. *ḥinnām* means "in vain" in Prov 1:17, Mal 1:10; "without reason" in Prov 3:30, Ezek 14:23; "without cause" in Prov 23:29, 24:28, 26:2, Ezek 6:10; "to no end" in Isa 52:5. Compare with David J. A. Clines, ed., *The Dictionary of Classical Hebrew. III. Zayin-Teth* (Sheffield: Sheffield Academic, 1996), 271–72.

12. E.g., "Does Job fear God for no reward?" Samuel E. Balentine, *Job* (Macon, Ga.: Smyth & Helwys, 2006), 54. Others (e.g., Rowley, *Job*, 32; Wilson, *Job*, 12, 23) also commend such a translation.

13. While other interpreters use a variant of the word "unconditionally" to describe that fear which *haśśāṭān* doubts Job displays, their interpretations fail (some more, some less) to articulate the notion of unconditionality aimed at here. C. Newsom comes closest; she reads the fear of God for naught as the "Fear of God as an absolute value," and when she sees what is at stake "not simply as the testing of a virtue but the testing of the conditions that make this virtue possible." *The Book of Job: A Contest of Moral Imaginations* (Oxford: Oxford University Press, 2003), 56.

14. I am deeply influenced by discussions of Kant's notion of the ethical in Alenka Zupančič, *Ethics of the Real: Kant, Lacan* (London, New York: Verso, 2000), and Joan Copjec, *Imagine There's No Woman: Ethics and Sublimation* (Cambridge, Mass.: MIT Press, 2002).

15. Gilles Deleuze, *Coldness and Cruelty*, trans. Jean McNeil (New York: Zone Books, 1991), 82.

16. Immanuel Kant, "Groundwork of The Metaphysics of Morals" in *Practical Philosophy* (Cambridge: Cambridge University Press, 1996), 56. Compare this with Lacan's exhortation not to miss the radicalism even to a point near insanity of the formula for the categorical imperative and Kant's second *Critique* more generally insofar as the ethical is therein divorced from the good: "That formula, which is, as you know, the central formula of Kant's ethics, is pursued by him to the limits of its consequences. His radicalism even leads to the paradox that in

the last analysis the *gute Wille*, good will, is posited as distinct from any beneficial action . . . one must have submitted oneself to the test of reading this text in order to measure [its] extreme, almost insane character." *The Seminar of Jacques Lacan, Book VII: The Ethics of Psychoanalysis, 1959–1960*, ed. Jacques-Alain Miller; trans. Dennis Porter (New York: W. W. Norton & Co., 1992), 77.

17. Kant, "Groundwork," e.g., 78.

18. Kant, "Groundwork," 55.

19. Kant, "Groundwork," 45.

20. See, for example, Immanuel Kant, "Critique of Practical Reason" in *Practical Philosophy* (Cambridge: Cambridge University Press, 1996), 237. De Kesel writes, "Desires, sorrow, passion (also the most noble ones) are 'pathological' in the sense that they affect and move people." Marc De Kesel, *Eros and Ethics: Reading Jacques Lacan's Seminar VII*, trans. Sigi Jöttkandt (Albany: State University of New York Press, 2009), 300n.8. See also Zupančič, *Ethics*, 7.

21. Alenka Zupančič, "The Subject of the Law" in *Cogito and the Unconscious*, ed. S. Žižek (Durham, N.C.: Duke University Press, 1998), 49.

22. This evacuation of any motivating content from the fear of God reverses the later tradition that the Satan is cast out of heaven by God's angels (cf. Rev 12:7–9). Since the fear of God epitomizes wisdom (cf. Job 28:28; Prov 1:7; 9:10), it is fair to say that *haśśāṭān* here reaches up into heaven to cast out Woman-Wisdom as a temptress who can only lead to inauthentic wisdom and make fools of sages—by her encouragement of wise activity on the basis of her qualities, her appeals to the self-interest of the sages, to their notion of the good, and so on.

23. Immanuel Kant, "The Metaphysics of Morals," in *Practical Philosophy* (Cambridge; New York: Cambridge University Press, 1996), 383.

24. Zupančič, *Ethics*, 16.

25. Zupančič, *Ethics*, 12.

26. Weiss, *Story*, 45, "There is in Satan's question no rejection, nor even any doubt, of God's claim that Job is God-fearing." Others recognize this as well, e.g., Clines, *Job 1–20*, 25; and J. Gerald Janzen, *Job* (Atlanta: John Knox, 1985), 39.

27. This is to arrive at a conclusion that is quite close to Newsom's (*Contest*, 56), albeit on a path guided by a different set of philosophical categories. She calls *haśśāṭān* a "proto-Nietzschean figure" whose question proposes a "clever genealogy of piety. . . . In this surprisingly philosophical tale, what is at stake is not simply the testing of a virtue but the testing of the conditions that make this virtue possible." Of course, describing the question as one about "conditions of possibility" cannot help but make us think she has Kant in mind even if she does not pursue the allusion as this book tries to do.

28. Newsom, *Contest*, 54.

29. Wilson, *Job*, 19–20.

30. Ellen Van Wolde, "The Development of Job: Mrs Job as Catalyst," in *A Feminist Companion to Wisdom Literature*, ed. A. Brenner (Sheffield: Sheffield Academic, 1995), 202.

31. "Je vous dirai brièvement que le sacrifice n'est pas du tout destiné à l'offrande ni au don, qui se propagent dans une bien autre dimension, mais à la capture de l'Autre dans le réseau de désir," Jacques Lacan, *Le Séminaire de Jacques*

Lacan, Livre X: Angoisse, 1962–1963, ed. Jacques-Alain Miller (Paris: Éditions du Seuil, 2004), 320.

32. Lacan, *Livre X,* 321; see also *The Seminar of Jacques Lacan, Book X: Anxiety, 1962–1963* (Unpublished Typescript), 5.6.63.

33. Walter Brueggemann has amply appreciated this point about the surplus of God's desire over any act of sacrifice. About God's rejection of Cain's sacrifice in Gen 4 he writes, "Both brothers do what is appropriate. Both bring their best . . . Inexplicably, Yahweh chooses—accepts and rejects. Conventional interpretation is too hard on Cain and too easy on Yahweh. It is Yahweh who transforms a normal report into a life/death story for us and about us. Essential to the plot is the capricious freedom of Yahweh." *Genesis* (Atlanta: John Knox, 1982), 56.

34. For another of Lacan's meditations on sacrifice to which this discussion is indebted, see *The Seminar of Jacques Lacan, Book XI: The Four Fundamental Concepts of Psycho-Analysis, 1964,* ed. Jacques-Alain Miller; trans. Alan Sheridan (New York: W. W. Norton & Co., 1977), 275–76.

35. The standard citation here is Prov 3:19: "The Lord by wisdom founded earth, he established heaven by understanding."

36. The modality of the universal is that of an exclusion. For a discussion of various debates about universalism in resources to which my discussion here and below is inextricably tied, see Kenneth Reinhard, "Universalism and the Jewish Exception: Lacan, Badiou, Rosenzweig," *Umbr(a)* (2005): 43–71, and especially the work cited therein by Hegel, Freud, Lacan, Laclau, Badiou, Žižek, and Copjec.

37. Compare with E. Davis's recent comment: "The willingness to be ignorant in this deepest sense is what the biblical writers call 'the fear of YHWH.' It is 'the beginning of wisdom' (Prov 1:7), for its essence is the rejection of arrogance and intellectual dishonesty." *Scripture, Culture, and Agriculture: An Agrarian Reading of the Bible* (Cambridge: Cambridge University Press, 2009), 35.

38. Crenshaw, *Introduction,* can be taken as representative of the common conception that these are appropriate metaphors for wisdom; compare with Michael V. Fox, *Proverbs 1–9: A New Translation with Introduction and Commentary* (Garden City, N.Y.: Doubleday, 2000), 128–31, and Norman C. Habel, "Symbolism of Wisdom in Proverbs 1–9," *Interpretation* 26 (1972): 131–57.

39. My language here intentionally follows Immanuel Kant, *Religion and Rational Theology* (Cambridge, New York: Cambridge University Press, 1996), 109n. This part of Kant's teaching on morality is discussed in a particularly relevant way by Copjec (*Imagine,* ch.5), to whom I am here and throughout indebted.

40. Compare with Wilson, *Job,* 12, "The upshot of the double tests Job endures in the first two chapters is to show that, indeed, it is possible for a human like Job to continue to live in fear of God even when he loses everything and stands on the brink of death without the hope of restoration."

41. Carol A. Newsom, "The Book of Job," in *The New Interpreter's Bible Volume 4,* ed. L. Keck (Nashville: Abingdon, 1996), 348.

42. Janzen, *Job,* 41.

43. So, Clines, *Job 1–20,* 43.

44. Compare with Michael V. Fox, "Job the Pious," *Zeitschrift für die alttestamentliche Wissenschaft* 117 (2005): 362–63.

45. Newsom, "Job" (NIB), 347.

46. Clines, *Job 1–20*, 20.

47. Robert Alter, *The Art of Biblical Narrative* (New York: Basic, 1981), 74.

48. Newsom, "Job" (NIB), 358.

49. See Tod Linafelt, "The Undecidability of *BRK* in the Prologue to Job and Beyond," *Biblical Interpretation* 4 (1996): 162.

50. Compare with Linafelt, "Undecidability," 160. In 1 Kgs 21:13 it is unimaginable that Naboth would be charged, convicted, and sentenced to death for "blessing" God and king.

51. For a list and discussion of the representative resources, see Linafelt, "Undecidability."

52. Compare with Wolde, "Development," 204, "He can curse God, which might make God leave him and result in his death. Alternatively, Job can bless God and die with that blessing on his lips." C. L. Seow, "Job's Wife, with Due Respect," in *Das Buch Hiob und seine Interpretationen: Beiträge zum Hiob-Symposium auf dem Monte Verità vom 14.-19. August 2005*, ed. T. Krüger et al. (Zürich: Theologischer Verlag Zürich, 2007), 371–73, also concludes that 2:9 presents the only ambiguous case, the other five dividing into clear euphemistic or literal uses.

53. Linafelt, "Undecidability," 168.

54. Linafelt is not alone in his opinion. See also Cooper, "Reading," 77: "It seems to me that Job 1–2 is raising profound questions about what b-r-k really means. Is it, after all, so obvious what it means to bless, or to be blessed?"

55. Sigmund Freud, "Civilization and Its Discontents," in *SE XXI* (1961), 91–92. In the original, "eine Art Prothesengott," *Gesammelte Werke* (GW) (Frankfurt: Fischer Taschenbuch Verlag, 1999), band 14, p.451.

56. Although YHWH clearly confesses responsibility for "swallowing Job up" here in 2:3, and although *haśśāṭān* at least only acts on God's authority and at most should be understood as a hypostasis of divine doubt, YHWH places all that is Job's in *haśśāṭān*'s hand (1:12) rather than stretching forth his own hand, as *haśśāṭān* suggests (1:11). But, as Newsom, "Job" (NIB), 350, contends, "the difference is not significant. Yahweh and the *satan* have, metaphorically, joined hands to destroy Job."

57. E.g., Francis I. Andersen, *Job: An Introduction and Commentary* (Downers Grove, Ill.: Inter-Varsity, 1976), 90.

58. So, Newsom, "Job" (NIB), 354. Compare with Fox, "Pious," 363.

59. For a discussion of wounds that create, in a real, ontological sense, new subjects discontinuous with their previous selves, see Catherine Malabou, *The New Wounded: From Neurosis to Brain Damage* (New York: Fordham University Press, 2012).

60. The earth swallows the Egyptian pursuers after the exodus in Exod 15:12; the earth swallows the Korahites et al. in Num 16 and 26 (cf. Deut 11:6; Ps 106:17); Isaiah, in a typical poetic flourish, promises YHWH will swallow up death itself in Isa 25:7–8; Sheol is depicted as swallowing lives in several places (Num 16:30; Prov 1:12; cf. Ps 69:15); Lam 2 characterizes YHWH's destruction of Israel as a swallowing up (vv. 2, 5, 8, 16). Compare with Mathewson, *Death*, 29.

61. See also 19:13–19, translated and discussed on page 155, wherein Job describes his loss as God's alienation of him from all his social relationships.

62. Clines, *Job 1–20*, 64.

63. Although I suppose dependency cannot be ruled out, Giorgio Agamben's concept of "bare life" is more rigorous and famous than that found in Driver, *Job*, liii, which uses this term to refer to Job in the quotation cited on page 42; see Agamben, *Homo Sacer: Sovereign Power and Bare Life*, trans. D. Heller-Roazen (Stanford, Calif.: Stanford University Press, 1995).

64. Mathewson, *Death*, 51. Balentine, *Job*, 56, makes the same point.

65. Sam Meier, "Job I-II: A Reflection of Genesis I-III," *Vetus Testamentum* 39 (1989): 187–88, opposes the movement in Genesis from chaos to a "very good" cosmos to the prose tale's disintegration of Job's perfect world. He therefore names what takes place in the prose tale a "de-creation," which, although my concern is strictly immanent to the tale, is not a bad name for what I am describing.

66. The formal and grammatical parallelism between Job's first and second statements "invites one to treat the two statements as part of a paradigmatic set, with the similar terms analogous to one another. The going forth and returning of birth and death are simply one way of describing what can also be expressed as YHWH's giving and taking. Thus, the two verbs, 'give' and 'take,' negotiate the space between the first and final nakedness. One is naked, and YHWH gives those things that clothe life; YHWH takes those things, and one returns naked to death" (Newsom, *Contest*, 59).

67. Compare with Newsom, *Contest*, 58.

68. This difference between a positive or substantial ego and a negative or substance-less subject is not only something I will return to below, it is also foundational to the philosophical and psychoanalytic coordinates of this book. For the most thorough discussion of the Lacanian/Hegelian conception of subjectivity that informs my work, see Adrian Johnston, *Žižek's Ontology: A Transcendental Materialist Theory of Subjectivity* (Evanston, Ill.: Northwestern University Press, 2008).

69. Robert A. Di Vito, "Old Testament Anthropology and the Construction of Personal Identity," *Catholic Biblical Quarterly* 61 (1999): 217–38, discusses biblical perspectives on personal identity and their treatments by scholars.

70. See also David J. A. Clines, ed., *The Dictionary of Classical Hebrew. V. Mem-Nun* (Sheffield: Sheffield Academic, 2001), 724–33.

71. "*Entre deux morts*" is how Lacan famously characterized Antigone who, in her act to bury her brother Polynices, defies Creon and is carried beyond her ties to the imaginary–symbolic world of the city. Lacan's commentary on *Antigone* can be found in *Seminar VII*, 241–83. The normal order, of course, is that the biological body dies first and then, some time later, the person dies a symbolic death as their legacy is forgotten. Funerals can thus be seen as affirmations of the symbolic life that survives biological death. One reason figures such as Antigone and Job seem so uncanny, therefore, is because they reverse this order. They become "dead (wo)men walking," alive even after their symbolic deaths.

72. Job's appearance, in other words, is uncanny in the sense described by Sigmund Freud, "The Uncanny" in *SE XVII* (1955 [1919]). One of Freud's examples is of a time when he, riding in a train car, misrecognized his own image in the mirror as another passenger who had mistakenly barged into his compartment. After getting up to redirect this passenger whose appearance he did not

like, he realized he was looking at a mirror. The uncanny is not simply unfamiliar, it is the familiar once its familiarity has been sucked out of it.

73. Although understandable on the basis of my exegesis and without knowledge of the use of such terms in the work of J. Lacan and others influenced by Lacan, especially the French philosopher Alain Badiou, I should indicate their influences and acknowledge my debt to their important explorations of concepts such as an "event" or an "act." Badiou's major, immense works, recently translated into English, are *Being and Event*, trans. O. Feltham (London: Continuum, 2005); and *Logics of Worlds*, trans. A. Toscano (London: Continuum, 2009). His shorter monograph on Paul may be of more interest to biblical critics, *Saint Paul: The Foundation of Universalism*, trans. R. Brassier (Stanford, Calif.: Stanford University Press, 2003). For Lacan's part, he spoke in several places about a notion of the psychoanalytic act, but most significantly devoted an entire year's seminar to explicating it (and it was a significant year in Paris to explore what is involved in an act), *The Seminar of Jacques Lacan, Book XV: The Psychoanalytic Act, 1967–68* (Unpublished Typescript).

74. The tradition about Job sitting upon a dunghill comes from LXX, which has κοπρίας.

75. See also Copjec, *Imagine*, 154.

76. In CHAPTER 3 I argue that *the* message of Eliphaz's first speech (chs. 4–5) is contained in the "instruction" that he admonishes Job not to reject in 5:17.

77. Such a notion of harmony is especially prominent in Fox's article "The Epistemology of the Book of Proverbs," *Journal of Biblical Literature* 126 (2007).

78. Not unrelatedly, Lacan says in *Seminar XI*, 128, "the cause of the unconscious . . . must be conceived as, fundamentally, a lost cause"; or, "In short, there is cause only in something that doesn't work." *Seminar XI*, 22. For a discussion of causality in Lacan, philosophy, and psychoanalysis, see Adrian Johnston, *Time Driven: Metapsychology and the Splitting of the Drive* (Evanston, Ill.: Northwestern University Press, 2005), 37–42, and Alenka Zupančič, *Why Psychoanalysis: Three Interventions* (Uppsala, Sweden: NSU Press, 2008), 33–58.

79. These two structures of universality I take primarily from Jacques Lacan, *The Seminar of Jacques Lacan, Book XX: Encore, 1972–1973*, ed. Jacques-Alain Miller; trans. Bruce Fink (New York: W. W. Norton & Co., 1998), which defines masculine and feminine being according to them, but also from Copjec's commentary on Lacan's formulas of sexuation that connects them with the Kantian antinomies of pure reason: *Read My Desire: Lacan against the Historicists* (Cambridge, Mass.: MIT Press, 1994), ch. 8. To make explicit the feminist insight that undergirds the logic of this entire book, I understand JOB's transformation of the wisdom tradition as a feminization of the tradition's (masculine) structure of wisdom. See Davis Hankins, "Woman and the Plasticity of Wisdom: Reconsidering Wisdom Literature and Feminism," in *Imagination, Ideology, and Inspiration: Biblical Studies after Walter Brueggemann*, ed. R. Williamson and J. Kaplan (Sheffield: Sheffield Phoenix, forthcoming).

80. Newsom, *Contest*, 57.

81. See Mathewson, *Death*, 53n.65.

82. Newsom, *Contest*, 57. The observation is not unique to Newsom. See also Walter Vogels, "Job's Empty Pious Slogans (Job 1,20–22; 2,8–10)," in *The Book of*

Job, ed. W. A. M. Beuken (Leuven: Leuven University Press, 1994), 370, "[The actions] may, however, express sorrow or despair, faith or disbelief." But Newsom's thesis that the prose tale is interested in Job's "moral imagination" (and not his piety) does bring her argument closer to my own—that the test tests Job's wisdom as a surplus dimension over his piety—than most others.

83. In a discussion of cause in Aristotle and Kant, Lacan (*Seminar XI*, 22) notes "that the problem of cause has always been an embarrassment to philosophers . . . Cause is to be distinguished from that which is determinate in a chain . . . [from] what is pictured in the law of action and reaction."

84. Clines, *Job 1–20*, 49.

85. Vogels, "Empty," 372.

86. Mathewson, *Death*, 45.

87. Mathewson, *Death*, 24, defines culture as a system of symbols that gives individuals "a sense of life and vitality *in light of the knowledge of death*, a sense of life that Lifton names 'symbolic immortality'" (emphasis added). Life comes to be because of death, in the social coordination of individual drives for immortality and eternity in the face of mortality and finitude. The psychohistorian R. J. Lifton informs much of Mathewson's theoretical orientation.

88. Mathewson, *Death*, 40–41.

89. Mathewson, *Death*, 49. This theological and moral position would not be unique to Job; one can find ample textual support in the Bible for the pairing of abundant life with right living. The texts that Mathewson cites (*Death*, 41–44) come mainly from Deuteronomy, Psalms, and Proverbs.

90. E.g., Clines, *Job 1–20*, 15; Alan Cooper, "The Sense of the Book of Job," *Prooftexts* 17 (1997): 232; Rowley, *Job*, 29; Hartley, *Job*, 70.

91. Jean Laplanche, *The Unconscious and the Id: A Volume of Laplanche's Problematiques*, trans. L. Thurston and L. Watson (London: Rebus, 1999), 198; see also Johnston, *Žižek's Ontology*, 45, and the other resources cited therein that speak of "a profound relation between obsessional neurosis and mortality."

92. Mathewson, *Death*, 47.

93. Roland Barthes, *La Chambre Claire: Note sur la Photographie* (Paris: Gallimard/Seuil, 1980), 144–45, "La Vie/la Mort: le paradigme se réduit à un simple déclic, celui qui sépare la pose initiale du papier final."

94. Mathewson, *Death*, 46.

95. Mathewson, *Death*, 54.

96. Mathewson, *Death*, 17–18. The notion that the particular, positive meanings given to death are "deflections" derives from K. Burke. The early philosophy of M. Heidegger undoubtedly informs the sense of authenticity and of death as a horizon that makes life possible.

97. *Pace* Mathewson, *Death*, 53.

98. Compare with Clines, *Job 1–20*, 36–37.

99. Mathewson, *Death*, 57.

100. Mathewson, *Death*, 61.

101. Mathewson, *Death*, 63.

102. Such an internal, limiting force of incoherence is another form of the unsayable, discussed in §7.

103. I have offered a simplified description in ontogenetic terms but do not mean to imply any sense of conscious intentionality behind the "choice" of the symbolic order. For a more precise and detailed discussion of these issues, see Johnston, *Žižek's Ontology*, part 1; and Copjec, *Imagine*, ch. 1.

104. To say that a form of life "persists" need not imply that it pre-exists the subject's entry into the symbolic order as a substantial entity. See, for example, Slavoj Žižek, *Tarrying with the Negative: Kant, Hegel, and the Critique of Ideology* (Durham: Duke University Press, 1993), 180–82.

105. On Lacan's notion of *jouissance*, see the discussion in footnote 72 on pages 239–40.

106. Slavoj Žižek, *The Plague of Fantasies* (London: Verso, 1997), 89.

107. Compare with Johnston, *Time*, 165; 238.

108. Copjec, *Imagine*, 32.

109. Mathewson, *Death*, 55.

110. E.g., "It is the very formula of oriental resignation. The only course is to allow the sovereign Ruler of the world to act as He wills." Dhorme, *Job*, 13.

111. E.g., referring at first to Job's second response, "It is rather some kind of trustfulness that God knows what he is doing, and the very same piety we have witnessed in Job's blessing the Yahweh who had given and taken away (1:21)." Clines, *Job 1–20*, 54.

112. Thinking Job continues to relate to God as an unfathomable Other, some, e.g., Wolde ("Development," 204), disparage his first response as cocksure.

113. A relevant discussion of this example can be found in Gilles Deleuze, *The Logic of Sense*, trans. Mark Lester (New York: Columbia University Press, 1990), 100–102. For a somewhat similar statement on Job, see Clines, *Job 1–20*, 54.

114. Compare Fox, "Epistemology," 671.

115. Driver, *Job*, 22.

116. Clines, *Job 1–20*, 9.

117. Carol A. Newsom, "Job," in *The Women's Bible Commentary*, 2nd ed. (Louisville: Westminster/John Knox, 1998), 139.

118. Compare Newsom, "Job" (NIB), 356; Janzen, *Job*, 49–51; and Mathewson, *Death*, 57n.81.

119. Newsom, "Job" (WBC), 139–40.

120. Newsom, "Job" (NIB), 356.

121. In this sense what Mathewson and Job's wife share is that any action that they allow for Job depends upon what psychoanalysis calls the superego. The superego is not the psychical representative of society's laws but the vicious agent who commands and accuses without concern for the law. Mathewson's superego injunction would be: "Job, if you want to live, one more resymbolization!" Job's wife's position illustrates how the superego operates above every law so that any action, regardless of its lawfulness, automatically makes the subject guilty.

122. Žižek draws numerous consequences out of Freud's vague notion of the death drive: "In trying to explain the functioning of the human psyche in terms of the pleasure principle, reality principle, and so on, Freud became increasingly aware of a radical non-functional element, a basic destructiveness and excess of negativity, that couldn't be accounted for. And that is why Freud posed

the hypothesis of death drive." Slavoj Žižek and Glyn Daly, *Conversations with Žižek* (Cambridge, Eng.: Polity, 2004), 61. Žižek repeatedly links the death drive to the human being's "radical and fundamental *dis*–adaptation, *mal*–adaptation, to his environs. . . . The 'death drive' means that the organism is no longer fully determined by its environs, that it 'explodes/implodes' into a cycle of autonomous behavior." *The Parallax View* (Cambridge: MIT Press, 2006), 231. Compare Johnston, *Žižek's*, ch. 13, 222–23.

123. The topological image here is that of the Möbius band, wherein one can go from one side to another side on the same surface.

124. To return to a question raised but deferred on pages 45–46, piety must not be defined by the prose tale, because the tale's very conception of WISDOM demands that piety remain open to transformation by an act of WISDOM.

125. Leo G. Perdue et al. (eds.), *In Search of Wisdom: Essays in Memory of John G. Gammie* (Louisville, Ky.: Westminster/John Knox Press, 1993), 82, emphasis added. Compare Balentine, *Job*, 57–58: "Job remains what he has always been."

126. Newsom, *Contest*, 64–65.

127. Newsom, *Contest*, 65–71.

128. The idea that the voyeur's gaze is disturbed by the rustling of leaves, or some other sensible form, was an insistence of the famous analysis of the voyeur by Jean-Paul Sartre in *Being and Nothingness*, trans. H. Barnes (New York: Washington Square, 1992).

129. Newsom, *Contest*, 70, suggests that the reader may feel "contaminated."

Chapter 3

1. I learned about it from Patrick Creadon's 2006 documentary *Wordplay*.

2. Quoted in Coral Amende, *The Crossword Obsession* (New York: Berkley Books, 2001), 302.

3. For a discussion of the differences among the arguments of the three friends, see Carol A. Newsom, *The Book of Job: A Contest of Moral Imaginations* (Oxford: Oxford University Press, 2003), 96–129, and David J. A. Clines, "The Arguments of Job's Three Friends," in *Art and Meaning: Rhetoric in Biblical Literature*, ed. D. Clines, D. Gunn, and A. Hauser (Sheffield: JSOT, 1982), 199–214.

4. Gustavo Gutiérrez, *On Job: God-talk and the Suffering of the Innocent* (Maryknoll, N.Y.: Orbis Books, 1987), 21.

5. John E. Hartley, *The Book of Job* (Grand Rapids, Mich.: Eerdmans, 1988), 103.

6. Hartley, *Job*, 103.

7. Furthermore, according to some scholars—e.g., Samuel E. Balentine, *Job* (Macon, Ga.: Smyth & Helwys, 2006), 103—Eliphaz is probably the oldest and most respected of the friends because he is honored with the first position in the dispute.

8. Carol A. Newsom, "The Book of Job," in *The New Interpreter's Bible Volume 4*, ed. L. Keck (Nashville, Tenn.: Abingdon, 1996), 363.

9. Kemper Fullerton, "Double Entendre in the First Speech of Eliphaz," *Journal of Biblical Literature* 49 (1930): 320–74. Fullerton's work is supplemented

some fifty years later in a short article by Yair Hoffman, "The Use of Equivocal Words in the First Speech of Eliphaz (Job IV-V)," *Vetus Testamentum* 30 (1980): 114–19.

10. Such is the conclusion of the majority of interpreters including, for example, David J. A. Clines, *Job 1–20* (Dallas: Word, 1989), 121–25; Norman C. Habel, *The Book of Job* (Philadelphia: Westminster, 1985), 121, which reverses Habel's previous position in *The Book of Job* (Cambridge: Cambridge University Press, 1975), 26.

11. While a minority conclusion, it is ancient (strongly articulated by Rashi) and still advanced by well-respected scholars, e.g., Balentine, *Job*, 104–5; Edwin M. Good, *In Turns of Tempest: A Reading of Job, with a Translation* (Stanford, Calif.: Stanford University Press, 1990), 208–13.

12. The hermeneutical nature of the problem is recognized by many who nonetheless enter into the debates; see Clines, *Job 1–20*, 121; Yair Hoffman, *A Blemished Perfection: The Book of Job in Context* (Sheffield: Sheffield Academic, 1996), 116–17.

13. See Hans-Georg Gadamer, *Truth and Method*, 2nd ed., trans. J. Wiensheimer and D. G. Marshall (London, New York: Continuum, 2004), 268–73. To seek a solution to the present hermeneutical impasse by turning to Gadamer, patron saint of hermeneutics, is to adhere to the old adage "only the spear that smote you can heal your wound." This ancient notion receives a properly dialectical analysis in Slavoj Žižek, *Tarrying with the Negative: Kant, Hegel, and the Critique of Ideology* (Durham: Duke University Press, 1993), ch. 5.

14. These divisions are generally uncontroversial. Pieter van der Lugt, *Rhetorical Criticism and the Poetry of the Book of Job* (Leiden: Brill, 1995), 65–66, provides a list of critics and their particular divisions.

15. It is supposed that v.17 reports the content of the word mentioned in v.12, though it is not necessary to take this as a direct citation. Verses 18–21, at any rate, describe what happened indirectly, in more summary fashion.

16. See, for example, Clines, *Job 1–20*, 124–25; Balentine, *Job*, 105–6.

17. See Gerhard von Rad, *Wisdom in Israel*, trans. James D. Martin (Nashville, Tenn.: Abingdon, 1972), ch. 4.

18. The range of scholarly opinions can be represented by the antithetical positions of Joachim Becker, *Gottesfurcht im Alten Testament* (Rome: Ist Biblico, 1965, Analecta Biblica), and David J. A. Clines, "'The Fear of the Lord Is Wisdom' (Job 28:28): A Semantic and Contextual Study," in *Job 28: Cognition in Context*, ed. E. van Wolde (Leiden: Brill, 2003), 57–92. David Cromwell Knauert, "The Limits of Wisdom and the Dialectic of Desire" (PhD diss., Duke University, 2009), 185–96, reframes the question, demonstrating that the paradigmatic or structuring function of the signifier "fear" is strictly a function of its gradual *loss* of significance.

19. Michael V. Fox, "Words for Folly," *Zeitschrift für Althebraistik* 10 (1997): 8.

20. Franz Delitzsch, *Biblical Commentary on the Book of Job*, 2nd ed., trans. F. Bolton (Edinburgh: T. & T. Clark, 1872), 91.

21. Fox, "Words for Folly," 8.

22. Compare Good, *Tempest*, 210. The masculine form *kesel* means "confidence" in Ps 78:7 and Job 31:24, but "folly" in Qoh 7:25.

23. The fool's confidence may be less important than the sage's fear but both are central to Proverbs. Dame Folly's final appellation in Prov 1–9 is "the woman of k^esîlût" (9:13); the book's final poem that praises the Woman of Substance teaches that "Charm is deceptive and beauty ephemeral, but a woman who yir'at YHWH is to be praised" (31:30). For the inherent connections between Woman-Wisdom in Prov 1–9 and the Woman of Substance in Prov 31:10–31, see Christine Roy Yoder, *Wisdom as a Woman of Substance: A Socioeconomic Reading of Proverbs 1–9 and 31:10–31* (Berlin: Walter de Gruyter, 2001).

24. The ambiguity of the vision and its implications receive detailed attention in James E. Harding, "A Spirit of Deception in Job 4:15? Interpretive Indeterminacy and Eliphaz's Vision," *Biblical Interpretation* 13 (2005): 137–66.

25. Harding, "Spirit," 159.

26. As noted and elaborated by Harding, "Spirit," 152–53.

27. David J. A. Clines, "Verb Modality and the Interpretation of Job IV 20–21," *Vetus Testamentum* 30 (1980): 354; compare Clines, "Arguments," 204, and David W. Cotter, *A Study of Job 4–5 in the Light of Contemporary Literary Theory* (Atlanta: Scholars Press, 1992), 196.

28. There is no reason to accept Clines's conclusion in "Arguments," 204–5, that the subject that could actually receive the potential predicate in these verses is the cultivators of trouble and sowers of misery mentioned in v.8.

29. Others agree that Eliphaz makes "unrighteous" a universal predicate of humankind; see, for example, Driver, *Job*, 48; Pope, *Job*, 39; Habel, *Job*, 120.

30. Gerhard von Rad, *Old Testament Theology, Vol. 1: The Theology of Israel's Historical Traditions*, trans. D. M. G. Stalker (New York: Harper & Row, 1962), 410.

31. Carol A. Newsom, "'The Consolations of God': Assessing Job's Friends Across a Cultural Abyss," in *Reading from Right to Left: Essays on the Hebrew Bible in Honour of David J. A. Clines*, ed. J. C. Exum and H. G. M. Williamson (London: Sheffield, 2003), 349.

32. Newsom, "Consolations," 356.

33. Newsom, "Consolations," 354.

34. Newsom, "Consolations," 356.

35. Newsom, "Consolations," 356.

36. See, for example, Dhorme, *Job*, 57; and Driver, *Job*, 49–50.

37. Compare HALOT, 491.

38. Compare HALOT, 1110–1111.

39. The division at this "strophic" level is basically the same as in, for example, Friedrich Horst, *Hiob* (Neukirchen-Vluyn: Neukirchener Verlag, 1968), 58–60; Samuel L. Terrien, *Job* (Neuchâtel: Delachaux et Niestlé, 1963), 74–78; Habel, *Job*, 113–15; Cotter, *Job 4–5*, 127–28, cf. 117–28; Balentine, *Job*, 104; and van der Lugt, *Rhetorical*, 70–79, who includes a list of different divisions and the interpreters who proposed them on pp.75–76. Cotter, *Job 4–5*, 122, writes, "The sections described by Horst (4:1–11, 12–21, 5:1–7, 8–16, 17–27) emerge as the most typical of the results achieved by scholars working on a great variety of theoretical bases." See van der Lugt, *Rhetorical*, 76n.1 for several of Horst's predecessors with similar sections.

40. Compare Habel, *Job*, 118–19.

41. Terrien, *Job*, 75, however, thinks they are set apart as crowns on two strophes of three triads: 8–10, 11–13, 14–16 + 17; 18–20, 21–23, 24–26 +27. As nice as Terrien's symmetry is, I side with the majority who read 5:17 as an introductory rather than a concluding line; see also Cotter, *Job 4–5*, 122.

42. The root is usually translated "to root" and has a similar range of meaning in Hebrew as it does in English, having first to do with a plant, but most often used to various figurative ends. It signifies a source (Deut 29:17; Job 19:28; Ezek 17:9), an anchor to the ground (2 Kgs 19:30; Job 8:17, 14:8, 28:9; Isa 40:24; Ezek 17:6), and more generally something riveted, stable (Prov 12:3; Jer 12:2), anchored to a social body (Job 29:19), or a history (Judg 5:14; Isa 37:31), and, contrastively, the displacement of some such fixed position, as in "uproot" (Ps 52:7; Job 31:8), as well as the acts of digging (Ps 80:10) and spreading (Jer 17:8).

43. Bildad twice characterizes the root of the wicked as dry, weak, ephemeral (Job 8:17–18, 18:16), and Proverbs opposes the root of the righteous, which will not totter, to wickedness, which will not be established (12:3).

44. For a fuller treatment of the psychoanalytic use of this term, see J. Laplanche and J.-B. Pontalis, *The Language of Psycho-Analysis*, trans. D. Nicholson-Smith (New York: W. W. Norton & Company, 1973), 162–65.

45. Verse 5 is impossible to make sense of as it stands. As for the part referred to here, the consonantal text, *qṣrw* could be read either as a qal perfect 3cp whose subject is the children of v.4 ("what they harvested . . ."), as in LXX, or a noun with the 3ms suffix ("whose harvest . . ."), as in the MT (the *mater* is the Masoretes' attempt to clarify this ambiguity). The relative particle beginning the verse works either way. Whether it is the fool or his children whose harvest is eaten by another, the fool is obviously not in a position to do anything about it with his head in the ground. This part of this verse is just a glimpse of the difficulties of 5:1–7. Newsom, "Job" (NIB), 379, writes, "This passage is the most difficult part of Eliphaz's speech to understand. First, the text is garbled in v.5; second, it is not clear how the verses fit together; third, vv.6–7 can be interpreted in contradictory ways. Any interpretation must therefore be tentative." For these reasons I have tried to stick to the consonantal text and focus more on the images structuring the passage than the precise meaning it produces.

46. See Clines, *Job 1–20*, 141–42.

47. Many repoint the MT to read a hiphil imperfect instead of a *pual* imperfect so that Eliphaz actually says "a human begets suffering." This reading is further supported by the presence of many manuscripts that have *yld*. While this is possible, it requires the *lᵉ*-preposition to mark the accusative, which it often does, only not with the verb *yld*. *yld* often occurs with *lᵉ*-, and these cases include both defective and full spellings of the verb, but nowhere does the *lᵉ*-preposition mark the direct object of the verb *yld*. See Gen 24:15; 35:26; 36:5; Deut 23:9; 2 Sam 3:2, 5; 5:13; Prov 17:7, 21; Job 1:2.

48. Compare Balentine, *Job*, 115.

49. E.g., Habel, *Job*, 120: "This El is the creator God of wisdom tradition, the master mind whose strategies are superior to those of the wisest schemers on earth and who intervenes to thwart their ingenius plans."

50. Compare Cotter, *Job 4–5*, 217, 219–20: "One of the puzzling things about the sorts of people to whom Eliphaz takes exception here is the fact that, by

and large, the qualities he objects to are held in esteem in the rest of the Hebrew Bible . . . A tightly crafted unity, this section of Eliphaz's first speech leaves the reader more confused than ever about him . . . [H]e seems to condemn the wise. At least he speaks of them, in vv.12–14, in such ambiguous terms that a reader who did not know that Eliphaz fancied himself to be one of the wise himself could hardly guess." Numerous interpreters miss this because they project a negative moral value onto these qualities. See, for example, Balentine, *Job*, 117.

51. *Pace* Habel, *Job*, 135, who refers to God here as "the grand controller of all cosmic events that affect human lives"; or Balentine, *Job*, 119, who calls God the one who "has revealed the blueprint for creation" to Eliphaz.

52. On this important term, see Habel, *Job*, 134–35.

53. *Pace* Balentine, *Job*, 118, "What Eliphaz envisions as Job's restitution is tantamount to a return to the paradisiacal harmony of Eden (vv.23–26)."

54. So, Clines, *Job 1–20*, 147: "The didacticism of the imperatives [in vv.17b and 27b] sounds a note of uncertainty; that is, there *is* a blessed future for Job, but *only if* he will meet certain conditions."

55. Newsom, "Job" (NIB), 381: "Read more sympathetically, and with more appreciation of the nature of poetic language, Eliphaz's imagery evokes something of the life-giving power of God, which sustains a person even in calamity, the inextinguishable source of strength that prevents a person who is gravely suffering from shattering entirely and even enables that person to flourish again."

56. Compare Deut 32:39; Hos 6:1.

57. What follows is an over-simplification of the basic problem of self-consciousness confronted repeatedly over the history of Western philosophy. This problem is lucidly discussed by Adrian Johnston in *Time Driven: Metapsychology and the Splitting of the Drive* (Evanston, Ill.: Northwestern University Press, 2005) and *Žižek's Ontology: A Transcendental Materialist Theory of Subjectivity* (Evanston, Ill.: Northwestern University Press, 2008).

58. Clines, *Job 1–20*, 121.

59. So, Žižek writes, "In short, the intimate link between the *subject* and *failure* lies not in the fact that 'external' material social rituals and/or practices forever fail to reach the subject's innermost kernel, to represent it adequately . . . but, on the contrary, in the fact that the 'subject' itself is nothing but the failure of signification, of its own symbolic representation—the subject is nothing 'beyond' this failure, it emerges through this failure." Judith Butler, Ernesto Laclau, and Slavoj Žižek, *Contingency, Hegemony, and Universality: Contemporary Dialogues on the Left* (London: Verso, 2000), 119–20.

60. See, for example, Jacques Lacan, *The Seminar of Jacques Lacan, Book XI: The Four Fundamental Concepts of Psycho-Analysis, 1964*, ed. Jacques-Alain Miller; trans. Alan Sheridan (New York: W. W. Norton & Co., 1977), 203–15.

61. Compare J. Maxwell Miller and John H. Hayes, *A History of Ancient Israel and Judah*, 2nd ed. (Louisville: Westminster John Knox, 2006), 320–25.

62. Jacques Lacan, *The Seminar of Jacques Lacan, Book III: The Psychoses, 1955–1956*, ed. Jacques-Alain Miller; trans. Russell Grigg (New York: W. W. Norton & Co., 1993), 262.

63. Lacan, *Seminar III*, 267, 268.

64. Slavoj Žižek, *For They Know Not What They Do: Enjoyment as a Political Factor*, 2nd ed. (London: Verso, 2002), 17.

65. Compare Woman-Wisdom's statement in Prov 8:33: "Hear instruction and be wise; and do not let it go."

66. For differences among the friends' speeches, see Newsom, *Contest*, 96–129; and Clines, "Arguments."

67. See the bulleted points in Balentine, *Job*, 229.

68. Eliphaz contrasts the righteous and the wicked on the same scale of durability in 4:7–9.

69. Zophar's account of a "doubled insight"—*kiplayim l'tûšîâ*—lends itself readily to the Kantian categories of noumena and phenomena discussed at length in part 1, so that Job's unbearable suffering can be read as a category error. Job foolishly mistakes the phenomenal *Objekt* for the noumenal *Ding*.

Chapter 4

1. Excerpt from Philip Larkin, "Aubade," from *Collected Poems*, ed. A. Thwaite (London: Faber and Faber, 1990 [1988]), 208–9. Reprinted by permission of Faber and Faber.

2. For a well-documented discussion of this issue and how it continues to inform scholarship, see Carol A. Newsom, "Re-considering Job," *Currents in Biblical Research* 5 (2007): 155–82.

3. On the intersubjective dynamics involved in lament psalms, see Amy C. Cottrill, *Language, Power, and Identity in the Lament Psalms of the Individual* (New York: T. & T. Clark, 2008).

4. Claus Westermann, *The Structure of the Book of Job: A Form-Critical Analysis* (Philadelphia: Fortress, 1981), 67.

5. Westermann, *Structure*, 69.

6. Westermann, *Structure*, 69, 70, emphasis added.

7. Norman C. Habel, *The Book of Job* (Philadelphia: Westminster, 1985), 351.

8. Habel, *Job*, 351.

9. See Habel, *Job*, 348.

10. Carol A. Newsom, *The Book of Job: A Contest of Moral Imaginations* (Oxford: Oxford University Press, 2003), 16, claims that the author of JOB "wrote by juxtaposing and intercutting certain genres and distinctly stylized voices, providing sufficient interconnection among the different parts to establish the sense of the 'same' story but leaving the different parts sharply marked and sometimes overly disjunctive." She then describes the author's work as a "manipulation of genre."

11. This characteristic may be a generic convention since the dialogue shares it with the *Babylonian Theodicy*. See Carol A. Newsom, "The Book of Job," in *The New Interpreter's Bible Volume 4*, ed. L. Keck (Nashville, Tenn.: Abingdon, 1996), 330–31.

12. As discussed on page 82, the ambiguity in this statement cannot be eliminated. This word means "confidence" in its other two occurrences (Ps 85:9; 143:9) but the masculine form of the substantive means both "confidence"

(e.g., Job 8:14; 31:24; Ps 78:7) and "folly" or "stupidity" (e.g., Qoh 7:25), which is how some ancient versions took it (LXX and Jerome). In both places in JOB where it occurs meaning confidence, it parallels *mbṭḥ* (cf. Prov 1:33). The second line, and especially the parallel here with hope (*tqwh*), certainly attenuate the possible double entendre. See, for example, David J. A. Clines, *Job 1–20* (Dallas: Word, 1989), 109.

13. The NRSV takes the uncharacteristically expansionist step to insert "of God" into its translation.

14. David J. A. Clines, "The Fear of the Lord Is Wisdom (Job 28:28): A Semantic and Contextual Study," in *Job 28: Cognition in Context*, ed. E. van Wolde (Leiden: Brill, 2003), 70, recently made a similar point, though I disagree with his conclusion that the terms for fear "mean no more and no less that the emotion of fear."

15. Compare Prov 15:33: "The fear of YHWH is the instruction (*mûsar*) of wisdom, just as humility precedes honor."

16. This sense of the difference between fear and terror was implicit in my description of the former as a positve *power* and the latter as a negative *force*. The difference between a force and a power can be described as a function of the presence or absence of an agent wielding it; power is wielded by an agent, a force lacks any apparent agent behind it. In the present context, then, one can say that the positive fear is available only to the conscious intention of the sapiential agent whereas the negative fear characteristically afflicts, comes upon, or overcomes its victim. The friends do not say that *no* agent wields the negative force of fear; they rather say that *no human* agent wields it. They attribute the negative force to the unique agency of God (e.g., 25:2). The distinction between a power and a force, therefore, is only meant to apply from the perspective of the human, who has the one at hand but experiences the other as a heavy-handed imposition.

17. *yqwṭ* is a hapax that has occasioned various emendations. See Clines, *Job 1–20*, 199–200. This translation follows a meaning of *qwṭ* in accord with the readings of the Targum and Syriac versions of the Hebrew Bible.

18. MT points the verb as a singular, as is *tškwn* in v.15. That both verbs are feminine has led some (e.g., JPSV) to take the feminine noun "terrors" as an intensive plural and the subject of the verb. In v.11, the same word is clearly the subject of the two verbs in each line, both of which are defectively pointed as plurals. Being in the hiphil and feminine, as opposed to the niphal and masculine as is the verb in the first line, this appears to be the best option even though it leaves the problem of what it means for terrors to "march one off to the king." For most the king, constructed with the terrors, refers to the god of the underworld (see the discussion in Clines, *Job 1–20*, 406). Most important for my purposes is that the terrors control the steps of the wicked and rip him from his secure dwelling, much as Bildad says in v.11.

19. This is a product of the friends' adherence to "one of the most widespread and fundamental beliefs in the ancient Near East . . . that good and evil have a different relation to reality. The resilient, enduring quality of good derives from its participation in the structures of creation itself, whereas evil, no matter how powerful and vital it appears, is actually fragile and subject to disintegration

because it has no root in that order of creation . . . What this view claims is significant is simply the qualitative difference between good and evil consequent upon
the ontological status of each." Newsom, *Contest*, 121.

20. Although *'ml* is pointed here as a personal noun ("laborer, sufferer"),
I follow most who read it as an abstract noun with the LXX and the Vulg. See
Clines, *Job 1–20*, 477.

21. The image of hands spread out to God is commonly used to represent
prayer or supplication. See Exod 9:29; 1 Kgs 8:22, 38; Jer 4:31; Ps 143:6; Lam
1:17; Ezra 9:5.

22. The pointing in the MT (*muṣāq*) renders the defective spelling of the
hophal participle of either *yṣq* or *ṣwq*, meaning "to be poured out" or "to be oppressed," respectively. Many go with the former—"You will be cast, strong, a man
of steel, and you will not fear" (see Clines, *Job 1–20*, 269; cf. NEB: "a man of iron";
NRSV: "secure"). One could repoint it as the defective spelling of the noun meaning hardship or anguish—*māṣôq* in Jer 19:9; in its feminine form *mᵉṣûqâ* in Job
15:24. It is certainly possible, especially in light of the above discussion of the end
of Eliphaz's first speech, that Zophar intends to tell Job that he will be oppressed,
in anguish, or poured out, and not fear. It may be best to read with other Hebrew
manuscripts that have a doubled middle consonant, which could be taken as an
indication of the *min* preposition prefixed to the nominal form of the root *ṣwq*,
found in both masculine (Dan 9:25), as here, and feminine forms (Isa 8:22; 30:6;
and Prov 1:27). This reading nicely renders two successive, parallel uses of the
preposition—"you will lift your face *without* blemish, you will be *without* anguish;"
see Isa 2:10, 19, 21; Ps 91:5—and a semantic parallel between the final phrases—
"you will be without anguish, and you will not fear."

23. While this verb (*hpr*) usually means "to be ashamed," it also means "to
dig" (e.g., Gen 21:30; Deut 23:14) or "search" (e.g., Job 3:21; 39:29; Deut 1:2),
which seems more likely here.

24. The reference to "tents" may thus be a recognition of a transsubjective
dimension to identity that is supposedly absent from certain western accounts of
the autonomous individual.

25. In CHAPTER 2, I discussed this structure as that of an All constituted on
the basis of an exception. Here one should note the important role prohibition
plays in the establishment of such a structure. While the prohibition may appear
merely superfluous, its superfluousity is precisely what allows the establishment
of the appearance of a beyond and, thus, the constitution of the order.

26. I should not miss the opportunity to state explicitly the difference
between this interpretation and another, much more common one, according
to which a quite knowable and known retribution theology functions as the support for the friends' recognitions of an epistemological limit. See for example,
Clines, *Job 1–20*, 272, which characterizes Zophar in ch. 11 as one "in the academy
of the wise . . . with his own personal chair in Divine Epistemology." On the contrary, I am arguing that the friends' epistemology exists only insofar as it includes
a negation of itself within itself.

27. In addition to those texts by Newsom in which she defines the friends'
theology as a "masochistic sublime" (*Contest*, 138–50; cf. *The Self as Symbolic Space:*

Constructing Identity and Community at Qumran [Leiden: Brill, 2004], 220), or understands the whirlwind speeches under the category of "the tragic sublime" (*Contest*, ch. 9), the sublime has also been drawn on by Tod Linafelt—first, briefly, in Linafelt, "The Undecidability of *BRK* in the Prologue to Job and Beyond," *Biblical Interpretation* 4 (1996): 170–71, and then more extensively in "The Wizard of Uz: Job, Dorothy, and the Limits of the Sublime," *Biblical Interpretation* 14 (2006): 94–109—and Kathleen M. O'Connor, "Wild, Raging Creativity: The Scene in the Whirlwind (Job 38–41)," in *A God So Near: Essays on Old Testament Theology in Honor of Patrick D. Miller*, ed. B. A. Strawn and N. R. Bowen (Winona Lake, Ind.: Eisenbrauns, 2003), 171–79. For Timothy K. Beal (*Religion and Its Monsters* [New York: Routledge, 2002]), Rudolf Otto's notion of the holy is central, but its roots in the sublime are acknowledged and clearly in the background. As is evident in these citations, the category of the sublime has been mostly used in readings of the divine speeches. I discuss it further in my treatment of these speeches below.

28. See Alenka Zupančič, *Ethics of the Real: Kant, Lacan* (London: Verso, 2000), whose influence is obvious throughout the following analysis.

29. Sigmund Freud, "Humour," in *SE XXI* (1961 [1927]), 164.

30. See Zupančič, *Ethics*, 150–52.

31. Zupančič, *Ethics*, 151.

32. "Someone who is afraid can no more judge about the sublime in nature than someone who is in the grip of inclination and appetite can judge about the beautiful . . . Bold, overhanging, as it were threatening cliffs, thunder clouds towering up into heaven, bringing with them flashes of lightening and crashes of thunder, volcanoes with their all-destroying violence, hurricanes with the devastation they leave behind, the boundless ocean set into a rage, a lofty waterfall on a mighty river, etc., make our capacity to resist into an insignificant trifle in comparison with their power. But the sight of them only becomes all the more attractive the more fearful it is, as long as we find ourselves in safety." Immanuel Kant, *Critique of the Power of Judgment*, trans. P. Guyer and E. Matthews (New York: Cambridge University Press, 2000), 144.

33. P. Nemo offers a similar description of Job's experience when he explains why he says, apropos the "dialogue" between Job and the friends (the reason for the scare quotes is obvious from the quotation), "We cannot really say that the two parties 'disagree . . . All combat presupposes a site where adversaries can confront each other face to face. Therefore all combat is communication; and all solitude that results from rejection is a communication in the same way. However, the solitude of Job is even less than this minimal communication. For there is no common ground. It is the ground itself that has collapsed under him." Philippe Nemo, *Job and the Excess of Evil*, trans. Michael Kigel (Pittsburgh: Duquesne University Press, 1998), 37.

34. C. L. Seow, *Job 1–21: Interpretation and Commentary* (Illuminations; Grand Rapids: Eerdmans, 2013), 508–9, is one of many scholars who read this with the preceding verse ("death to my bones [that] I reject"). While he makes a good argument and while leaving it on its own makes the statement somewhat indeterminate, I do so, as it is in the MT, because this verb is elsewhere in JOB on its own and without an object (cf. 34:33; 36:5; 42:6), and because reading it on its

258

own does not limit its object to Job's bones, which is more appropriate in light of the larger function the verb assumes in the dialogue (see for example, 5:17; 8:20; 9:21; 10:3).

35. "Look; he snatches away; who can turn him? Who can say to him, 'What are you doing?'"

36. Translators often render this clause fairly loosely, but some rightly insist upon a literal reading. See Habel, *Job*, 183; Newsom, "Job" (NIB), 412; and Samuel E. Balentine, *Job* (Macon, Ga.: Smyth & Helwys, 2006), 170.

37. So, for example, Habel, *Job*, 179. For discussions of the issue, see Clines, *Job 1–20*, 235–36; and Yair Hoffman, *A Blemished Perfection: The Book of Job in Context* (Sheffield: Sheffield Academic, 1996), 149–50; and Marvin H. Pope, *Job*, 3rd ed. (Garden City, N.Y.: Doubleday, 1973), 72–73. F. Rachel Magdalene, *On the Scales of Righteousness: Neo-Babylonian Trial Law and the Book of Job* (Providence, R.I.: Brown Judaic Studies, 2007), 191–92, notes the anagram this word forms with *'šq*, "to oppress," which suggests that Job experiences his perversion as oppressive.

38. So, for example, Robert Gordis, *The Book of Job: Commentary, New Translation, and Special Studies* (New York: The Jewish Theological Seminary of America, 1978), 96, and Clines, *Job 1–20*, 218.

39. That is, these texts do not testify to the "death of the subject" such as is described in certain post-structuralist or new historicist discourses.

40. Compare Harry G. Frankfurt, "Freedom of the Will and the Concept of a Person," *The Journal of Philosophy* 68 (1971): 5–20.

41. Others have also drawn on Freud's notion of the uncanny in their readings of JOB. See, for example, Beal, *Religion*, 4–5, 55.

42. Sigmund Freud, "The Uncanny," in *SE XVII* (1955 [1919]b), 220. He draws especially on the direction indicated by Schelling who says, Freud summarizes, "everything is *unheimlich* that ought to have remained secret and hidden but has come to light" ("Uncanny," 225).

43. Habel, *Job*, 196.

44. Newsom, "Job" (NIB), 413; compare with *Contest*, 144.

45. This is to describe the anxiety that is the affective avatar of Job's experience of God in the sense Lacan gives it in his tenth seminar where, for example, he says, "anxiety is not the signal of a lack but of something that you must manage to conceive of at this redoubled level as being the absence of this support of the lack." *The Seminar of Jacques Lacan, Book X: Anxiety, 1962–1963* (Unpublished Typescript), 12.5.1962. Anxiety begins at the moment the lack (desire) that supports the subject goes lacking (*Le Séminaire de Jacques Lacan, Livre X: Angoisse, 1962–1963*, ed. Jacques-Alain Miller [Paris: Éditions du Seuil, 2004], 53). The importance of this observation will become more apparent as this chapter proceeds. See also *Seminar X*, 11.28.62, where Lacan exhorts his students to (re)read Freud's article on the *Unheimlich*, which he calls "the absolutely indispensable hinge for approaching the question of anxiety . . . I will approach the anxiety this year by the *Unheimlichkeit*."

46. This argument distances my reading from Nemo's, which describes the ground beneath Job's feet as unsettled or absent. To support my critique of Nemo via Levinas, in his early evocation of the whistle that Charlie Chaplin swallows in

City Lights, Levinas describes anxiety as the experience of being riveted to one's being as to something one cannot assume; *On Escape: de l'évasion*, trans. B. Bergo (Stanford, Calif.: Stanford University Press, 2003), 64–65.

47. Joan Copjec, "The Censorship of Interiority," *Umbr(a)* (2009): 178. See Žižek, *Tarrying*, ch. 6, especially 208–11, for a lengthy discussion and numerous social, cultural, and historical examples supporting the Lacanian thesis that the subject's enjoyment always appears as something foreign to her.

48. I encountered the notion of an other who lives the subject in Deleuze's description of the double, which is "not a doubling of the One, but a redoubling of the Other. It is not a reproduction of the Same, but a repetition of the Different. It is not the emanation of an 'I,' but something that places in immanence an always other or a Non-self. It is never the other who is a double in the doubling process, it is a self that lives me as a double of the other: I do not encounter myself on the outside, I find the other in me." Gilles Deleuze, "Foldings, or the Inside of Thought (Subjectivation)," in *Foucault*, trans. S. Hand (Minneapolis: University of Minneapolis Press, 1988), 98.

49. The prevalence of Job's use of siege imagery for God is well-documented. Some of the best examples come in ch. 19; see especially vv.6, 8, 10, 12.

50. Copjec, "Censorship," 174, refers to this anxious sense of "the unbearable opaqueness we are to ourselves" as an experience of "being stuck to an inalienable alienness."

51. Philippe Nemo's study of JOB relies on some of the same intellectual tradition as this book and often arrives at similar sounding conclusions, which makes it crucial to understand the differences between the two studies. Nemo describes anxiety, which also functions as a defining category for his analysis, as a transformation of the person. In reference to Job's descriptions of himself as "drunk with pain" (10:15), "inebriated" with "delirium" (7:4), and of his words as "thoughtless" (6:3), he says we should not take these to be superlatives or metaphors painting "the portrait of a man suffering in the extreme while still basically remaining who he is . . . Job is not altogether 'there.' He is 'elsewhere,' in some 'other' place not related to the normal place. Anxiety has caused him to take leave of himself, has fractured his being, has derailed him" (*Job*, 35). While I agree that we must not collapse the "other" place into reality or the "normal" place, it is equally crucial that we do not separate the two, which will be especially apparent in my analysis of shame. Job is dis-placed into an elsewhere whose only quality is that it *is* not-the-normal-place. In other words and in direct contradiction to Nemo's penultimate statement, its *only* characteristic is that *it is related to the normal place.*

52. To Job 16:8 I could add other texts in which Job suffers God's disintegrating presence, is impeded in his attempt to establish a mediating distance through a symbolic order, and suffers an experience of shame when he finds himself implicated in his violent experience, that is, when he finds no space to differentiate God from himself. In ch. 9 Job confronts the impossibility of relating to God from within a symbolic order and then vows in 10:1ac, "My spirit (*nepeš*) is loathed by my life . . . I will speak in the bitterness of my soul" (cf. 7:11). Recall that this "bitterness" is precisely what he accuses God of stuffing

him with in 9:18. The shame associated with such confusions between self and other as regards agency carries important resonances with the testimony of some victims of sexual abuse. Freud's article entitled "A Child is Being Beaten" would be a helpful resource to pursue in this regard. Incidentally, it was published in 1919, the same year as "The Uncanny."

53. Newsom, *Contest*, 162.

54. Newsom, *Contest*, 163, "Although the device is not made explicit until verse 27 (the reference to 'your thoughts'), the second half of the speech is a series of four objections and replies (v.16/vv.17–18; v.19/vv.20–21; v.22/vv.23–26; vv.27–28/vv.29–33)."

55. Some translations preface this quotation with a remark, e.g., "You say . . ." so as to clarify that Job's statement seems to be a quotation or sentiment to which he is responding. It is not clear, however, whether Job disapproves of what the sentiment avers or disagrees with it, as the clarification suggests. Thus it is better not to insert it into the text.

56. Many translations take the participle as a reference to high or exalted ones such as the friends. However, I think it is better to take the heights as a reference to what the friends consider to be the locus of the divine presence for two reasons in particular. First, it occurs in the context of their references to God as one who judges and dwells from on high. Such references are present elsewhere in JOB (e.g., 22:12) and beyond (e.g., Ps 113:5). Second, in this speech Job is here citing sentiments of the friends in order to object to them.

57. For a discussion of the third line of this verse, see Clines, *Job 1–20*, 291–92. Some are reticent to believe that Job calls God the protector of God's own provocateurs but this seems less surprising in light of what has thus far been said.

58. My evocation of skepticism intends to allude to the work of Katharine J. Dell, *The Book of Job as Sceptical Literature* (Berlin: Walter de Gruyter, 1991), 171: "The sentiments of Job in the dialogue are 'sceptical' in that they doubt and question tradition. He attacks the reasoning of the traditionalists who hold certain dogmas about God and his action in the world and puts experience before beliefs which do not begin to answer his questions." If Job is only a skeptic who exposes the limits of traditional wisdom with respect to his experience, then he would appear to entrench the idea that this wisdom forms the ultimate, albeit now more clearly limited, horizon of thought and action.

59. One often finds this either/or interpretation in the claim that Job's position differs from the friends' only with respect to their shared conviction about a doctrine of retribution. Cooper, "The Sense of the Book of Job," *Prooftexts* 17 (1997): 234, adopts and summarizes this position, which goes at least as far back as Maimonides: "Maimonides states, 'If you now consider the discourse of the five [Job, his three friends, and Elihu] in the course of their conversation, you may almost think that whatever one of them says is said also by all the others, so that the same notions are repeated and overlap.' After saying that, of course, Maimonides goes on to find subtle differences among the characters, and to suggest that each one represents a particular philosophical school.

"I see little basis for such differentiation. Job and his friends share a common theology of retributive justice: God rewards people for their virtue and punishes them for their sins. The only question at issue is how that principle applies to the particular case of Job" (Cooper's brackets). There are several problems with this position. Not only have I tried to demonstrate that the universal adopted by the friends is not an all-encompassing retribution theology that can be applied to particular cases—it is rather a universal constituted by an exception which makes room within the theology for cases that contradict it—I have also set up a robust account of the difference between Job's and the friends' theologies that, I hope, would give one pause before agreeing that Cooper's is in fact "the only question."

60. The prepositions indicating this relationship (*bᵉyādô, 'immô, lô*) all denote a relationship of ownership.

61. E.g., Clines, *Job 1–20*, 296, and Newsom, "Job" (NIB), 429.

62. Clines, *Job 1–20*, 296.

63. Gerhard von Rad, *Old Testament Theology, Vol.2: The Theology of Israel's Prophetic Traditions*, trans. D. M. G. Stalker (New York: Harper & Row, 1965), 415, in response to Henning Graf Reventlow, "Grundfragen der alttestamentlighen Theologie im Lichte der neueren deutschen Forschung," *Theologische Zeitschrift* 17 (1961): 96.

64. At the risk of stating the obvious, Job's sense that his increased anxiety corresponds to God's proximity is neither unique to him nor the wisdom literature. One thinks especially of the priestly tradition's holiness theologies in which God's presence is particularly antagonistic to human life. Newsom also recognizes the connection: "In narrative texts the outbreak of the holy against the profane may take the form of annihilating violence (e.g., Lev 10:1–4; Num 11:31–34; 2 Sam 6:6–8)" (*Contest*, 142).

65. Mayer I. Gruber, "Fear, Anxiety and Reverence in Akkadian, Biblical Hebrew and Other North-West Semitic Languages," *Vetus Testamentum* XL (1990): 418–19.

66. Willard Gaylin, *Feelings: Our Vital Signs* (New York: Ballantine, 1979), 21, 22.

67. Paul Kielholz, "Psychopharmacology Measurement of Emotions in Medical Practice" in *Emotions: Their Parameters and Measurement*, ed. L. Levi and U. S. von Euler (New York: Raven, 1975), 748–49.

68. I do not mean to suggest that the student's ego has consciously elected the test; the election is rather something that takes place at the level of the drive. The same distinction is at work in the difference between the milk and the breast according to the psychoanalytic account of the oral drive (see pages 36–37). A human baby seeks milk to fill its stomach. However, the oral drive is posited to account for the fact that the baby is, on the one hand, not satisfied by the milk alone and, on the other, satisfied by something more than the milk, which psychoanalysis names "the breast." The milk is split from itself by the drive's investment, so that the breast is not an object opposed to it but is rather that object in it that makes it something more, that makes it the locus of the subject's enjoyment. There is a brief discussion of this in Lacan, *Seminar X*, 12.12.1962; compare with Jacques Lacan, *The Seminar of Jacques Lacan, Book XI: The Four Fundamental Concepts of Psycho-Analysis, 1964*, ed. Jacques-Alain Miller; trans. Alan Sheridan (New York: W. W. Norton & Co., 1977), 180.

69. Lacan, *Seminar X*, 12.19.1962.

70. "The most striking manifestation, the signal of the intervention of this *objet a*, is anxiety . . . and this object, of which we have to speak under the term *a*, is precisely an object which is outside any possible definition of objectivity." Lacan, *Seminar X*, 1.9.1963. In other words, Lacan deduces the object *(a)* from his elaboration of anxiety, not vice versa.

71. Lacan, *Seminar X*, 1.9.1963.

72. Compare Jacques Lacan, *The Seminar of Jacques Lacan, Book XVII: The Other Side of Psychoanalysis, 1969–1970*, ed. Jacques-Alain Miller; trans. Russell Grigg (New York: W. W. Norton & Co., 2007), 58.

73. Kierkegaard says, of the object of anxiety about sin: "its nothing is an actual something." He goes on to say, "No matter how deep an individual has sunk, he can sink still deeper, and this 'can' is the object of anxiety." *The Concept of Anxiety: A Simple Psychologically Orienting Deliberation on the Dogmatic Issue of Hereditary Sin* (Princeton, N.J.: Princeton University Press, 1980 [1844]), 111, 113.

74. Freud wrote numerous, not altogether consistent theses on anxiety. It is clear that for him anxiety is experienced by the ego as a signal of danger, and that the signal is a (privileged) affect, not a signal constituted by a signifying order. See the later chapters of Sigmund Freud, "Inhibitions, Symptoms, and Anxiety" in *SE XX* (1959 [1926]), 77–172.

75. "That in the face of which one has anxiety is not an entity within-the-world. . . . That in the face of which one is anxious is completely indefinite. Not only does this indefiniteness leave factically undecided which entity within-the-world is threatening us, but it also tells us that entities within-the-world are not 'relevant' at all. Nothing which is ready-to-hand or present-at-hand within the world functions as that in the face of which anxiety is anxious. . . . Accordingly when something threatening brings itself close, anxiety does not 'see' any definite 'here' or 'yonder' from which it comes. That in the face of which one has anxiety is characterized by the fact that what threatens is *nowhere*. Anxiety 'does not know' what that in the face of which it is anxious is. 'Nowhere', however, does not signify nothing. . . . *[T]he world as such is that in the face of which one has anxiety. . . . Being-in-the-world itself is that in the face of which anxiety is anxious.*" Martin Heidegger, *Being and Time*, trans. J. Macquarrie and E. Robinson (New York: Harper, 1962), 232–33, emphasis in original.

76. As he admits, it is a difficult notion, "This object without which anxiety is not can still be addressed in some other way. It's precisely this that over the course of the years I have given more and more form to. I have in particular given many chatterboxes the opportunity to rush hastily into print on the subject of what I may have had to say with the term 'object *a*,'" Lacan, *Seminar XVII*, 147.

77. My phrasing here intentionally evokes the accounts of anxiety cited above in Copjec (on page 259n50) and Levinas (on page 258n46).

78. As Sartre says about "the look," God reveals Job to himself as unrevealed; see *Being and Nothingness*, trans. H. Barnes (New York: Washington Square, 1992), 359.

Chapter 5

1. The pair "shame/guilt" should be folded onto those other, massive oppositions by which this book traces new fault lines for interpretations of the contours of JOB—e.g., desire/drive, sacrifice/satisfaction, All/not-All, exclusion/subtraction, fear/anxiety.

2. The Septuagint and Syriac both have "like" and some scholars have proposed reading the *kᵉ* preposition instead of *min*, finding it unimaginable that those who long for death search for treasure. But reading the comparative *min* need not imply that they dig for treasures, just that they seek death more than they would seek treasures. See David J. A. Clines, *Job 1–20* (Dallas: Word, 1989), 74.

3. Katharine J. Dell, *The Book of Job as Sceptical Literature* (Berlin: Walter de Gruyter, 1991), 181.

4. Samuel E. Balentine, *Job* (Macon, Ga.: Smyth & Helwys, 2006), 182.

5. See C. L. Seow, *Job 1–21: Interpretation and Commentary* (Illuminations; Grand Rapids: Eerdmans, 2013), 497, on 7:16: "Some interpreters think this call to God to desist is an outright rejection of God, a call for divine absence (so Clines). It is in fact a cry for God to stop paying him undue attention, perhaps meaning the potentially destructive attention."

6. This is true of many more scholars than Norman C. Habel, *The Book of Job* (Philadelphia: Westminster, 1985), 308 (cf. 230), who names as "one of the conditions" of Job's desire for a trial "that God remove his intimidating 'terror' from the court so that Job would not need to hide from his 'face' (13:20–21)." Yair Hoffman, *A Blemished Perfection: The Book of Job in Context* (Sheffield: Sheffield Academic, 1996), 167–68, provides a refreshingly self-aware account of his prioritization of the trial motif. The most extreme example is provided by F. Rachel Magdalene, *On the Scales of Righteousness: Neo-Babylonian Trial Law and the Book of Job* (Providence, R.I.: Brown Judaic Studies, 2007), 191–92, which refers to Job's demands for space from God as demands for a pre-trial settlement!

7. Recall that on page 108, I showed that Claus Westermann, *The Structure of the Book of Job: A Form-Critical Analysis* (Philadelphia: Fortress, 1981), 69, goes so far as to say that Job's third wish—that his cause might be heard and that he might find an advocate despite his death—is "logically incompatible with the first"—with Job's wish to die.

8. See footnote 45 on page 258, where I allude to Lacan's acute formula according to which anxiety arises when *le manque vient à manquer*, "the lack comes to lack" (*Le Séminaire de Jacques Lacan, Livre X: Angoisse, 1962–1963*, ed. Jacques-Alain Miller [Paris: Éditions du Seuil, 2004], 53).

9. For a more intuitive example, imagine the similar effect of looking through binoculars into an abyss of darkness (pure absence) or the over-proximity of lens covers (pure presence). In both cases, without any illuminated distance to distinguish subject/seer and object/seen, one can only see nothing.

10. Bruce Fink, *The Lacanian Subject: Between Language and Jouissance* (Princeton: Princeton University Press, 1995), 25.

11. Immanuel Kant, *Critique of Pure Reason*, trans. and ed. Paul Guyer and Allen W. Wood (Cambridge: Cambridge University Press, 1998).

12. F. P. Ramsey, "Universals," *Mind* 34 (1925): 404.

13. In the above example, the premise is the assumption that the world exists. The first *Critique* as a whole could be read as the articulation of a third option that gets its start by negating the shared, false premise of rationalism and empiricism. Compare with Jacques Lacan, *The Seminar of Jacques Lacan, Book XX: Encore, 1972–1973*, ed. Jacques-Alain Miller; trans. Bruce Fink (New York: W. W. Norton & Co., 1998), 43, who connects the illicit belief in the world with the illicit belief in the sexual relationship. Both beliefs, he insists, "must be abandoned."

14. When capitalized as here and elsewhere, Symbolic, Imaginary, and Real refer to the Lacanian registers first introduced on page 30.

15. Catherine Malabou, *Plasticity at the Dusk of Writing: Dialectic, Destruction, Deconstruction*, trans. C. Shread (New York: Columbia University Press, 2010), 66, names "'plasticity' the logic and economy of such a formation: the movement of the constitution of an exit, there, where no such exit is possible."

16. For a justly classic treatment of the the Imaginary and Symbolic registers see Fredric Jameson, "Imaginary and Symbolic in Lacan," in *The Ideologies of Theory* (London: Verso, 2008), 77–124. Especially relevant to my interpretation of Job's "mood swings" are those places where Jameson uncovers the coeval emergence of aggressivity and narcissism: "The mirror state, which is the precondition for primary narcissism, [i.e., the jubilation the infant feels upon grasping their independence from their situation] is also, owing to the equally irreducible gap it opens between the infant and its fellows, the very source of human aggressivity; and indeed, one of the original features of Lacan's early teaching is its insistence on the inextricable association of these two drives" (87).

17. Carol A. Newsom, *The Book of Job: A Contest of Moral Imaginations* (Oxford: Oxford University Press, 2003), 140.

18. Newsom, *Contest*, 143.

19. I phrase this masochistic position as a *pursuit* so as to avoid the common confusion of masochism with passivity. There is a dialectic at work in masochism on account of which activity and passivity, subject and object are displaced or transposed. The masochist appears to give his partner, the torturess, every right over him, and so appears to assume the role of object vis-à-vis a subject. However, the scene is determined by the position of the masochist. So, Gilles Deleuze, *Coldness and Cruelty*, trans. Jean McNeil (New York: Zone Books, 1991), 41, "The woman torturer of masochism . . . is *in* the masochistic situation, she is an integral part of it, a realization of the masochistic fantasy." Although the fantasy appears to begin in mutuality—a consenting victim and an willing torturer—and subsequently to be determined by the activity of the latter, it is clear that the masochist is the one who determines the scene, persuading and training his torturer in how to act, determining the other's enjoyment by supplying himself as its object. Melissa Febos testifies to her realization of this dynamic in an interview with Terry Gross. Febos, who worked for four years as a dominatrix in a dungeon under midtown Manhattan, admits, "In the beginning, it did feel pretty powerful, you know, to act out those roles. . . . After a little while, you

know, it wasn't my fantasy in most cases, you know? And in a lot of ways, it felt more humiliating to me than it did to them. I mean, I think it was satisfying for them. And for me, to enact a sexual fantasy that wasn't my own fantasy was uncomfortable in a lot of ways." (Melissa Febos. Interview with Terry Gross. *Fresh Air.* 8 March 2010.)

20. Newsom, *Contest*, 150.

21. God's act of creation, as recounted in the Priestly tradition, famously turns on the question of the shared image (the Hebrew *ṣelem* of Gen 1:27 supremely conveying the qualities of Imaginary identification) and on the particular axis this common image is understood to reside in.

22. Newsom, *Contest*, 147.

23. Newsom, *Contest*, 146.

24. The verb Job uses here to describe what God has done to him, *bl'* ("to swallow"), is the same verb God uses to characterize the affliction to *haśśāṭān* in 2:3. Here, however, Job does not account for that dimension of God's act which God characterized as *ḥinnām*.

25. Newsom, *Contest*, 147.

26. Although he perhaps fails to maintain his insistence, Levinas insists that this "narrative" is misleading to the extent that it is formulated ontogenetically. But, Newsom and I are justified in recounting it narratively by Levinas himself: "It is necessary to begin with the concrete relationship between an I and the world." *Totality and Infinity: An Essay on Exteriority*, trans. A. Lingis (Pittsburgh: Duquesne University Press, 1969), 37. After proceeding from this necessary point of origin, however, Levinas argues that it is not that one gets along as an ego that is then interrupted by the encounter, but rather that one's getting along is always already a response to such an encounter. This "primacy of the Other" is intended by a number of Levinasian/Derridean conclusions, e.g., "ontology presupposes metaphysics" or "truth presupposes justice."

27. Levinas, *Totality*, 75–76, "To recognize the Other is to give. . . . The presence of the Other is equivalent to this calling into question of my joyous possession of the world."

28. Levinas, *Totality*, 87, "The relationship with the Other does not move (as does cognition) into enjoyment and possession, into freedom; the Other imposes himself as an exigency that dominates this freedom."

29. Emmanuel Levinas, *Difficult Freedom: Essays on Judaism*, trans. S. Hand (Baltimore: Johns Hopkins University Press, 1990), 98.

30. Newsom, *Contest*, 149.

31. Newsom, *Contest*, 147.

32. Newsom, *Contest*, 147–48.

33. Newsom, *Contest*, 149.

34. Joan Copjec, *Read My Desire: Lacan against the Historicists* (Cambridge, Mass.: MIT Press, 1994), 3, supplies a distinction of some help here by saying that "the first is subject to a predicative judgment as well as to a judgment of existence; that is, it is an existence whose character or quality can be described. The existence implied by the second is subject *only* to a judgment of existence; we can say only that it does or does not exist, without being able to say what it is, to describe

it in any way." Copjec uses the distinction to explain similar statements by Lacan about "the" woman, and Foucault about "the" pleb.

35. Although I have, for consistency's sake, defined this unique "object" that is the Levinasian Other according to Lacan's *objet petit a*, I do not want to suggest that they are two names for the same object. Žižek, among others, has attempted to articulate the difference in some recent works, e.g., Slavoj Žižek, "Neighbors and Other Monsters: A Plea for Ethical Violence," in Slavoj Žižek, Eric L. Santner, and Kenneth Reinhard, *The Neighbor: Three Inquiries in Political Theology* (Chicago: The University of Chicago Press, 2005), 134–90, and *Did Somebody Say Totalitarianism?: Five Interventions in the (Mis)use of a Notion* (London: Verso, 2001), ch. 4.

36. *yp'* literally means "to shine forth" and is predicated of God in several texts, e.g., Deut 33:2; Ps 50:2; and Job 37:15. Enjoyment is often present when God's "shining" is at stake. Here its opposition to *m's* and parallel enveloping function with "Is it good for you" led me to agree with the NRSV's decision to translate it as "favor."

37. Newsom, *Contest*, 148.

38. Recall the quotation cited on page 143 from Levinas, *Difficult*, 98: "Subjectivity as such is primordially a hostage, responsible to the extent that it becomes the sacrifice for others."

39. Newsom writes of "mutual disclosure" (*Contest*, 159) and elsewhere claims, "Job negotiates the dangerous terrain of alterity by establishing the common ground upon which the divine and the human can meet—the ground of justice. Job's strategy is indeed to reduce the alterity of the divine and the human by stressing the common moral nature of God and human beings" (150); "Legal appeal shifts the ground to an objective set of values both sides take as normative, privileging reasoned argument" (156); "Legal disputes . . . require the provisional setting aside of inequality" (157).

40. Biblical scholars note a similar dynamic when they recognize that enunciating innocence to God communicates more than its enunciated content—it also communicates a call for justice. See, for example, Magdalene, *Scales*, 163–64; Walter Brueggemann, *The Message of the Psalms: A Theological Commentary* (Minneapolis, Minn.: Augsburg, 1984), 55.

41. Newsom, *Contest*, 145.

42. Newsom, *Contest*, 152–53.

43. Newsom, *Contest*, 153.

44. Newsom, *Contest*, 158–60, fittingly identifies and elaborates the "hermeneutical" character of Job's desire for a Third.

45. See, for example, David J. A. Clines, *Job 21–37* (Nashville: Thomas Nelson, 2006), 593–96 and Balentine, *Job*, 362–66.

46. Emmanuel Levinas, *Time and the Other and Additional Essays*, trans. R. A. Cohen (Pittsburgh: Duquesne University Press, 1987), 45, compares his approach to existence with Heidegger's notion of *Dasein*'s "Throwness" (*Geworfenheit*). For a reflection on Levinas's relation to Heidegger, especially in Levinas's early writings, see Jacques Rolland's introduction to Levinas's *On Escape: de l'évasion*, trans. B. Bergo (Stanford, Calif.: Stanford University Press, 2003). For a slight complication of this simplified account, see Levinas, *Escape*, 69–70.

47. Although it has apparently been lost on her readers, Newsom also recognizes this violence inherent to Job's desire and the ethically problematic character (for Levinas's position) of Job's demands. First, in her phenomenology of the courtroom (*Contest,* 160) and, second, in a brief footnote (*Contest,* 278n.49). Incidentally, Hegel anticipates Levinas's position when he saw in self-consciousness's pleasure the movement of desire that "does not aim so much at the destruction of objective being in its entirety, but only at the form of its otherness or its independence." *Phenomenology of Spirit,* trans. A. V. Miller (Oxford: Clarendon, 1977), 218.

48. Compare with Martin Hägglund, *Radical Atheism: Derrida and the Time of Life* (Stanford, Calif.: Stanford University Press, 2008), ch. 3. Hägglund advances a similar though much more polemical argument against the common tendency to assimilate Derrida's work into a Levinasian ethical framework.

49. So, Jacques Derrida, *Adieu to Emmanuel Levinas,* trans. P.-A. Brault and M. Naas (Stanford, Calif.: Stanford University Press, 1999), 32: "The third does not wait; its illeity calls from as early as the epiphany of the face in the face to face."

50. Derrida, *Adieu,* 33. On the following page Derrida says, in his characteristic style, "the proceedings that open both ethics and justice are in the process of committing quasi-transcendental or originary, indeed, pre-originary perjury. One might even call it *ontological,* once ethics is joined to everything that exceeds and betrays it (ontology, precisely, synchrony, totality, the State, the political, etc.)."

51. Derrida designates the other as "faceless" in "Faith and Knowledge: The Two Sources of 'Religion' at the Limits of Reason Alone," in *Acts of Religion,* trans. S. Weber, ed. G. Anidjar (New York and London: Routledge, 2002), 59.

52. As recognized by Newsom, *Contest,* 143, cited on pages 141–42.

53. This verse is quite difficult and various different proposals have been made. Its symmetry with v.32 and Job's other statements about not being at one with himself (e.g., 9:21 and 10:1) favor the more literal reading: "Truly [it is] not so [that] I am with myself."

54. Newsom, *Contest,* 154.

55. In §61 I discuss a number of other texts in which Job follows his expressions of this desire with explicit statements concerning its impossibility; e.g., 13:17–23 followed by vv.24–27; 14:13, 16 followed by vv.19–20; and, definitively, 19:6–10.

56. For example, Newsom, *Contest,* 150, says one scholar's "decision to maximize the presence and shaping of legal language obscures a more complex and subtle situation. Though Job on occasion uses unmistakably technical legal expressions, much of the language in question is at home both in legal and more general discourse." She does not want to disavow the significance of legal language, only to insist on its "subtle and exploratory" nature. She acknowledges that "explicitly legal speech actually occurs rather infrequently" (*Contest,* 154).

57. Compare with Lauren Berlant, *Cruel Optimism* (Durham: Duke University Press, 2011).

58. See, for example, Giorgio Agamben, *State of Exception,* trans. K. Attell (Chicago: The University of Chicago Press, 2005).

59. The following discussion of shame relies heavily on several recent treatments, including Giorgio Agamben, *Remnants of Auschwitz: The Witness and the Archive*, trans. D. Heller-Roazen (New York: Zone Books, 2002); and, most importantly, several recent works by Joan Copjec. Both take their departures from the early and excellent analyses of shame by Levinas and Sartre, and both end with similar results even though their theoretical approaches are finally oriented around two different thinkers: Foucault for Agamben, Lacan for Copjec. Agamben, *Remnants*, 107, refers to shame as "nothing less than the fundamental sentiment of being *a subject.*"

60. On the root *qr'* as a summons, see Deut 25:8; 1 Sam 22:11; 1 Kgs 20:7. Compare Magdalene, *Scales*, 141.

61. Compare 10:8: "Your hands shaped me and made me, and afterward you swallowed me up all-around."

62. Compare 14:19: "Water wears down stones, its torrrents wash away the earth's soil, so you destroy a human's hope."

63. See HALOT, 807.

64. Or, "life/spirit."

65. The cohortative is elsewhere used to introduce a conditional clause, as in 16:6, where it accompanies *'im*. See also Clines, *Job 1–20*, 429.

66. *Pace* KJV, NIV, JPSV, this correction is made by, for example, NRSV, Pope, Habel, Gordis, and Clines, *Job 1–20*, 429, who notes, "The transfer seems supported by 11QtgJob which has no 'and' preceeding 'my servant-girl(s)'," i.e., "maidservants" in v.15a.

67. Such a notion of two things intersecting at a point that belongs to neither was famously put forward by Jacques Lacan in *The Seminar of Jacques Lacan, Book XI: The Four Fundamental Concepts of Psycho-Analysis, 1964*, ed. Jacques-Alain Miller, trans. Alan Sheridan (New York: W. W. Norton & Co., 1977), 203–15, as a way to understand the structure of the subject's alienation from himself upon entry into the Symbolic order, an entry that also alienates the Symbolic order from itself. This obverse side of alienation is why Lacan could put forward slogans such as "There is no Other of the Other"; "There is no such thing as metalanguage"; and, finally, "The Other does not exist." See also the discussion in Fink, *Subject*, 33–68, and the post-Lacanian use to which this paradoxical topology is put in the excellent work of Mladen Dolar, *A Voice and Nothing More* (Cambridge, Mass.: MIT Press, 2006).

68. Lacan, *Seminar XI*, 204, 214, refers to this topology as the overlapping or superimposition of two lacks.

69. The discussions of this sense of shame are many and complex in biblical, anthropological, and historical studies. An excellent discussion and list of resources can be found in Gale A. Yee, *Poor Banished Children of Eve: Women as Evil in the Hebrew Bible* (Minneapolis, Minn.: Fortress, 2003), 40–48.

70. Julian Pitt-Rivers, "Honour and Social Status," in *Honor and Shame: The Values of Mediterranean Society*, ed. J. G. Peristiany (Chicago: The University of Chicago Press, 1966), 21, 42.

71. See the discussion and resources cited in Joan Copjec, "The Censorship of Interiority," *Umbr(a)* (2009): 166–67.

72. Copjec, "Censorship," 167.

73. This verse is admittedly difficult. The final word is pointed as an imperative *r*ᵉ*'ê* (cf. Lam 1:9) whereas one expects an adjective, like the identically pointed *ś*ᵉ*baʿ*, "sated." But *r*ᵉ*'ê* is not only an imperative; it functions elsewhere as a stereotyped interjection like *hinnê* (e.g., Deut 1:8; Qoh 7:27). See Wilhelm Gesenius, *Gesenius' Hebrew Grammar* (Mineola, N.Y.: Dover, 2006 [1909, 1813]), §105b. Thus, while my translation permits one to read it either as an imperative or an interjection, the context favors the latter since it does not seem to issue a return to direct discourse ("look at my misery!"), but instead functions more like an adjective describing his condition as one who is sated with shame and showing his misery ("behold, my misery"). Others argue that this is not the root *r'h* but, as occurs in some words e.g., *g'h*, a case of medial *'/w* switch. *rwh* is a synonym of *śb'*, which would read "and saturated with my misery." Emendations that produce such (admittedly) nice harmonies between parallel lines usually heighten critical suspicions.

74. One could define these terms differently and come to different understandings of them, ones that may support saying "I am ashamed of what I have done" or "I am as such guilty." My description draws on an analysis of shame by Steven Connor, "The Shame of Being a Man," http://www.bbk.ac.uk/english/skc/shame/ (2000), who writes, "guilt relates to actions, shame to being. . . . The sinner can abhor her sin and the malefactor loathe the guilt in him. But the one in shame is always on the side of his shame, there being no other side for him to take." As with the opposition between guilt and anxiety discussed in CHAPTER 4, in practice it may be very difficult to separate such affects on the basis of any hard-and-fast distinction. For a nuanced discussion of affects, emotions, feelings, as well as of the possibility of unconscious affects, misfelt feelings, and so on, see Adrian Johnston, "Misfelt Feelings: Unconscious Affect Between Psychoanalysis, Neuroscience, and Philosophy," in *Self and Emotional Life: Philosophy, Psychoanalysis, and Neuroscience* (New York: Columbia University Press, 2013), 73–210.

75. Copjec, "Censorship," 167–68, emphasis added.

76. For other uses of the idiom "to lift one's head," see Judg 8:28; Ps 110:7; Zech 1:21.

77. Compare Ps 83:17, which implies that there remains one place for the one in shame to turn: "Fill their faces with shame, so that they may seek your name, O YHWH."

78. See Job 3:26, and the emphasis given this term throughout Newsom, *Contest.*

79. Friedrich Nietzsche, *Beyond Good and Evil: Prelude to a Philosophy of the Future,* trans. W. Kaufmann (New York: Vintage Books, 1989), 213.

80. The epithet "pure immanence" intends to evoke deep associations with Gilles Deleuze's work. In the context of Job's torment it seems especially important to restrain ourselves from reaching any settled evaluation of shame, which by no means strips Job of his life. Deleuze allows one to re-think what is normally meant by a life (i.e., something imbued with consistency, meaning, a "project") under the new sign of immanence: "a *life,* no longer dependent on a Being or submitted to an Act—it is an absolute immediate consciousness whose very activ-

ity no longer refers to a being but is ceaselessly posed in a life." *Pure Immanence: Essays on Life*, trans. Anne Boyman (New York: Zone Books, 2001), 27.

81. Paradigmatically, I think of chapters 29–31 and 22:6–11 as texts in which Job and the friends—here, Eliphaz—assume this posture of guilt.

82. This is, in other words, yet another instance where JOB renders God immanent to the limits of phenomena, not as their transcendent or unlimited noumena.

83. Literally, "my formed parts." See the discussion in Clines, *Job 1–20*, 373.

84. I write "non-phenomenal" to capture the darkness in its invisibility, the sense in which it surfaces within the phenomenal field without thereby taking on a phenomenal or visible form. See further, Joan Copjec, "The Phenomenal Non-phenomenal: Private Space in Film Noir," in *Shades of Noir: A Reader* (London: Verso, 1993), esp. 188–90.

85. A wonderful illustration occurs when the invisibility cloak is donned in the Harry Potter films. Others in its presence manifest their awareness of it in an anxious look or pause. Sometimes the videography even indicates this non-phenomenal manifestation of presence by smudging the image. The viewer is thus encouraged to imagine that nothing is added to or subtracted from phenomenal reality by virtue of its presence, and yet others can "sense" its non-sensible presence. Freud called this sense of the non-sensible "the uncanny," discussed on page 123.

86. Compare with Agamben, *Remnants*, 53.

87. Compare with 9:25: "My days are swifter than a runner; they flee and see (*r'h*) no good (*lō' ṭôbāh*)."

88. One thinks here of Shoah survivors' testimony to the impossibility of gazing upon the *Muselmänner*. Levi refers to them as a "faceless presence" in whose image "all the evil of our time," if it were possible, could be enclosed (Agamben, *Remnants*, 44). Another survivor wrote that they are those for whom sympathy was impossible: "The other inmates, who continually feared for their lives, did not even judge him worthy of being looked at. For the prisoners who collaborated, [they] were a source of anger and worry; for the SS, they were merely useless garbage" (Agamben, *Remnants*, 43). Agamben also relates the story of Aldo Carpi, a painting professor who was deported to Gusen and remained there for over a year: "He managed to survive because the SS began to commission paintings and drawings from him once they discovered his profession. They mostly commissioned family portraits . . . Italian landscapes and 'Venetian nudes' . . . Carpi was not a realistic painter, and yet one can understand why he wanted to paint the actual scenes and figures from the camp. But his commissioners had absolutely no interest in such things; indeed, they did not even tolerate the sight of them. 'No one wants camp scenes and figures,' Carpi notes in his diary, 'no one wants to see the *Muselmann*'" (Agamben, *Remnants*, 50). Agamben (*Remnants*, 51) concludes, "As Elias Canetti has noted, a heap of dead bodies is an ancient spectacle, one which has often satisfied the powerful. But the sight of *Musselmänner* is an absolutely new phenomenon, unbearable to human eyes." Although I do not mean to suggest that the *Musselmann* provides a paradigm for understanding Job's experience, I do think that he similarly presents a "new phenomenon" upon which it is impossible to gaze.

89. The unique ontological status of the "object" that appears to Job is the same as that of Lacan's *objet petit a*, discussed in §55. About the *objet petit a*, see Jacques Lacan, "The Subversion of the Subject and the Dialectic of Desire in the Freudian Unconscious," in *Écrits*, trans. B. Fink (New York: W. W. Norton & Co., 2006), 693: "A common characteristic of these objects as I formulate them is that they have no specular image. . . . It is to this object that cannot be grasped in the mirror that the specular image lends its clothes."

90. Levinas, *Escape*, 63.

91. Similarly, Agamben, *Remnants*, 107, "[Shame] is nothing less than the fundamental sentiment of being *a subject*, in the two apparently opposed senses of this phrase: to be subjected and to be sovereign. Shame is what is produced in the absolute concomitance of subjectification and desubjectification, self-loss and self-possession, servitude and sovereignty."

92. In Jean-Paul Sartre, *Being and Nothingness*, trans. H. Barnes (New York: Washington Square, 1992).

93. Lacan, *Seminar XI*, 84.

94. Copjec, "Censorship," 176.

95. See, for example, Levinas, *Escape*, 64, "What appears in shame is thus precisely the fact of being riveted to oneself, the radical impossibility of fleeing oneself to hide from oneself, the unalterably binding presence of the I to itself [*du moi à soi-même*]." See also Joan Copjec, "May '68, the Emotional Month," in *Lacan: The Silent Partners*, ed. S. Žižek (London: Verso, 2006), 103.

96. This is to say that Job testifies to an experience of shame that departs from Levinas and Sartre and is captured only once we account for Lacan's contribution to the analysis of shame. For a discussion of Lacan's contribution, see Copjec, "Censorship"; and "May '68." For a more general discussion of shame and affect in psychoanalysis in relation to recent neuroscientific findings, see Adrian Johnston, "Misfelt Feelings."

97. This verse and the next are quite difficult and have given rise to various emendations. Here I read with most others who think this word (*mwršy*) is not from *yrš* (i.e., "property, inheritance") but *'rš*, meaning desire. However, I do not want to rule out the rather obvious play evoking the numerous connections between property and desire and that, incidentally, may also be present in Mic 1:14.

98. Many translations struggle with this verse, which is not in the Old Greek. Some (e.g., NRSV) take the *l*–preposition as a marker of a datival goal, as it sometimes functions with things made—i.e., "they make light into day." (See Mic 1:6; Bruce K. Waltke and M. O'Connor, *An Introduction to Biblical Hebrew Syntax* [Winona Lake, Ind.: Eisenbrauns, 1990], §11.2.10e.) Given the context, I find other readings preferable, each of which corresponds to a different lexical sense of "day." First, there is a temporal sense like the terminative (see Waltke and O'Connor, *Syntax*, §11.2.10c)—i.e., Job rebukes the friends for thinking that the night is what endures *until* day, that is, for thinking of day and night as equal and alternating parts that together constitute a twenty-four hour period. Alternatively, the preposition could be read possessively—i.e., the night *belongs to* day, implying that they reckon day the genus in which night is a species (Waltke and O'Connor, *Syntax*, §11.2.10d). The parallel line does not help us decide between

the two in that the position it ascribes to the opponents—that light is proximate to darkness—supports both readings. But, perhaps the assumption shared by both of these readings is precisely what Job attacks as false, namely, the assumption of day as genus. In the possessive sense, day obviously functions as genus. In the temporal sense, however, this use is implicit. In order for day to be perceived as a complement of night, some neutral, universal background must be posited as the frame within which the equal alternation occurs. This background is also signified by day elsewhere. In other words, if the preposition is read in the temporal sense, then day must perform double duty, not only signifying the period that alternates with nightime, but also the twenty-four hour period in which day and night alternate (as in Gen 1:5, when God calls the light "day" and the darkness "night" and yet the day and the night together constitute "day" one). If Job rejects this assumption it is because he takes night to be a crack that runs through day, alienating day from itself, and preventing it from constituting a complete and delimited frame for subjective existence.

99. The conditional ("if" in vv.13–14, "then" in vv.15–16) does not suggest that the pit and the worm will not produce something new of Job, this he takes as axiomatic; it serves rather to admonish his opponents for their baseless assumption that Job could hope in the nature of what is to be. Because Job knows nothing of this nature, he is unable to hope in it.

100. *Pace* the MT ("to the bars of Sheol"), parallelism favors reading with the LXX (ἢ μετ ἐμου); see Clines, *Job 1–20*, 375.

101. For a discussion and a more precise description of the phenomenological connection between the onset of Job's anxiety and the disappearance of all his plans/projections and desires/hopes, see the Heideggerian description in Philippe Nemo, *Job and the Excess of Evil*, trans. Michael Kigel (Pittsburgh: Duquesne University Press, 1998), 24–27.

102. Job is not the only figure in the Hebrew Bible to think that newness emerges from a gap (dis)joining light and darkness, day and night. YHWH paradigmatically operates at this gap, either guaranteeing or overturning their particular conjunction. In Jer 33:20–21a, for example, YHWH says, "If you could break my covenant with the day and my covenant with the night so that they would not come at their time, only then could my covenant with my servant David be broken"; but Zech 14:6–7 imagines the day of YHWH as a day on which "there shall not be light . . . and it will be a day, known only to YHWH, without day and without night; and there will be light at evening time."

103. One cannot but think here of Job's similar statement in the prose tale (1:21: "Naked I came out of the womb of my mother, and naked I shall return there"), about which I made a similar point in CHAPTER 2 (see §24).

104. One of Lacan's fundamental insights (which, incidentally, anticipated recent neuroscientific and evolutionary-biological research) was into the way in which psychoanalysis problematizes any hard and fast distinction between the material, libidinal, and affective forces related to the body, and the more-than-material ideational and representational signifiers used by speaking beings. Lacan insists "language is not immaterial" in part because of his realization of the material effects produced by signifiers on speaking beings. "The Function

and Field of Speech and Language in Psychoanalysis" in *Écrits*, 248. On the connections between Lacanian metapsychology and the neurosciences, see Johnston, "Misfelt Feelings."

105. Habel, *Job*, 347, says that 23:17 "follows the poet's favorite practice of closing a speech with the theme of death or darkness (7:21; 10:21–22; 12:24–25; 14:18–20; 17:11–16)."

106. Copjec, "May '68," 111, discusses the distinction between a flight from and a flight into being vis-à-vis shame.

107. Newsom, *Contest*, 161.

108. Newsom, *Contest*, 165.

109. Newsom, *Contest*, 166.

110. Newsom, *Contest*, 167.

111. Newsom, *Contest*, 168.

Chapter 6

1. Edward L. Greenstein, "In Job's Face/Facing Job," in *The Labour of Reading: Desire, Alienation, and Biblical Interpretation*, ed. F. C. Black, R. Boer, and E. Runions (Atlanta: Society of Biblical Literature, 1999), 303: "It is by now fairly commonplace to regard the divine speeches as ambiguous and enigmatic. . . . Two things have become clear to many: God almost entirely avoids or evades the question of justice, but at the same time demonstrates his own knowledge of nature's intricacies."

2. Compare with Gerhard von Rad, *Wisdom in Israel*, trans. James D. Martin (Nashville, Tenn.: Abingdon, 1972), 225.

3. Shakespeare was the master of such word creation. His plays are riddled with words and combinations of words that had never before appeared in print. He was particularly fond of the prefix "un." "Unreal," for example, had not appeared in print prior to *Macbeth*. One knows the word "real" and the prefix "un-," but it takes some time to grasp what "unreal" might mean.

4. That is, by not responding directly to Job's political and juridical concerns, God excludes Godself from the discussion. See also David Robertson, *The Old Testament and the Literary Critic* (Philadelphia: Fortress, 1977), 48–50; and Jack Miles, *God: A Biography* (New York: Alfred A. Knopf, 1995), 315–16.

5. Many side with God and think that this change of subject is a step closer to the truth, whatever that may be. See R. N. Whybray, *Job* (Sheffield: Sheffield Academic, 1998); and Kathryn Schifferdecker, *Out of the Whirlwind: Creation Theology in the Book of Job* (Cambridge, Mass.: Harvard University Press, 2008).

6. For a quick overview, see Carol A. Newsom, "Re-considering Job," *Currents in Biblical Research* 5 (2007): 168–71. For a lengthier discussion, see Schifferdecker, *Whirlwind*, 3–11.

7. Compare with Jacques Rancière, *The Politics of Aesthetics: The Distribution of the Sensible*, trans. G. Rockhill (New York: Continuum, 2004).

8. For particular differences, see Pieter van der Lugt, *Rhetorical Criticism and the Poetry of the Book of Job* (Leiden: Brill, 1995), 369–70.

9. Compare with Susan Niditch, *Chaos to Cosmos: Studies in Biblical Patterns of Creation* (Chico, Calif.: Scholars, 1985).

10. Raymond C. Van Leeuwen, "Cosmos, Temple, House: Building and Wisdom in Mesopotamia and Israel," in *Wisdom Literature in Mesopotamia and Israel*, ed. R. J. Clifford (Atlanta: Society of Biblical Literature, 2007), 67–90. Of course, these points are made often and by many others. Van Leeuwen offers a particularly well-documented and concise presentation of the most relevant points. With respect to the privilege of temples, Brown writes, "the Priestly account of creation finds its home in the structural integrity of the sanctuary and its environs. The tabernacle is both the image projected onto the cosmos and the microcosmos lodged in the heart of Israel's own existence." *The Ethos of the Cosmos: The Genesis of Moral Imagination in the Bible* (Grand Rapids: W. B. Eerdmans, 1998), 385. See also Jon D. Levenson, *Creation and the Persistence of Evil: The Jewish Drama of Divine Omnipotence* (Princeton: Princeton University Press, 1994), 66–99.

11. Samuel E. Balentine, *Job* (Macon, Ga.: Smyth & Helwys, 2006), 645. See also Brown, *Ethos*, 341.

12. W. G. Lambert and A. R. Millard, *Atra-ḫasis: The Babylonian Story of the Flood* (Oxford, Eng.: Clarendon, 1969), 43, cf. 166n.

13. J. Gerald Janzen, *Job* (Atlanta: John Knox, 1985), 234.

14. Compare with Levenson, *Creation*.

15. Carol A. Newsom, "The Book of Job" in *The New Interpreter's Bible Volume 4*, ed. L. Keck (Nashville Tenn.: Abingdon, 1996), 603.

16. Norman C. Habel, *The Book of Job* (Philadelphia: Westminster, 1985), 532.

17. Habel, *Job*, 533.

18. For other examples, see John E. Hartley, *The Book of Job* (Grand Rapids: Eerdmans, 1988), 497; James L. Crenshaw, "When Form and Content Clash: The Theology of Job 38:1–40:5," in *Urgent Advice and Probing Questions: Collected Writings on Old Testament Wisdom* (Macon, Ga.: Mercer University Press, 1995), 457.

19. Schifferdecker, *Whirlwind*, 125; cf. 73.

20. Dan Mathewson, *Death and Survival in the Book of Job: Desymbolization and Traumatic Experience* (New York: T. & T. Clark, 2006), 157–58, provides another example of a study that, while paying attention to forces and figures of chaos in the speeches, claims that their message is a brute insistence on mastery: "The type of 'self' that Job must be in this type of universe is one who trusts unfailingly in God's direction of the universe—one who, though not understanding the world's operations, nevertheless knows that a master design ultimately undergirds all that surrounds him."

21. The similitude with the smoke and mirrors of the great and powerful Oz, which one can take surprisingly far, has been made by Tod Linafelt, "The Wizard of Uz: Job, Dorothy, and the Limits of the Sublime," *Biblical Interpretation* 14 (2006): 94–109. Žižek speaks in several places of the speeches as a massive display of God's impotence; e.g., Slavoj Žižek, *For They Know Not What They Do: Enjoyment as a Political Factor*, 2nd ed. (London: Verso, 2002), li. I discuss Žižek's interpretation in §**2**.

22. So, for example, Jacques Derrida, *Writing and Difference*, trans. A. Bass (Chicago: The University of Chicago Press, 1978), 203: "There is no life present *at first* which would *then* come to protect, postpone, or reserve itself."

23. For an ancient example, see Herodotus's account of Persian hegemony discussed in Pierre Briant, *From Cyrus to Alexander: A History of the Persian Empire*, trans. P. T. Daniels (Winona Lake, Ind.: Eisenbrauns, 2002), 393, 410. For the modern emergence of disciplinary power, see the forceful case made by Michel Foucault, *Discipline and Punish: The Birth of the Prison*, trans. A. Sheridan (New York: Vintage, 1995), 144.

24. See, for example, Catherine Malabou, *What Should We Do with Our Brain?*, trans. S. Rand (New York: Fordham University Press, 2008), 5.

25. Balentine, *Job*, 638.

26. William P. Brown, *The Seven Pillars of Creation: The Bible, Science, and the Ecology of Wonder* (London: Oxford University Press, 2010), 133.

27. Kathleen M. O'Connor, "Wild, Raging Creativity: The Scene in the Whirlwind (Job 38–41)," in *A God So Near: Essays on Old Testament Theology in Honor of Patrick D. Miller*, ed. B. A. Strawn and N. R. Bowen (Winona Lake, Ind.: Eisenbrauns, 2003), 175.

28. Even Brown, whose descriptions of the cosmos that these speeches present rarely imply any underlying sense of unity (and so approximate O'Connor's more than others discussed above), nonetheless ultimately links the cosmos to a "deeper" unity. In Brown, *Ethos*, 341, for example, he writes, "Preceding the extensive litany of wild creatures, the cosmic realm is limned with evocative descriptions of the basic elements of creation: earth, sea, and light (38:4–15), which then gives way to the specific manifestations of these elements," but then he insists, "Their respective functions and interrelationships serve to reestablish Yahweh's indomitable plan or design ('*ēṣâ* 38:2)."

29. See, for example, Ps 33:7, Ezek 26:19, Jonah 2:5.

30. Catherine Keller, *The Face of the Deep: A Theology of Becoming* (London: Routledge, 2003), 130.

31. Keller, *Face*, 131.

32. I intend to evoke Johnston's description ("Misfelt Feelings," 197; cited in footnote 75 on page 240) of recent researches in the cognitive sciences that describe the brain as being "hardwired to be rewired."

33. Brown, *Seven*, 129.

34. Keller, *Face*, 131.

35. Balentine, *Job*, 649.

36. Balentine, *Job*, 649.

37. Janzen, *Job*, 236, however, agrees with Balentine by wondering whether the "apparently rhetorical taunts of verses 16–18 in fact intend and convey a solicitation. . . . The language of verses 16–17, of deep, revelation, and deep darkness so resonates with the terms of 12:22 (not to say 10:21–22) that one finds oneself leaning forward in the posture of a kibbitzer, self-involvingly wanting to say, 'Say yes, Job, say yes! You *have* been there, as your own words attest'."

38. See, for example, Schifferdecker, *Whirlwind*, 145; ṣalmāwet ("darkness") first appears "in 3:5, where Job wishes that ṣlmwt and ḥšk would obliterate the day of his birth. In this verse [38:17] and in 38:19, God challenges Job's curse. Job has evoked ṣlmwt and ḥšk, but he cannot even claim to know their dwelling places. He has longed for death (*mwt*) numerous times (first in 3:21), but has never even been to its gates."

39. Hans Urs von Balthasar, *Theo-Drama: Theological Dramatic Theory, vol. I: Prolegomena,* trans. Graham Harrison (San Francisco: Ignatius, 1988), 626; as discussed by Walter Brueggemann, *The Covenanted Self* (Minneapolis, Minn.: Fortress, 1999), 1, 19. Brueggemann rightly extrapolates from these thinkers to the later developments of Levinas and Steiner.

40. Carol A. Newsom, *The Book of Job: A Contest of Moral Imaginations* (Oxford: Oxford University Press, 2003), 234–58; O'Connor, "Wild," 171–79; Keller, *Face,* 124–40. I should add to this list the closely related and independently written study of the divine speeches by Timothy K. Beal, *Religion and Its Monsters* (New York: Routledge, 2002), 35–56. Compare Beal's recent note considering several points of convergence and divergence between his study and Keller's: "Mimetic Monsters: The Genesis of Horror in the Face of the Deep," *Postscripts* 4 (2008): 85–93.

41. Prior to Kant there was, famously, Edmund Burke, *A Philosophical Enquiry into the Origin of Our Ideas of the Sublime and the Beautiful* (London: Routledge and Kegan Paul, 1958 [1757]).

42. Immanuel Kant, *Critique of the Power of Judgment,* ed. Paul Guyer, trans. Paul Guyer and Eric Matthews (New York: Cambridge University Press, 2000), 128, 129.

43. Kant, *Judgment,* 128.

44. Kant, *Judgment,* 129.

45. Kant, *Judgment,* 128–29.

46. Of course, the harmony that gives one pleasure in the experience of beauty does not come from the object either since it is a harmony between the subject's own faculties. Compare "It is in the negative space opened up by the failure of representation that this negative presentation takes place; it is through the breakdown of representation, the point at which our representative faculties are confronted with their immanent limit, that the realm of the supersensible is opened up as the beyond of representation itself. . . . The sublime can only be presented negatively, as the experience of a lack as the nonplace of the idea—a necessary absence that summons the presence-through-absence of the power of reason." George Hartley, *The Abyss of Representation: Marxism and the Postmodern Sublime* (Durham and London: Duke University Press, 2003), 35, 37.

47. "Even to be able to think the given infinite without contradiction requires a faculty in the human mind that is itself supersensible. . . . Nature is thus sublime in those of its appearances the intuition of which brings with them the idea of infinity. Now the latter cannot happen except through the inadequacy of even the greatest effort of our imagination in the estimation of the magnitude of an object." Kant, *Judgment,* 138.

48. Kant, *Judgment,* 144.

49. Kant, *Judgment,* 145, "The irresistibility of [nature's] power certainly makes us, considered as natural beings, recognize our physical powerlessness, but at the same time it reveals a capacity for judging ourselves as independent of [nature] and a superiority over nature on which is grounded a self-preservation of quite another kind than that which can be threatened and endangered by nature outside us."

50. Newsom, *Contest*, 242. Newsom's judgment is echoed by Linafelt, *Wizard*, 102.

51. Linafelt, *Wizard*, 103.

52. Newsom, *Contest*, 248.

53. Kant, *Judgment*, 134.

54. Newsom, *Contest*, 249–50.

55. "Since God's speeches begin with such attention to the order of the cosmos, I would not be inclined to see the speeches as a rejection of God's role as source of moral order in the social realm." Newsom, *Contest*, 252.

56. Robert Gordis, *The Book of God and Man* (Chicago: The University of Chicago Press, 1965), 187–88, "After God has spoken, Job is overcome. He is overwhelmed by the disclosure of the vast miracle and mystery of the world, of which man's existence and suffering constitute only a minor facet. In voicing his submission, Job repeats the Lord's opening challenge to him. . . . After each citation he adds his humble comment. In his humility there is a note of triumph that God has deigned to meet and argue with him." Gordis recognizes the indirect, doubled feeling of the sublime when he speaks about the "note of triumph" betrayed by each "humble comment."

57. Newsom, *Contest*, 255.

58. In particular, Elaine Scarry, *On Beauty and Being Just* (Princeton: Princeton University Press, 1999).

59. Linafelt, *Wizard*, 106, sees this as part of a larger movement: "there has been a recent spate of books that attempt to reclaim an aesthetics of beauty, over against the dominant tradition since Kant that has seen the beautiful as too mundane, too available, too this-worldly, too much in the service of pleasure and of love and domesticity, and too much the preserve of women." In addition to Scarry, he cites Wendy Steiner, *Venus in Exile* (New York: The Free Press, 2001); and Dennis Donoghue, *Speaking of Beauty* (New Haven: Yale University Press, 2003).

60. Scarry, *Beauty*, 82–86.

61. Immanuel Kant, *Observations on the Feeling of the Beautiful and Sublime*, trans. John T. Goldthwait (Berkeley: University of California Press, 1960).

62. Scarry, *Beauty*, 84.

63. I have benefited from the discussion of Scarry's work by Joan Copjec, *Imagine There's No Woman: Ethics and Sublimation* (Cambridge, Mass.: MIT Press, 2002), 169–71.

64. Scarry, *Beauty*, 93.

65. Rodolphe Gasché tries to correct the common misreading that ignores this aspect of Kant's notion of beauty: "if beauty is linked to an agreement of a manifold with a unity, such agreement is not to be understood in terms of regularity, symmetry, and uniformity. . . . Neither regularity and symmetry nor their opposites constitute the beautiful form; instead a certain richness of the form itself, its indeterminateness, or dynamis (of possibilities), constitutes that beauty. Rather than being opposed to content, form, in this sense, gestures toward what is otherwise than form and content—an exuberance of indeterminateness prior to any fixing of objective meaning and its constraining formal characteristics. . . .

The form that is thus judged beautiful is form in the wild." *The Idea of Form: Rethinking Kant's Aesthetics* (Stanford, Calif.: Stanford University Press, 2003), 65–66.

66. Recall that Newsom, *Contest*, 255, describes Job's sublime experience as "a profound loss of unity, a recognition of the deeply fractured nature of reality," that is itself displaced. This experience of the displacement of the experience of a loss of unity does not return Job to the previous unity but affords him a new experience of unity that somehow holds the loss of unity within itself.

67. In particular, see the deservedly classic study by Robert Alter, *The Art of Biblical Poetry* (New York: Basic, 1985), 85–110. One could also go back to the discussion of God's speeches in Johann Gottfried Herder, *The Spirit of Hebrew Poetry*, trans. J. Marsh (Burlington, Vt.: Edward Smith, 1833). O'Connor's work differs in that she does not treat the speeches' beauty as a hermeneutical clue that could dispel their incongruencies, but instead analyzes the beauty of these incongruencies.

68. O'Connor, "Wild," 179.

69. Linafelt, *Wizard*, 108. Compare William P. Brown, *Character in Crisis: A Fresh Approach to the Wisdom Literature of the Old Testament* (Grand Rapids: W. B. Eerdmans, 1996), 113–14.

70. O'Connor, "Wild," 179.

71. Scarry (*Beauty*, 96) likens the experience of beauty to "one term of an analogy actively call[ing] out for its missing fellow," that is, justice, and she explicitly opposes this to the weaker claim that the symmetries of beauty and justice are (passively) analogous: "An analogy is inert and at rest only if both terms are present in the world; when one term is absent, the other becomes an active conspirator for the exile's return." When given its proper Kantian background, justice for Scarry is structurally similar to the understanding for Kant in that both constitute the missing second term of an analogy whose first term is supplied by beauty.

72. Recall Scarry's statement, "The surfaces of the world are aesthetically uneven" (*Beauty*, 106).

73. Although she differentiates one from the other, Newsom, *Contest*, 138–50, predicates a notion of the sublime both to the friends and to God. The former she calls the "masochistic sublime," the latter, the "tragic sublime."

74. Kant, *Judgment*, 138.

75. Kant, *Judgment*, 138.

76. Kant, *Judgment*, 144.

77. Newsom, *Contest*, 253.

78. Newsom, *Contest*, 258.

79. My understanding of tragedy is indebted to Alenka Zupančič, *The Odd One In: On Comedy* (Cambridge, Mass.: MIT Press, 2008).

80. J. Hartley claims, for example, "Although the plot requires a word from God, his coming surprises everyone. The air is full of excitement. The greatest wonder of all is that God himself speaks to a mere man. Job has had to wait for the moment of Yahweh's choosing" (*Job*, 487).

81. Compare Whedbee, "Comedy," 22; David Robertson, "The Book of Job: A Literary Study," *Soundings* 56 (1973): 462–69.

82. With *yd* and in the Qal, *kbd* usually means "to weigh heavily upon" or "press down upon," with the sense of "oppress" (see HALOT, 455), as in Judg 1:35; 1 Sam 5:6, and 11. The scholarly discomfort with *yādî*, "my hand," which is evident in the commonplace emendation to "his [God's] hand," seems to stem from a general ignorance of Job's conception of his experience as an inherent antagonism. As discussed at length in §52 and as evident in 7:15: "my throat chooses strangulation"; in 9:20: "my mouth condemns me"; and in 16:8: "my leanness rises up against me," Job often describes his anguish as an experience of being divided against himself. Thus, yet again in chapter 23 Job describes suffering that arises from within, his experience of something that was previously on his side—his hand—turning into something that oppresses him as if in the service of another, and not just any other, as if it were God's own hand.

83. See, for example, Keller, *Face*, 131.

84. Newsom, *Contest*, 242, quoted on page 189.

85. Newsom, *Contest*, 248.

86. Brown, *Seven*, 126.

Chapter 7

1. "I believe that the *Nicomachean Ethics* is properly speaking the first book to be organized around the problem of an ethics." Jacques Lacan, *The Seminar of Jacques Lacan, Book VII: The Ethics of Psychoanalysis, 1959–1960*, ed. Jacques-Alain Miller; trans. Dennis Porter (New York: W. W. Norton & Co., 1992), 36.

2. In 1517, just before nailing his ninety-five theses to the church door in Wittenburg, Luther wrote another set entitled "Disputation against Scholastic Theology," which included these: "41: Virtually the entire *Ethics* of Aristotle is the worst enemy of grace." "43: It is an error to say that no man can become a theologian without Aristotle." "44: Indeed, no one can become a theologian unless he becomes one without Aristotle."

3. The revival of virtue ethics is usually traced to G. E. M. Anscombe, "Modern Moral Philosophy," *Philosophy* 33 (1958): 1–19. See, famously, Alasdair MacIntyre, *After Virtue: A Study in Moral Theory* (Notre Dame: University of Notre Dame Press, 1981); and its three sequels: *Whose Justice? Which Rationality?* (London: Duckworth, 1988); *Three Rival Versions of Moral Enquiry: Encyclopaedia, Genealogy, and Tradition* (London: Duckworth, 1990); *Dependent Rational Animals* (London: Duckworth, 1999). Compare the acclaimed study of MacIntyre's work by Kelvin Knight, *Aristotelian Philosophy: Ethics and Politics from Aristotle to MacIntyre* (Cambridge, Eng.: Polity, 2007). See also the theologian Stanley Hauerwas, *Character and the Christian Life: A Study in Theological Ethics* (San Antonio, Tex.: Trinity University Press, 1975); and *A Community of Character: Toward a Constructive Christian Social Ethic* (Notre Dame, Ind.: University of Notre Dame Press, 1981). Lara Denis, "Kant's Conception of Virtue," in *The Cambridge Companion to Kant and Modern Philosophy*, ed. Paul Guyer (Cambridge: Cambridge University Press, 2006), 536n82, recommends two works of constructive, neo-Aristotelian virtue ethics: Rosiland Hursthouse, *On Virtue Ethics* (New York: Oxford University Press,

1999); and Christine Swanton, *Virtue Ethics: A Pluralistic View* (New York: Oxford University Press, 2003).

4. For a concise, sweeping perspective on these changes, see Charles Taylor, "The Moral Order: The Transition to Political Modernity," in *Religion and Political Thought*, ed. M. Hoelzl and G. Ward (London: Continuum, 2006), 259–67. What follows is indebted to a number of other works that have been central to this book: Alenka Zupančič, *Ethics of the Real: Kant, Lacan* (London: Verso, 2000); Alain Badiou, *Ethics: An Essay on the Understanding of Evil*, trans. P. Hallward (London: Verso, 2001); Lacan, *Seminar VII*; Joan Copjec, *Imagine There's No Woman: Ethics and Sublimation* (Cambridge, Mass.: MIT Press, 2002); Marc De Kesel, *Eros and Ethics: Reading Jacques Lacan's Seminar VII*, trans. S. Jöttkandt (Albany: State University of New York Press, 2009), 57–82; and, finally, Todd May, *Gilles Deleuze: An Introduction* (Cambridge: Cambridge University Press, 2005), especially the introduction.

5. For a polemical but informative critique of modern ethics from a very different angle than that of virtue ethics, see Badiou, *Ethics*.

6. May, *Deleuze*, 6.

7. See William P. Brown, *Character in Crisis: A Fresh Approach to the Wisdom Literature of the Old Testament* (Grand Rapids: W. B. Eerdmans, 1996); *The Ethos of the Cosmos: The Genesis of Moral Imagination in the Bible* (Grand Rapids: W. B. Eerdmans, 1998), 379; and Brown, ed., *Character and Scripture: Moral Formation, Community, and Biblical Interpretation* (Grand Rapids: W. B. Eerdmans, 2002). Brown's work on wisdom literature has numerous parallels; see James L. Crenshaw, *Old Testament Wisdom: An Introduction*, rev. and enl. ed. (Louisville, Ky.: Westminster John Knox, 1998), which frames wisdom as a search. For another recent volume including an essay by Brown and an introduction with a short bibliography, see M. Daniel Carroll R. and Jacqueline E. Lapsley, eds., *Character Ethics and the Old Testament: Moral Dimensions of Scripture* (Louisville, Ky.: Westminster John Knox, 2007).

8. Brown, *Character*, 7, suggests that ethical character has much in common with literary character but, whereas literary qualities tend to "highlight a person's uniqueness, ethical character represents a *generalizing* aspect that sets in relief certain values and virtues that have a normative claim to be shared and embodied by others."

9. Brown, *Character*, 8, "Simply put, to alter one's perception of God and the world is to shape and reshape character, the goal of sapiential rhetoric."

10. Brown, *Character*, 9. This echoes the standard Brown associates with Aristotle, who speaks of virtues as "a deliberated and permanent disposition."

11. Brown, *Character*, 9, offers this quote from Aquinas.

12. Yet one should note that in Latin and thus in Aquinas, the word translated "virtue" is *habitus*. Immanuel Kant, "The Metaphysics of Morals," in *Practical Philosophy*, trans. and ed. Mary J. Gregor (Cambridge, New York: Cambridge University Press, 1996), 535, 593, defines habit as an aptitude for "uniformity in action that has become a necessity through frequent repetition," and "a lasting inclination apart from any maxim," whereas virtue presupposes a maxim that the subject freely adopts.

13. Brown, *Character*, 11, "Moral virtue is no guarantee of success, and success is not necessarily a sign of moral integrity. The appeal of virtuous life is in-

trinsic. Distinct from professional skills, moral virtue is characteristic of a 'unitary life' . . . moral virtues tend to cut across all situations of conduct, from professional to personal. . . . Virtues are by nature all encompassing." Many presentations of virtue ethics think Kant exemplifies the strand of modern ethics that defines the virtuous as the fulfillment of a duty regardless of its effects on human beings. Kant does define virtue "despite the benefits it confers on human beings" ("Metaphysics of Morals," 524). But on the same page he clearly states that he does not disregard happiness or consequences when he writes, "The happiness of others is . . . an end that is also a duty." Kant insists that if virtue is to be treated as "its own end and . . . also its own reward," it must also be an unconditional duty ("Metaphysics of Morals," 526).

14. Brown, *Character*, 152.

15. Brown, *Character*, 156.

16. Brown *Character*, 159, renders Qohelet a distant third: "Qoheleth's view of character is deficiently individualized and self-referential. By contrast, the ideals of the sagacious community are vividly portrayed in Proverbs and the end of Job."

17. Brown, *Character*, 158.

18. JOB is not alone in this regard. I also do not believe that Proverbs or Qohelet support Brown's attempt to treat "character formation as the central framework and goal of biblical wisdom" (*Character*, 4). While Qohelet will have to await a future project, an analysis of Proverbs that poses problems for a character-based ethic has been provided by David Cromwell Knauert, "The Limits of Wisdom and the Dialectic of Desire" (PhD diss., Duke University, 2009), part 3.

19. For other examples, see Žižek's various discussions of "concrete universals," and Agamben's discussions of *homo sacer* and the the *Muselmänner* in Shoah survivors testimony. I discussed Agamben's work in footnote 88 on page 270.

20. Brown, *Character*, 60, "Job's character unites the prose and poetry of his story as well as provides for the story's literary tension."

21. Brown, *Character*, 12, emphasis in original.

22. See, for example, the otherwise exceedingly problematic essay by Theodore Hiebert, "Beyond Heilsgeschichte," in *Character Ethics and the Old Testament*, ed. M. D. Carroll R. and J. E. Lapsley, 3–11. Compare the brief but effective engagement by Walter Brueggemann, foreword to *Character Ethics and the Old Testament*, x.

23. Brown, *Character*, 158, "Creation is an indispensable feature of biblical wisdom, but not in isolation. Necessarily rooted in the perception and worldview of the inquirer of wisdom, the cosmic perspective is embodied and lived out in conduct . . . both creation and community are bound up with worldview."

24. See the discussion on page 124.

25. Brown, *Character*, 158.

26. Brown, *Character*, 151, emphasis added.

27. Brown, *Character*, 154, 55.

28. Brown, *Character*, 151, "[T]he journeying self is no island. . . . The way of wisdom is the prescribed way of the community. . . . Character in and of itself is necessarily character *in relation* . . . the development of character is inevitable."

29. Brown, *Character*, 159.

30. Brown, *Character*, 159.

31. As Adrian Johnston says of Lacanian psychoanalysis in *Badiou, Žižek, and Political Transformations: The Cadence of Change* (Evanston, Ill.: Northwestern University Press, 2009), 149.

32. So, Van Wolde, "Job 42,1–6," 237: "In many semantic studies about Job 42,1–6 usually all attention is concentrated on verse 6. What is more, sometimes the content of the preceding verses is determined on the basis of verse 6."

33. So, Norman C. Habel, *The Book of Job* (Philadelphia: Westminster, 1985), 579, "The hero concedes Yahweh's superior wisdom and confesses that he spoke out of ignorance."

34. Van Wolde, "Job 42,1–6," 232–33, "Technically speaking only verse 4b is a quotation (see 38:3 and 40:7) and verse 4a is not. However, verse 4a is an introduction to this quotation and is essential in this situation since it exactly marks the syntactic reversal brought about by the switch in point of view."

35. Van Wolde, "Job 42,1–6," 242. For a list of representative works on this verse, see Samuel E. Balentine, *Job* (Macon, Ga.: Smyth & Helwys, 2006), 705n.21.

36. Compare David J. A. Clines, ed., *The Concise Dictionary of Classical Hebrew* (Sheffield: Sheffield Phoenix, 2009), 199–200.

37. The LXX has διὸ ἐφαύλισα ἐμαυτὸν καὶ ἐτάκην, "Therefore I have disparaged myself and dissolved."

38. Compare the discussion in Van Wolde, "Job 42,1–6," 243–44.

39. For a list and discussion of five, see Newsom, "Job" (NIB), 629; see also Balentine, *Job*, 694.

40. E.g., Exod 32:12, 14; Jer 8:6; 18:8, 10 (with *ṭbḥ*); Joel 2:13; Jonah 4:2; 1 Chr 21:15.

41. An example of a similar anaylsis can be found in Good, *Tempest*, 375–76.

42. Stephen Mitchell, *The Book of Job*, rev. ed. of *Into the Whirlwind* (New York: HarperCollins, 1987 [1979]), xxxii, 88.

43. David Robertson, "The Book of Job: A Literary Study," *Soundings* 56 (1973): 446–69; John Curtis Briggs, "On Job's Response to Yahweh," *Journal of Biblical Literature* 98 (1979): 497–511.

44. Unlike the others, this interpretation does not first ask whether Job is submissive or defiant. Here are two examples of the different forms it takes: for Van Wolde, Job "discovers that most things are beyond his scope, that he does not have insight, nor could have, in the masterplan of creation, and he briefly recognises YHWH's way of looking. Because Job's view changes, there can also be a reversal in his attitude: Job turns away from what is past and turns towards the future" ("Job 42,1–6," 250). For Balentine, Job's experience of God's perspective enables him not to turn away from the past but to assume responsibility for it insofar as Job is meant to identify with the animals that are given power and responsibility for their domains.

45. Balentine, *Job*, 698.

46. Carol A. Newsom, "Narrative Ethics, Character, and the Prose Tale of Job," in *Character and Scripture: Moral Formation, Community, and Biblical Interpretation*, ed. W. P. Brown (Grand Rapids: Eerdmans, 2002), 127.

47. Newsom, "Ethics," 128.

48. By naive, I mean the dual response many readers have of *relief* at Job's re-integration into the community, and *distress* at the tale's apparent attempt to conclude the story by "restoring" Job's possessions without dealing with the mistreatment that removed them. For an ethically sophisticated reading that responds to the prose tale with both consolation and rejection, see Newsom, "Ethics"; and *The Book of Job: A Contest of Moral Imaginations* (Oxford: Oxford University Press, 2003), chapter 2.

49. For a contemporary example, in the recent financial crisis think of all the blame ascribed to Wall Street greed, predatory practices, and so on. While these and other factors were undoubtedly involved, rendering them the cause of the crisis fails to appreciate how capitalism's own dynamic inevitably generates such crises. That is, appeal to particular guilty parties alone gives a false impression that capitalism would function smoothly if everyone played fairly.

50. The situation reported in 42:7–10 may appear to provide a point-by-point reversal of the prose introduction. There Job's sacrificial deeds are described in 1:5 and in 1:9–10 his piety is challenged and authentic piety and authentic worship are determined to be unconditional. By contrast, here God commands a human being to do what God wants, gives motivating conditions in the interest of the human being to carry out this activity, then reports that God's servant obediently carried out the sacrifice, which effectively abated God's anger and controlled God's activities. Yet such a reading considers the events of the conclusion in relation to the book's first ten verses and nothing else. It may be more instructive to consider this situation in light of the "immanent theology" I have uncovered throughout the dialogue and divine speeches. What does it matter that the God to whom Job sacrifices in the conclusion is different from the God to whom Job sacrifices prior to *haśśāṭān*'s challenge?

51. See the interpretations discussed in CHAPTER 6 by Newsom and O'Connor.

52. See Linafelt's quotation on page 192.

53. The latter scenario describes many readings that contend that God's speeches imply nothing other than such a mutually exclusive opposition. For many, YHWH's speeches demand Job's submission to YHWH's position. For others, the speeches tacitly subject YHWH to Job's position by YHWH's failure to engage the implications of Job's position.

54. Adrian Johnston, *Žižek's Ontology: A Transcendental Materialist Theory of Subjectivity* (Evanston, Ill.: Northwestern University Press, 2008); Martin Hägglund, *Radical Atheism: Derrida and the Time of Life* (Stanford, Calif.: Stanford University Press, 2008).

55. Johnston, *Žižek's Ontology*, xiv.

56. As Johnston acknowledges at the beginning of his preface, an important precursor to these works that similarly approaches Gilles Deleuze's corpus is Alain Badiou's *Deleuze: The Clamor of Being*, trans. L. Burchill (Minneapolis: University of Minnesota Press, 2000); for a critical engagement of Badiou's *Deleuze*, see Clayton Crockett, *Deleuze Beyond Badiou: Ontology, Multiplicity, and Event* (New York: Columbia University Press, 2013).

Works Cited

Agamben, Giorgio. *Homo Sacer: Sovereign Power and Bare Life.* Translated by Daniel Heller-Roazen. Stanford, Calif.: Stanford University Press, 1995.

———. *Remnants of Auschwitz: The Witness and the Archive.* Translated by Daniel Heller-Roazen. New York: Zone Books, 2002.

———. *State of Exception.* Translated by Kevin Attell. Chicago: The University of Chicago Press, 2005.

Alter, Robert. *The Art of Biblical Narrative.* New York: Basic, 1981.

Amende, Coral. *The Crossword Obsession.* New York: Berkley Books, 2001.

Andersen, Francis I. *Job: An Introduction and Commentary.* Downers Grove, Ill.: Inter-Varsity, 1976.

Anscombe, G. E. M. "Modern Moral Philosophy." *Philosophy* 33 (1958): 1–19.

Asad, Talal. *Genealogies of Religion: Discipline and Reasons of Power in Christianity and Islam.* Baltimore: The Johns Hopkins University Press, 1993.

Badiou, Alain. *Deleuze: The Clamor of Being.* Translated by Louise Burchill. Minneapolis: University of Minnesota Press, 2000.

———. *Ethics: An Essay on the Understanding of Evil.* Translated by Peter Hallward. London: Verso, 2001.

———. *Saint Paul: The Foundation of Universalism.* Translated by Ray Brassier. Stanford, Calif.: Stanford University Press, 2003.

———. *Being and Event.* Translated by Oliver Feltham. London: Continuum, 2005.

Balentine, Samuel E. *Job.* Macon, Ga.: Smyth & Helwys, 2006.

Balthasar, Hans Urs von. *Theo-Drama: Theological Dramatic Theory, Volume I: Prolegomena.* Translated by Graham Harrison. San Francisco: Ignatius, 1988.

Barthes, Roland. *La Chambre Claire: Note Sur La Photographie.* Paris: Gallimard/Seuil, 1980.

Beal, Timothy K. *Religion and Its Monsters.* New York: Routledge, 2002.

———. "Mimetic Monsters: The Genesis of Horror in the Face of the Deep." *Postscripts* 4 (2008): 85–93.

Becker, Joachim. *Gottesfurcht Im Alten Testament.* Rome: Ist Biblico, Analecta Biblica, 1965.

Berlant, Lauren. *Cruel Optimism.* Durham: Duke University Press, 2011.

Blanton, Ward. "Neither Religious nor Secular: On Saving the Critic in Biblical-Criticism." In *Secularism and Biblical Studies,* edited by Roland Boer, 141–62. London and Oakland, Conn.: Equinox, 2010.

Boer, Roland, ed. *Secularism and Biblical Studies.* London and Oakland, Conn.: Equinox, 2010.

Briant, Pierre. *From Cyrus to Alexander: A History of the Persian Empire.* Translated by P. T. Daniels. Winona Lake, Ind.: Eisenbrauns, 2002.

Briggs, John Curtis. "On Job's Response to Yahweh." *Journal of Biblical Literature* 98 (1979): 497–511.

Brown, F., S. Driver, and C. Briggs. *The Brown-Driver-Briggs Hebrew and English Lexicon.* Peabody, Mass.: Hendrickson, 1906.

Brown, William P. *Character in Crisis: A Fresh Approach to the Wisdom Literature of the Old Testament.* Grand Rapids, Mich.: W. B. Eerdmans, 1996.

———. *The Ethos of the Cosmos: The Genesis of Moral Imagination in the Bible.* Grand Rapids: W. B. Eerdmans, 1998.

———, ed. *Character and Scripture: Moral Formation, Community, and Biblical Interpretation.* Grand Rapids, Mich.: W. B. Eerdmans, 2002.

———. *The Seven Pillars of Creation: The Bible, Science, and the Ecology of Wonder.* London: Oxford University Press, 2010.

Brueggemann, Walter. *Genesis.* Atlanta: John Knox, 1982.

———. *The Message of the Psalms: A Theological Commentary.* Minneapolis, Minn.: Augsburg, 1984.

———. *The Covenanted Self.* Minneapolis, Minn.: Fortress, 1999.

———. "Foreword." In *Character Ethics and the Old Testament: Moral Dimensions of Scripture,* edited by M. Daniel Carroll R. and Jacqueline E. Lapsley, vii–xi. Louisville: Westminster John Knox, 2007.

Burke, Edmund. *A Philosophical Enquiry into the Origin of Our Ideas of the Sublime and the Beautiful.* London: Routledge and Kegan Paul, 1958 (1757).

Buss, Martin J. *Biblical Form Criticism in Its Context.* Sheffield: Sheffield Academic, 1999.

Butler, Judith, Ernesto Laclau, and Slavoj Žižek. *Contingency, Hegemony, and Universality: Contemporary Dialogues on the Left.* London: Verso, 2000.

Carroll R., M. Daniel, and Jacqueline E. Lapsley, eds. *Character Ethics and the Old Testament: Moral Dimensions of Scripture.* Louisville: Westminster John Knox, 2007.

Cartwright, Nancy. *The Dappled World: A Study of the Boundaries of Science.* Cambridge: Cambridge University Press, 1999.

Chesterton, G. K. *Introduction to the Book of Job.* London: S. Wellwood, 1907.

Chiesa, Lorenzo. *Subjectivity and Otherness: A Philosophical Reading of Lacan.* Cambridge, Mass.: MIT Press, 2007.

Clines, David J. A. "Verb Modality and the Interpretation of Job IV 20–21." *Vetus Testamentum* 30 (1980): 354–57.

———. "The Arguments of Job's Three Friends." In *Art and Meaning: Rhetoric in Biblical Literature,* edited by David J. A. Clines, David M. Gunn, and Alan J. Hauser, 199–214. Sheffield: JSOT, 1982.

———. "False Naivety in the Prologue to Job." *Hebrew Annual Review* 9 (1985): 127–36.

———. *Job 1–20.* Dallas: Word, 1989.

———, ed. *The Dictionary of Classical Hebrew. III. Zayin-Teth.* Sheffield: Sheffield Academic, 1996.

———, ed. *The Dictionary of Classical Hebrew. V. Mem-Nun.* Sheffield: Sheffield Academic, 2001.

————. "'The Fear of the Lord Is Wisdom' (Job 28:28): A Semantic and Contextual Study." In *Job 28: Cognition in Context*, edited by Ellen Van Wolde, 57–92. Leiden: Brill, 2003.

————. *Job 21–37*. Nashville: Thomas Nelson, 2006.

————, ed. *The Concise Dictionary of Classical Hebrew*. Sheffield: Sheffield Phoenix, 2009.

Connor, Steven. "The Shame of Being a Man." (2000). http://www.bbk.ac.uk/english/skc/shame/. This is an expanded version of the article in *Textual Practice* 15 (2001): 211–30.

Cooper, Alan. "Reading and Misreading the Prologue to Job." *Journal for the Study of the Old Testament* 46 (1990): 67–79.

————. "The Sense of the Book of Job." *Prooftexts* 17 (1997): 227–44.

Copjec, Joan. "The Phenomenal Nonphenomenal: Private Space in Film Noir." In *Shades of Noir: A Reader*. 167–98. London: Verso, 1993.

————. *Read My Desire: Lacan against the Historicists*. Cambridge, Mass.: MIT Press, 1994.

————. *Imagine There's No Woman: Ethics and Sublimation*. Cambridge, Mass.: MIT Press, 2002.

————. "May '68, the Emotional Month." In *Lacan: The Silent Partners*, edited by Slavoj Žižek, 90–114. London: Verso, 2006.

————. "The Censorship of Interiority." *Umbr(a)* (2009): 165–86.

Cotter, David W. *A Study of Job 4–5 in the Light of Contemporary Literary Theory*. Atlanta: Scholars Press, 1992.

Cottrill, Amy C. *Language, Power, and Identity in the Lament Psalms of the Individual*. New York: T. & T. Clark, 2008.

Crenshaw, James L. "When Form and Content Clash: The Theology of Job 38:1–40:5." In *Urgent Advice and Probing Questions: Collected Writings on Old Testament Wisdom*, 455–67. Macon, Ga.: Mercer University Press, 1995.

————. *Old Testament Wisdom: An Introduction*. Rev. ed. Louisville: Westminster John Knox, 1998.

Crockett, Clayton. *Radical Political Theology*. New York: Columbia University Press, 2011.

————. *Deleuze Beyond Badiou: Ontology, Multiplicity, and Event*. New York: Columbia University Press, 2013.

Davis, Ellen F. *Scripture, Culture, and Agriculture: An Agrarian Reading of the Bible*. Cambridge: Cambridge University Press, 2009.

Deleuze, Gilles. *Foucault*. Translated by Seán Hand. Minneapolis: University of Minneapolis Press, 1988.

————. *The Logic of Sense*. Translated by Mark Lester. New York: Columbia University Press, 1990.

————. *Coldness and Cruelty*. Translated by Jean McNeil. New York: Zone Books, 1989.

————. *Pure Immanence: Essays on Life*. Translated by Anne Boyman. New York: Zone Books, 2001.

Delitzsch, Franz. *Biblical Commentary on the Book of Job*. Translated by F. Bolton. 2nd ed. Edinburgh: T. & T. Clark, 1872.

Dell, Katharine J. *The Book of Job as Sceptical Literature*. Berlin: Walter de Gruyter, 1991.

Denis, Lara. "Kant's Conception of Virtue." In *The Cambridge Companion to Kant and Modern Philosophy*, edited by Paul Guyer. Cambridge: Cambridge University Press, 2006.

Derrida, Jacques. *Writing and Difference*. Translated by Alan Bass. Chicago: The University of Chicago Press, 1978.

———. *Adieu to Emmanuel Levinas*. Translated by Pascale-Anne Brault and Michael Naas. Stanford, Calif.: Stanford University Press, 1999.

———. "Faith and Knowledge: The Two Sources of 'Religion' at the Limits of Reason Alone." Translated by S. Weber. In *Acts of Religion*, edited by Gil Anidjar. New York and London: Routledge, 2002.

Dhorme, E. *A Commentary on the Book of Job*. Nashville: T. Nelson, 1984.

Di Vito, Robert A. "Old Testament Anthropology and the Construction of Personal Identity." *Catholic Biblical Quarterly* 61 (1999): 217–38.

Dolar, Mladen. *A Voice and Nothing More*. Cambridge, Mass.: MIT Press, 2006.

Donoghue, Dennis. *Speaking of Beauty*. New Haven, Conn.: Yale University Press, 2003.

Driver, Samuel R., and George Buchanan Gray. *A Critical and Exegetical Commentary on the Book of Job*. Edinburgh: T. & T. Clark, 1921.

Duhm, B. *Das Buch Hiob erklärt*. Tübingen: Mohr, 1897.

Febos, Melissa. Interview with Terry Gross. *Fresh Air*. 8 March 2010, accessed 6 May, 2010. Transcript available at http://www.npr.org/templates/transcript/transcript.php?storyId=124369913.

Fink, Bruce. *The Lacanian Subject: Between Language and Jouissance*. Princeton: Princeton University Press, 1995.

———. *A Clinical Introduction to Lacanian Psychoanalysis: Theory and Technique*. Cambridge, Mass.: Harvard University Press, 1997.

Fontaine, Carole R. *Smooth Words: Women, Proverbs, and Performance in Biblical Wisdom*. Sheffield: Sheffield Academic, 2002.

Foucault, Michel. *Discipline and Punish: The Birth of the Prison*. Translated by Alan Sheridan. New York: Vintage, 1995.

Fox, Michael V. "Ideas of Wisdom in Proverbs 1–9." *Journal of Biblical Literature* 116 (1997): 613–33.

———. "Words for Folly." *Zeitschrift für Althebraistik* 10 (1997): 4–17.

———. *Proverbs 1–9: A New Translation with Introduction and Commentary*. Garden City, N.Y.: Doubleday, 2000.

———. "Job the Pious." *Zeitschrift für die alttestamentliche Wissenschaft* 117 (2005): 351–66.

———. "The Epistemology of the Book of Proverbs." *Journal of Biblical Literature* 126 (2007): 669–84.

Frankfurt, Harry G. "Freedom of the Will and the Concept of a Person." *The Journal of Philosophy* 68 (1971): 5–20.

Freud, Sigmund. *The Standard Edition of the Complete Psychological Works of Sigmund Freud (SE)*. Translated by James Strachey. 24 vols. London: Hogarth Press and the Institute of Psycho-Analysis, 1953–1974.

———. *Gesammelte Werke*. 18 vols. Frankfurt: Fischer Taschenbuch Verlag, 1999.

———. "Instincts and Their Vicissitudes." In *SE XIV*, 109–40, 1955 (1915).

————. "A Metapsychological Supplement to the Theory of Dreams." In *SE XIV*, 218–35, 1955 (1917).

————. "'A Child Is Being Beaten': A Contribution to the Study of the Origin of Sexual Perversions." In *SE XVII*, 175–204, 1955 (1919).

————. "The Uncanny." In *SE XVII*, 217–56, 1955 (1919).

————. "Inhibitions, Symptoms, and Anxiety." In *SE XX*, 77–172, 1959 (1926).

————. "The Future of an Illusion." In *SE XXI*, 1–56, 1961 (1927).

————. "Humour." In *SE XXI*, 159–66, 1961 (1927).

————. "Civilization and Its Discontents." In *SE XXI*, 57–145, 1961 (1929).

Fullerton, Kemper. "Double Entendre in the First Speech of Eliphaz." *Journal of Biblical Literature* 49 (1930): 320–74.

Gadamer, Hans-Georg. *Truth and Method.* Translated by Joel Wiensheimer and Donald G. Marshall. 2nd ed. London, New York: Continuum, 2004.

Gasché, Rodolphe. *The Idea of Form: Rethinking Kant's Aesthetics.* Stanford, Calif.: Stanford University Press, 2003.

Gaylin, Willard. *Feelings: Our Vital Signs.* New York: Ballantine, 1979.

Gesenius, Wilhelm. *Gesenius' Hebrew Grammar.* Mineola, N.Y.: Dover, 2006 (1909, 1813).

Good, Edwin M. *In Turns of Tempest: A Reading of Job, with a Translation.* Stanford, Calif.: Stanford University Press, 1990.

Gordis, Robert. *The Book of God and Man.* Chicago: The University of Chicago Press, 1965.

————. *The Book of Job: Commentary, New Translation, and Special Studies.* New York: The Jewish Theological Seminary of America, 1978.

Greenstein, Edward L. "In Job's Face/Facing Job." In *The Labour of Reading: Desire, Alienation, and Biblical Interpretation,* edited by Fiona C. Black, Roland Boer, and Erin Runions, 301–17. Atlanta: Society of Biblical Literature, 1999.

Gruber, Mayer I. "Fear, Anxiety and Reverence in Akkadian, Biblical Hebrew and Other North-West Semitic Languages." *Vetus Testamentum* XL (1990): 411–22.

Gutiérrez, Gustavo. *On Job: God-Talk and the Suffering of the Innocent.* Maryknoll, N.Y.: Orbis Books, 1987.

Habel, Norman C. "Symbolism of Wisdom in Proverbs 1–9." *Interpretation* 26 (1972): 131–57.

————. *The Book of Job.* Cambridge: Cambridge University Press, 1975.

————. *The Book of Job.* Philadelphia: Westminster, 1985.

Hägglund, Martin. *Radical Atheism: Derrida and the Time of Life.* Stanford, Calif.: Stanford University Press, 2008.

Hankins, Davis, and Brennan Breed. "The Book of Job." In *The Oxford Encyclopedia of the Books of the Bible, Vol. 1,* edited by M. Coogan, 434–50. New York: Oxford University Press, 2011.

Hankins, Davis. "Woman and the Plasticity of Wisdom: Reconsidering Wisdom Literature and Feminism." In *Imagination, Ideology, and Inspiration: Exploring Walter Brueggemann's Influence in Biblical Studies,* edited by R. Williamson and J. Kaplan. Sheffield: Sheffield Phoenix, 2014.

————. Introduction to *Ice Axes for Frozen Seas: A Biblical Theology of Provocation,* by Walter Brueggemann. Edited by Davis Hankins. Waco, Texas: Baylor University Press, 2014.

————. "Wisdom as an Immanent Event in Job 28, Not a Transcendent Ideal." *Vetus Testamentum* 63 (2013): 210–35.

Hankins, Davis, and David Knauert. "Desire and Ideology in Wisdom's Inaugural Address: Proverbs 1:22–33." In *Imagination, Ideology, and Inspiration: Exploring Walter Brueggemann's Influence in Biblical Studies*, edited by R. Williamson and J. Kaplan. Sheffield: Sheffield Phoenix, forthcoming.

Harding, James E. "A Spirit of Deception in Job 4:15? Interpretive Indeterminacy and Eliphaz's Vision." *Biblical Interpretation* 13 (2005): 137–66.

Hartley, George. *The Abyss of Representation: Marxism and the Postmodern Sublime.* Durham and London: Duke University Press, 2003.

Hartley, John E. *The Book of Job.* Grand Rapids, Mich.: Eerdmans, 1988.

Hauerwas, Stanley. *Character and the Christian Life: A Study in Theological Ethics.* San Antonio: Trinity University Press, 1975.

————. *A Community of Character: Toward a Constructive Christian Social Ethic.* Notre Dame: University of Notre Dame Press, 1981.

Hegel, Georg Wilhelm Friedrich. *Phenomenology of Spirit.* Translated by A. V. Miller. Oxford: Clarendon, 1977.

————. *Hegel's Science of Logic.* Translated by A. V. Miller. Atlantic Highlands, N.J.: Humanities Press International, 1989.

————. *The Encyclopædia Logic: Part 1 of the Encylopædia of Philosophical Sciences with the Zusätze.* Translated by T. F. Geraets, W. A. Suchting, and H. S. Harris. Indianapolis: Hackett, 1991.

Heidegger, Martin. *Being and Time.* Translated by J. Macquarrie and E. Robinson. New York: Harper, 1962.

Herder, Johann Gottfried. *The Spirit of Hebrew Poetry.* Translated by James Marsh. Burlington, Vt.: Edward Smith, 1833.

Hiebert, Theodore. "Beyond Heilsgeschichte." In *Character Ethics and the Old Testament: Moral Dimensions of Scripture*, edited by M. Daniel Carroll R. and Jacqueline E. Lapsley, 3–11. Louisville: Westminster John Knox, 2007.

Hoffman, Yair. "The Use of Equivocal Words in the First Speech of Eliphaz (Job IV–V)." *Vetus Testamentum* 30 (1980): 114–19.

————. *A Blemished Perfection: The Book of Job in Context.* Sheffield: Sheffield, 1996.

Horst, Friedrich. *Hiob.* Neukirchen-Vluyn: Neukirchener Verlag, 1968.

Hursthouse, Rosiland. *On Virtue Ethics.* New York: Oxford University Press, 1999.

Jameson, Fredric. "Imaginary and Symbolic in Lacan." In *The Ideologies of Theory*, 77–124. London: Verso, 2008.

————. "The Vanishing Mediator; or, Max Weber as Storyteller." In *The Ideologies of Theory*, 309–43. London: Verso, 2008.

Janzen, J. Gerald. *Job.* Atlanta: John Knox, 1985.

Johnston, Adrian. *Time Driven: Metapsychology and the Splitting of the Drive.* Evanston, Ill.: Northwestern University Press, 2005.

————. "Ghosts of Substance Past: Schelling, Lacan, and the Denaturalization of Nature." In *Lacan: The Silent Partners*, edited by Slavoj Žižek, 34–55. London: Verso, 2006.

————. "Conflicted Matter: Jacques Lacan and the Challenge of Secularizing Materialism." *Pli: The Warwick Journal of Philosophy* 19 (2008): 166–88.

———. *Žižek's Ontology: A Transcendental Materialist Theory of Subjectivity.* Evanston, Ill.: Northwestern University Press, 2008.

———. *Badiou, Žižek, and Political Transformations: The Cadence of Change.* Evanston, Ill.: Northwestern University Press, 2009.

———. "The Weakness of Nature: Hegel, Freud, Lacan, and Negativity Materialized." In *Hegel and the Infinite: Religion, Politics, and Dialectic,* edited by Slavoj Žižek, Clayton Crockett, and Creston Davis, 159–80. New York: Columbia University Press, 2011.

———. "Misfelt Feelings: Unconscious Affect Between Psychoanalysis, Neuroscience, and Philosophy." In *Self and Emotional Life: Merging Philosophy, Psychoanalysis, and Neurobiology,* 73–210. New York: Columbia University Press, 2013.

———. *Prolegomena to Any Future Materialism: Volume 1, The Outcome of Contemporary French Philosophy.* Evanston, Ill.: Northwestern University Press, 2013.

Johnston, Adrian, and Catherine Malabou. *Self and Emotional Life: Philosophy, Psychoanalysis, and Neuroscience.* New York: Columbia University Press, 2013.

Kant, Immanuel. *Observations on the Feeling of the Beautiful and Sublime.* Translated by John T. Goldthwait. Berkeley: University of California Press, 1960.

———. "Critique of Practical Reason." In *Practical Philosophy.* Translated and edited by Mary J. Gregor, 133–271. Cambridge, New York: Cambridge University Press, 1996.

———. "Groundwork of the Metaphysics of Morals." In *Practical Philosophy.* Translated and edited by Mary J. Gregor, 37–108. Cambridge, New York: Cambridge University Press, 1996.

———. "The Metaphysics of Morals." In *Practical Philosophy.* Translated and edited by Mary J. Gregor, 353–603. Cambridge, New York: Cambridge University Press, 1996.

———. *Religion and Rational Theology.* Translated by Allen W. Wood. Cambridge, New York: Cambridge University Press, 1996.

———. *Critique of Pure Reason.* Translated and edited by Paul Guyer and Allen W. Wood. Cambridge: Cambridge University Press, 1998.

———. *Critique of the Power of Judgment.* Edited by Paul Guyer. Translated by Paul Guyer and Eric Matthews. New York: Cambridge University Press, 2000.

Keller, Catherine. *The Face of the Deep: A Theology of Becoming.* London: Routledge, 2003.

Kesel, Marc de. *Eros and Ethics: Reading Jacques Lacan's Seminar VII.* Translated by Sigi Jöttkandt. Albany: State University of New York Press, 2009.

Kielholz, Paul. "Psychopharmacology Measurement of Emotions in Medical Practice." In *Emotions: Their Parameters and Measurement,* edited by L. Levi and U. S. von Euler, 748–49. New York: Raven, 1975.

Kierkegaard, Soren. *The Concept of Anxiety: A Simple Psychologically Orienting Deliberation on the Dogmatic Issue of Hereditary Sin.* Translated by Reidar Thomte. Princeton, N.J.: Princeton University Press, 1980 (1844).

Knauert, David Cromwell. "The Limits of Wisdom and the Dialectic of Desire." PhD diss., Duke University, 2009.

Knight, Kelvin. *Aristotelian Philosophy: Ethics and Politics from Aristotle to Macintyre.* Cambridge, Eng.: Polity, 2007.

Koehler, Ludwig, and Walter Baumgartner. *The Hebrew and Aramaic Lexicon of the Old Testament (*HALOT*).* 2 vols. Leiden: Brill, 2001.

Lacan, Jacques. *The Seminar of Jacques Lacan, Book III: The Psychoses, 1955–1956.* Edited by Jacques-Alain Miller. Translated by Russell Grigg. New York: W. W. Norton & Company, 1993.

———. *Le Séminaire de Jacques Lacan, Livre IV: La Relation D'objet, 1956–1957.* Edited by Jacques-Alain Miller. Paris: Éditions du Seuil, 1994.

———. *The Seminar of Jacques Lacan, Book VII: The Ethics of Psychoanalysis, 1959–1960.* Edited by Jacques-Alain Miller. Translated by Dennis Porter. New York: W. W. Norton & Company, 1992.

———. *Le Séminaire de Jacques Lacan, Livre X: Angoisse, 1962–1963.* Edited by Jacques-Alain Miller. Paris: Éditions du Seuil, 2004.

———. "The Seminar of Jacques Lacan, Book X: Anxiety, 1962–1963." Unpublished Typescript.

———. *The Seminar of Jacques Lacan, Book XI: The Four Fundamental Concepts of Psycho-Analysis, 1964.* Edited by Jacques-Alain Miller. Translated by Alan Sheridan. New York: W. W. Norton & Company, 1977.

———. "The Seminar of Jacques Lacan, Book XII: Crucial Problems for Psychoanalysis, 1964–1965." Unpublished Typescript.

———. "The Seminar of Jacques Lacan, Book XIV: The Logic of Fantasy, 1966–1967." Unpublished Typescript.

———. "The Seminar of Jacques Lacan, Book XV: The Psychoanalytic Act, 1967–1968." Unpublished Typescript.

———. *The Seminar of Jacques Lacan, Book XVII: The Other Side of Psychoanalysis, 1969–1970.* Edited by Jacques-Alain Miller. Translated by Russell Grigg. New York: W. W. Norton & Company, 2007.

———. *The Seminar of Jacques Lacan, Book XX: Encore, 1972–1973.* Edited by Jacques-Alain Miller. Translated by Bruce Fink. New York: W. W. Norton & Company, 1998.

———. "Le Triomphe de la religion." In *Le triomphe de la religion, précédé de Discours aux aatholiques,* edited by Jacques-Alain Miller, 67–102. Paris: Éditions du Seuil, 2005.

———. "The Function and Field of Speech and Language in Psychoanalysis." In *Écrits,* translated by Bruce Fink, 197–268. New York: W. W. Norton & Company, 2006.

———. "The Mirror Stage as Formative of the *I* Function as Revealed in Psychoanalytic Experience." In *Écrits,* translated by Bruce Fink, 93–100. New York: W. W. Norton & Company, 2006.

———. "Position of the Unconscious." In *Écrits,* translated by Bruce Fink, 671–702. New York: W. W. Norton & Company, 2006.

———. "The Subversion of the Subject and the Dialectic of Desire in the Freudian Unconscious." In *Écrits,* translated by Bruce Fink, 671–702. New York: W. W. Norton & Company, 2006.

Lambert, W. G., and A. R. Millard. *Atra-Ḥasis: The Babylonian Story of the Flood.* Oxford: Clarendon, 1969.

Laplanche, Jean. *The Unconscious and the Id: A Volume of Laplanche's Problematiques.* Translated by L. Thurston and L. Watson. London: Rebus, 1999.

Laplanche, J., and J.-B. Pontalis. *The Language of Psycho-Analysis.* Translated by D. Nicholson-Smith. New York: W. W. Norton & Company, 1973.

Leeuwen, Raymond C. Van. "Cosmos, Temple, House: Building and Wisdom in Mesopotamia and Israel." In *Wisdom Literature in Mesopotamia and Israel,* edited by R. J. Clifford, 67–90. Atlanta: Society of Biblical Literature, 2007.

Levenson, Jon D. *Creation and the Persistence of Evil: The Jewish Drama of Divine Omnipotence.* Princeton: Princeton University Press, 1994.

Levinas, Emmanuel. *Totality and Infinity: An Essay on Exteriority.* Translated by Alphonso Lingis. Pittsburgh: Duquesne University Press, 1969.

———. "The Trace of the Other." Translated by Alphonso Lingis. In *Deconstruction in Context: Literature and Philosophy,* edited by Mark C. Taylor. Chicago: The University of Chicago Press, 1986.

———. *Time and the Other and Additional Essays.* Translated by Richard A. Cohen. Pittsburgh: Duquesne University Press, 1987.

———. *Difficult Freedom: Essays on Judaism.* Translated by Seán Hand. Baltimore: Johns Hopkins University Press, 1990.

———. *Otherwise than Being or Beyond Essence.* Translated by Alphonso Lingis. Pittsburgh: Duquesne University Press, 1998.

———. *On Escape: De L'évasion.* Translated by Bettina Bergo. Stanford, Calif.: Stanford University Press, 2003.

Linafelt, Tod. "The Undecidability of *BRK* in the Prologue to Job and Beyond." *Biblical Interpretation* 4 (1996): 154–72.

———. "The Wizard of Uz: Job, Dorothy, and the Limits of the Sublime." *Biblical Interpretation* 14 (2006): 94–109.

Lugt, Pieter van der. *Rhetorical Criticism and the Poetry of the Book of Job.* Leiden: Brill, 1995.

MacIntyre, Alasdair. *After Virtue: A Study in Moral Theory.* Notre Dame: University of Notre Dame Press, 1981.

———. *Whose Justice? Which Rationality?* London: Duckworth, 1988.

———. *Three Rival Versions of Moral Enquiry: Encyclopaedia, Genealogy, and Tradition.* London: Duckworth, 1990.

———. *Dependent Rational Animals.* London: Duckworth, 1999.

Magdalene, F. Rachel. *On the Scales of Righteousness: Neo-Babylonian Trial Law and the Book of Job.* Providence, R.I.: Brown Judaic Studies, 2007.

Malabou, Catherine. *What Should We Do with Our Brain?* Translated by Sebastian Rand. New York: Fordham University Press, 2008.

———. *Plasticity at the Dusk of Writing: Dialectic, Destruction, Deconstruction.* Translated by Carolyn Shread. New York: Columbia University Press, 2010.

———. *The New Wounded: From Neurosis to Brain Damage.* Translated by Steven Miller. New York: Fordham University Press, 2012.

Masuzawa, Tomoko. *The Invention of World Religions: Or, How European Universalism Was Preserved in the Language of Pluralism*. Chicago and London: The University of Chicago Press, 2005.

Mathewson, Dan. *Death and Survival in the Book of Job: Desymbolization and Traumatic Experience*. New York: T. & T. Clark, 2006.

May, Todd. *Gilles Deleuze: An Introduction*. Cambridge: Cambridge University Press, 2005.

Meier, Sam. "Job I–II: A Reflection of Genesis I–III." *Vetus Testamentum* 39 (1989): 189–93.

Miles, Jack. *God: A Biography*. New York: Alfred A. Knopf, 1995.

Miller, J. Maxwell, and John H. Hayes. *A History of Ancient Israel and Judah*. 2nd ed. Louisville: Westminster John Knox, 2006.

Mitchell, Stephen. *The Book of Job*. Rev. ed. of *Into the Whirlwind* (1979). New York: HarperCollins, 1987.

Moore, Stephen D., and Yvonne Sherwood. *The Invention of the Biblical Scholar: A Critical Manifesto*. Minneapolis, Minn.: Fortress, 2011.

Morrow, William. "Consolation, Rejection, and Repentance in Job 42:6." *Journal of Biblical Literature* 105 (1986): 211–25.

Nancy, Jean-Luc. *Dis-Closure: The Deconstruction of Christianity*. Translated by Bettina Bergo et al. New York: Fordham University Press, 2008.

Nemo, Philippe. *Job and the Excess of Evil*. Translated by Michael Kigel. Pittsburgh: Duquesne University Press, 1998.

Newsom, Carol A. "The Book of Job." In *The New Interpreter's Bible, Volume 4*, edited by L. Keck. Nashville: Abingdon, 1996.

———. "Job." In *The Women's Bible Commentary*, edited by Carol A. Newsom and Sharon H. Ringe. 138–45. Louisville: Westminster/John Knox, 1998.

———. "Narrative Ethics, Character, and the Prose Tale of Job." In *Character and Scripture: Moral Formation, Community, and Biblical Interpretation*, edited by William P. Brown, 121–34. Grand Rapids, MI: Eerdmans, 2002.

———. *The Book of Job: A Contest of Moral Imaginations*. New York: Oxford University Press, 2003.

———. "'The Consolations of God': Assessing Job's Friends across a Cultural Abyss." In *Reading from Right to Left: Essays on the Hebrew Bible in Honour of David J. A. Clines*, edited by J. C. Exum and H. G. M. Williamson, 347–58. London: Sheffield, 2003.

———. *The Self as Symbolic Space: Constructing Identity and Community at Qumran*. Leiden: Brill, 2004.

———. "Re-Considering Job." *Currents in Biblical Research* 5 (2007): 155–82.

Niditch, Susan. *Chaos to Cosmos: Studies in Biblical Patterns of Creation*. Chico, Calif.: Scholars, 1985.

Nietzsche, Friedrich. *Beyond Good and Evil: Prelude to a Philosophy of the Future*. Translated by Walter Kaufmann. New York: Vintage Books, 1989.

O'Connor, Kathleen M. *The Wisdom Literature*. Collegeville, Minn.: The Liturgical Press, 1990.

———. "Wild, Raging Creativity: The Scene in the Whirlwind (Job 38–41)." In *A God So Near: Essays on Old Testament Theology in Honor of Patrick D. Miller*, edited by B. A. Strawn and N. R. Bowen, 171–79. Winona Lake, Ind.: Eisenbrauns, 2003.

Panksepp, Jaak. *Affective Neuroscience: The Foundations of Human and Animal Emotions*. Oxford: Oxford University Press, 1998.

Perdue, Leo G., Bernard Brandon Scott, and William Johnston Wiseman, eds. *In Search of Wisdom: Essays in Memory of John G. Gammie*. Louisville: Westminster/John Knox Press, 1993.

Pitt-Rivers, Julian. "Honour and Social Status." In *Honor and Shame: The Values of Mediterranean Society*, edited by J. G. Peristiany. Chicago: The University of Chicago Press, 1966.

Pope, Marvin H. *Job*. 3rd ed. Garden City, N.Y.: Doubleday, 1973.

Rad, Gerhard von. *Old Testament Theology, Vol. 1: The Theology of Israel's Historical Traditions*. Translated by D. M. G. Stalker. New York: Harper & Row, 1962.

———. *Old Testament Theology, Vol. 2: The Theology of Israel's Prophetic Traditions*. Translated by D. M. G. Stalker. New York: Harper & Row, 1965.

———. *Wisdom in Israel*. Translated by James D. Martin. Nashville: Abingdon, 1972.

Ramsey, F. P. "Universals." *Mind* 34 (1925): 401–17.

Rancière, Jacques. *The Politics of Aesthetics: The Distribution of the Sensible*. Translated by Gabriel Rockhill. New York: Continuum, 2004.

Reinhard, Kenneth. "Universalism and the Jewish Exception: Lacan, Badiou, Rosenzweig." *Umbr(a)* (2005): 43–71.

Reventlow, Henning Graf. "Grundfragen Der Alttestamentlighen Theologie Im Lichte Der Neueren Deutschen Forschung." *Theologische Zeitschrift* 17 (1961): 81–98.

Robbins, Jeffrey W. *Radical Democracy and Political Theology*. New York: Columbia University Press, 2011.

Robertson, David. "The Book of Job: A Literary Study." *Soundings* 56 (1973): 462–69.

———. *The Old Testament and the Literary Critic*. Philadelphia: Fortress, 1977.

Rowley, H. H. *Job*. London: Nelson, 1970.

Rubenstein, Mary-Jane. "Dionysius, Derrida, and the Critique of Ontotheology." In *Division I Faculty Publications* (2008). http://wesscholar.wesleyan.edu/div1facpubs/98.

Sartre, Jean-Paul. *Being and Nothingness*. Translated by Hazel E. Barnes. New York: Washington Square, 1992.

Scarry, Elaine. *On Beauty and Being Just*. Princeton: Princeton University Press, 1999.

Schifferdecker, Kathryn. *Out of the Whirlwind: Creation Theology in the Book of Job*. Cambridge, Mass.: Harvard University Press, 2008.

Seow, Choon-Leong. "Job's Wife, with Due Respect." In *Das Buch Hiob Und Seine Interpretationen: Beiträge Zum Hiob-Symposium Auf Dem Monte Verità Vom 14.–19. August 2005*, edited by Thomas Krüger et al., 351–73. Zürich: Theologischer Verlag Zürich, 2007.

———. *Job 1–21: Interpretation and Commentary*. Grand Rapids, Mich.: Eerdmans, 2013.

Smith, Anthony Paul, and Daniel Whistler, eds. *After the Postsecular and the Postmodern: New Essays in Continental Philosophy of Religion*. Cambridge, Eng.: Cambridge Scholars Press, 2010.

Steiner, Wendy. *Venus in Exile*. New York: The Free Press, 2001.

296

WORKS CITED

Swanton, Christine. *Virtue Ethics: A Pluralistic View.* New York: Oxford University Press, 2003.
Taylor, Charles. "The Moral Order: The Transition to Political Modernity." In *Religion and Political Thought,* edited by Michael Hoelzl and Graham Ward, 259–67. London: Continuum, 2006.
Terrien, Samuel L. *Job.* Neuchâtel: Delachaux et Niestlé, 1963.
Vito, Robert A. Di. "Old Testament Anthropology and the Construction of Personal Identity." *Catholic Biblical Quarterly* 61 (1999): 217–38.
Vogels, Walter. "Job's Empty Pious Slogans (Job 1,20–22; 2,8–10)." In *The Book of Job,* edited by W. A. M. Beuken. Leuven: Leuven University Press, 1994.
Waltke, Bruce K., and M. O'Connor. *An Introduction to Biblical Hebrew Syntax.* Winona Lake, Ind.: Eisenbrauns, 1990.
Weiss, Meir. *The Story of Job's Beginning: Job 1–2: A Literary Analysis.* Jerusalem: Magness Press, Hebrew University, 1983.
Westermann, Claus. *The Structure of the Book of Job: A Form-Critical Analysis.* Philadelphia: Fortress, 1981.
Whedbee, J. William. "The Comedy of Job." *Semeia* 7 (1977): 1–39.
Whybray, R. N. *Job.* Sheffield: Sheffield Academic, 1998.
Williamson, R., and Kaplan, J., eds. *Imagination, Ideology, and Inspiration: Biblical Studies after Walter Brueggemann.* Sheffield: Sheffield Phoenix, forthcoming.
Wilson, Gerald H. *Job.* Peabody, Mass.: Hendrickson, 2007.
Wolde, Ellen Van. "Job 42,1–6: The Reversal of Job." In *The Book of Job,* edited by W. A. M. Beuken, 223–50. Leuven: Leuven University Press, 1994.
———. "The Development of Job: Mrs Job as Catalyst." In *A Feminist Companion to Wisdom Literature,* edited by Athalya Brenner, 201–21. Sheffield: Sheffield, 1995.
Yee, Gale A. *Poor Banished Children of Eve: Women as Evil in the Hebrew Bible.* Minneapolis, Minn.: Fortress, 2003.
Yoder, Christine Roy. *Wisdom as a Woman of Substance: A Socioeconomic Reading of Proverbs 1–9 and 31:10–31.* Berlin: Walter de Gruyter, 2001.
Žižek, Slavoj. *Tarrying with the Negative: Kant, Hegel, and the Critique of Ideology.* Durham: Duke University Press, 1993.
———. *The Indivisible Remainder: An Essay on Schelling and Related Matters.* London: Verso, 1996.
———. *The Plague of Fantasies.* London: Verso, 1997.
———. *Did Somebody Say Totalitarianism?: Five Interventions in the (Mis)Use of a Notion.* London: Verso, 2001.
———. *On Belief.* London: Routledge, 2001.
———. *For They Know Not What They Do: Enjoyment as a Political Factor.* 2nd ed. London: Verso, 2002.
———. *The Puppet and the Dwarf: The Perverse Core of Christianity.* Cambridge, Mass.: MIT Press, 2003.
———. *Organs without Bodies: On Deleuze and Consequences.* New York: Routledge, 2004.
———. *The Parallax View.* Cambridge, Mass.: MIT Press, 2006.
———. *In Defense of Lost Causes.* London: Verso, 2008.
Žižek, Slavoj, and Glyn Daly. *Conversations with Žižek.* Cambridge, Eng.: Polity, 2004.

Žižek, Slavoj, Eric L. Santner, and Kenneth Reinhard. *The Neighbor: Three Inquiries in Political Theology.* Chicago: The University of Chicago Press, 2005.

Žižek, Slavoj, and John Milbank, *The Monstrosity of Christ: Paradox or Dialectic?* Edited by Creston Davis. Cambridge, Mass.: MIT Press, 2009.

Zupančič, Alenka. "The Subject of the Law." In *Cogito and the Unconscious,* edited by Slavoj Žižek, 41–73. Durham, N.C.: Duke University Press, 1998.

———. *Ethics of the Real: Kant, Lacan.* London, New York: Verso, 2000.

———. *The Odd One In: On Comedy.* Cambridge, Mass.: MIT Press, 2008.

———. *Why Psychoanalysis?: Three Interventions.* Uppsala, Sweden: NSU Press, 2008.

Index of Names and Subjects

Aaron, 197
Abihu, 31
Abner, 96–97
Abu Ghraib, 157
aesthetics, 175, 183–204, 223, 277n59, 278n72
Agamben, Giorgio, 4, 245n63, 267–68nn58–59, 270n86, 270n88, 271n91, 281n19
Ahaziah, 96
Alter, Robert, 51, 237n46, 244n47, 278n67
ambiguity, 13, 51–52, 69, 77–98, 122, 125, 251n24, 254n12
Amende, Coral, 249n2
Andersen, Francis, 244n57
Anscombe, G. E. M., 279n3
Antigone, 197, 245n71
anxiety, 18, 20, 73, 114–18, 120–38, 145, 165–66, 226, 259nn50–51, 262nn70–77, 263n1, 269n74, 270n85. *See also* fear; fear of God/YHWH; Freud, anxiety; Lacan, anxiety; terror
Aquinas, Thomas, 206, 280nn11–12
Aristotle, 205–6, 210, 247n83, 279nn2–3, 280n10
Asad, Talal, 233n4
Athaliah, 96–97

Badiou, Alain, 4, 243n36, 246n73, 280nn4–5, 283n56
Bakhtin, Mikhail, 23–29
Balentine, Samuel, 137, 176–77, 180, 184, 218, 241n12, 245n64, 249n125, 249n7, 250n11, 250n16, 251n39, 252n48, 253nn50–51, 253n53, 254n67, 258n36, 263n4, 266n45, 274n11, 275n25, 275nn35–37, 282n35, 282n39, 282nn44–45

Barthes, Roland, 62, 247n93
Beal, Timothy, 257n27, 258n41, 276n40
beauty/beautiful, the, 182, 185–95, 198, 223–24, 251n23, 257n32, 276n46, 277n59, 277n65, 278n67, 278n71
Becker, Joachim, 250n18
Behemoth, 21–22, 176, 183, 189, 193, 204
Berlant, Lauren, 267n57
biblical criticism, 3–4, 18–19
biblical studies. *See* biblical criticism
Bildad, 79, 84, 99–103, 115, 170, 252n43, 255n18
Blanton, Ward, 233nn6–7
bless/curse, 41, 43, 50–53, 68–69, 72, 82, 93, 244n50, 244n52, 244n54
Bloch, Ernst, 4
Boer, Roland, 233n7
Breed, Brennan, 236n15
Briant, Pierre, 275n23
Briggs, Charles, 230n8
Briggs, John Curtis, 282n43
Brown, Francis, 230n8
Brown, William, 180, 182, 204, 208–14, 274n10, 275n26, 275n28, 275n33, 278n69, 279n86, 280nn7–11, 280–81nn13–17, 281nn20–21, 281n23, 281–82nn25–30
Brueggemann, Walter, 234n18, 243n33, 266n40, 276n39, 281n22
Buber, Martin, 170, 185, 236n16
Burke, Edmund, 276n41
Burke, Kenneth, 247n96
Buss, Martin, 18, 236n16

Cain, 48, 243n33
Canetti, Elias, 270n88
capitalism, 8, 283n49
Carpi, Aldo, 270n88

Carroll R., M. Daniel, 280n7
Cartwright, Nancy, 233n2
chaos, 176–82, 202, 274n20
Chaplin, Charlie, 258–59n46
character ethics. *See* virtue ethics
Chesterton, G. K., 5, 234n12
Chiesa, Lorenzo, 238n51
Clines, David, 42–43, 84, 95, 230n17,
    230n18, 231n19, 231n22, 240nn3–
    4, 241n8, 241n11, 242n26, 243n43,
    244n46, 245n62, 245n70, 247n84,
    247n90, 247n98, 248n111, 248n113,
    248n116, 249n3, 250n10, 250n12,
    250n16, 250n18, 251nn27–28,
    252n46, 253n54, 253n58, 254n66,
    255n12, 255n14, 255nn17–18,
    256n20, 256n22, 256n26,
    258nn37–38, 260n57, 261nn61–62,
    263n2, 266n45, 268nn65–66,
    270n83, 272n100, 282n36
Clinton, Bill, 77–78
cognitive dissonance, 171
comedy/comic, the, 16, 185–86
consolation and mourning, 85–87, 91, 217
Congo, 6
Connor, Steven, 269n74
Cooper, Alan, 241n9, 244n54, 247n90,
    260–61n59
Copjec, Joan, 157–58, 240n78, 241n14,
    243n36, 243n39, 246n75, 246n79,
    248n103, 248n108, 259n47, 259n50,
    262n77, 265–66n34, 268n59,
    268–69n71–72, 269n75, 270n84,
    271nn94–96, 273n106, 277n63, 280n4
cosmos/cosmological, 176–83, 206, 209,
    212, 224, 256n19, 275n28, 281n23.
    See also world
Cotter, David, 230nn8–10, 231n20,
    251n27, 251n39, 252n41, 252n50
Cottrill, Amy, 254n3
Creadon, Patrick, 249n1
creation. *See* cosmos/cosmological
Crenshaw, James, 240n4, 241n6, 243n38,
    274n18, 280n7
Creon, 245n71
Crockett, Clayton, 233n3, 283n56

Dahood, M. J., 230n11
Daly, Glyn, 234n10, 237n45, 240n82,
    249n122

Damasio, Antonio, 32
Daniel, 51
darkness. *See under* Job
David, 197, 272n102
Davis, Ellen, 243n37
death. *See* life (and death)
death drive, the, 65–66, 71, 240n72, 248–
    49n122
deconstruction
    of the secular, 3, 233n4
    of the subject, 122
Deleuze, Gilles, 241n15, 248n113,
    259n48, 264n19, 269–70n80, 283n56
Delitzsch, Franz, 83, 250n20
Dell, Katharine, 241n6, 260n58, 263n3
Denis, Lara, 279n3
Derrida, Jacques/Derridean, 40, 148,
    225–26, 265n26, 267nn48–51,
    274n22
Descartes, René, 25
desire, 18, 207, 242n20, 243n33, 263n1,
    267n47, 271n97. *See also under*
    Lacan; Job
Dhorme, Édouard, 215n5, 230n14,
    230n18, 231n22, 241n6, 248n110,
    251n36
Di Vito, Robert, 245n69
Dolar, Mladen, 268n67
Dole, Bob, 77–78
Donoghue, Dennis, 277n59
drive. *See under* Lacan
Driver, Samuel, 68, 230n8, 240n5,
    245n63, 248n115, 251n29, 251n36
Duhm, B., 230n18

Ebner, Ferdinand, 185
Eckhart, Meister, 11
Eden, 253n53
Elihu, 84, 221, 235n15, 260n59
Elijah, 197
Eliphaz, 78–103, 115, 222, 224, 227–31,
    246n76, 249n7, 251n29, 252n45,
    252n47, 252n50, 253n51, 253n53,
    253n55, 254n68, 256n22, 270n81
ethics. *See under* Job
event. *See under* Lacan
exile, 43, 129

fear, 18, 20, 81–83, 92, 97, 105–35, 226,
    251n23, 255n14, 255n16, 256n22,

263n1. *See also* anxiety; fear of God/
YHWH; terror
fear of God/YHWH, 41–54, 58–59, 68,
72, 82–83, 96–98, 104, 111–21,
209, 211, 241n13, 242n22,
242n26, 243n37, 243n40, 250n18,
255nn15–16
Febos, Melissa, 264–65n19
feminism, 246n79
Fink, Bruce, 32–33, 238n55, 263n10,
268n67
finitude, 15, 25, 58, 65, 147–49, 165–66,
218, 220, 225, 247n87
fixation, 33, 72, 88–89, 98, 110, 164,
228
folly/fool, 82–84, 88–89, 91, 103–4, 125,
230n9, 230n17, 242n22, 251n23,
252n45
Fontaine, Carole, 234n2
Foucault, Michel, 236n17, 266n34,
268n59, 275n23
Fox, Michael, 11–14, 82–83, 234n1,
234–35nn3–7, 243n38, 243n44,
244n58, 246n76, 248n114, 250n19,
250n21
Frankfort, Harry, 258n40
Freud, Sigmund/Freudian, 6–7, 29,
32, 35–36, 52, 65, 234n16, 238n52,
239n62, 239n67, 239n69, 243n36,
244n55, 248n122, 257n29, 260n52
anxiety, 134, 262n74
libido, 239n72
psychoanalysis, 118, 240n72
superego, 119, 164, 248n121
uncanny, the, 123, 134, 213,
245–46nn71–72, 258nn41–42,
258n45, 260n52, 270n85
Fullerton, Kemper, 79, 99, 249n9

Gadamer, Hans-Georg, 80, 250n13
Gasché, Rodolphe, 277n65
Gaylin, Willard, 132, 261n66
gaze, the, 144–45, 158, 162–65, 168, 202,
204, 249n128, 270n88. *See also under*
Lacan
German Idealism, 14–15, 29, 38, 118
Gesenius, Wilhelm, 269n73
Girard, René, 4
Good, Edwin, 215n5, 250n11, 250n22,
282n41

Gordis, Robert, 190, 230n16, 230n18,
231nn19–20, 231n22, 258n38,
268n66, 277n56
Gorgon, the, 161
Gray, George Buchanan, 240n5
Greenstein, Edward, 273n1
grief, 59–60, 86
Gross, Terry, 264–65n19
Grotius, Hugo, 206
Gruber, Mayer I., 132, 261n65
guilt, 20, 69–70, 72–73, 135–51, 153–54,
156–60, 164–66, 199, 222, 226,
248n121, 263n1, 269n74, 270n81
Gunkel, Hermann, 18, 236n16
Gutiérrez, Gustavo, 4, 249n4

Habel, Norman, 42, 108–10, 123, 137,
178–80, 230n11, 231n19, 241nn6–
7, 243n38, 250n10, 251n29,
251nn39–40, 252n49, 253nn51–52,
254nn7–9, 258nn36–37, 258n43,
263n6, 268n66, 273n105,
274nn16–17, 282n33
Hägglund, Martin, 225–26, 237n38,
237n41, 267n48, 283n54
Hankins, Davis, 234n18, 235–36n12,
235n15, 246n79
Harding, James, 251nn24–26
Harry Potter, 270n85
Hartley, George, 276n46
Hartley, John, 215n5, 241n6, 247n90,
249nn5–6, 274n18, 278n80
haśśāṭān, 19, 25, 41–54, 64, 68–69, 105,
209, 236n20, 240nn3–4, 241n9,
241n13, 242n22, 242nn26–27,
244n56, 265n20, 283n50
Hauerwas, Stanley, 206, 279n3
Hayes, John, 253n61
Hebrew Bible, 4, 16, 56, 85, 112, 130,
234n1, 253n50, 255n17, 272n102
Hegel, Georg Wilhelm Friedrich/
Hegelian, 6, 11, 14–15, 38, 179,
235nn10–11, 235n14, 240n83,
243n36, 245n68, 267n47
Heidegger, Martin/Heideggerian, 134,
247n96, 262n75, 266n46, 272n101
Herder, Johann Gottfried von, 18,
278n67
hermeneutics, 80, 84–85, 183–86,
250nn12–13, 266n44, 278n67

Herodotus, 275n23
Hezekiah, 51
Hiebert, Theodore, 281n22
ḥinnam, 41–60, 67, 72, 241n11, 265n20
Hoffman, Yair, 250n9, 250n12, 258n37,
    263n6
Holocaust. *See* Shoah
Hopkins, Gerard Manley, 233n2
Horst, Friedrich, 251n39
Hursthouse, Rosiland, 279n3

ideology, 3–8, 77–104, 117–18, 163–64,
    171–72, 236n17
imagination, the, 186–89, 195, 246n47.
    See also Lacan, the Imaginary
immanence, 7–8, 11–15, 20–21, 159,
    163–64, 204, 219–26, 259n48,
    269n80. *See also* immanent theology;
    theology
immanent theology, 7–8, 11–15, 19,
    67, 79, 106, 124–25, 129–31, 134,
    149, 160–69, 171–72, 210, 219–26,
    234n18, 270n82, 283n50
individualism, 207, 223

Jameson, Fredric, 235n13, 264n16
Janzen, Gerald, 50, 177, 242n26, 243n42,
    248n118, 274n13, 275n37
Jehoiada, 96–97
Jehosheba, 96
Jehu, 96
Jerusalem, 43, 158
Jesus, 40–41
Joash, 96
Job
    anxiety of, 120–38, 145–47, 150, 153,
        161–62, 212, 226, 261n64, 272n101.
        See also anxiety
    body of, 168–69, 171–72, 211, 218–19
    darkness and, 153–55, 159–69,
        273n105, 275n38
    daughters of, 192, 194, 222–23
    desire of, 106–57, 166, 212, 226, 263n6,
        266n44, 267n47, 267n55, 272n101
    ethics and, 21–23, 59–60, 70–73,
        143–51, 205–26
    God's speeches, 4–6, 21, 175–204, 209,
        215, 257n27, 273n1, 274nn20–21,
        278n67, 278n80, 277n55, 283n50,
        283n53

friends of, 4–6, 16–21, 99–103, 128–31,
    149, 167, 170–71, 195, 211, 222,
    249n3, 254n66, 255n16, 255n19,
    256nn26–27, 257n33, 260n56, 260–
    61n59, 270n81
hope and, 151, 167–69, 213–14,
    220–21, 226, 272n99, 272n101
justice and, 79–80, 107, 123–24,
    145–52, 159–60, 171, 175, 260–
    61n59, 265n26, 266nn39–40, 273n1,
    273n4. *See also* justice; law
poetic dialogue, 4, 16–22, 26–29, 73,
    84, 98, 105–6, 108, 111, 130–31, 194,
    198, 202, 209, 212–14, 217, 219–22,
    254n11, 257–58nn33–34, 260n58,
    283n50
prose conclusion, 21–22, 205, 209, 215,
    221–26
prose introduction, 19, 28–29, 40–73,
    105–6, 208–14, 219–20, 247n82,
    249n124, 272n103, 283n48;
salvation and. *See* salvation
shame and. *See* shame
skepticism and, 127–28
subjectivity of, 55–66, 70–73, 120–25,
    151–56, 212–14, 274n20, 278n66
theology and, 66–68, 70–73, 89–93,
    121–31, 134, 160–69, 171–72,
    212–13, 215–26, 283n50. *See also* im-
    manent theology
truth and, 223–25
wife of, 64, 68–71, 105, 210, 244n52,
    248n121
Johnston, Adrian, 7, 225–26, 233n2,
    234n17, 235n11, 237n42,
    238nn51–52, 239n60, 239n64,
    239n66, 240nn72–73, 240n75,
    240n77, 240n82, 245n68, 246n78,
    247n91, 248n103, 248n107,
    249n122, 253n57, 269n74, 271n96,
    273n104, 275n32, 283n31,
    283nn54–56
J(eh)oram, 96
Jung, Carl, 4
justice, 43, 191–94, 265n26, 267n50,
    278n71. *See also under* Job

Kant, Immanuel/Kantian, 6, 14–16, 29,
    38, 44–46, 118–20, 138–39, 179,
    186–89, 191, 194, 206, 208, 210,

235n11, 235n14, 240n83, 241n14,
241–42nn16–20, 242n23, 242n27,
243n39, 246n79, 247n83, 254n69,
257n32, 264n11, 276nn41–45,
276nn47–49, 277n53, 277n59,
277n61, 277n65, 278n71,
278nn74–76, 280–81nn12–13
Keller, Catherine, 181–82, 184–85,
275nn30–31, 275n34, 276n40, 279n83
Kesel, Marc De, 242n20, 280n4
Kielholz, Paul, 132, 261n67
Kierkegaard, Søren, 134, 262n73
kislāh/ksl, 82–83
Knauert, David, 235n12, 250n18, 281n18
Knight, Kelvin, 279n3
knowledge
  belief and, 112–18
  folly and, 83
  God and, 100
  See also under Lacan; wisdom
Korahites, 244n60

Lacan, Jacques/Lacanian: 6–8,
  234n8, 234n16, 236n17, 236n18,
  237n43, 237n47, 238n52, 239n58,
  239nn60–61, 239n65, 239n68,
  240n76, 240n79, 241–42n16,
  243n32, 243n36, 247n83, 253n60,
  253nn62–63, 264n13, 268n59,
  271n93, 271n96, 279n1, 280n4,
  282n31
  anxiety, 47–48, 133–34, 145, 226,
    258n45, 262nn69–72, 262n76,
    263n8, 268nn67–68
  "between two deaths," 245n71
  Borromean knot, 31
  desire, 20, 34–39, 68–73, 86, 93, 95, 98,
    124, 226, 242n31, 258n45
  drive(s), 18, 20, 34–39, 65–66, 70–73,
    226, 237n50, 239n60, 239n63,
    239–40nn70–72, 261n68, 263n1
  event, 246n73
  formulas of sexuation, 245n79
  four discourses, 18–19
  gaze, the, 165. *See also* gaze
  half-said truth, 203–4, 223–25
  hysteria, 239n57
  Imaginary, the, 29–34, 124, 139–43,
    145, 194, 238n51, 245n71, 264n14,
    264n16, 265n21. *See also* imagination

jouissance, 18, 65, 70–73, 124, 133–34,
  160, 202, 239n71, 248n105, 259n47,
  261n68, 263n1
knowledge/meaning (S$_2$), 70, 73,
  94–96
lamella, 65
Master Signifier (S$_1$), 94–98
materialism, 31–33, 238n51, 272n104
mirror stage, the, 141–42, 240n74,
  264n16
narcissism, 36, 191, 193, 264n16
object *a* (*objet petit a*), 34–38, 110,
  133–34, 211, 239n59, 239n68, 261n68,
  262n70, 262n76, 266n35, 271n89
Other, the (big), 6, 95, 268n67
quilting point (*point de capiton*), 97
Real, the, 6, 29–34, 65, 117–18, 134,
  140–45, 207, 237n48, 238n51,
  264n14
repetition, 35
sacrifice, 47–48, 243n34
satisfaction. *See* Lacan, *jouissance*
self/ego/subjectivity, 33, 94–96,
  237n50, 239n57, 245n68
structuralism, 18
subject, barred/split ($), 33–38, 93–96,
  124, 214, 237n49, 238n56, 245n68
sublimation, 36–38, 70, 113, 137,
  239n70
Symbolic, the, 29–34, 64–65, 95,
  134, 138–41, 145–47, 204, 238n51,
  240n75, 245n71, 259n52, 264n14,
  264n16, 268n67
transference, 35
unconscious, the, 35, 237n50, 246n78
woman, the, 266n34
Laclau, Ernesto, 243n36
Lambert, W. G., 274n12
lament literature, 107–10, 254n3
Laplanche, Jean, 62, 247n91, 252n44
Lapsley, Jacqueline, 280n7
Larkin, Philip, 105, 254n1
law, the/legality, 31, 44–50, 69, 71, 107,
  109–10, 135, 137–51, 154, 156–57,
  163–65, 170–71, 206, 223, 248n121,
  263n6, 266n39, 266n44, 267n47,
  267nn49–50, 267n56
LeDoux, Joseph, 32
Levenson, Jon, 177, 274n10, 274n14
Levi, Primo, 270n88

Leviathan, 21–22, 176, 189–90, 193, 204
Levinas, Emmanuel/Levinasian, 4, 24–29,
    34, 143–50, 164–66, 213, 236n26,
    236n28, 237nn29–31, 237n33,
    237n38, 237n40, 258–59n46, 262n77,
    265nn26–29, 266n35, 266n38,
    266–67nn46–49, 268n59, 271n90,
    271nn95–96, 276n39
life (and death), 6, 28, 42, 48, 52, 55–66,
    70–71, 122, 124, 136, 155–56, 165–69,
    180–82, 199–200, 206–7, 209, 211,
    226, 243n33, 245n63, 245n66,
    245n71, 247n87, 247n89, 247n93,
    247n96, 248n104, 253n55, 261n64,
    269–70n80, 274n22, 280–81n13
Lifton, Robert, 62, 247n87
Linafelt, Tod, 51–52, 192, 244nn49–51,
    244nn53–54, 257n27, 274n21,
    277nn50–51, 277n59, 278n69,
    283n52
Lugt, Pieter van der, 250n14, 251n39,
    273n8
Luther, Martin, 206, 279n2

Macbeth, 273n3
MacIntyre, Alisdair, 206, 279n3
Magdalene, F. Rachel, 258n37, 263n6,
    266n40, 268n60
Maimonides, 260–61n59
Malabou, Catherine, 180, 238n51,
    238n54, 244n59, 264n15, 275n24
Marcel, Gabriel, 185
Marx, Karl, 133
masochism, 141–42, 256n27, 264–65n19,
    278n73
Masuzawa, Tomoko, 233n4
materialism, 7–8, 31, 238n54. See also
    under Lacan
Mathewson, Dan, 55, 61–66, 69–70,
    241n6, 244n60, 245n64, 246n81,
    247nn86–89, 247n92, 247nn94–97,
    247nn99–101, 248n109, 248n118,
    248n121, 274n20
May, Todd, 280n4, 280n6
Meier, Sam, 245n65
Miles, Jack, 273n4
Millard, A. R., 274n12
Miller, Jacques-Alain, 37
Miller, Maxwell, 253n61
Mitchell, Stephen, 282n42

Möbius band, 203, 223–24, 249n123
Monty Python, 119
Moore, Stephen, 233nn5–6
Morrow, William, 215n6
Moses, 197
mourning. See consolation and mourning

Naboth, 244n50
Nadab, 31
Nancy, Jean-Luc, 233n8
Negri, Antonio, 4
Nemo, Philippe, 4, 236n26, 257n33,
    258n46, 259n51, 272n101
nepeš, 56–58, 71–72, 122, 210–11, 259n52
New Testament, 4
New York Times, 77–78
Newsom, Carol, 23–30, 60, 69, 72–73,
    85–87, 95–96, 123, 140–50, 170–71,
    185–86, 189–90, 192, 196, 203–4,
    215nn5–6, 225, 236nn21–27, 237n32,
    237nn34–39, 241n13, 242nn27–28,
    243n41, 244n45, 244n48, 244n56,
    244n58, 245nn66–67, 246n80,
    246–47n82, 248nn117–120,
    249nn126–127, 249n129, 249n3,
    249n8, 251nn31–35, 252n45, 253n55,
    254n66, 254n2, 254nn10–11, 255–
    56n19, 256–57n27, 258n36, 258n44,
    260nn53–54, 261n61, 261n64,
    264nn17–18, 265n20, 265nn22–23,
    265nn25–26, 265nn30–33,
    266n37, 266n39, 266nn41–44,
    267n47, 267n52, 267n54, 267n56,
    269n78, 273nn107–11, 273n6,
    274n15, 276n40, 277n50, 277n52,
    277nn54–55, 277n57, 278n66,
    278n73, 278nn77–78, 279nn84–85,
    282n39, 282–83nn46–48, 283n51
Newton, Adam Zachary, 24
Niditch, Susan, 274n9
Nietzsche, Friedrich/Nietzschean, 159,
    205, 219, 242n27, 269n79
Nineveh, 158
"not-All" and "All," 6, 58–60, 67, 263n1.
    See also universality.

O'Connor, Kathleen, 13, 180, 185–86,
    190–93, 235n9, 257n27, 275nn27–28,
    276n40, 278nn67–68, 278n70,
    283n51

O'Connor, M., 230n8, 271n98
Oedipus, 196–97
Old Testament. *See* Hebrew Bible
ontology/ontological, 3, 6–8, 22, 25,
    27, 29, 39, 114–16, 125–27, 133–34,
    149, 159, 168, 181, 189, 206, 223–25,
    237n39, 244n59, 256n19, 265n26,
    267n50, 271n89. *See also* world
Otto, Rudolf, 257n27

Panksepp, Jaak, 32, 238n53
Paul, the apostle, 4, 40–41, 233–34n8,
    246n73
Perdue, Leo, 249n125
Pitt-Rivers, Julian, 156–57, 268n70
plastic/plasticity, 21, 115, 169, 180,
    238n54, 264n15
Plato/Platonism, 4, 11, 25, 56
pleasure/the pleasure principle, 33,
    36–37, 59, 65–66, 71, 116, 142,
    187–88, 191, 196, 209, 239n72,
    248n122, 267n47, 276n46, 277n59
Plotinus, 25
Polynices, 245n71
Pontalis, J.-B. 252n44
Pope, Marvin, 215n5, 240n2, 241n6,
    251n29, 258n37, 268n66
public and private, 153–56, 158, 165

Racine, Jean, 96
Rad, Gerhard von, 98, 103, 129, 250n17,
    251n30, 261n63, 273n2
Ramsey's maxim (F. P. Ramsey), 138–39,
    264n12
Rancière, Jacques, 273n7
Rashi, 230n11, 250n11
Rawls, John, 191
reality principle, the, 33, 71, 248n122
reason, 7, 73, 138, 159, 186–89, 195,
    235n14, 246n79, 276n46
Reinhard, Kenneth, 243n36
retributive theology/retribution ide-
    ology, 47, 52, 73, 80–91, 99–104,
    256n26, 260–61n59
Reventlow, Henning Graf, 130, 261n63
Robbins, Jeffrey, 233n3
Robertson, David, 273n4, 278n81,
    282n43
Rolland, Jacques, 266n46
Rosenzweig, Franz, 185

Rowley, H. H., 231n22, 241n6, 241n12,
    247n90
Rubenstein, Mary-Jane, 40, 240n1

sacrifice, 25, 46–48, 58–59, 61, 69–70,
    73, 117, 119, 143, 145, 148, 222,
    226, 242n31, 243nn33–34, 263n1,
    266n38, 283n50. *See also under* Lacan
salvation, 20, 89, 135, 168–69, 172, 213
Sartre, Jean-Paul, 165–66, 249n128,
    262n78, 268n59, 271n92, 271n96
satan, the. See *haśśāṭān*
Scarry, Elaine, 185, 191–93, 277nn58–60,
    277nn62–64, 278nn71–72
Schelling, 258n42
Schifferdecker, Kathryn, 179–80,
    273nn5–6, 274n19, 275n38
science/scientism, 3, 7, 31–32
self-consciousness, 116–17, 253n57,
    267n47
Seow, Choon-Leong, 229nn2–3,
    229nn6–7, 230n10, 230nn16–17,
    231nn23–24, 244n52, 257n34, 263n5
Shakespeare, William, 273n3
shame, 20, 73, 100–101, 135, 151,
    156–66, 194, 214, 219–20, 226,
    256n23, 259–60nn51–52, 263n1,
    268n59, 268n69, 269nn73–74,
    269n77, 269n80, 271n91,
    271nn95–96, 273n106
Sheol, 63, 66, 115, 118, 130, 167, 244n60,
    272n100
Sherwood, Yvonne, 233nn5–6
Shoah, 6, 270n88, 281n19
Shortz, Will, 78
Smith, Anthony Paul, 233n3
Sophocles, 196
sovereignty, 21, 151, 179, 198, 200, 218,
    248n110, 271n91
Steiner, George, 276n39
Steiner, Wendy, 277n59
subjectivity, 3, 206–8, 237–38n50,
    244n59, 248n104, 258n39, 265n26,
    266n38, 268n59, 271n91. *See also*
    under Job; Lacan
sublime, the, 16, 100, 118–20, 185–
    204, 226, 256–57n27, 257n32,
    276nn46–47, 277n56, 278n66,
    278n73. *See also* Lacan, sublimation
Swanton, Christine, 280n3

Taylor, Charles, 280n4
Terrien, Samuel, 55, 88, 230n18, 251n39, 252n41
terror, 92, 98, 109, 111–18, 120, 124, 126, 128, 131, 147, 162, 171, 189, 255n16, 255n18, 263n6. *See also* anxiety; fear; fear of God/YHWH; Freud, anxiety; Lacan, anxiety
theology, 3–8, 66–68, 142, 216, 225, 247n89. *See also* immanent theology; Job, theology; retributive theology/ retribution ideology
Third, the. *See* law
tragedy/tragic, the, 16, 185–86, 188, 195–98, 203–4, 257n27, 278n73, 278n79
transcendence, 3, 6–8, 11–15, 20–21, 27–34, 58–59, 125, 164, 188–89, 204, 218–26, 237n40, 270n82. *See also* immanence; immanent theology
trauma/traumatic, 5, 20, 29, 31, 68, 93, 159, 164, 169, 205, 214
type-scene, 30, 237n46

uncanny, the. *See under* Freud.
understanding, the, 186–89
universal/universality, 4, 11–15, 48, 59, 72, 129–31, 143–50, 193, 206, 210, 243n36, 246n79, 256n25, 260–61n59, 281n19. *See also* "not-All"
Urs von Balthasar, Hans, 185, 276n39

Vann Leeuwen, Raymond, 176–77, 274n10
Venn diagram, 156, 163
vexation, 87–89, 93, 98
virtue, 208, 241n13, 242n27, 280n8, 280n10, 280–81nn12–13
virtue ethics, 22, 205–14, 241n13, 242n27, 279–80n3, 280n5
Vogels, Walter, 246n82, 247n85

Wall Street, 283n49
Waltke, Bruce, 230n8, 271n98
Weiss, Meir, 241n6, 242n26
Westermann, Claus, 108–10, 137, 254nn4–6, 263n7
Whedbee, William, 278n81
Whistler, Daniel, 233n3

Whybray, R. N., 273n5
wickedness/wicked, the, 101–3, 113–18, 125–28, 170–71, 177–78, 230n16, 252n43, 254n68, 255n18
Wilson, Gerald, 47, 241n6, 241n12, 242n29, 243n40
wisdom, 11–19, 82–85, 234n1, 234n2, 235n6, 235n7, 242n22, 243n35, 247n82
instruction and, 92–93, 97–98
Job's radical reconceptualization of, 44–46, 58–60, 70–73, 105–6, 172, 204, 205, 209–212, 218–26, 246n79
knowledge and, 11–14, 47–48, 58–59, 70, 102–4
as limited, 12–19, 21, 27, 38, 48, 58–59, 90, 93, 98–104, 106, 117–20, 127–31, 144, 149, 160, 172, 189, 204, 210, 218–20, 222, 225–26, 235n14, 256n26
traditional, 3, 11–15, 48, 58–59, 80–104, 106, 113–18, 130–31, 170–71, 209, 234n4, 260n58
as a Woman, 11–12, 242n22, 251n23, 254n65
Wolde, Ellen van, 51, 215n6, 242n30, 244n52, 248n112, 282n32, 282nn34–35, 282n38, 282n44
world, as ontologically incomplete, 6, 180–83, 202–4, 212, 223–25. *See also* cosmos

Yee, Gale, 268n69
Yoder, Christine Roy, 251n23
Yom Kippur, 40

Žižek, Slavoj, 4–6, 15, 29–30, 37–39, 97, 225–26, 233–34nn8–15, 235n11, 237n42, 237n44, 237n45, 238n52, 239n72, 240nn80–83, 243n36, 248n104, 248n106, 248–49n122, 250n13, 253n59, 254n64, 259n47, 266n35, 274n21, 281n19
Zupančič, Alenka, 119, 241n14, 242nn20–21, 242nn24–25, 246n78, 257n28, 257nn30–31, 278n79, 280n4
Zophar, 79, 84, 99–103, 115–18, 128, 170, 254n69, 256n22, 256n26

Index of Ancient Sources

This book includes several abbreviations of different versions and translations of the Hebrew Bible, including:

LXX   Septuagint Bible
MT   Masoretic Text Bible

Tg.   Aramaic translation
Vulg. Latin translation

The Hebrew Bible

Genesis

1:5, 272n98
1:21, 182
1:27, 265n21
4, 243n33
9:2, 240n3
16:6, 240n3
20:11, 111
21:30, 256n23
23:8, 56
24:15, 252n47
29:15, 43
34:3, 56
35:26, 252n47
36:5, 252n47
46:2, 229n5

Exodus

3:8, 240n3
3:20, 240n3
9:15, 240n3
9:29, 256n21
19–20, 31
19:16–20:18, 197
20:21, 181
21:2, 43
32:12, 282n40
32:14, 282n40

Leviticus

10:1–4, 261n64

Numbers

1:17, 230n16
11:5, 43
11:31–34, 261n64
12:6, 229n5
16, 244n60
16:30, 244n60
26, 244n60

Deuteronomy

Book of, 247n89
1:2, 256n23
1:8, 269n73
4:11, 181
5:22, 181
11:6, 244n60
23:9, 252n47
23:14, 256n23
25:8, 268n60
29:17, 252n42
31:18, 160
31:27, 230n8
32:19, 87
32:24, 231n19

32:27, 87
32:29, 253n56
33:2, 266n36
34:7, 231n23

Judges

1:35, 279n82
5:14, 252n42
8:28, 269n76

Ruth

3:9, 177

1 Samuel

1:6, 87
1:16, 87
5:6, 279n82
5:11, 279n82
19:5, 241n10
22:11, 268n60
25:31, 241n10

2 Samuel

3:2, 252n47
3:5, 252n47
5:13, 252n47
6:6–8, 261n64
13:39, 217
22:8–18, 197
24:24, 43

1 Kings

2:31, 241n10
8:12, 181
8:22, 256n21
8:38, 256n21
19:11–18, 197
20:7, 268n60
21:13, 244n50

2 Kings

Book of, 96
8:26, 96
8:27, 96

11:1, 96
19:1–4, 51
19:30, 252n42

1 Chronicles

16:41, 230n16
21:15, 282n40

2 Chronicles

20:29, 112
22:11, 96

Ezra

9:5, 256n21

Job

1–2, 243n40, 244n54
1, 106
1:1–5, 41
1:1, 82, 100
1:2, 252n47
1:4–5, 46, 61
1:5, 46, 51, 103, 117, 283n50
1:8, 41, 55
1:9–11, 41
1:9–10, 283n50
1:9, 19, 43, 49, 50, 209
1:10, 50, 51
1:11, 51, 52, 244n56
1:12, 56, 244n56
1:14–17, 62
1:19, 61
1:20, 60
1:21, 51, 61, 64, 66, 248n111, 272n103
1:21a, 55
1:22b, 55
2, 99, 106
2–37, 221
2:3, 54, 55, 57, 244n56
2:3b, 54, 68
2:5, 51, 68
2:6, 56
2:8, 60
2:9, 51, 68, 244n52
2:10, 42, 64, 68
2:11–13, 55

2:11, 217
2:12, 57
2:13, 120
2:23, 127
2:36, 67
3, 88, 97, 106, 110, 135, 162, 194
3:3a, 136, 162
3:4b, 136
3:5, 275n38
3:9, 201
3:10, 88, 162
3:11a, 136
3:11, 88
3:20–23, 136
3:20–22, 184
3:20, 88
3:21, 256n23, 275n38
3:23, 111
3:25–26, 92, 111
3:26, 269n78
4–5, 19, 78, 79, 80, 94, 95, 99, 100,
    227–31, 246n76
4, 80–82, 86, 87, 88, 89, 98, 100
4:1–11, 251n39
4:2–11, 81, 84
4:2–6, 81
4:3–4, 111
4:5, 92, 111
4:5–6, 81
4:6, 82, 83, 84, 111, 112
4:6a, 79
4:7–11, 81
4:7–9, 254n68
4:7, 81, 84
4:7a, 79
4:8, 81, 89
4:9, 84, 89
4:11, 80
4:12–21, 81, 84, 251n39
4:12–16, 81
4:12, 84
4:13–14, 113
4:15, 251n24
4:17–21, 81
4:17, 84, 141, 250n15
4:18–21, 250n15
4:18–19, 84
4:19–21, 84
4:20, 84
4:20–21, 84

4:21, 230n11
5, 87–93, 129
5:1–2, 88
5:1–7, 90, 91, 230n17, 251n39,
    252n45
5:1, 89
5:2, 89
5:3–5, 88
5:3, 89
5:4–5, 89
5:4, 89, 252n45
5:5, 89, 252n45
5:6–7, 88, 89, 230n18, 252n45
5:6, 89
5:7, 89
5:8–27, 95
5:8–16, 90, 251n39
5:8–10, 252n41
5:8, 90, 231n20, 251n28
5:8a, 129
5:9, 90
5:10, 231n20
5:11–13, 252n41
5:11, 91
5:11a, 129
5:12–14, 253n50
5:12–13, 91
5:12, 90
5:13, 90
5:14–16, 252n41
5:14, 90, 91
5:16, 90, 91
5:16a, 129
5:17–27, 88, 251n39
5:17–18, 93
5:17, 88, 91, 112, 217, 246n76, 252n41,
    258n34
5:17b, 112, 253n54
5:18–22, 91
5:18–20, 252n41
5:18, 91
5:19–20, 91
5:19, 91
5:20, 91
5:21–23, 252n41
5:21–22, 91, 92
5:21, 112
5:21b, 112, 115
5:22a, 116
5:23–26, 253n53

5:23–25, 92
5:24–26, 252n41
5:24a, 112, 116
5:24b, 116
5:26, 92
5:27, 88, 93, 252n41
5:27b, 253n54
6:3, 259n51
6:20–21, 162
6:21b, 162
7, 162, 167
7:1. 200
7:4, 159, 259n51
7:6a, 136
7:7–11, 168
7:7, 162
7:7a, 136
7:8b, 136
7:11, 165, 259n52
7:11a, 136
7:12, 143, 202
7:13–16, 121
7:13, 217
7:14, 109, 143, 162
7:15, 279n82
7:16, 136, 216, 217, 263n5
7:17–19, 143
7:20–23, 136
7:20–21, 184
7:21, 273n105
7:21b, 143
8, 99, 100
8:14, 229, 255n12
8:17–18, 252n43
8:17, 252n42
8:20–22, 99
8:20, 217, 258n34
9–10, 102
9, 127, 259n52
9:2, 84, 142, 151
9:2a, 200
9:4a, 200
9:6–10, 200
9:8, 159
9:10, 90
9:11, 160
9:12, 122
9:14–24, 123
9:16–20, 198
9:16–18, 121

9:17, 229n6, 241n10
9:18, 260n52
9:19a, 199
9:20–21, 121
9:20, 279n82
9:20a, 153
9:21, 258n34, 267n53
9:22–24, 127
9:24, 217
9:25, 270n87
9:27–29, 123, 154
9:30–31, 123
9:30a, 153
9:31, 123, 153
9:32–35, 145, 149
9:32, 267n53
9:34–35, 136
9:34, 109
10, 142
10:1, 153, 154, 165, 259n52, 267n53
10:1b, 154
10:1c, 154
10:2–7, 144
10:2, 146, 158
10:3, 142, 217, 258n34
10:4–7, 143
10:6, 142, 144
10:8–11, 202
10:8–9, 142
10:8, 142, 268n61
10:13–15, 157
10:13–14, 157
10:14–17, 143
10:15, 158, 162, 259n51
10:15a, 158
10:18–22, 184
10:18, 168
10:20–22, 166
10:20–21, 109
10:20, 136
10:21–22, 273n105, 275n37
10:22, 167
11, 256n26
11:4–9, 101
11:7, 118
11:8, 115, 118, 130, 148
11:13–16a, 116
11:13, 128
11:15–16, 112
11:15, 112

11:15a, 116
11:15b, 115
11:18–19a, 116
11:18, 128
11:18a, 116
11:19a, 116
11:20, 118
11:36, 101
12, 128, 130
12:2b, 128
12:3a, 128
12:6, 127
12:10, 128, 129, 200
12:13, 128, 129
12:14–15, 128
12:16, 128, 129
12:17–22, 129
12:17–21, 129
12:22, 129, 161, 275n37
12:23, 129
12:24–25, 129, 273n105
13, 131, 151, 168
13:6, 147, 158
13:9, 131
13:10, 131
13:11, 131
13:13–16a, 168
13:17–27, 267n55
13:17–23, 151
13:17–18, 147, 158
13:18–23, 145
13:19a, 152
13:20–21, 109, 136, 263n6
13:20, 160
13:21–22, 108
13:22a, 152
13:23, 147, 153, 158
13:23a, 152
13:24–27, 152
13:24, 160
13:26, 152, 153
13:27, 202
13:28, 200
14, 152
14:1, 136, 159, 200
14:2, 200
14:5–6, 136
14:5, 202
14:8, 252n42
14:13, 143, 267n55

14:13ab, 152
14:15, 108
14:16, 152, 153, 267n55
14:18–20, 273n105
14:19–20, 152, 199, 267n55
14:19, 268n62
15, 48
15:4, 112
15:14–16, 100
15:14, 84
15:15–16, 230n8
15:20–22a, 115
15:20–21, 112
15:21, 112, 126
15:24, 112, 256n22
15:24a, 115
15:29–34, 126
15:29, 126
15:30, 126
16, 120
16:2, 217
16:6–7a, 120
16:6, 268n65
16:8, 124, 259n52, 279n82
16:12, 125
16:15–17, 184
16:16, 161, 166
16:18–22, 145
17:1–2, 184
17:7, 161
17:9, 48
17:10b–16, 167
17:11–16, 184, 273n105
17:13–16, 270n99
18:5–7, 126
18:11, 113, 114, 255n18
18:13–14, 126
18:13b–15, 114
18:14–15, 126
18:14, 112, 113, 114, 255n18
18:16, 252n43
18:19, 126
19, 152, 160, 163, 259n49
19:3, 160
19:6–10, 153, 267n55
19:6, 122, 259n49
19:8, 161, 166, 259n49
19:9, 153, 199
19:10, 259n49
19:12, 259n49

19:13–19, 153, 155, 160, 165, 244n61
19:13–14, 155
19:14–15, 155
19:14a, 155
19:14b, 155
19:15–17, 155
19:15a, 155, 268n66
19:18–19, 155
19:21, 199
19:23–27, 145
19:28, 252n42
20, 102
20:4–7, 101
20:6–11, 126
20:8, 229n5
20:10, 126
20:15, 115, 126
20:22, 115
20:23–25, 126
20:25, 112
20:27, 115
20:28, 126
20:29, 115
21, 125, 126, 127, 128
21:6, 109
21:7, 126
21:8–9
21:9, 126
21:10, 126
21:11–13, 126
21:11, 126
21:16–33, 260n54
21:16a, 126
21:17, 126
21:19a, 126
21:19b–20a, 126
21:21a, 126
21:22, 127
21:25–26, 127
21:34, 217
22:3, 48
22:4, 112
22:6–11, 270n81
22:10, 112
22:12–14, 181
22:12, 260n56
23, 109, 153, 169, 279n82
23:2b, 199
23:4–7, 109
23:6, 230n11

23:8–9, 153, 160, 161
23:11, 48
23:13–17, 147
23:15–17, 169
23:15–16
23:15, 153
23:16, 153
23:17, 153, 165, 273n105
24, 112, 171
24:1–17, 171
24:18–25, 170
24:18–24, 170
24:25, 170
25:2–6, 100
25:2, 115, 255n16
25:4, 84
25:5–6, 230n8
27, 171
27:12–23, 170
27:12, 170
27:13, 229n6
27:20, 170
28, 235n15
28:9, 252n42
28:23, 48
28:28, 45, 111, 242n22
29–31, 194, 195, 196, 270n81
29:19, 252n42
29:25, 217
30:2, 231n23
30:19, 123
31, 109
31:7, 48
31:8, 252n42
31:24, 229, 250n22, 255n12
31:35–37, 109
32–37, 235n15
33:15, 229n5
34:33, 216, 257n34
36:5, 216, 257n34
37:3, 177
37:5, 90
37:15, 266n36
38, 175, 178, 181, 189, 202
38:1–3, 198
38:1, 175
38:2–3, 175
38:2, 190, 215, 222, 275n28
38:2b, 200
38:3, 175, 282n34

38:3b, 190, 215
38:4–38, 176
38:4–15, 275n28
38:4–7, 176
38:4, 181
38:4a, 180
38:5b, 180
38:6, 200
38:6a, 176, 180
38:8–11, 177, 181
38:8–9, 181
38:8, 177, 200
38:9, 181
38:10b–11, 177
38:12–15, 177, 178, 181
38:12–13, 200
38:12, 201
38:13, 177
38:15, 177
38:16–18, 181, 184, 275n37
38:16–17, 201
38:16, 181, 182
38:17, 275n38
38:18, 184
38:19, 275n38
38:20–30, 182
38:21, 184, 200
38:22, 182
38:23, 181
38:26–27, 182
38:31–33, 182, 200
38:36–37, 176
38:37, 200
38:39–39:30, 176
38:41, 183
39–41, 189
39:4, 183
39:12, 183
39:13–18, 180
39:13–17, 183
39:22, 183
39:29, 256n23
40, 175, 198
40:1–14, 193
40:6–14, 175
40:6–8, 198
40:6, 175
40:7, 175, 282n34
40:7b, 190, 215
40:9, 199

40:10, 199
40:14, 199
40:15–24, 176
40:19a, 189, 204
40:20, 183
40:22, 183
40:23, 183
40:25–41:26, 176
41:1–34, 176
41:25–26, 190, 204
42, 21, 175, 224
42:1–6, 190, 205, 215, 218, 220, 282n32
42:1, 215, 220
42:2–5, 216
42:2, 216, 224
42:2a, 215, 220
42:2b, 215, 220
42:3, 224
42:3a, 190, 215, 216, 220
42:3b, 215, 220
42:3bc, 216, 218
42:3c, 190, 215, 218, 220
42:4, 215, 216
42:4a, 215, 220, 282n34
42:4b, 190, 215, 220, 282n34
42:5, 192, 215, 216, 218, 224
42:5a, 215, 220
42:5b, 215, 220
42:6, 192, 216, 217, 219, 257n34, 282n32
42:6a, 215, 220
42:6b, 215, 218, 220
42:7–17, 215, 221
42:7–10, 222, 283n50
42:7–9, 192
42:7, 222. 224
42:8, 222, 224
42:9, 222
42:10, 222
42:11, 217, 222
42:12, 222
42:13–15, 223
47:7–17, 205, 223

Psalms

Book of, 247n89
18:8–18, 197
18:44, 215

33:7, 275n29
35:7, 241n10
37, 234n1
48:1–4, 177
49:11, 229
49:14, 229
50:2, 266n36
52:7, 252n42
69:4, 241n10
69:15, 244n60
78:7, 229n1, 250n22, 255n12
80:10, 252n42
83:17, 269n77
85:5, 87
85:9, 229, 254n12
89:38, 216
90:13, 217
91:5, 256n22
97:1–2, 181
104:27–30, 200
106:12, 230n9
106:17, 244n60
109:3, 241n10
110:7, 269n76
113:5, 259n56
116:6, 230n16
119:130, 230n16
119:161, 241n10
139:13–15, 63
143:6, 256n21
143:9, 229, 254n12
145:15–16, 200

Proverbs

Book of, 82, 208, 209, 234n1, 234n4,
     235n6, 247n89, 281n16, 281n18
1–9, 81, 104, 251n23
1:7, 45, 82, 104, 242n22, 243n37
1:11, 241n10
1:12, 244n60
1:15, 48
1:17, 241n11
1:22, 230n16
1:27, 256n22
1:32, 230n16
1:33, 255n12
2:8, 48
3:5, 13, 48
3:7, 13

3:17, 48
3:19, 243n35
3:25, 230n16
3:30, 241n11
4:18–19, 48
5:21, 48
6:15, 230n16
7, 48
7:22, 230n16
7:27, 48
8:5, 230n16
8:29ab, 177
8:32, 48
8:33, 254n65
9:6, 48, 230n16
9:10, 45, 82, 104, 242n22
9:13, 251n23
11:31, 230n8
12, 13, 48
12:3, 252n42, 252n43
12:15, 13, 48
12:16, 87
12:28, 48
13, 48
13:25, 56
15:33, 255n15
16, 13, 48
16:2, 13, 48
17:7, 252n47
17:21, 252n47
20, 48
21:2, 13, 48
21:31, 13, 103
23:29, 241n11
24:28, 241n11
26:2, 241n11
26:4a, 13
26:5, 13, 48
26:5a, 13
27:1, 103
27:3, 87
28:11, 13, 48
31:10–31, 251n23
31:30, 251n23

Ecclesiastes/Qohelet

Book of, 234n1, 235n14, 281n16, 281n18
2:2, 230n9
7:9, 87

7:25, 229, 250n22, 255n12
7:27, 269n73

Isaiah

2:10, 256n22
2:19, 256n22
2:21, 256n22
8:22, 256n22
11:3, 215
11:12, 177
25:7–8, 244n60
30:6, 256n22
37:31, 252n42
40:24, 252n42
41:22, 230n11
52:5, 241n11

Jeremiah

1:9, 240n3
4:31, 256n21
8:6, 282n40
12:2, 252n42
13:23, 158
17:8, 252n42
18:8, 282n40
18:10, 282n40
19:9, 256n22
22:13, 43
31:15, 217
33:20–21a, 272n102
51:26, 176

Lamentations

1:9, 269n73
1:17, 256n21
2:2, 244n60
2:5, 244n60
2:8, 244n60
2:16, 244n60
3:45, 40
3:52, 241n10

Ezekiel

6:10, 241n11
14:20, 43
14:23, 43, 241n11

17:6, 252n42
17:9, 252n42
20:28, 87
26:19, 275n29
32:31, 217
47:3, 176

Daniel

2:19, 229n5
6:11, 51
6:24, 51
7:2, 229n5
7:7, 229n5
7:13, 229n5
9:25, 256n22

Hosea

6:1, 253n56

Joel

2:13, 282n40

Amos

6:1, 230n16

Jonah

2:5, 275n29
4:2, 282n40

Micah

1:14, 271n97

Nahum

3:5, 158

Zephaniah

1:15, 181

Zecheriah

1:21, 269n76
14:6–7, 270n81

Sirach

Book of, 234n1

Wisdom of Solomon

Book of, 234n1

The New Testament

1 Corinthians

3:7, 41
4:11, 40
4:13, 40
4:16, 41

Revelation

12:7–9, 242n22

James

Book of, 233n8

Ancient Cognate Literature

11QtgJob, 268n66
Atra-ḥasis, 177

The Babylonian Theodicy, 254n11